Data Analytics

Data Analytics
Concepts, Techniques, and Applications

Edited by
Mohiuddin Ahmed and Al-Sakib Khan Pathan

CRC Press
Taylor & Francis Group
Boca Raton London New York

CRC Press is an imprint of the
Taylor & Francis Group, an **Informa** business

CRC Press
Taylor & Francis Group
6000 Broken Sound Parkway NW, Suite 300
Boca Raton, FL 33487-2742

Library of Congress Cataloging-in-Publication Data

Names: Ahmed, Mohiuddin (Computer scientist), editor. | Pathan, Al-Sakib Khan, editor.
Title: Data analytics : concepts, techniques and applications / edited by Mohiuddin Ahmed, Al-Sakib Khan Pathan.
Other titles: Data analytics (CRC Press)
Description: Boca Raton, FL : CRC Press/Taylor & Francis Group, 2018. | Includes bilbliographical references and index.
Identifiers: LCCN 2018021424 | ISBN 9781138500815 (hb : acid-free paper) | ISBN 9780429446177 (ebook)
Subjects: LCSH: Quantitative research. | Big data.
Classification: LCC QA76.9.Q36 D38 2018 | DDC 005.7—dc23
LC record available at https://lccn.loc.gov/2018021424

Visit the Taylor & Francis Web site at
http://www.taylorandfrancis.com

and the CRC Press Web site at
http://www.crcpress.com

Dedicated to

My Loving Parents

—Mohiuddin Ahmed

My two little daughters: Rumaysa and Rufaida

—Al-Sakib Khan Pathan

Contents

SECTION III   DATA ANALYTICS APPLICATIONS

Acknowledgments

I am grateful to the Almighty Allah for blessing me with the opportunity to work on this book. It is my first time as a book editor and I express my sincere gratitude to Al-Sakib Khan Pathan for guiding me throughout the process. The book editing journey enhanced my patience, communication, and tenacity. I am thankful to all the contributors, critics, and the publishing team. Last but not least, my very best wishes for my family members whose support and encouragement contributed significantly to the completion of this book.

Mohiuddin Ahmed
Centre for Cyber Security and Games
Canberra Institute of Technology, Australia

Preface

Introduction

Big data is a term for datasets that are so large or complex that traditional data processing applications are inadequate for them. The significance of big data has been recognized very recently and there are various opinions on its definition. In layman's terms, big data reflects the datasets that cannot be perceived, acquired, managed, and processed by the traditional information technology (IT) and software/hardware tools in an efficient manner. Communities such as scientific and technological enterprises, research scholars, data analysts, and technical practitioners have different definitions of big data. Due to a large amount of data arriving at a fast speed, a new set of efficient data analysis techniques are required. In addition to this, the term data science has gained a lot of attention from both the academic research community and the industry. Therefore, data analytics becomes an essential component for any organization. For instance, if we consider health care, financial trading, Internet of Things (IoT) smart cities, or cyber-physical systems, one can find the role of data analytics. However, with these diverse application domains, new research challenges are also arising. In this context, this book on data analytics will provide a broader picture of the concepts, techniques, applications, and open research directions in this area. In addition, the book is expected to serve as a single source of reference for acquiring knowledge on the emerging trends and applications of data analytics.

Objective of the Book

This book is about compiling the latest trends and issues of emerging technologies, concepts, and applications that are based on data analytics. It is written for graduate students in the universities, researchers, academics, and industry practitioners working in the area of data science, machine learning, and other related issues.

About the Target Audience and Content

The target audience of this book is comprised of students, researchers, and professionals working in the area of data analytics and is not focused on any specific application. This book includes chapters covering the fundamental concepts, relevant techniques, and interesting applications of data analysis. The chapters are categorized into three groups with a total of 16 chapters. These chapters have been contributed by authors from seven different countries across the globe.

SECTION I: Data Analytics Concepts
   Chapter 1: An Introduction to Machine Learning
   Chapter 2: Regression for Data Analytics
   Chapter 3: Big Data-Appropriate Clustering via Stochastic Approximation and Gaussian Mixture Models
   Chapter 4: Information Retrieval Methods for Big Data Analytics on Text
   Chapter 5: Big Graph Analytics

SECTION II: Data Analytics Techniques
   Chapter 6: Transition from Relational Database to Big Data and Analytics
   Chapter 7: Big Graph Analytics: Techniques, Tools, Challenges, and Applications
   Chapter 8: Application of Game Theory for Big Data Analytics
   Chapter 9: Project Management for Effective Data Analytics
   Chapter 10: Blockchain in the Era of Industry 4.0
   Chapter 11: Dark Data for Analytics

SECTION III: Data Analytics Applications
   Chapter 12: Big Data: Prospects and Applications in the Technical and Vocational Education and Training Sector
   Chapter 13: Sports Analytics: Visualizing Basketball Records in Graphical Form
   Chapter 14: Analysis of Traffic Offenses in Transportation: Application of Big Data Analysis
   Chapter 15: Intrusion Detection for Big Data
   Chapter 16: Health Care Security Analytics

Section I contains six chapters that cover the fundamental concepts of data analytics. These chapters reflect the important knowledge areas, such as machine learning, regression, clustering, information retrieval, and graph analysis. Section II has six chapters that cover the major techniques of data analytics, such as transition from regular database to big data, big graph analysis tools and techniques, and game theoretical approaches for big data analysis. The rest of the chapters in this section cover topics that lead to newer research domains, i.e., project management,

Industry 4.0, and dark data. These topics are considered as the emerging trends in data analytics. Section III is dedicated to the applications of data analytics in different domains, such as education, traffic offenses, sports data visualization and, last but not the least, two interesting chapters on cybersecurity for big data analytics with specific focus on the health care sector.

Mohiuddin Ahmed and Al-Sakib Khan Pathan

List of Contributors

Mohiuddin Ahmed obtained his PhD from UNSW Australia and is currently working as a lecturer in the Canberra Institute of Technology at the Centre for Cyber Security and Games. His research interests include big data mining, machine learning, and network security. He is working to develop efficient and accurate anomaly detection techniques for network traffic analysis to handle the emerging big data problems. He has made practical and theoretical contributions toward data summarization in network traffic analysis. His research also has high impact on critical infrastructure protection (SCADA systems, smart grid), information security against DoS attacks, and complicated health data (heart disease, nutrition) analysis. He has published a number of journals and conference papers in reputed venues of computer science. Dr. Ahmed holds a bachelor of science degree in computer science and information technology with high distinction from Islamic University of Technology, OIC.

Adam A. Alli received his PhD in computer science and engineering from the Islamic University of Technology, Dhaka, Bangladesh. He completed his MSc in computer science (2008) from the University of Mysore, India, and his BSc in computer science (2002) from the Islamic University in Uganda. He also received a Postgraduate Diploma in Management and Teaching at Higher Education (2015) from the Islamic University in Uganda and a Graduate Diploma in ICT Leadership and Knowledge Society (2013) from the Dublin City University through the GeSCI program. He was Dean, Faculty of Science at the Islamic University in Uganda from 2011 to 2016. He is a lecturer of computer science and engineering at both Islamic University in Uganda and Uganda Technical College in Bushenyi.

C. Narendra Babu graduated with a BE in computer science engineering (CSE) from Adichunchanagiri Institute of Technology, Chikmagalur, in 2000. He received his MSc in MTech (CSE) from M. S. Ramaiah Institute of Technology, Bangalore, in 2004. He received a PhD degree from JNT University, Anantapur. He is an associate professor in the department of CSE at M. S. Ramaiah University of Applied Sciences, Bangalore. His research interests include time series data analysis and mining and soft computing. He has published four papers in reputed international journals and in two international conferences, and has also received the best author award from IEEE-ICAESM International Conference in 2012 held at Nagapattinam. He has been a member of IEEE since 2009. His email address is narendrababu.c@gmail.com.

M. Saiful Bari likes to solve mathematical problems and build intelligent systems. He completed his bachelor of science from the Islamic University of Technology (IUT) in 2016. His undergraduate life at IUT was spent participating in different programming contests and in coaching university students for competitive programming. After his graduation, he started his job as a lecturer at Southeast University, Bangladesh. He is currently (March 2018) working as a research assistant at Nanyang Technological University under the supervision of Dr. Shafiq Joty. His research objective involves developing models by deep learning that have the notion of humanity. Currently, he is working on deep learning-based adversary models. He wants to explore the application of deep learning in an unsupervised manner. In the future, he wants to explore the possibility of combining reinforcement learning and deep learning for a more robust intelligent system.

Abu Saleh Shah Mohammad Barkat Ullah is working as senior lecturer in the Canberra Institute of Technology with the department of ICT and library studies. He obtained his PhD from UNSW, Australia, with significant contribution in the areas of computational intelligence, genetic computing, and optimization. He is currently the principal investigator of a health care cyber security research project. He has published in reputed venues of computer science and is actively involved in both academia and industry. He holds a bachelor of science degree in computer science with outstanding results and has achieved a Gold Medal for such performance. He is also one of the pioneers in introducing false data injection attacks in the health care domain.

Abhay Kumar Bhadani holds his PhD (decision and data sciences in telecom) from the Indian Institute of Technology, Delhi, India. He has more than 6 years of experience in industry and research in the government as well as the IT sector. Currently, he is associated with Yatra Labs, Gurgaon, as the senior tech lead—data sciences. He has more than ten publications in top international computer science and decision sciences conferences and journals. In his spare time, he conducts different meetings, loves to teach, and also mentors different technology start-ups. His interests are in Natural Language Processing, Machine Learning, Decision Sciences, Recommender Systems, Linux, Open Source, and working for social causes. He can also be contacted at his personal email: abhaybhadani@gmail.com.

Robert Biddle is Professor of Human–Computer Interaction at Carleton University in Ottawa, Canada, where he is appointed both at the School of Computer Science and the Institute of Cognitive Science. His qualifications are in Mathematics, Computer Science, and Education, and he has worked at universities and with the government and industry partners in Canada and New Zealand. His recent research is primarily on human factors in cybersecurity and software design, especially in creating and evaluating innovative designs for computer security software. In particular, his research projects have addressed novel forms of authentication, user understanding of security, security operation centers, and tools for collaborative security analysis. He has led research themes for cross-Canada research networks on human-oriented computer security, for software engineering for surface applications, and for privacy and security in new media environments.

Biozid Bostami finished his Bachelor of Science in Computer Science and Information Technology with High Distinction from the Islamic University of Technology, OIC. He is working in the area of Big Data Mining, Machine Learning, and Network Security in collaboration. He is working to develop efficient and accurate Anomaly Detection techniques for network traffic analysis to handle the emerging Big Data problems.

Gerry Chan is a PhD student in the School of Information Technology at Carleton University located in Ottawa, Canada. He has a background in human–computer interaction and psychology. His research interests include visual analytics, computer-aided exercise, and player pairings in digital games. Recently, he has been working on the research involving the use of wearable technologies, gamification principles, and matchmaking methods for encouraging a more active lifestyle. Chan is particularly interested in the social and motivational aspects of the gaming experience. He believes that games are valuable learning tools and offer ways for building stronger social relationships with others.

Prasenjit Choudhury is an assistant professor in the department of computer science and engineering at the National Institute of Technology, Durgapur, India. He has completed his PhD in computer science and engineering from the same institute. He has published more than 40 research papers in international journals and conferences. His research interests include wireless network, data analytics, complex networks, and recommendation systems.

Malka N. Halgamuge is a researcher in the department of electrical and electronic engineering at the University of Melbourne, Australia. She has also obtained her PhD from the same department in 2007. She is also the adjunct senior lecturer (casual) at the Charles Sturt University, Melbourne. She is passionate about research and teaching university students (life sciences, big data/data science, natural disaster, wireless communication). She has published more than 80 peer-reviewed technical articles attracting over 780 Google Scholar Citations with h-index = 14 and her Research Gate RG Score is 31.69. She is currently supervising two PhD students at the University of Melbourne—three PhD students completed their theses in 2013 and 2015 under her supervision. She successfully sought seven short-term research fellowships at premier universities across the world.

Abid Hasan is a final year student in the Institute of Business Administration, Dhaka University, Dhaka, Bangladesh. He is studying bachelor of business administration there. He completed his secondary and higher secondary education from Jhenidah Cadet College. His research interests include dark data, health sector data, business analytics, and survey research. As a business student, he is studying data analytics with practical business value. He has published a journal in the 1st International Conference on Business and Management (ICBM 2017) in BRACU.

Charitha Subhashi Jayasekara graduated in 2017 from Charles Sturt University, with a master's degree in information technology specializing in networking. Also, in 2014, she obtained her bachelor's degree in software engineering from the Informatics Institute of Technology, Sri Lanka, collaborated with the University of Westminster, London. She is currently working as a project-based developer at Spatial Partners Pvt. Ltd, Melbourne, Australia. Her work is focused on maps and spatial data analysis and geographic information system. She is passionate about data science and big data analysis. Also, she has published one book chapter reviewing security and privacy challenges of big data.

 **Muye Jiang** is a master of computer science student at the University of Ottawa, Canada, supervised by Dr. Jochen Lang and Dr. Robert Laganiere. His major research field is computer vision, specifically in improving object tracking techniques' speed and accuracy. Currently, he is using traditional methods for object tracking, such as correlation filter, but he is also learning some new popular methods, such as Machine Learning with Convolutional Neural Network.

Andrew Thomas Jones received a bachelor of engineering (mechatronics) degree with honors in 2010, a bachelor of arts in mathematics with first-class honors in 2011, and a PhD in statistics in 2017, all from the University of Queensland, St. Lucia, Australia. His main areas of research interest include the efficient implementation of statistical algorithms in the context of big data, image clustering and analysis, statistical models for differential gene expression, and population genetics modeling. He is also an accomplished programmer in a number of languages including C++, R, Python, and Fortran, and is the author of a number of R packages. Since late 2016, he has been working as a postdoctoral research fellow at the University of Queensland.

 **Md. Shahadat Hossain Khan** completed his PhD at the University of Sydney, Australia. He has been working as an assistant professor of the department of Technical and Vocational Education, at the Islamic University of Technology, Bangladesh, since 2006. He was awarded the Australian Leadership Award Scholarship (Australia) and Skill-Road Scholarship (Seoul University, South Korea) based on his outstanding academic results, teaching, and research expertise. His research area mainly includes ICT-enhanced teaching and learning, professional development with a particular focus on scholarship in teaching (student-centered teaching, ICT integration), Technical and Vocational Education and Training (TVET) pedagogy, technology integration in TVET sectors, and Technological Pedagogical Content Knowledge in national and international contexts.

Santoshi Kumari graduated with a BE in computer science engineering (CSE) from Rural Engineering College, Bhalki, India, in 2009. She received her MTech degree in software engineering from AMC Engineering College, Bangalore, in 2011. She is an assistant professor in the department of CSE, M. S. Ramaiah University of Applied Sciences, Bangalore. She is currently pursuing her PhD degree from the department of computer science. Her research interests are in the areas of big data and data stream analytics, with an emphasis on data mining, statistical analysis/modeling, machine learning, and social media analytics. Her email address is santoshik29@gmail.com.

Tamanna Motahar is a lecturer at the electrical and computer engineering department of North South University. She completed her master's degree in electrical engineering from the University of Alberta, Canada. She graduated summa cum laude with a BSc in computer engineering from the American International University, Bangladesh. Her high-school graduation is from Mymensingh Girls' Cadet College, Bangladesh. Her interdisciplinary research works are based on optical electromagnetics and nano optics. Her current research areas include Internet of Things, human–computer interaction, and big data. She is taking Junior Design classes for computer science engineering students in the North South University and is also mentoring several groups for their technical projects. Her email address is tamanna.motahar@northsouth.edu.

Mohammad Muhtady Muhaisin attained his bachelor of science degree from the Islamic University of Technology, Bangladesh, in 2016. He has coauthored two research publications on signal processing. His undergraduate thesis was on the application of game theory in devising a custody transfer mechanism in wireless sensor networks. His research interest includes game-theoretic approach in modeling energy transaction in smart grids and microgrids.

Nambobi Mutwalibi is a research member at the department of technical and vocational education, Islamic University of Technology, Gazipur, Bangladesh. He specialized in computer science and engineering. He has published and presented papers on big data and learning analytics, skill development, MOOCs, and online learning tools.

 **Ankur Narang** holds a PhD in computer science engineering (CSE) from the Indian Institute of Technology, Delhi, India. He has more than 23 years of experience in senior technology leadership positions across MNCs including IBM Research India and Sun Research Labs & Sun Microsystems (Oracle), Menlo Park, California, USA. He leads the Data Science & AI Practice at Yatra Online Pvt. Ltd, Gurgaon, India, as senior vice president for Technology & Decision Sciences. He has more than 40 publications in top international computer science conferences and journals, along with 15 approved US patents, with five filed patents pending approval. His research interests include artificial general intelligence, machine learning, optimization, approximation and randomized algorithms, distributed and high-performance computing, data mining, and computational biology and computational geosciences. He is a senior member of IEEE and a member of ACM (including the Eminent Speaker Program), has held multiple Industrial Track and Workshop Chair positions, and has spoken in multiple conferences. He completed both BTech and PhD in CSE from IIT, Delhi, India, and MS from Santa Clara University, Santa Clara, California, USA.

Hien D. Nguyen holds a bachelor of economics degree and a bachelor of science (statistics; first-class honors) degree, both granted by the University of Queensland. He obtained his PhD in image analysis and statistics from the University of Queensland in 2015. Also, in 2015, Dr. Nguyen was the recipient of the prestigious A. K. Head Travelling Scholarship from the Australian Academy of Science, which he utilized to build collaborations with the SIMEXP group at the Centre de recherche de l'Institut universitaire de gériatrie de Montreal, Canada. In 2017, Dr. Nguyen was appointed lecturer at La Trobe University, Australia, and was the recipient of an Australian Research Council (ARC) DECRA Fellowship. In the same year, he also spent time as a visiting scholar at the Lab of Mathematics, Nicolas Oresme, Universite de Caen Normandie, France. Starting from 2018, Dr. Nguyen will commence work on his ARC Discovery Project, entitled "Classification methods for providing personalized and class decisions." Dr. Nguyen's work revolves around the interplay between artificial intelligence, machine learning, and statistics. To date, he has published more than 30 research articles and software packages.

Asma Noor graduated in 2017 from Charles Sturt University with a master's degree in information technology, specializing in networking and system analysis. In 2011, she obtained her master's degree in international relations from the University of Balochistan, Pakistan. In 2007, she obtained a bachelor's degree in business administration from Iqra University, Pakistan, specializing in marketing. Her hobbies include reading and writing. Her interests in the field of information technology include cloud computing, information security, Internet of Things, and big data analytics.

Mark A. Norrie has over 35 years of experience in research, statistics, administration, and computing. He specializes in consulting, statistical programming, data management, and training. He has spent (as have other experienced data scientists) half his life on data munging and preparation, but it has all been worth it. Clients he has worked with are numerous, including the Shanghai Stock Exchange, Citibank, and the Australian Taxation Office. His current work includes prediction of workplace accidents, natural language processing for client sentiment analysis, and building a decision support system to classify injuries using semantic methods for icare, the social insurer for the State of New South Wales.

Md. Mehedi Hassan Onik is a master's degree student and is working as a research assistant in the Computer and Communication Lab at Inje University, South Korea. His research focuses particularly on blockchain technology, multipath transmission (MPTCP), and energy-efficient communication. He also worked as a software engineer in Bangladesh. He holds a bachelor of science degree in computer science and engineering from the Islamic University of Technology, OIC.

Pijush Kanti Dutta Pramanik is a PhD research scholar in the department of computer science and engineering at the National Institute of Technology, Durgapur, India. He has acquired a range of professional qualifications in the core and allied fields of information technology, namely, MIT, MCA, MBA (information technology), MTech (computer science engineering), and MPhil (computer science). He is actively engaged in research in the domains of the Internet of Things, grid computing, fog computing, crowd computing, and recommendation systems, and has published a number of research articles and book chapters in these areas.

Ahsanur Rahman is an assistant professor of the electrical and computer engineering department at the North South University. He completed his PhD in computer science from Virginia Tech, Blacksburg, VA. Before that he has worked as a lecturer in the computer science and engineering department at the American International University Bangladesh. He obtained his bachelor's degree in computer science and engineering from Bangladesh University of Engineering and Technology. His research interest lies in the areas of computational systems biology, graph algorithms, hypergraphs, and big data. He is mentoring several groups of NSU for their research projects. His email address is ahsanur.rahman@northsouth.edu.

Taseef Rahman completed his BSc in electrical and electronics engineering from the Islamic University of Technology, Bangladesh, in 2016. He is currently working at a sister concern of Axway Inc. as a cross platform support engineer. His research interests include big data analytics, human–computer interaction, and mobile computing.

Ather Saeed is the course coordinator for CSU (networking programs) at the Study Centre Melbourne, Australia. Currently, he is pursuing his PhD (thesis titled "Fault-Tolerance in the Healthcare Wireless Sensor Networks"). He has a master's degree in information technology and a graduate diploma (information technology) from the University of Queensland, Australia, along with a master's degree in computer science (Canadian Institute of Graduate Studies). He has been involved in the tertiary education since 1999 (prior to joining CSU, he was the course coordinator at the Federation University for IT Program) and has published several research papers in journals and international conferences (held in the United States, the United Kingdom, and Germany).

Munir Ahmad Saeed is currently enrolled in the professional doctorate of project management at the University of New South Wales, Australia. His research is focused on investigating project benefits realization practices. He is working as lecturer at the College of Business, Canberra Institute of Technology, Canberra, Australia. Saeed has worked as a journalist in Pakistan for 10 years and has abiding interest in politics and current affairs. He holds a bachelor of arts, bachelor of business, master of English literature, and master of project management (with distinction) degrees from Pakistani and Australian universities.

Dhananjay Kumar Singh received his MTech degree in computer science and engineering from the department of computer science and engineering, National Institute of Technology, Silchar, India, in 2016. He is currently pursuing his PhD degree in computer science and engineering at the National Institute of Technology, Durgapur, India. His primary research interests include complex networks, social networking, graph mining, and recommendation systems.

DATA ANALYTICS
CONCEPTS

Chapter 1

An Introduction to Machine Learning

Mark A. Norrie

icare

Contents

1.1 A Definition of Machine Learning

It is useful to begin with the definition of machine learning (ML). ML is, in effect, a computer program or system that can learn specific tasks such as discrimination or classification without being explicitly programmed to do so. Learning is the key word here.

So how did it all start?

There are many strands for this particular story. The modern discipline of data science (of which supervised learning is a part) has grown in a complex and interesting way and has had inputs from numerous other disciplines and fields. These days, ML is thought of as a distinct Computer Science subject or discipline.

Another way to look at ML is that it is a process that involves the use of a computer (machine) to make decisions (or recommendations) based on (usually) multiple data inputs.

We can see the overall relationships shown in Figure 1.1.

Data science has a substantial overlap with computer science that subsumes artificial intelligence (AI). AI includes ML and the learning types, supervised and unsupervised. Data science also includes ML, but not AI as such.

1.1.1 Supervised or Unsupervised?

Some ML methods are effective statistical modeling such as various types of regression (the dependent variable is also known in ML parlance as the target, while the independent variables are the predictors that determine the value of the target). These are among the supervised methods. Other methods can involve determining

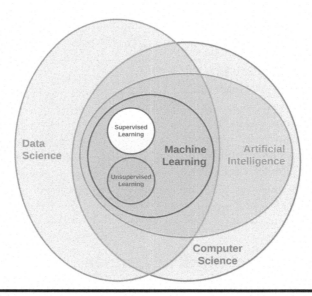

Figure 1.1   Data science, ML, and related disciplines.

the structure or group membership (e.g., classification and/or clustering). Such methods are also known as unsupervised learning.

There also exists a hybrid method, which is known as semisupervised ML. Currently, this hybrid method is of great research interest. It is useful especially when only a modest set of identified or labeled data exists as part of a much larger dataset. Cost is frequently a factor. Lastly, some programs use an algorithm to learn by being presented with examples, much like a human being does. This is the so-called reinforcement learning.

A number of important algorithms or methods are involved and statistical analogs for this process exist and, in reality, constitute a substantial part of ML because ML essentially emerged from the field of statistics. Disciplines that have contributed to the field as well as the research problems that stimulated people to look for solutions in the first place are well worth examining as they will round out our understanding and allow us to make the best and most appropriate use of what we have available to us.

1.2 Artificial Intelligence

The two main disciplines involved predate computers by quite a margin. They are artificial intelligence (AI) and classical statistics. Interest in AI extends historically all the way back to classical antiquity. Once the Greeks convincingly demonstrated that thought and reason are basic physical processes, it was hoped that machines could also be built to demonstrate thought, reason, and intelligence.

One of the key milestones in the development of AI came from the well-known pioneer of information systems, Alan Turing. In 1950, Turing suggested that it should be possible to create a *learning machine* that could learn and become artificially intelligent.

A couple of years after this, people began to write programs to play games with humans, such as checkers on early IBM computers (rather large computers at that, as the transistor hadn't been invented yet, and Integrated Circuits (ICs) and Complementary metal-oxide-semiconductors (CMOS) were so far ahead in the future that nobody had given the matter much thought).

Leading thinkers, such as John von Neumann, long advocated thinking of (and designing) computer and information systems architectures based on an understanding of the anatomy and physiology of the brain, particularly its massively parallel nature. In the Silliman lectures of 1956, which the dying von Neumann was too ill to give, this approach is set out in detail. The lectures were published posthumously as *The Computer and the Brain, (1958)* by Yale University Press, New Haven and London [1].

In the year 1957, Frank Rosenblatt, a research psychologist, invented the Perceptron, a single layer neural network while working at the Cornell Aeronautical Laboratory. In Figure 1.2, we can see Dr. Rosenblatt's original Perceptron design.

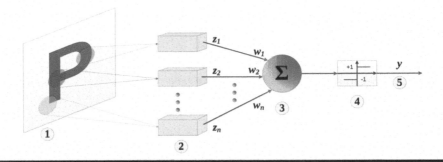

Figure 1.2 Frank Rosenblatt's original Perceptron.

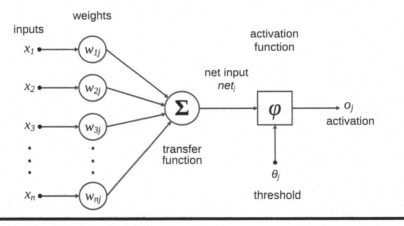

Figure 1.3 The architecture of a Perceptron.

The components of the Perceptron are as follows:

1. Input pattern—a letter or shape, such as a triangle or a circle
2. Random Boolean Units
3. Linear threshold gate (LTG)
4. Bipolar binary output function
5. Decision/classified instance

This design is shown as a basic schematic in Figure 1.3.

Naturally, this invention created an enormous amount of excitement and articles appeared in both *The New York Times* [2] and *The New Yorker*. *The New York Times* article [2] is quoted in Box 1.1:

BOX 1.1   AN EARLY EXAMPLE OF HYPE

NEW YORK TIMES, 1958

NEW NAVY DEVICE LEARNS BY DOING

Psychologist Shows Embryo of Computer Designed to Read and Grow Wise

WASHINGTON. July 7 (UPI)—The Navy revealed the embryo of an electronic computer today that it expects will be able to walk, talk, see, write, reproduce itself and be conscious of its existence.

The embryo—the Weather Bureau's $2,000,000 "704" computer—learned to differentiate between right and left after fifty attempts In the Navy's demonstration for newsmen.

The service said it would use this principle to build the first of its Perceptron thinking machines that will be able to read and write. It is expected to be finished in about a year at a cost of $100,000.

Dr. Frank Rosenblatt, designer of the Perceptron, conducted the demonstration. He said the machine would be the first device to think as the human brain. As do human beings, Perceptron will make mistakes at first, but will grow wiser as it gains experience, he said.

Dr. Rosenblatt, a research psychologist at the Cornell Aeronautical Laboratory, Buffalo, said Perceptrons might be fired to the planets as mechanical space explorers.

WITHOUT HUMAN CONTROLS

The Navy said the Perceptron would be the first non-living mechanism "capable of receiving, recognizing and identifying its surroundings without any human training or control."

The *brain* is designed to remember images and information it has perceived itself. Ordinary computers remember only what is fed into them on punch cards or magnetic tape.

Later Perceptrons will be able to recognize people and call out their names and instantly translate speech in one language to speech or writing in another language, it was predicted.

Mr. Rosenblatt said in principle it would be possible to build brains that could reproduce themselves on an assembly line and which would be conscious of their existence. In today's demonstration, the "704" was fed two cards, one with squares marked on the left side and the other with squares on the right side.

LEARNS BY DOING

In the first fifty trials, the machine made no distinction between them. It then started registering a Q for the left squares and O for the right squares.

> Dr. Rosenblatt said he could explain why the machine learned only in highly technical terms. But he said the computer had undergone a ***self-induced change in the wiring diagram***.
> The first Perceptron will have about 1,000 electronic ***association cells*** receiving electrical Impulses from an eye-like scanning device with 400 photo-cells. The human brain has 10,000,000.000 responsive cells, including 100,000,000 connections with the eyes.

Interestingly, the IBM 704 computer they were using was state-of-the-art and would be worth over $17M USD in today's money. Five months later, in the December 6th issue of the New Yorker an article appeared where Dr Rosenblatt was also interviewed [3]. The article was imaginatively entitled ***Rival***. He was quoted saying similar things to what had appeared in the earlier New York Times article. This was the first true hype around AI. This hype when it finally came off the rails was also the cause of the first *AI Winter*.

There is absolutely no doubt that the Perceptron was an astonishing intellectual and engineering achievement. For the first time ever, a non-human agent (and non-biological for that matter) could actually demonstrate learning by trial and error.

Rosenblatt published a paper (1958) [4] and a detailed report, later published as a book on the Perceptron and used this in his lecture classes for a number of years (1961, 1962) [5,6].

1.2.1 The First AI Winter

Seven years after that, in 1969, Marvin Minsky and Seymour Papert published a book on the Perceptron [7], and this was widely quoted. They proved that the Perceptron could not perform an XOR function and was therefore severely limited in its functions.

This shortcoming was partly used by James Lighthill, in 1973, to recommend the withdrawal of funding by the British Government for the United Kingdom's AI research [8]. As is common in science and engineering, all funding in AI came from public sources, so when the funding plug was pulled, it really was the end for most of this research work.

Only three UK universities were allowed to continue with AI research: Edinburgh, Essex, and Sussex. Lighthill's report is somewhat controversial these days, as it appears he did not understand the primary aim of AI researchers, which was to actually understand problem solving completely divorced from living systems, that is to say, as an abstract process.

Since the early days of computing, there has been a close association between the United Kingdom and the United States, and Lighthill's report had a profound effect on the Advanced Research Projects Agency (ARPA or DARPA as it is known these days), and they also pulled the plug on major research funding. In the 1960s, enormous amounts of money had been given to various AI researchers (Minsky, Rosenblatt, etc.) pretty much to spend as they liked.

In 1969, the Mansfield Amendment was passed as part of the Defense Authorization Act of 1970. This required the DARPA to restrict its support for basic research to only those things that were directly related to military functions and operational requirements. All major funding for basic AI research was withdrawn.

While it is true that there had been a number of high profile failures, in hindsight it can be seen that the optimism was partly correct. Today almost all the advanced technologies have elements of AI within them, as Ray Kurzweil has remarked in his 2006 book *The Singularity Is Near*: "many thousands of AI applications are deeply embedded in the infrastructure of every industry." [9]

To Kurzweil, the AI winter has ended, but there have been two very highly significant ones, the first from 1974 to 1980 and the second from 1987 to 1993. There have also been a host of minor incidents or episodes, e.g., the failure of machine translation in 1966 and the abandonment of connectionism in 1970.

It is still the case, apparently, that venture capitalists as well as government officials get a bit nervous at the suggestion of AI, and so most of the AI research undertook a rebranding exercise. They also refocused research on smaller, more tractable problems. This reminds one of what Dennis Ritchie said about why he invented the UNIX operating system—to concentrate on *doing one thing at a time and doing it well*.

1.3 ML and Statistics

ML and Statistics are closely related fields. According to Michael I. Jordan, the ideas of ML, from methodological principles to theoretical tools, have had a long prehistory in statistics [10]. He has also suggested the term data science as a placeholder to call the overall field, at least for the stage that we are in right now.

You could say that (in relation to ML) statistics is running on a parallel track. Although there are many similarities between ML theory and statistical inference, they use different terms. This can be quite important and will be more fully explored later on.

In terms of the statistical element of our story, the timeline extends as far back as the early 19th century and starts with the invention of the least squares linear method. It is impossible to overstate the importance of the least squares method as it is the single most important technique used in modern statistics.

In 1805 and 1806 [11], Adrien-Marie Legendre published *Nouvelles Méthodes pour la Détermination des Orbites des Comètes (Courcier, Paris)*.

He was studying cometary orbits and on the bottom of page 75 stated: *On voit donc que la méthode des moindres carrés fait connaître en quelque sorte le centre autour duquel viennent se ranger tous les résultats fournis par l'expérience de manière à s'en écarter le moins possible.* This sentence translates to English as "This shows that the least squares method demonstrates the center around which the measured values from the experiment are distributed so as to deviate as little as possible."

Gauss also published on this method in 1809 [12]. A controversy erupted (similar to the one between Newton and Leibnitz about the primacy of invention of the calculus). It turns out that although it is highly likely that Gauss knew about this method before Legendre did, he didn't publish on it or talk about it widely, so Legendre can be rightly regarded as the inventor of the least squares method (Stigler, 1981) [13].

Stigler also states: "When Gauss did publish on least squares, he went far beyond Legendre in both conceptual and technical development, linking the method to probability and providing algorithms for the computation of estimates."

As further evidence of this, Gauss's 1821 paper included a version of the Gauss–Markov theorem [14].

The next person in the story of least squares regression is Francis Galton. In 1886, he published *Regression towards Mediocrity in Hereditary Stature,* which was the first use of the term *regression* [15]. He defined the difference between the height of a child and the mean height as a *deviate.*

Galton defined the law of regression as: "The height deviate of the offspring is on average two thirds of the height deviate of its mid-parentage" where mid-parentage refers to the average height of the two parents. Mediocrity is the old term for average. Interestingly, it has taken on a vernacular meaning today as *substandard*; however, the correct meaning is *average.* For Galton, regression was only ever meaningful in the biological context.

His work was further extended by Udny Yule (1897) [16] and Karl Pearson (1903) [17]. Yule's 1897 paper on *the theory of correlation* introduced the term *variables* for numerical quantities, since he said *their magnitude varies.* He also used the term *correlation* and wanted this to be used instead of *causal relation*, presaging the long debate that correlation does not imply causation. In some cases, this debate still rages today.

As an interesting sidenote, Pearson's 1903 paper was entitled "The Law of Ancestral Heredity," and it was published in the then new journal, *Biometrika,* which he had cofounded. There was a debate on the mechanics of evolution raging at that time, and there were two camps, the biometricians (like Pearson and Raphael Weldon) and the Mendelians (led by William Bateson, who had been taught by Weldon). There exists a fascinating letter from Raymond Pearl written to Karl Pearson, about their robust disagreement on hereditary theory and Pearl's removal as an editor of *Biometrika* (1910). This controversy continued until the modern synthesis of evolution was established in the 1930s [18].

Yule and Pearson's work specified that linear regression required the variables to be distributed in a Gaussian (or normal) manner.

They assumed that the joint distribution of both the independent and dependent variables was Gaussian; however, this assumption was weakened by Fisher, in 1922, in his paper: *The goodness of fit of regression formulae, and the distribution of regression coefficients* [19].

Fisher assumed that the dependent variable was Gaussian, but that the joint distribution needn't be. This harkens back to the thoughts that Gauss was expressing a century earlier.

Another major advance was made by John Nelder and Robert Wedderburn in 1972, when they published the seminal paper "Generalised Linear Models" in the *Journal of the Royal Statistical Society* [20]. They developed a class of generalized linear models, which included the normal, poisson, binomial, and gamma distributions.

The link function allowed a model with linear and nonlinear components. A maximum likelihood procedure was demonstrated to fit the models. This is the way we do logistic regression nowadays, which is the single most important statistical procedure employed by actuaries and in modern industry (particularly the finance industry).

The multiple linear regression model is given by

$$y_i = \beta_0 + \beta_1 x_{1i} + \beta_2 x_{2i} + \cdots + \beta_k x_{ki} + \epsilon_{i\,(1)} \tag{1.1}$$

where

y_i is the dependent variable for the ith observation

β_0 is the Y intercept

$\beta_1, \beta_2, \ldots, \beta_k$ are the population partial regression coefficients

$x_{1i}, x_{2i}, \ldots, x_{ki}$ are the observed values of the independent variables $x_1, x_2, \ldots, x_k$ and $k = 1, 2, 3, \ldots, K$ are the explanatory variables

The model written in vector form is shown as

$$\mathbf{y} = \mathbf{X}\boldsymbol{\theta} + \boldsymbol{\varepsilon} \tag{1.2}$$

where $\mathbf{y}$ is an $(n \times 1)$ vector of observations, $\mathbf{X}$ is an $(n \times k)$ matrix of known coefficients (with $n > k$), $\boldsymbol{\theta}$ is a $(k \times 1)$ vector of parameters, and $\boldsymbol{\varepsilon}$ is an $(n \times 1)$ vector of error *random* variables $\boldsymbol{\varepsilon}_j$, shown as,

$$E(\boldsymbol{\varepsilon}) = \mathbf{0} \tag{1.3}$$

This embodies the assumption that the $\boldsymbol{\varepsilon}_j$ are all uncorrelated, i.e., they have zero means and the same variance σ^2.

If we assume that a set of n observations comes from distributions with differing means, such that

$$\mu_j = \sum_{i=1}^{k} x_{ij}\theta_i, \quad j = 1,\, 2,\ldots,n \tag{1.4}$$

We now have to minimize

$$\sum_{j}\left(y_j - \sum_i x_{ij}\theta_i\right)^2 \tag{1.5}$$

which is the *sum of squares* (Eq. 1.5) in the least squares method [21].

Figure 1.4 graphically demonstrates a line of best fit, i.e., the line which minimizes the squared distance between all the points and the line. This is the basis of linear regression. The slope of the line corresponds to the regression coefficients and the intercept is the first term in our model above. Note that this corresponds to the well-known equation of a straight line: $y = ax + b$, where the slope is given by a and b is the intercept.

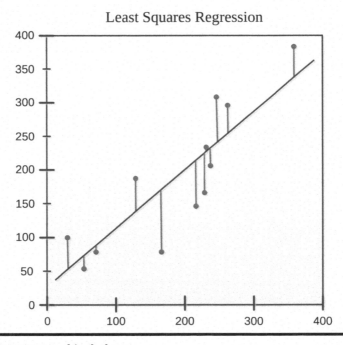

Figure 1.4 LSR graphical plot.

Regression methods have been a continuing part of statistics and, even today, they are being used and extended. Modern extensions include things such as ridge regression and lasso regression.

1.3.1 Rediscovery of ML

In a sense to take up the slack, expert systems came into vogue during the first AI Winter. By the end of it, they were waning in popularity and are hardly used these days.

After about a 15-year hiatus, ML was revived with the invention of backpropagation. This took the Perceptron model to a new level. This helped break the logjam where it was assumed that neural nets would never amount to anything. The key paper in 1986 was by David Rumelhart, Geoff Hinton, and Ronald J Williams [22]. It was entitled "Learning Representations by Back-Propagating Errors" and was published in *Nature*, the world's most prestigious scientific journal.

In Figure 1.5, the essential architecture and the process of backpropagation are shown. The network topology has three layers (there may be more than this, but three layers is a fairly common arrangement). The weights propagate forward

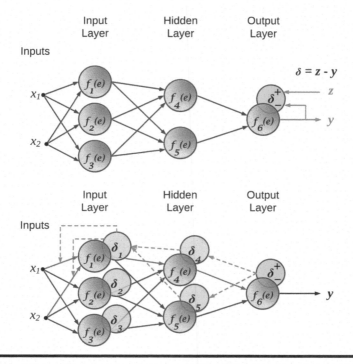

Figure 1.5 The architecture and process of backpropagation.

through the layers. Each node in the network has two units: a summing function (for the weights) and an activation unit that uses a nonlinear transfer function. Common transfer functions include the log-sigmoid which outputs 0 to 1 and the tan-sigmoid which outputs −1 to 1.

The weights are rolled up to predict y, and this is compared with the actual target vector z. The difference is known as the error signal, and it is transmitted back through the layers, which cause re-weighting that runs forward for another comparison. The algorithm proceeds to find an optimal value for the output by means of gradient descent. Sometimes, local minima in the error surface can disrupt the process of finding a global minimum, but if the number of nodes is increased, this problem resolves, according to Rumelhart, Hinton, and Williams (1986).

Research on neural nets exploded. Three years after that, Kur Hornik, Maxwell Stinchcombe, and Halber White published *Multilayer Feedforward Networks Are Universal Approximators* [23]. As they said, "backpropagation is the most common neural net model used today it overcomes the limitations of the Perceptron by using a combination of a hidden layer and a sigmoid function."

Development in neural nets has expanded enormously, and today the current interest is in deep belief networks, which are neural networks with multiple hidden layers and are topologically quite complex. They have enjoyed recent success in allowing images to be classified accurately as well as in many other use cases. Today, it is fair to say that Google makes an extensive use of neural nets (almost exclusively) and they have also open-sourced such important technologies as TensorFlow and Google Sling, which are natural language frame semantics parsers of immense power.

1.4 Critical Events: A Timeline

This list of critical events (Table 1.1) is by no means exhaustive; readers who want to know more can find a huge amount of material on the web about the history of computers and ML.

Table 1.1   Critical Events: A Timeline

Year	Event	Details
1945	von Neumann architecture	A draft report that John von Neumann wrote on Eckert and Mauchly's EDVAC proposal was widely circulated and became the basis for the *von Neumann architecture*. All digital electronic computers today use this architecture [24].
1950	Turing test	In a famous paper, "Computing Machinery and Intelligence" published in the journal, *Mind*, Alan Turing introduces what he calls *The Imitation Game* [25]. Later on, this becomes a more generalized proposition which in effect states that if a person were unable to tell a machine apart from a human being though a remote terminal, then we could say that artificial intelligence has been achieved.
		In his paper, Turing proposed a *learning machine*, which could learn as much as a child does with rewards and punishments. This becomes a stimulus to develop genetic algorithms and reinforcement learning.
1952	Computer checkers programs	Arthur Samuel created a program to play checkers at IBM's Poughkeepsie Laboratory.
1957	Perceptron	Frank Rosenblatt invents the Perceptron. This is the first time that a machine can be said to *learn* something. This invention creates a massive amount of excitement and is widely covered in influential media (*The New York Times*, *The New Yorker* magazine, and many others).
		Some of the claims made are quite extraordinary examples of hyperbole and this will be the direct cause of the first *AI Winter*.

(Continued)

Table 1.1 (*Continued*) Critical Events: A Timeline

Year	Event	Details
1969	*Perceptrons*	Marvin Minsky and Seymour Papert publish their book *Perceptrons*, which outlines a number of limitations to the use of Perceptrons, most notably their inability to execute an XOR function. The XOR, or exclusive OR, is a logical operation that outputs as true only when the inputs differ (one being true, the other false). This is in practice a severe limitation for case or conditional logic in programming. This work was seen by many as the major trigger in bringing about the *AI Winter*.
1973	Lighthill report	James Lighthill is commissioned by the British Science Research Council. He published this report as "Artificial Intelligence: A General Survey" in 1973. Lighthill was extremely (and unfairly) pessimistic about what AI research has achieved to date. For example, he stated: "in no part of the field have discoveries made so far produced the major impact that was then promised." However, he also failed to understand that the main purpose of AI research is "studying the structure of information and the structure of problem solving processes independently of applications and independently of its realization in animals or humans." (John McCarthy, 1974). The Lighthill report was flawed; however the damage had been done, and after this, the first AI Winter (which went for at least 15 years) began.

(*Continued*)

Table 1.1 (*Continued*) Critical Events: A Timeline

Year	Event	Details
1986	Backpropagation	It is described by David Rumelhart, Geoff Hinton, and Ronald J. Williams, in a paper in *Nature* entitled "Learning Representations by Back-Propagating Errors." In effect, they designed a system that involves repeated adjustment of weights of connections in a hidden layer until they have minimized the overall difference between the actual output vector and the desired output vector. They stated that at the end of the process, the hidden layer comes to represent important features, and therefore, the ability to create these features distinguishes backpropagation from earlier simpler methods, such as Perceptrons.
1995	Random forests	Tin Kam Ho published the first paper describing a random forest [26]. In the abstract, it was stated that decision trees are attractive classifiers because of their computational efficiency, but that traditional trees often can't be grown to an arbitrary complexity because generalization starts to break down. In other words, overfitting occurs. A stochastic modeling method was devised where multiple trees are built in randomly selected subspaces of the overall feature space. These multiple trees can then be combined to give a stable estimator. The algorithm was demonstrated on the NIST handwriting data.

(Continued)

Table 1.1 (*Continued*) Critical Events: A Timeline

Year	Event	Details
1995	Support vector machines	Corinna Cortes and Vladimir Vapnik published the paper establishing support vector machines [27]. In the paper, they gave a history, starting with Fisher's linear discriminant function and then moving on to Rosenblatt's Perceptron and the recently discovered backpropagation algorithm. They proposed a support vector network as a new learning machine for two-group classification problems. The key idea is that input vectors are nonlinearly mapped to a high dimensional feature space, where a linear hyperplane can be constructed that gives maximum separation of the groups. Using dot products as well as the very clever kernel trick, the solution becomes computationally feasible. SVMs that are known these days give very good performance and generalizability. They concluded the paper by demonstrating success with the NIST character recognition data.
1997	Machine defeats chess grand master	Garry Kasparov is defeated by IBM's Deep Blue chess machine.
2011	Machine wins at Jeopardy!	IBM's Watson defeats two human experts in a Jeopardy! Competition. The system is extremely sophisticated and uses a hybrid combination of information retrieval, natural language processing, and machine learning.
2015	Machine beats a human Go champion.	An expert human Go player is defeated by Google's AlphaGo. This system is based on a combination of tree search and machine learning.

1.5 Types of ML

There are basically four important types of ML. They are supervised learning, semisupervised learning, unsupervised learning, and reinforcement learning.

Essentially in supervised learning a known target or label is modeled. The purpose of algorithms that are used in supervised learning is to predict the likelihood of a specific event or outcome.

A typical example of SL would be a consumer credit risk model employed by a bank.

Unsupervised learning is where the data are investigated for particular patterns or structure, a common example of this is cluster analysis, commonly used in market segmentation operations. Unsupervised learning is commonly known to statisticians as a *hypothesis-generating technique*.

A typical example of UL is given by market segmentation. This has been found to be especially valuable for marketing campaigns.

Semisupervised learning falls between supervised and unsupervised learning, as one might expect. There are a variety of approaches, and one commonly taken is to use unsupervised techniques to ascertain a class structure and then switch to supervised learning to verify the structure/target. This process can occur iteratively.

A typical example of SSL would be the use of a hidden Markov model or HMM, together with a Baum-Welch learning procedure in speech recognition [28].

Reinforcement learning is characterized by agent-based processes that use current knowledge to make a decision where the aim is to maximize a reward. They proceed in discrete time intervals and usually involve Markov processes.

An example of RL would be teaching a computer to play backgammon and other games.

1.5.1 Supervised Learning

Supervised learning is the most prevalent form of ML. The key point in supervised learning is that you have a known target or label. The modeling process involves prediction of the new label or target, based on the characteristics of the dependent variables in the training set. In a sense, supervised learning is like regression in statistics. It involves the estimation of new possible cases from known, understood targets or labels.

Most ML uses supervised learning techniques. Essentially, we have an input vector with the goal of approximating the mapping function so well that we can predict the output with a high degree of precision.

The two subtypes of supervised machines are classification and regression. Classification is when the output variable is a category that is binary, ternary, or a higher number. Either way it is categorical (grouped outcome). The point of regression is the output variable which is a real number, such as cost or height. Good examples of supervised ML techniques include linear regression, random forests, and support vector machines.

Let's look at the different types of supervised learning algorithms.

A good place to start is the set of supervised learning algorithms listed in scikit-learn, which is a very popular Python ML library. The list is as follows:

1. Generalized linear models
2. Linear and quadratic discriminant analysis
3. Kernel ridge regression
4. Support vector machines
5. Stochastic gradient descent
6. Nearest neighbors
7. Gaussian processes
8. Cross decomposition
9. Naive Bayes
10. Decision trees
11. Ensemble methods
12. Multiclass and multi-label algorithms
13. Feature selection
14. Semisupervised
15. Isotonic regression
16. Probability calibration

Most commercial propensity models involve supervised learning. An example is the use of a number of inputs, such as age, sex, income, type of housing, and marital status to predict creditworthiness. Banks use such models (usually derived using logistic regression) all the time. The model is trained with a set of bad and good customers. When sufficient accuracy has been achieved, the model is then deployed into production.

1.5.2 Unsupervised Learning

By contrast, unsupervised learning is a technique in which you have inputs that have no specific output. The goal is to understand the structure or groupings in the data. There are two subtypes of unsupervised learning: clustering and association. Clustering is used to discover inherent groupings in the data; usually confirmatory discriminant analysis is required as a follow-up to determine the validity of the discovered structure.

Association rules are about co-occurrence of different attributes. Recommender systems are usually based on this type of analysis. Past purchase co-occurrences are used to suggest appropriate additional purchases to a customer. Amazon uses such techniques very heavily. The other term for association rules is market basket analysis. This has been used extensively in retail settings, particularly in store layout and redesign.

scikit-learn unsupervised learning algorithms include the following:

1. Gaussian mixture models
2. Manifold learning

3. Clustering
4. Biclustering
5. Decomposing signals in components (matrix factorization problems)
6. Covariance estimation
7. Novelty and outlier detection
8. Density estimation
9. Neural network models (unsupervised)

A classic example of clustering is market or customer segmentation. The point is that the sort of conversation or presentation a marketer might make to a 76-year-old woman is almost certainly going to be different from that to a 22-year-old male. Market segmentation is used to allow marketers to engage meaningfully with distinctly different parts of the customer base.

There are plenty of biological examples, where biometric measurement has been used to separate closely related species. These have been around since the early 20th century.

1.5.3 Semisupervised Learning

Semisupervised learning is a hybrid of the two techniques: supervised and unsupervised learning. It is commonly used where it is impractical or too expensive to label all of the input data so we only have some of it labeled.

One approach to semisupervised learning involves using the known labeled data and projecting it into the other data attributes and then testing to see how good this is. The second approach involves using unsupervised learning to discover structure, then validating how closely the assigned structure matches with the existing labeled data. Both approaches converge on a similar outcome.

Support vector clustering can be used for semisupervised learning. This is often used in industrial applications either when data is not labeled or when only some data is labeled as a preprocessing operation for a classification pass. Another good example of semisupervised learning is in the use of HMM, which is commonly employed with a Baum-Welch learning procedure. This is used in both speech recognition and bioinformatics.

1.5.4 Reinforcement Learning

In reinforcement learning the most important thing is characterization of the learning problem. A key difference between reinforcement learning and supervised learning is that outcomes are not determined, but the system learns from its own experience.

Two competing processes are set up, commonly referred to as exploitation: the reapplication of a prior decision and exploration and the search through the solution space for a better performing decision function. These two operate against each other in a classic trade-off, and the configuration of agents is important to optimize both, otherwise convergence is unlikely.

Key points for this approach usually taken are as follows:

1. An agent is established (an agent is a semi-independent piece of software or code).
2. Various environmental states are presented to the agent.
3. Actions (decision outcomes) are produced by the agent.
4. State transition rules operate.
5. Reward rules/principles that are related to the transition are activated.
6. Rules for the agent to interpret observation are invoked.
7. Repeat from step 2 onward until a stable estimate is reached.

A key aspect of this learning method is the discrete time dimension. The major enabling algorithmic process is a Markov decision process.

Currently, there is a tremendous interest in reinforcement learning. It can be applied in numerous disciplines and contexts, e.g., control engineering, game theory, and economics.

An example of reinforcement learning would be to set up a computer to play backgammon or other games. Building elevator control is another use case.

1.6 Summary

We covered an introduction to both the nature and history of ML. The complex and, sometimes, convoluted way in which things developed was briefly discussed, especially the development of AI, which has a fascinating history of stops and starts, i.e., the so-called AI winter where funding was literally cut off midstream. This is not uncommon with other types of computer technology development, but it was especially pronounced in the case of AI. Neural net methods are well established in the mainstream these days and form the major part of what is being done at Google, among other tech giants.

We looked at one of the most important methods in statistics, least squares regression—how it came about historically and just how it works. Statistics and ML have a long and intertwined history.

The critical timeline from 1945 (the dawn of the Computer and Atomic Age) to 2015 with the defeat of a Go master by a computer gives us a detailed understanding of some of the broad sweep of history.

Lastly, we had a brief exposition on the various types of ML, including supervised, unsupervised, semisupervised, and reinforcement learning. Finally, some of the algorithms available in the scikit-learn Python ML library were listed to give one an idea of where to start the journey to learn how to apply these methods. An entire and detailed book could be written on this topic, but hopefully the interested readers will have gained some idea about where to start their search for further knowledge.

1.7 Glossary

Term	Acronym	Meaning
Agent		A software program which acts for another, either an individual or another software program. These are often bots and are also used in complex simulations, particularly of network topology and behavior.
AI Winter		Hiatus in AI Research, the first one was from 1973 to 1986, with others less serious since then.
Artificial intelligence	AI	The ability to get a computer (machine) to mimic intelligent behavior often in very sophisticated ways.
Association		A statistical technique where related items are grouped together, such as in market basket analysis.
Backpropagation		An algorithm where repeated adjustment of weights of connections in a hidden layer is carried out iteratively until they have minimized the overall difference between the actual output vector and the desired output vector.
Clustering		A multivariate statistical technique to group related cases together, commonly used in market segmentation studies.
Correlation		A statistical technique to determine the strength of the linear relationship between two numeric variables.
Defense Advanced Research Projects Agency	DARPA	A US Government agency, created in the panic after the Soviet Union launched the first artificial satellite, Sputnik 1 (Спутник-1), using a P-7 Semyorka (Семёрка) rocket designation 8K71PS, on October 4, 1957, from Baikonur Cosmodrome (Космодро́м Байкону́р) Site No. 1.

(Continued)

Term	Acronym	Meaning
Data science	DS	A modern and rapidly growing synthesis of large-scale database operations, ML, and statistics. It also includes unstructured data analysis such as text mining, which involves an understanding of both computational linguistics and natural language processing.
Decision trees		Tools that use human-understandable graphs to process data to provide a classification or decision point. There are a variety of methods, the most common being recursive partitioning. Both categorical and numeric variables can be used in the construction of trees.
Deep belief networks	DBN	A complex type of neural network with multiple layers. They have recently been found to be good at discrimination and classification of images. DBNs are the most resistant technique which is able to classify images that have been deliberately modified.
Dependent variable		A variable which is estimated or predicted using a regression equation.
Deviate		A normally distributed random variable with a mean of 0 and a standard deviation of 1.
Electronic Discrete Variable Automatic Computer	EDVAC	The first ever general-purpose computer, designed by J. Presper Eckert and John Mauchly. They went on to build it as the Electronic Numerical Integrator and Computer, which was commissioned at the University of Pennsylvania on February 15, 1946. It was also Turing-complete. They went on to found the Eckert-Mauchly Computer Corporation, which survives today as Unisys.
Expert systems		The first successful AI endeavor. Expert systems are designed to mimic a human expert and consist of a knowledge base component as well as an inference engine. These are usually rule-based systems using if-then-else type of statements.

(Continued)

Term	Acronym	Meaning
Gaussian distribution		Also known as normal distribution. A symmetrical bell-shaped curve with the probability density function given by $f\left(x\mid\mu,\sigma^2\right)=\dfrac{1}{\sqrt{2\sigma^2\pi}}\,e^{-\frac{(x-\mu)^2}{2\sigma^2}}$.
Gauss–Markov theorem		The Gauss–Markov theorem states that in a linear regression model in which the errors have expectation of zero and are uncorrelated with equal variances, the best linear unbiased estimator of the coefficients is given by the ordinary least squares estimator. The error distribution does not necessarily need to be normal (Gaussian) or IID (independent and identically distributed), only uncorrelated with a mean of zero and having the same finite variance.
Generalized linear model	GLM	A flexible generalization of ordinary linear regression that allows response variables that have error distribution models other than a normal distribution. It was proposed by Nelder and Wedderburn in 1972. Distributions covered in their original paper included the normal, poisson, binomial, and gamma distributions.
Google Sling		A natural language frame semantics parser. To quote from their GitHub page: "The parser is a general transition-based frame semantic parser using bi-directional LSTMs for input encoding and a Transition Based Recurrent Unit (TBRU) for output decoding."
Linear threshold gate	LTG	A device used to discriminate between vectors belonging to two classes. An LTG maps an input vector x into a single binary output y. A threshold constant is used to set the gate. In effect, it is a binary switch.
Long short-term memory	LSTM	A type of recurrent neural network. It has the property of being able to transmit some state information across the layer boundary, thus mimicking a Markov process.

(Continued)

Term	Acronym	Meaning
Machine learning	ML	The field where computer programs or systems can learn specific tasks, such as discrimination or classification, without being explicitly programmed to do so.
Markov decision process	MDP	A discrete time stochastic control process. It provides the ability to model decision-making in a situation where the outcome is partly random and partly under the control of a decision maker. It is used in dynamic programming and reinforcement learning and has been known since 1957, when Richard Bellman published his paper: "A Markovian Decision Process" [29].
Markov process		A stochastic process in which the conditional probability distribution of future states depends only upon the present state, and not on the events that preceded it. A Markov chain is the usual representation.
Natural language processing	NLP	Afield of computer science, AI, and computational linguistics that deals with interactions between computers and human language. Its products are machine translation and voice-to-text. The AI Winter had a big impact on this field. Today it is going well. The voice-to-text product dragon can be traced back to the Stanford Research Institute.
Perceptron		The first type of artificial neural net devised by Dr. Frank Rosenblatt in 1957. The Perceptron was specifically designed as a (simplified) copy of the human retina. It consisted of a detector array, a weight summing function, and a transfer function. When it functioned correctly Dr. Rosenberg said that an internal change in the wiring diagram had occurred. This was the first instance of successful ML.

(Continued)

Term	Acronym	Meaning
Predictive modeling		The process of building or creating a mathematical model to determine a specific outcome, e.g., linear regression. When new values are put into the regression equations, it can be said that a prediction is being made.
Python		A high-level, general-purpose, interpreted, and dynamic programming language. It is explicitly designed for code readability, and its syntax allows programmers to express concepts in fewer lines of code than other languages. Python supports multiple programming paradigms, including object-oriented, imperative, and functional programming. It also has a dynamic type system, automatic memory management, and late binding.
Random Boolean units		A component of Rosenblatt's initial Perceptron design. These were, in effect, hidden layer units, which mapped a given nonlinearly separable training set of patterns onto the vectors of a high-dimensional feature space for that training set to become linearly separable. LTGs were used for the output.
Random forests		An ensemble learning method for classification, regression and, other tasks that are operated by constructing many decision trees during training. They output either the class mode or the mean (regression) of the individual trees. They are very robust and do not overfit. They were first proposed by Tin Kam Ho, but were extended and made famous by Leo Breiman and Adele Cutler.
Regression		A term first introduced by Galton in his 1886 paper: "Regression towards Mediocrity in Hereditary Stature." Galton defined the law of regression as the height deviate of the offspring is on average two thirds of the height deviate of its mid-parentage.

(Continued)

Term	Acronym	Meaning
Reinforcement learning	RL	In this technique, the system learns from its own experience. There are two processes, exploration and exploitation (decision function). These two processes are set up to trade off against each other and cause the system to iteratively search the solution space for a better performing function. Good configuration is important to yield convergence of the algorithm.
Semisupervised learning	SSL	A hybrid of supervised and unsupervised learning. It is commonly used where it is impractical or too expensive to label all of the input data so that only some of it is labeled. The two approaches commonly involve using known labeled data, projecting, then testing or using unsupervised learning to discover structure, and then validating how closely the assigned structure matches the existing labeled data.
Supervised learning	SL	It involves the use of a known target or label. The modeling process for supervised learning involves prediction of the new label or target in new data, based on the characteristics of the dependent variables that were determined in the training set (or as is often said "during training").
Support vector machines	SVMs	Also known as support vector networks. They are supervised learning models that are used for classification and regression analysis. SVM maps values into high dimensional space where the hyperplane of maximum linear separation is determined. Computational tractability is afforded by the use of the clever kernel trick as well as by dot products.
Target		Also known as a dependent variable or label. It is the known outcome that a regression or other model is designed to predict by use of a training set.

(*Continued*)

Term	Acronym	Meaning
TensorFlow	TF	To quote Wikipedia: "TensorFlow is an open-source software library for dataflow programming across a range of tasks…It is used for both research and production at Google." A variant of this, using LSTMs, can effectively apply a Markov process to an enormous dataset.
Unsupervised learning	UL	Also known as a hypothesis generating technique. It involves grouping observations in the case of clustering or co-occurrence in the case of association analysis.
Variables		A measured quantity. There are four main types used in statistics: nominal (e.g. male/female), ordinal (an ordered list where the order is more important than the size of the interval), interval (an ordinal sequence with equal-sized intervals), and continuous (quantities such as a person's weight and height).
von Neumann architecture		The basic architecture of modern digital computers. There are three basic components: an input device, an output device, and a central processing unit that contains a control unit, an arithmetic logic unit, and an attached memory module. The design is also known as the Princeton architecture.
Exclusive OR function or gate	XOR	A digital logic gate that implements an exclusive OR. That means a true (1) is output if one, and only one, of the inputs to the gate is true. If both inputs are false (0) or both are true, a false output is obtained. A good way to remember this is "one or the other, but not both."

References

1. Von Neumann, John (1958) *The Computer & the Brain*, Yale University Press, New Haven and London.
2. Anonymous (1958) New Navy Device Learns by Doing; Psychologist Shows Embryo of Computer Designed to Read and Grow Wiser, *The New York Times*, July 1958, 25.

3. Mason, Harding, Stewart, D., Gill, Brendan (1958) *The Talk of the Town: Rival*, The New Yorker, December 1958 Issue, pp. 44–45.
4. Rosenblatt, Frank (1958) The Perceptron: A probabilistic model for information storage and organization in the brain, *Psychological Review*, Vol. 65, No. 6, pp. 386–408.
5. Rosenblatt, Frank (1961) *Principles of Neurodynamics: Perceptrons and the Theory of Brain Mechanisms*, Cornell Aeronautical Laboratory, Inc., Cornell University, New York.
6. Rosenblatt, Frank (1962) *Principles of Neurodynamics: Perceptrons and the Theory of Brain Mechanisms*, Spartan books, Washington, DC, pp. xvi, 616.
7. Minsky, Marvin and Papert, Seymour (1969) *Perceptrons: An Introduction to Computational Geometry*, MIT Press, Cambridge, MA.
8. Lighthill, James (1973) Artificial Intelligence: A General Survey, *Artificial Intelligence: A Paper Symposium*, Science Research Council.
9. Kurzweil, Ray (2006) *The Singularity Is Near*, Viking Press, New York.
10. Jordan, Michael Irwin (2014) Comments in Relation to Statistics and Machine Learning, www.reddit.com/r/MachineLearning/comments/2fxi6v/ama_michael_i_jordan/; 09 Sep 2014.
11. Legendre, Adrien-Marie (1805, 1806) *Nouvelles Méthodes pour la Détermination des Orbites des Comètes*, Courcier, Paris.
12. Gauss, Carl Friedrich (1809) *Theoria Motus Corporum Coelestium in Sectionibus Conicis Solem Ambientum*, Friedrich Perthes and I.H. Besser, Hamburg.
13. Stigler, Stephen M. (1981) Gauss and the invention of least squares, *The Annals of Statistics*, Vol. 9, No. 3, pp. 465–474.
14. Gauss, Carl Friedrich (1821) *Theoria Combinationis Observationum Erroribus Minimis Obnoxiae*, H. Dieterich, Gottingen.
15. Galton, Francis (1886) Regression towards mediocrity in hereditary stature, *The Journal of the Anthropological Institute of Great Britain and Ireland*, Vol. 15, No. 1886, pp. 246–263.
16. Yule, George Udny (1897) On the theory of correlation, *Journal of the Royal Statistical Society*, Vol. 60, No. 4, pp. 812–854.
17. Pearson, Karl (1903) The law of ancestral heredity, *Biometrika*, Vol. 2, No. 2, pp. 211–236.
18. Pearl, Raymond (1910) Letter Raymond Pearl letter to Karl Pearson, about disagreement on hereditary theory and his removal as an editor of Biometrika (2/15/1910), www.dnalc.org/view/12037-Raymond-Pearl-letter-to-Karl-Pearson-about-disagreement-on-hereditary-theory-and-his-removal-as-an-editor-of-Biometrika-2-15-1910-.html.
19. Fisher, Ronald Aylmer (1922) The goodness of fit of regression formulae, and the distribution of regression coefficients, *Journal of the Royal Statistical Society*, Vol. 85, No. 4, pp. 597–612.
20. Nelder, John and Wedderburn, Robert William Maclagan (1972) Generalised linear models, *Journal of the Royal Statistical Society. Series A (General)*, Vol. 135, No. 3, pp. 370–384.
21. Stuart, Alan and Ord, J. Keith (1991) Kendall's advanced theory of statistics. Volume 2, *Classical Inference and Relationship*, 5th edition, Edward Arnold, London.
22. Rumelhart, David; Hinton, Geoff and Williams, Ronald J. (1986) Learning representations by back-propagating errors, *Nature*, Vol. 323, pp. 533–536.
23. Hornik, Kur; Stinchcombe, Maxwell and White, Halber (1989) Multilayer feedforward networks are universal approximators, *Neural Networks*, Vol. 2, pp. 359–366.

24. Von Neumann, John (1945) First Draft of a Report on the EDVAC, Contract No. W–670–ORD–4926 Between the United States Army Ordnance Department and the University of Pennsylvania, Moore School of Electrical Engineering, University of Pennsylvania, June 30, 1945.

25. Turing, Alan Mathison (1950) Computing machinery and intelligence, *Mind*, Vol. LIX. No. 236, pp. 433–460.

26. Ho, Tin Kam (1995) Random Decision Forests, *Proceedings of the Third International Conference on Document Analysis and Recognition*. Montreal, Quebec: IEEE. 1: 278–282.

27. Cortes, Corinna and Vapnik, Vladimir (1995) *Support-vector Networks, Machine Learning*, Kluwer Academic Publishers, Dordrecht, 20 (3), pp. 273–297.

28. Baum, Leonard E., Petrie, Ted, Soules, George and Weiss, Norman (1970) A maximization technique occurring in the statistical analysis of probabilistic functions of Markov chains, *The Annals of Mathematical Statistics*, Vol. 41, No. 1, pp. 164–171.

29. Bellman, Richard (1957) A Markovian decision process, *Journal of Mathematics and Mechanics*, Vol. 6, No. 5, pp. 679–684.

Chapter 2

Regression for Data Analytics

M. Saiful Bari

Southeast University
Nanyang Technological University

Contents

2.1 Introduction

The world is getting smaller, but in the process of doing so, we are producing a lot of data (by using data oriented technology, i.e. social network, e-commerce etc.). Throughout the development of modern civilization, we can divide the whole procedure into multiple stages. Agriculture (around 1980), industrialization (around 1900–1960) and information technology (around 1960–2007) are the major footprints of human civilization. Now we have entered into the fourth industrial revolution: artificial intelligence. In the next decade, the advancement of technology and programming philosophy of the existing field will change drastically and we will get much closer to the human level intelligence for a lot of tasks without actually telling a computer what to do. It will be possible only through the amount of data that we are producing in our day-to-day life. Philosophically, people will develop intelligent systems by learning from their previous stories and activities. To make a long story short, people will be able to analyze the huge amount of data more systematically so that they can take the correct decision based on statistical data. The stage of information technology gives us a complete platform to gather the necessary data through Internet of Things (IoT) devices and products. We will explore new methods in the coming decades to gather and take decisions and solve some major problems of our society.

To be able to cope up with the change that is happening right now, we should have proper knowledge of understanding data and analyze it so that we can take a more educative guess, which will be so perfect that we cannot differentiate it from that of a human. This art of exploration is known as data science. Analyzing big data is more difficult in terms of technique and usability because of the need for memory and computational power. To be able to do that, we need more sophisticated algorithms that can also be implemented in real life.

Data science is not "rocket science." In response to a bigger picture of the relevant subject, we can safely assume it to be the analysis of pattern exploration in higher dimension—the dimension that can only be visualized by vectors. Although data science is full of attractive, mouthful names, the basic intuitions are so simple that anyone can grasp the beauty of this so-called MAGIC, given a proper and focused direction.

2.1.1 Chapter Roadmap

This chapter aims to provide the fundamental idea of a data exploration methodology, *regression*. Without a proper understanding of regression, we will not be able to go further and explore more opportunities to play with the data. Data science is nothing but exploiting the features of machine learning with proper visualization. No matter what advanced model [1–3] we might develop in the future, the core of the model will lie in understanding regression. At the start of the chapter, we will be learning about linear regression and its intuitions. We will be asking the question "why?" instead of "how?" We will see some examples and try to understand what is going on. Later on, we will develop some mathematical thinking based on our intuitions and begin the question "how?" Finally, we will derive the complete probabilistic analysis of linear regression. Then we will add a condition on the linear regression model and see how we can derive logistic regression from linear regression. We will also discuss the probable mathematical solution of optimization techniques, though we will not go into details of their optimization algorithms.

2.1.2 What Is Regression?

Regression is the process of estimating a relationship between variables. An event can be represented by statistical data where multiple variables participate to explain sub-events. Sometimes these variables might have a correlation between them. Say, given that you have sufficient knowledge about the perspective, if you know the age and geographical area of a certain person, you may guess the height of that person in most cases. If you consider age, geographic area, and height as variables, then you can correlate them to guess one value, given other values. Regression helps us to do such things.

In relevance to data science, we will look into linear regression and logistic regression.

2.2 Linear Regression

When the variables are linearly dependent on each other, we can estimate one variable from the other by linear regression. Assume X and Y are two variables. If they are linearly dependent on each other, we can write

$$Y \propto X$$
$$Y = mX \tag{2.1}$$

If we write the equation in the form of an equation of a line (for proper mathematical analysis), then it will become

$$Y = mX + b \tag{2.2}$$

So, the relation between X and Y can be defined by m and b. Now given enough statistical data, our objective will be finding a suitable m and b that support the statistical data most of the time. But why do we want to do that? Remember that we want to learn from our actual data. Before going through the formal process, let's have some good intuitions about what types of problems we will be solving by linear regression.

A classic example of linear regression is housing price estimation [4]. Suppose you have some detailed statistical information such as house size, door type, utilities, style, roof type, number of kitchens, and most importantly price. The variable we want to predict is called label. In this case, the price of the house is the label and the rest of the variables are called feature(s). So, house size, door type, utilities, style, roof type, number of kitchens are features.

Let's consider another interesting example. Suppose you have the honest dataset of a student's total daily average time of study in hours. Can you estimate the student's grade (in number) from the amount of study hours? So, here the student's grade is the label and the study hour is the feature.

Linear regression is a supervised problem. You must have the label on the data for training. For housing price estimation, we need the price of the house and for student grade estimation, we need the actual grades of the students.

2.2.1 Dataset Description

Let's assume you have the relevant data. Now our challenge is to generate a function *f* and feed the function with data in a *proper* way and expect some results. Let *X* be our data and *Y* be the output. So, we can write

$$f : X \rightarrow Y \tag{2.3}$$

Our objective is to design this function *f*. Before designing such a function, let's introduce our dataset in a more definitive manner:

$$\mathcal{D}\left\{x_i, y_i\right\}_{i=1}^{N}$$

where

$\mathcal{D}$ is the complete dataset.
N is the number of examples of data.
x_i is a D-dimensional vector of features/input.
y_i is the response variable/label/output.

Now, we can formally define the problem.

2.2.2 Problem Definition

Given a set of pair $\mathcal{D}\left\{x_i, y_i\right\}_{i=1}^{N}$ where y_i is the dependent variable against x_i, can you predict the value of y_i for an arbitrary given $\hat{x}$?

A graphical view of the problem is worth a lot.

In Figure 2.1, 1D regression is shown. Here the number of statistical features is 1 (only *x*). Ten points are shown in Figure 2.1a). We can easily see in the figure that most of the time for a point (*x*, *y*), while the value of *x* increases, *y* also increases. This is the correlation between the points. Figure 2.1b shows the regression line

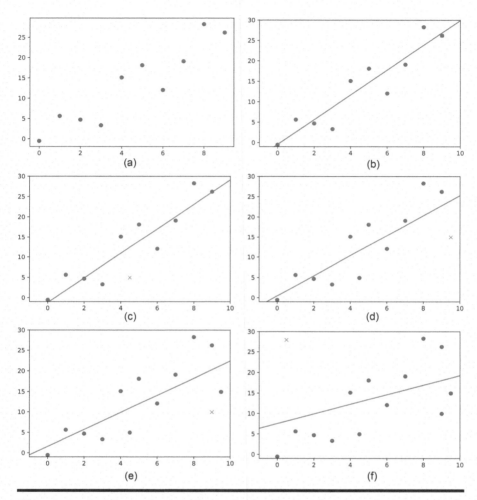

Figure 2.1 **(a) Some points are drawn in the 2D coordinate system. The x-axis is the feature and the y-axis is the response variable. (b) A regression line is drawn based on the given points. (c–f) a new point (pointed as x) is added in each of the figures, and based on the new points, a new regression line is drawn.**

based on the correlation of ten points that are in Figure 2.1a. From Figure 2.1c–f, each time a new point (showed as cross) is added, a new regression line is drawn. Notice how the line changes direction while adding a new point in Figure 2.1c–f. These four continuous figures help us to understand how the correlation is represented by the regression line. See Figure 2.1f more carefully. An outlier (strongly oppose the correlation) point causes a bad regression line. We will see some techniques at the end of the chapter to resolve the issue. For the time being, let's make sure that we get an idea of how to represent the correlation of points with the regression line.

For any arbitrary given $\hat{x}$, the value $\hat{y}$ (^ (hat) represents it's not from the dataset) on the line is the estimation. We call this line as the best fitted line (considering the given points). The line actually explains the best linear relationship for the given data points. As we learn the line (How? There's no need to think about that now.) that shows the relationship between x and y of the data points, we can use this relationship (equation of line) to generate $\hat{y}$ for any given $\hat{x}$. From Figure 2.1, now we understand that we have to draw some line (line → linear) to estimate some points (as they have linear relation).

Assume we have higher dimensions of data. Like, for each x, it's not one point. There could be D points. Note that higher dimension does not mean a higher order of relationship. Two D-dimensional points could have a linear relationship. Just think about it a bit and don't skip this if you have any confusion.

When you are expressing something in the higher dimension, the only good mathematical tools we have are the *vector* and *linear algebra* operations. For the rest of the explanation, we will be explaining everything in terms of *vector*. If you are weak in the basics of *linear algebra*, now it is a good time for a recap.

If we express the equation of a line in linear algebra, it will be as follows:

$$Y = \begin{bmatrix} w_0 \\ w_1 \\ \vdots \\ w_D \end{bmatrix}^T * \begin{bmatrix} x_0 \\ x_1 \\ \vdots \\ x_D \end{bmatrix} = W^T X \tag{2.4}$$

$$\in = Y - \hat{Y} \tag{2.5}$$

where the superscript T represents the transpose operation and * represents the matrix multiplication. $X = \begin{bmatrix} x_0 & x_1 & x_2 \dots x_D \end{bmatrix}^T$ is the input of the model. You need to find a vector W such that Y gets its original value in the dataset. In short, W actually relates X to Y. $\hat{Y}$ is the predicted value (the value our model will generate) for X and Y is the original label in the dataset. Assume $\in$ is the residual error. Notice W^T*X is scalar. Now here is the trick. If we take a random matrix for W (as we don't know the relation between X and Y, we initialize it randomly), the probability will be very low that W^T*X can estimate the correct $\hat{Y}$ that is close to Y. It will predict something greater or lesser than our expected output Y. Mathematically, $\hat{Y} \gg Y$ or $\hat{Y} \ll Y$. So, what can we do? We can just add an error $\in$ term to make the prediction correct. Let's write the equation:

$$\hat{Y} = W^T * X + \in \tag{2.6}$$

Now, according to the preceding equation, $Y \sim \hat{Y}$. As long as we select the residual error ∈ properly, our prediction $\hat{Y}$ gets right. So, how should we calculate the *residual error* ∈? Remember X is our input. We want to change X to Y by W. Based on W, our error will be calculated. If we visualize our error in our previous data, our objective is to reduce the error ∈ or the total sum of the lengths of the vertical lines of Figure 2.2.

2.2.2.1 To Wrap Up the Whole Thing

We have a dataset $\mathcal{D}\{x_i, y_i\}_{i=1}^{N}$ where $X = \{x_i\}_{i=1}^{N}$ is the D-dimensional input and $Y = \{y_i\}_{i=1}^{N}$ is the output/label. For learning function f that defines the mapping between X and Y, we have a model as follows:

$$\hat{Y} = W^T * X + \in \tag{2.7}$$

For a random initialization of W, our residual error ∈ will be much higher. We need to change (iteratively or algebraically) W in such a way so that the residual error ∈ gets lower. We can only calculate the residual error ∈ when we have a W (guessed or calculated):

$$\in = \hat{Y} - W^T * X \tag{2.8}$$

Now intuitively, it's quite clear that we need to *optimize* the residual error ∈ or some form of the residual error. For analyzing which *function* of ∈ needs to be optimized, let's interpret the model by probability distribution.

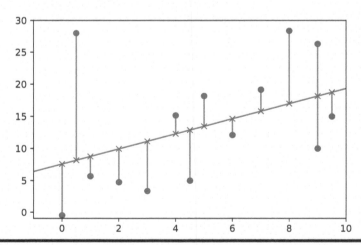

Figure 2.2 Crosses are the predicted values on the regression line. The line from the given points to cross shows the distance between the predicted and given points.

2.2.3 Probabilistic Interpretation

For a data scientist, the main objectives are to implement and visualize the model cleverly so that one may get the chance to extract useful information from the predictive model. For that a basic mathematical understanding of the model is the building block. For readers' suitability, the mathematical explanation in this chapter is derived in a simple X manner and in details without skipping any calculation. The readers are encouraged to reason every mathematical form of explanation from this chapter as these mathematical understandings will be the building blocks for the more advanced models.

There are two types of probabilistic model:

1. **Generative model:** A generative model asks the question—which category is most likely to generate the data? This interpretation works well only with large amounts of data. It calculates the complete probability model, performing inference condition on the data and model.
2. **Discriminative model:** A discriminative model doesn't care about how data is generated, but it only classifies the data. Its elegance is *simplicity*. Compared to the generative approach, most of the time discriminative model can work with small amounts of data.

For the problem discussed previously, we can decide that we need a discriminative probabilistic model. As we are not working on data generation, only the discriminative model will suffice.

We can represent the problem as $p(y|x)$ that implies, what is the probability of outcome y given an input x?

We assume that *residual error* $\in$ follows normal distribution ($\mathcal{N}$) with zero mean ($\mu = 0$) and constant variance (σ), which implies the conditional probability of y given x:

$$\in \sim \mathcal{N}\left(\mu = 0, \sigma^2\right) \tag{2.9}$$

$$p\left(y|x,\{W,\sigma^2\}\right) = \mathcal{N}\left(y|\mu(x), \sigma^2(x)\right) \tag{2.10}$$

Here, σ and W are the parameters of the model. σ is constant (constant noise). For linear regression, we assume that $\mu(x) = W^T x$. Suppose the input is one-dimensional. Then we define $\mu(x)$ as

$$\mu(x) = w_1 x + w_0 = W^T x \tag{2.11}$$

where

$$W^T = [\begin{array}{cc} w_0 & w_1 \end{array}]$$

$$x = \left[\begin{array}{c} 1 \\ x \end{array}\right]$$

As we are calculating everything in vector, we took $x = \begin{bmatrix} 1 & x \end{bmatrix}^T$ for robust implementation of Eq. (2.2). Note that x is a vector and x is a scalar. The conversion of x to x is called basis function expansion. With basis function expansion, we can make a linear model nonlinear. Basis function is generally written as ϕ(x). General basis function is

$$\phi(x,d) = \begin{bmatrix} 1 & x & x^2 & \ldots & x^d \end{bmatrix}$$

If we visualize the model based on normal distribution, we get the representation as shown in Figure 2.3.

Now we will be calculating the likelihood of our model. Likelihood is one kind of probability where we have the data before calculating probability. We have data *y*, and we assume it comes from some distribution and the data examples are *independent and identically distributed* (IID). This means all the examples of data have the same probability distribution as the others and all are mutually independent. Linear regression follows normal distribution. It is an *inductive bias* of the model.

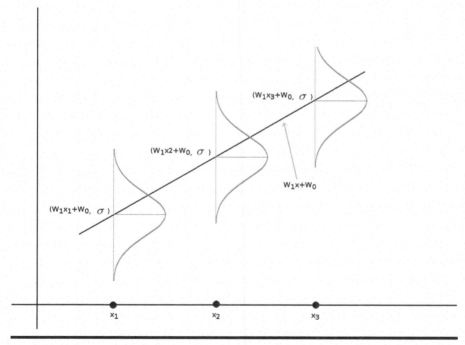

Figure 2.3   A regression line is drawn. Based on Eq. (2.10), each point on the line is calculated based on the zero mean of the normal distribution of the points around it.

Inductive bias is the assumption that your model takes into account before learning/ computation. The total likelihood is the product of the likelihood for each point y_i

$$p(y,\theta) = \prod_i^N p(y_i,\theta) \tag{2.12}$$

where θ is the model parameter. The total log likelihood is

$$p(y,\theta) = l(\theta) = \sum_i^N \log\left(p(y_i,\theta)\right) \tag{2.13}$$

As log is a monotonically increasing function, log-likelihoods have the same relations of order as the likelihoods. But applying log will make the model easier to calculate and more precise. As an example, we can see the simplification by taking log of the *probability density function* (p.d.f) of the normal distribution. If x is the random variable,

$$p(x,\,\theta) = \mathcal{N}(\mu,\sigma) = \frac{1}{\left(\sqrt{(2\pi \det \Sigma)}\right)^d} e^{-\frac{1}{2}(x-\mu)^T \Sigma^{-1}(x-\mu)} \tag{2.14}$$

$$\log p(x,\theta) = -\frac{d}{2}\log(2\pi) - \frac{d}{2}\log(\det \Sigma) - \frac{1}{2}(x-\mu)^T \Sigma^{-1}(x-\mu) \tag{2.15}$$

As we are working on 1D data points (two values in x), our p.d.f for normal distribution will be

$$\mathcal{N}(\mu,\sigma^2) = \frac{1}{2\pi\sigma^2} e^{-\frac{1}{2\sigma^2}(y - W^T x)^2} \tag{2.16}$$

Now, according to the definition of log likelihood in Eq. (2.13),

$$l(\theta) \triangleq \log\left(p(\mathcal{D}|\theta)\right) = \sum_{i=1}^N p(y_i \,|\, x_i,\theta) = \sum_{i=1}^N \log\left(\mathcal{N}(\mu,\sigma^2)\right)$$

$$l(\theta) \triangleq \sum_{i=1}^N \log\left[\frac{1}{2\pi\sigma^2} e^{-\frac{1}{2\sigma^2}(y_i - W^T x_i)^2} \right]$$

$$-l(\theta) \triangleq \frac{N}{2}\log\left(2\pi\sigma^2\right) + \frac{1}{2\sigma^2} RSS(W)$$

$$RSS(W) \triangleq \sum_{i=1}^{N} \left(y_i - W^T x_i \right)^2 = \sum_{i=1}^{N} \|\epsilon\|^2 \qquad (2.17)$$

Here, RSS means *residual sum of squares*. This is also called *Sum of squared errors* (SSE). If we take the mean, it will be

$$MSE = \frac{1}{N} SSE \qquad (2.18)$$

MSE is the *mean squared error* or l_2 norm. This is considered as the loss of the model (remember ϵ; We finally get the function of ϵ that must be reduced/optimized according to Eq. (2.8)).

For the discriminative model, we calculate the *maximum likelihood estimation (MLE)* $\hat{\theta}$ to estimate the value. Minimizing error is equivalent to maximizing likelihood as the likelihood defines how likely it is for y to be selected for a given x, which means that we can also calculate the value of the parameter θ for which the loss will be minimized. According to Eq. (2.17), parameter θ is W.

$$\hat{\theta} \triangleq \arg\max_{\theta} \log \left(p(\mathcal{D}, \theta) \right) \qquad (2.19)$$

where $\mathcal{D}$ is the dataset. So, for linear regression,

$$\hat{\theta} \triangleq \arg\max_{\mu} \log \left(\mathcal{N} \left(\mu, \sigma^2 \right) \right) = \arg\max_{\theta} l(\theta)$$

Note that for a better model, we need to reduce the residual error ϵ according to Eq. (2.5). Reducing ϵ is the same as maximizing likelihood. Maximizing likelihood is the same as maximizing *log likelihood* and minimizing *negative log likelihood*.

If we can convert the same problem to a minimization problem by taking negative log-likelihood,

$$\hat{\theta} \triangleq \arg\min_{\theta} \left(-l(\theta) \right)$$

From Eq. (2.17), we get

$$\hat{\theta} = \arg\min_{w} RSS(w)$$

$$\hat{\theta} = \arg\min_{w} \sum_{i=1}^{N} \left(y_i - W^T x_i \right)^2 = \sum_{i=1}^{N} \|\epsilon\|^2 \qquad (2.20)$$

Remember at the end of Section 2.2.2 that we need to optimize the residual error. Equation (2.20) is the final form of the equation that we need to optimize.

This equation also works for a higher dimension. You may need to tweak the size of W according to the dimension of x, for a higher dimension.

After optimizing the loss function, we will have such a representation of W that maps the data X to Y. Actually, W will contain such a value for which if you take a new example that is not in the dataset, W will be able to estimate the value of y based on its experience (training process) with the dataset. The accuracy of the linear regression will depend on the size of the dataset and the design of the model. In a real-life scenario, linear regression is not the feasible solution. You may need to try nonlinear regression or extend the concept of linear regression to further advanced models.

2.2.4 Optimization Method

For the calculation of arg min part, we need an optimization method. There are two types of optimization methods for linear regression.

1. **Iterative method:** Use some learning algorithms such as gradient descent, stochastic gradient descent [5], Adam [6], and Newton's optimization method.
2. **Closed-form solution:** Use vector algebra to derive the solution.

The discussion of the learning algorithms such as stochastic gradient descent, Adam etc. is out of the scope of this chapter. In this chapter, we will be discussing the closed form solution. For the closed-form solution, we will be doing some algebraic derivation and we will try to minimize negative log-likelihood by *vector algebra*.

From Eq. (2.15), taking negative log-likelihood,

$$-l(\theta) = \frac{d}{2}\log(2\pi) + \frac{d}{2}\log(\det \Sigma) + \frac{1}{2}(x - \mu)^T \Sigma^{-1}(x - \mu) \qquad (2.21)$$

For our case, $\frac{d}{2}\log(2\pi) + \frac{d}{2}\log(\det \Sigma)$ and Σ^{-1} terms are constant. So, we can ignore these terms. Remember, for our model, $\mu(x) = W^T x$. Our reduced *negative log-likelihood* (*NLL*) term will be (In Eq. [2.21], x is the random variable. In our problem, y is the random variable that we want to predict. Equation [2.21] is just an example of normal distribution.):

$$-l(\theta) = NLL(W) = (y - xW)(y - xW) \quad \left[as \ W^T x = xW \right]$$

With some *vector algebra*, we can easily simplify the equation as follows:

$$NLL(W) = (y - xW)^T (y - xW)$$

$$= \left(y^T - (\mathrm{x}W)^T \right)(y - \mathrm{x}W) \left[\text{ as } (A+B)^T = A^T + B^T \right]$$

$$= \left(y^T - W^T \mathrm{x}^T \right)(y - \mathrm{x}W) \left[\text{ as } (AB)^T = B^T A^T \right]$$

$$= y^T y - y^T \mathrm{x}W - W^T \mathrm{x}^T y + W^T \mathrm{x}^T W$$

$$= y^T y - 2W^T \mathrm{x}^T y + W^T \mathrm{x}^T \mathrm{x}W \left[\text{ as } A^T (BC) = (BC)^T A \right]$$

$$NLL(w) = y^T y - 2W^T \mathrm{x}^T y + W^T \mathrm{x}^T \mathrm{x}W \qquad (2.22)$$

Now, we need to minimize the *NLL* with respect to its parameter *w*:

$$\hat{\theta} = \arg \min_W \left(y^T y - 2W^T \mathrm{x}^T y + W^T \mathrm{x}^T \mathrm{x}W \right)$$

Taking derivative with respect to *W*,

$$\frac{\delta}{\delta w} NLL(W) = -2\mathrm{x}^T y + \mathrm{x}^T \mathrm{x}W$$

For minimization according to calculus,

$$-2\mathrm{x}^T y + \mathrm{x}^T \mathrm{x}W = 0$$

$$W = \left(2 \left(\mathrm{x}^T \mathrm{x} \right)^{-1} \mathrm{x}^T y \right)$$

$$\hat{\theta} = \left(\left(\mathrm{x}^T \mathrm{x} \right)^{-1} \mathrm{x}^T y \right) \qquad (2.23)$$

We can drop 2 as it is a constant term.

2.2.5 Block Diagram

Block diagram is a way of representing the model in a brief way. In this diagram, the variables that are open to access by the model are shaded.

Step 1: At the beginning of the experiment, feature *X* is observed. We assume *W* is the transformation matrix such that multiplying W^T with *X*, we get *Y*. But *W* is unknown (initialized randomly). So, at this stage, *W* is hidden (Figure 2.4).

Step 2: Together with *X* and *Y*, we train the model to estimate the best fitting. At this point, *Y* is observed and *W* is converging to its best solution (Figure 2.5).

Step 3: Now with trained *W* and a given $\hat{X}$, we can estimate any $\hat{Y}$. As *W* is trained, we can access *W*. At this stage, there's no need to access *Y* (Figure 2.6).

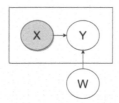

Figure 2.4 *Y* is hidden and *X* is observed.

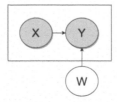

Figure 2.5 *X* and *Y* is observed. Together, they train *W*.

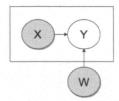

Figure 2.6 Now after training W, we can predict *Y* for any given *X*.

2.2.6 Overview of the Model

The basic assumption of the model is called inductive bias. For the short view of a model, we need to explain some key features of the model: *inductive bias*, *basis function*, *cost/loss function*, and *training algorithm*. Before implementing any model, you may need to follow up these key features of the models.

- **Inductive bias:** Error maintains *Gaussian distribution* with mean 0 and constant variance. Training examples are IID.
- **Basis function:** $\phi(x) = [\ 1\ x\ ]$
- **Cost/loss function:** $MSE = \dfrac{1}{N} \sum\limits_{i=1}^{N} \left(y_i - W^T x_i \right)^2 = \dfrac{1}{N} \sum\limits_{i=1}^{N} \|\in\|^2$
- **Training:**
  - Iterative method
  - Closed-form solution

2.3 Logistic Regression

Linear regression is a regression model where the dependent variable (DV) is continuous. Logistic regression or logit regression or logit model is a regression model where the dependent variable (DV) is categorical.

Suppose you have the last 5 years' daily weather information (if it is rainy or not) of a specific geographic region. Can you estimate if tomorrow's weather will be rainy or not (yes or no question)?

Another example will be, suppose you have the honest dataset of a student's total daily average time of study. Can you predict if the student will pass the exam or not from his/her amount of study hours (yes or no question)?

Logistic regression is also a supervised problem. You need to have the label of the data about which you want to predict.

2.3.1 Problem Definition

Given a set of pairs $\mathcal{D}\{x_i, y_i\}_{i=1}^{N}$ where y_i is the dependent binary or dichotomous variable against x_i, can you predict the category $\hat{y}$ (either 0 or 1) for an arbitrary given $\hat{x}$?

Logistic regression predicts either 0 or 1. The probability distribution of linear regression is Gaussian distribution. We will change the distribution to the Bernoulli distribution as the Bernoulli distribution is discrete and it categorizes the data as either 0 or 1.

$$p(y|x, W) = Ber(y \mid \mu(x)) \qquad (2.24)$$

We will implement the Bernoulli feature by using *sigmoid* function. It is also known as logistic or logit function.

2.3.2 Logistic Function

The equation of sigmoid/logistic/logit function is

$$\text{sigmoid}(\eta) \triangleq \frac{1}{1+e^{-\eta}} = \frac{e^{\eta}}{1+e^{\eta}} \qquad (2.25)$$

The term *sigmoid* means S-shaped squashing function. Look at Figure 2.7.

From the figure, you may see that all the outputs of the sigmoid function are between 0 and 1.

$$0 \leq \text{sigmoid}(x) \leq 1$$

So, by applying the logistic function, we squash the value from 0 to 1.

This gives us the advantage to calculate the Bernoulli random variable.

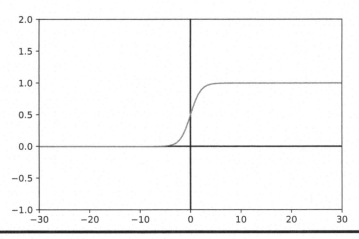

Figure 2.7   S-shaped logit curve.

Let's evaluate some important values:

$$\text{sigmoid}(-\inf) = 0$$

$$\text{sigmoid}(0) = 0.5$$

$$\text{sigmoid}(\inf) = 1$$

We often utilize these features and set a range to classify

$$p(y_i = 1|x, W) = \text{sigmoid}(w_0 + w_1 x_i) \qquad (2.26)$$

$$\hat{y} = 1 \quad \text{if } p(y_i = 1|x, W) > 0.5$$

$$\hat{y} \in \{0,1\}$$

2.3.3 *Probabilistic Interpretation*

Logistic regression is a discriminative model. The parameter descriptions are given in the text that follows:

As logistic regression follows the Bernoulli distribution, the log-likelihood will be the probability mass function (p.m.f) of the Bernoulli distribution.

$$p(y|x, W) = Ber(y \mid \mu(x))$$

$$\phi(x) = x = [\,1\ x\,]$$

where μ is the linear function of x and $\phi(x)$ is the basis function. As we apply the logit/logistic function over the equation of linear regression, we call this procedure as logistic regression.

The *MLE* derivation for the loss function is given below. The derivation is similar to linear regression. The only difference is the use of the *Bernoulli distribution* instead of the *Gaussian distribution*.

$$l(\theta) \triangleq \log\big(p(\mathcal{D}|\theta)\big) = \sum_{i=1}^{N} \log\big(p(y_i|x_i,\theta)\big) = \sum_{i=1}^{N} \log Ber\big(y \,|\, \text{sigmoid}\big(W^T x\big)\big)$$

$$-l(\theta) = -\sum_{i=1}^{N} \log Ber\big(y \,|\, \text{sigmoid}\big(W^T x\big)\big) \tag{2.27}$$

We can also write the same equation in plain form as

$$-l(\theta) = \sum_{i=1}^{N} \Big[y_i \log(\mu_i) + (1 - y_i)\log(1 - \mu_i) \Big] \tag{2.28}$$

where $y_i \in \{0,1\}$. This is also called cross entropy, which is the loss function. We need to optimize this function.

2.3.4 Optimization Method

We cannot write down the *MLE* optimization of logistic regression in closed form. So, we will have to use an iterative method such as gradient descent and Newton's optimization method. These iterative methods of learning will be discussed later.

2.3.5 Overview of the Model

- **Inductive bias:** Maintains the Bernoulli distribution. Training examples are IID.
- **Basis function:** $x = [\ 1\ x\ ]$
- **Cost/loss function:** $-l(\theta) = \sum_{i=1}^{N} \Big[y_i \log(\mu_i) + (1 - y_i)\log(1 - \mu_i) \Big]$, where $y_i \in \{0,1\}$
- **Training:**
  - Iterative method: using a convex optimizer such as gradient descent and Newton's optimization method.

The basic operation of linear and logistic regression is very similar. The difference is the assumption or inductive bias on the probability distribution which derives the loss function. A good example of this could be, suppose you have a huge collection of labeled images of digits (0–9) [7]. Given a new image of a digit, can you predict the digit number in it? Observe carefully, here the number of categorical values is 10. So, is this a logistic regression? No, this is called *softmax* regression or *multinomial* regression. Here we use multinomial distribution as the likelihood function to predict the outcomes. The whole procedure of designing such a model is the same, except that in place of *sigmoid* function, another specialized function named *softmax* (for multinomial distribution) is used.

$$\text{softmax}(x): R^K \rightarrow [0,1]^K$$

$$\text{softmax}(x)_i = \frac{e^{x_i}}{\sum_{k=1}^{K} e^{x_k}} \quad \text{for } i = 1, 2, \dots, k \tag{2.29}$$

2.4 Problems of Regression

Regression is a very naïve model that is heavily dependent on data. The performance of regression depends on how the statistical variables are correlated and, more importantly, on the amount and quality of data. Here, we discuss some of the specific problems of regression.

2.4.1 Underfitting and Overfitting

Curve fitting [9,10] is always a hard problem. In regression, we basically want to calculate the best fitting curve based on the statistical data. Regression is highly data oriented. If the features and label are not linearly dependent, a line cannot predict the value properly. Maybe a nonlinear curve (like degree 4 in Figure 2.8) can fit the data properly. On the contrary, if we have a higher degree curve that fits all the points perfectly, then we may not be able to get a good prediction from that. From Figure 2.8, we saw a degree 15 curve which overfits the data. If we predict y for an arbitrary given $\hat{x}$ based on degree 15 curve in the Figure 2.8, then there is a high probability that it will be miss-classified or will estimate a wrong value. It is always a hectic job to find the right degree of curve to fit the data properly. We need to use good intuition, visualization technique, and evaluation method to solve this problem.

2.4.2 Outlier

Outliers are the points that oppose the correlation of the points in the dataset (Figure 2.9). The cost function of regression is the square difference of the real value and predicted value. We can see from Figure 2.2 that our objective is to reduce the

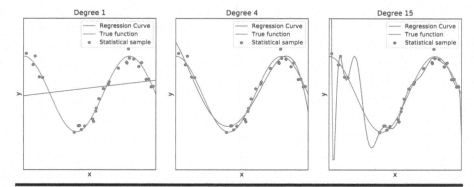

Figure 2.8 The same data distribution is mapped by three different degrees of curves. The Degree 1 curve is a straight line that cannot fit the data properly. The Degree 15 curve perfectly fits the data, but it's accuracy in predicting a value correctly will be very low. But the Degree 4 curve can properly fit the data and more accurately predict the value for some unknown data that is not in the training/given data [8].

length of the vertical segments. But one outlier dominates the total length of the vertical line, thus creating a bad regression curve. To attack this type of a problem, we change the loss function a bit. The changed loss function is called Huber loss. For calculating Huber loss, a threshold distance is taken into account. If any segment length crosses the threshold, we assume it as an outlier and take the absolute value of the output instead of squaring. Other than that, we take half of the regular square distance. The loss function of Huber loss is

$$L_\delta\left(y, f\left(x\right)\right) = \begin{cases} \dfrac{1}{2}\left(y - f\left(x\right)\right)^2 & \text{for } \left|y - f\left(x\right)\right| \le \delta \\[2ex] \delta\left|y - f\left(x\right)\right| - \dfrac{1}{2}\delta^2 & \text{otherwise} \end{cases} \tag{2.30}$$

where δ is the threshold.

2.4.3 Hyper-Parameter

Hyper-parameters are the parameters whose values are set before the learning process begins. In Eq. (2.4), we took a $D \times 1$ dimensional weight matrix. Before the learning procedure begins, you must fix the value of D. D is the number of parameters that you will be learning by the learning algorithm. If D is higher, the computation gets higher. If D is smaller, then we may not be able to learn the correlation between the points properly. To solve a specific problem, we may need to check different values of D for a better model (you may have to change other parameters of the model also). There are also some algorithms for hyper-parameter optimization [11,12].

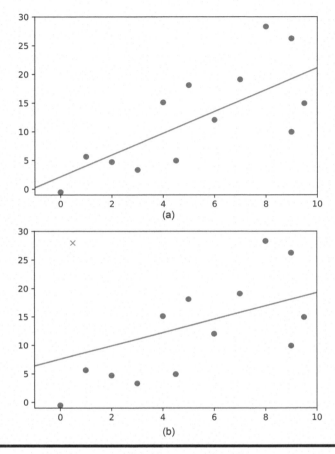

Figure 2.9 **(a) A set of points with their regression line. (b) An outlier is added (marked by cross) in the graph and a regression line is drawn.**

2.5 Conclusion

The main context of this chapter is to realize how different kinds of probabilistic analysis lead to different kinds of regression. However, readers should also grow strong intuitions about the applicability and about the types of problems that regression can solve. In the era of deep learning, linear regression and logistic regression are hardly used as a single unit. These two are considered the most preliminary model of machine learning. Most advanced discriminative models (that perform far better than these two models) actually consist of one of these two basic models. These two are like the smallest LEGO® bricks among a lot of complex problems. Before going to the next chapters, the readers are requested to make their concepts clear of linear regression and logistic regression.

References

1. Alex Krizhevsky, Ilya Sutskever, Geoffrey E. Hinton. ImageNet Classification with Deep Convolutional Neural Networks, Advances in neural information processing systems, 2012.
2. Sepp Hochreiter, Jurgen Schmidhuber. Long short-term memory, *Neural Computation* 9(8):1735–1780, 1997.
3. Ian J. Goodfellow, Jean Pouget-Abadie, Mehdi Mirza, Bing Xu, David Warde-Farley, Sherjil Ozair, Aaron Courville, Yoshua Bengio. Generative Adversarial Nets. Advances in neural information processing systems, 2672–2680, 2014.
4. Dean De Cock. Ames, Iowa: Alternative to the Boston housing data as an end of semester regression project, *Journal of Statistics Education* 19(3), 2011. doi = 10.1080/ 10691898.2011.11889627.
5. Léon Bottou. *Proceedings of COMPSTAT'2010*, 177–186, 2014.
6. Diederik Kingma, Jimmy Ba. Adam: A method for stochastic optimization, *International Conference on Learning Representation*, San Diego, CA, 2015.
7. Yann LeCun, Léon Bottou, Yoshua Bengio, and Patrick Haffner. Gradient-based learning applied to document recognition, *Proceedings of the IEEE* 86(11):2278–2324, 1998.
8. Fabian Pedregosa, Gaël Varoquaux, Alexandre Gramfort, Vincent Michel, Bertrand Thirion, Olivier Grisel, Mathieu Blondel, Peter Prettenhofer, Ron Weiss, Vincent Dubourg, Jake Vanderplas, Alexandre Passos, David Cournapeau, Matthieu Brucher, Matthieu Perrot, Edouard Duchesnay. Scikit-learn: Machine learning in {P}ython, *Journal of Machine Learning Research* 12:2825–2830, 2011.
9. Sandra Lach Arlinghaus. *PHB Practical Handbook of Curve Fitting*. CRC Press, 1994, 249pp. Persistent URL (URI): http://hdl.handle.net/2027.42/58759.
10. William M. Kolb. *Curve Fitting for Programmable Calculators*. Syntec, Incorporated, 1984.
11. James Bergstra, Yoshua Bengio. Random search for hyper-parameter optimization, *Journal of Machine Learning Research* 13:281–305, 2012.
12. James Bergstra, Remi Bardenet, Yoshua Bengio, Balazs Kégl. Algorithms for Hyper-Parameter Optimization, Advances in neural information processing systems, 2546–2554, 2011.

Chapter 3

Big Data-Appropriate Clustering via Stochastic Approximation and Gaussian Mixture Models

---

Hien D. Nguyen
La Trobe University
Andrew Thomas Jones
University of Queensland

Contents

3.1 Introduction

Let $\mathbf{Z}^n = \{\mathbf{Z}_i\}_{i=1}^n$ be an IID (independent and identically distributed) random sample of $n \in \mathbb{N}$ observations, where $\mathbf{Z}_i^T = (\mathbf{X}_i^T, Y_i)$, $\mathbf{X}_i \in \mathbb{X} \subset \mathbb{R}^p$ and $Y_i \in [q] = \{1, \ldots, q\} (i \in [n])$. Here, $p, q \in \mathbb{N}$, where $\mathbb{N}$ is the set of natural numbers (zero exclusive), $\mathbb{R}$ is the set of real numbers, and $(\cdot)^T$ is the matrix transposition operator. We call $\mathbf{X}_i$ and Y_i the feature vector and label of the ith observation from the sample $\mathbf{Z}^n$, respectively.

We suppose that the data generating process (DGP) of $\mathbf{Z}^n$ is unknown, but that each observation $\mathbf{Z}_i$ is generated by the following mechanism:

(A1) First, generate Y_i from a distribution with probabilities $\mathbb{P}(Y_i = y) = \pi_y > 0$, where $\sum_{y=1}^{q} \pi_y = 1$.

(A2) Given $Y_i = y$, generate $\mathbf{X}_i$ from a probability density function (PDF) $f_y(\mathbf{X})$. We call $f_y(\mathbf{X})$ the component PDF of the yth mixture component.

(A3) Concatenate the vector components $\mathbf{X}_i$ and Y_i to obtain the observation vector $\mathbf{Z}_i^T = (\mathbf{X}_i^T, Y_i)$.

Utilizing the usual convention of uppercase for random variables and lowercase for realizations, we suppose that we only observe the realization $\mathbf{x}^n = \{\mathbf{x}_i\}_{i=1}^n$ of the feature vectors $\mathbf{X}^n = \{\mathbf{X}_i\}_{i=1}^n$, but not the corresponding set of labels $\mathbf{Y}^n = \{Y_i\}_{i=1}^n$. Each $y \in [q]$ can be viewed as one of the q subpopulations of the DGP. We can then propose to estimate the realized labels $\mathbf{y}^n$ (corresponding to $\mathbf{x}^n$) by some set $\mathbf{y}_*^n = \{y(\mathbf{x}_i)\}_{i=1}^n$, where each $y(\mathbf{x}_i) \in [q]$ is a function that estimates the label Y_i. Here, we seek labelings $\mathbf{y}_*^n$ that are optimal in some sense, with respect to a mathematical criterion, or that are sensible with respect to some scientific hypothesis or theory. This is the problem of clustering (or vector quantization).

A model-based approach to clustering is one where the DGP that yields either $\mathbf{X}^n$ is modeled directly. This approach is advocated in the well-referenced books [1,2]. A common and popular probabilistic model used when applying the model-based clustering approach is the Gaussian mixture model (GMM).

GMMs are one of the earliest proposed techniques for clustering and they date back to the famous work of [3]. Since then, GMM-based methods have been among the most influential and successful methods for solving the aforementioned clustering problem. For examples regarding applications and implementations of GMMs, refer to the works and the results of [1,2,4,5]. In particular, we note the great success of the *mclust* software package [6–9] for the R statistical programming language [10], over many years. Unfortunately, when faced with big data (which we define in the sequel), traditional software packages, such as *mclust*, which rely on older computation paradigms, such as batch expectation-maximization (EM; [11]) algorithms (cf. [12]), cannot be applied due to computational and storage limitations.

We note that model-based clustering is not the only available paradigm for solving the problem of data clustering. Examples of other popular clustering paradigms include centroid-based clustering, hierarchical clustering, and modal clustering. Good and instructive references regarding clustering algorithms and their application in general include [13–16]. For brevity of exposition, we shall forgo further discussions of such alternative clustering paradigms.

There are many available notions of big data in the literature. We choose to define the big data analysis context via the "three Vs" [17]. The three Vs stand for variety, velocity, and volume, and each can be defined as follows:

Variety: The data arise from multiple subpopulations that exhibit heterogeneous behaviors with differing idiosyncrasies.

Velocity: The data are not available as a static batch, but rather arrives to the analyst in a continuous stream or in chunks or mini-batches.

Volume: The data are large to the point that they cannot be contained within the storage of a single computing unit and cannot be manipulated upon by said computer, in their entirety.

In this chapter, we consider the clustering of data using GMMs, fitted via the maximum likelihood (ML) criterion using a bespoke stochastic approximation algorithm (SAA). The algorithm that we utilize is a specialization of the SAA that [18] derived for the fitting of mixtures of exponential power family distributions, a class of distributions that include the GMM as a special case. The original algorithm was developed for the fitting of the aforementioned mixture distributions in the context of medium-sized and low-dimensional biomedical data analytic problems; see also [19]. We shall demonstrate that the SAA of [18] is also applicable in the big data setting. That is, we demonstrate that the derived SAA allows for the rapid fitting of GMMs in a low-memory and stream-suitable manner.

Although a powerful paradigm, the presented specialization of the SAA of [18] only allows for the estimation of spherical-covariance GMMs. Thus, it cannot estimate the entire spectrum of covariance matrix specifications and restrictions that software packages, such as *mclust,* allow. However, it is well known that clusterings via a spherical-covariance and homoskedastic GMM, estimated via the ML criterion, and clustering via the k-means algorithm share many similarities in algorithmic construction and in paradigm (cf. [20]). Thus, the presented SAA can instead be considered as comparable to the k-means algorithm of [21] and its many big data variants, such as those of [22–26].

Along with the presentation of the SAA for fitting spherical-covariance GMMs, we also briefly describe the theoretical framework behind the SAA paradigm of [18]. This then allows us to present a discussion regarding the convergence of the presented SAA algorithm. A set of numerical simulations are also presented to demonstrate the capability of the SAA when applied to clustering problems of various sizes and specifications. For a real-world demonstration of our methodology, we then apply the SAA to fit a GMM for the clustering of data from the famous MNIST handwritten digits dataset of [27].

3.1.1 Chapter Roadmap

The rest of the chapter proceeds as follows: the theoretical framework surrounding the SAA approach of [18] is briefly described in Section 3.2. The GMM is described in Section 3.3, along with its usage in model-based clustering. The specialization of the SAA of [18] for ML fitting of spherical-covariance GMMs is then presented in Section 3.4. Reports of conducted simulation studies are presented in Section 3.5. The SAA for GMM-based clustering is demonstrated via clustering of the MNIST dataset in Section 3.6. Conclusions are drawn and future directions are discussed in Section 3.7.

3.2 Stochastic Approximation Algorithm

Suppose that we wish to solve an optimization problem that can be phrased as the maximization or minimization of some function.

$$g(\boldsymbol{\psi}) = \mathbb{E}_{\mathbf{W}}\big[H(\boldsymbol{\psi};\mathbf{W})\big], \tag{3.1}$$

where $\mathbf{W} \in \mathbb{W} \subset \mathbb{R}^p$ is a random variable and $\boldsymbol{\psi} \in \Psi \subset \mathbb{R}^d$ is a parameter vector $(d, p \in \mathbb{N})$. Here, $\mathbb{E}_{\mathbf{W}}(\cdot)$ indicates the expectation with respect to the DGP of $\mathbf{W}$ and $H(\boldsymbol{\psi};\mathbf{w})$ is a measurable function in $\mathbf{w}$, for all $\boldsymbol{\psi}$, and is continuously differentiable in $\boldsymbol{\psi}$, for all $\mathbf{w}$. Let the partial derivative $\nabla H(\boldsymbol{\psi};\mathbf{w})$ (with respect to the parameter vector $\boldsymbol{\psi}$) exist for every $\mathbf{w} \in \mathbb{W}$ and $\boldsymbol{\psi} \in \Psi$. To maximize or minimize (3.1), we can consider obtaining a root of the system

$$\mathrm{h}(\boldsymbol{\psi}) \equiv \mathbb{E}_{\mathbf{W}}\big[\nabla H(\boldsymbol{\psi};\mathbb{W})\big] = \mathbf{0}, \tag{3.2}$$

where $\mathbf{0}$ is a zero vector of appropriate dimensionality.

Suppose that the DGP of $\mathbf{W}$ is unknown, but well-behaved in a manner that will be made clearer in the sequel. Given a sequence of IID observations from the same DGP as $\mathbf{W}$ that is increasing in size, $\mathbf{W}^n = \{\mathbf{W}_i\}_{i=1}^n$, we can obtain a root of (3.2) via the iterative scheme

$$\boldsymbol{\psi}^{(i+1)} = \boldsymbol{\psi}^{(i)} + \gamma_i \nabla H\big(\boldsymbol{\psi}^{(i)}; \mathbf{W}_{i+1}\big), \tag{3.3}$$

where $\{\boldsymbol{\psi}^{(i)}\}_{i=0}^n$ is a sequence of solutions that iterate with the index i and $\gamma_i > 0$ is a gain factor that will be explained in the sequel. Here $\boldsymbol{\psi}^{(0)}$ is an initial value of the parameter vector that is selected arbitrarily over the parameter space Ψ. The problem can further be made concrete when the sequence $\mathbf{W}^n$ is replaced by some observed stream of data $\mathbf{w}^n = \{\mathbf{w}_i\}_{i=1}^n$.

The iterative scheme (3.3) is generally referred to as an SAA for obtaining a root of equation system (3.2). The study of SAAs date back to the early works of [28,29]. Good expositions regarding the modern theory of SAAs can be found in [30,31]. A recent review of the literature can be found in [32].

3.2.1 Convergence Result

The appeal of the SAA of [18] is that the conditions under which convergence can be established are quite simple to state and verify. We first begin by supposing that the sequence $\mathbf{W}^n$ consists of n IID observations drawn uniformly with replacement from some finite (but potentially very large) set of N observations $\bar{\mathbf{w}}^N = \left\{ \bar{\mathbf{w}}_j \right\}_{j=1}^N$. Here, we can consider that $\bar{\mathbf{w}}^N$ is itself a realization of a sample of N observations from some other higher level DGP. Under this scenario, by equiprobability, we can write $\mathbf{h}(\psi) = N^{-1} \sum_{j=1}^N \nabla H\left(\psi; \bar{\mathbf{w}}_j \right)$.

Let $\|\cdot\|$ denote the usual Euclidean norm. Assume that there exists an objective function of interest $\bar{g}(\psi)$ with stationary points that correspond to the elements of the set $\Psi^* = \left\{ \psi \in \Psi : \mathbf{h}(\psi) = 0 \right\}$. Define the sets

$$\Psi_0 = \left\{ \psi_0 \in \Psi : \mathbf{h}(\psi) \text{ is not continuous at } \psi_0, \text{ or } \bar{g}(\psi) \text{ is not differentiable at } \psi_0 \right\}$$

and

$$\Xi = \left\{ \left\{ \psi^{(i)} \right\}_{i=1}^{\infty} : \text{there exists a closed subset } Q \text{ of } \Psi \setminus \Psi_0 \text{ such that } \psi^{(i)} \in Q, \right.$$

$$\left. \text{for all } i \in \mathbb{N} \right\}.$$

Further, let $\mathbf{B}_{i+1} = \nabla H\left(\psi^{(i)}; \mathbf{W}_{i+1} \right) - \mathbf{h}\left(\psi^{(i)} \right)$, so that the SAA scheme (3.3) can be rewritten as

$$\psi^{(i+1)} = \psi^{(i)} + \gamma_i \left[\mathbf{h}\left(\psi^{(i)} \right) + \mathbf{B}_{i+1} \right].$$

Make the following assumptions regarding the sequences $\{\gamma_i\}_{i=1}^n$ and $\{\mathbf{B}_i\}_{i=1}^n$: (B1) $\gamma_i > 0$ for all $i \in \mathbb{N}$ and $\lim_{i \to \infty} \gamma_i = 0$, (B2) $\lim_{n \to \infty} \sum_{i=1}^n \gamma_i = \infty$, (B3) $\lim_{n \to \infty} \sum_{i=1}^n \gamma_i^2 < \infty$, and (B4) $\sup_i \mathbf{B}_i^2 < \infty$. Furthermore, make the following regularity assumption on $\bar{g}(\psi)$ and $\mathbf{h}(\psi)$: (C1) $\bar{g}(\psi)$ is continuous and differentiable, and for any $\psi \in \Psi$,

$-\mathbf{h}(\psi) = \nabla \overline{g}(\psi)$, and (C2) $\sup_{\psi \in Q} -\mathbf{h}(\psi) < 0$ for any compact subset Q of $\Psi \setminus \Psi^*$. Under assumptions (B1)–(B4), (C1) and (C2), [18] presented the following result regarding the scheme (3.3).

Theorem 1. *If we assume that (B1)—(B4), (C1), and (C2) hold, then as $n \to \infty$, we have* $\lim_{n \to \infty} dist\left(\psi^{(n)}, \Psi^*\right) = 0$ *almost surely on* Ξ, *where* $dist\left(\psi^{(n)}, \Psi^*\right) = \inf_{\psi \in \Psi^*} \psi^{(n)} - \psi$.

We note that [18], in fact, states a more general result that replaces assumptions (B1) with a criterion regarding the generalized gradient of $\overline{g}(\psi)$ in the sense of [33]. This allows for the maximization or minimization of functions that may not be continuously differentiable. As we do not require such a strong result, we have chosen to simplify the assumptions for brevity of exposition.

3.3 Gaussian Mixture Model

Assume that data $\mathbf{Z}^n$ are generated according to a DGP that follows the structure described by (A1)–(A3). For each $y \in [q]$, replace the component PDFs $f_y(\mathbf{x})$ in (A2) by the multivariate Gaussian density function

$$\phi\left(\mathbf{x}; \mu_y, \Sigma_y\right) = \left|2\pi \Sigma_y\right|^{-1/2} \exp\left[-\frac{1}{2}\left(\mathbf{x} - \mu_y\right)^T \Sigma_y^{-1}\left(\mathbf{x} - \mu_y\right)\right],$$

where $\mu_y \in \mathbb{R}^p$ is a mean vector and $\Sigma_y \in \mathbb{R}^{p \times p}$ is a positive, definite, and symmetric covariance matrix, for each $y \in [g]$. We then say that the data $\mathbf{X}^n$ arise from a GMM in the sense that the marginal PDF of each $\mathbf{X}_i$ $(i \in [n])$ can be written as the convex combination of q Gaussian PDFs:

$$f(\mathbf{x}; \theta) = \sum_{y=1}^{q} \pi_y \phi\left(\mathbf{x}; \mu_y, \Sigma_y\right), \tag{3.4}$$

where θ is a parameter vector that contains the unique elements of π_y, μ_y, and Σ_y.

Suppose it is know that the DGP of $\mathbf{Z}^n$ is a GMM, as described above, or can be approximated by a GMM with the parameter vector θ_0 containing the unique elements of the parameter components π_{0y}, μ_{0y}, and Σ_{0y} $(y \in [q])$. Suppose that we observe only the realizations $\mathbf{x}^n$ of the feature vectors $\mathbf{X}^n$. We can utilize the usual maximum a posteriori (MAP) rule for model-based clustering in order to compute the estimated labels $\mathbf{y}_*^n$ that best predict the labels $\mathbf{Y}^n$. The MAP rule for mixture models is to predict Y_i $(i \in [n])$ by the label that yields the highest a posteriori probability based on Bayes' rule (cf. [2]). For GMMs, the MAP rule for the prediction of the label Y_i based on the observed feature $\mathbf{x}_i$ can be written as

$$y(\mathbf{x}_i) = \arg \max_{y \in [q]} \pi_{0y} \phi\left(\mathbf{x}_i; \mu_{0y}, \Sigma_{0y}\right). \tag{3.5}$$

Upon computing y ($\mathbf{x}_i$) for each i, we can concatenate the predicted label in order to obtain the set of cluster allocations $\mathbf{y}_*^n$ for the observed feature vectors $\mathbf{x}_n$.

Note that the application of rule (3.5) requires that we know the parameter vector $\boldsymbol{\theta}_0$ and that we know the number of clusters or labels q. Using the SAA that was described in Section 3.2, we shall demonstrate how an estimate for $\boldsymbol{\theta}_0$ can be obtained in the big data context. The determination of q is however outside of the scope of this chapter.

There are numerous ways by which q can be determined. Recent results of [34] suggests that the Bayesian information criterion of [35] asymptotically correctly selects the true number of labels under generous regularity conditions. For a finite number of observations, Maugis and Michel [36] utilized an oracle result of [37] that can be combined with the computational technique of [38] in order to compute an estimate of q with good penalized loss properties. The aforementioned methods are all probability based. Yet other methods for choosing q exist outside of such a setting. A good recent reference for such methods is [39]. We refer the interested reader to [40] for an excellent summary on the topic of determining q in the context of GMMs.

3.4 An SAA for Maximum Likelihood Estimation of GMMs

We now narrow our attention to the restricted class of spherical-covariance GMMs. That is, we shall only consider the case where $\boldsymbol{\Sigma}_y = \lambda_y^2/2\mathbf{I}$, for each $\boldsymbol{\Sigma}_y$ in (3.4) $\left(y \in [q] \right)$. Here, $\lambda_y > 0$ and $\mathbf{I}$ is an identity matrix of appropriate dimensionality. As a result, we can write (3.4) as

$$f(\mathbf{x};\boldsymbol{\theta}) = \sum_{y=1}^{q} \pi_y \phi\left(\mathbf{x}; \boldsymbol{\mu}_y, \frac{\lambda_y^2}{2}\mathbf{I} \right)$$

$$= \sum_{y=1}^{q} \pi_y \left| \pi\lambda_y^2\mathbf{I} \right|^{-\frac{1}{2}} \exp\left[-\frac{1}{\lambda_y^2}(\mathbf{x} - \boldsymbol{\mu}_y)^{\top}(\mathbf{x} - \boldsymbol{\mu}_y) \right],$$

(3.6)

where $\boldsymbol{\theta}$ now contains the elements of the parameter components π_y, $\boldsymbol{\mu}_y$, and λ_y. The parameter components λ_y control the volume of the confidence sets of each of the respective mixture component PDFs.

Suppose that we are given a realization $\mathbf{x}^n$ of $\mathbf{X}^n$ that arises from a DGP that can be characterized by a GMM with a PDF of form (3.6) with the parameter vector $\boldsymbol{\theta}_0$ or can be well-approximated by a GMM with a PDF of form (3.6) with the parameter vector $\boldsymbol{\theta}_0$. We are then required to estimate the parameter vector $\boldsymbol{\theta}_0$ from the data in order to obtain the best possible fitting GMM. Traditionally, this is achieved via ML.

Define the log-likelihood function (or more correctly, the quasi-log-likelihood function when the model is used only as an approximation; cf. [41]) of $\mathbf{x}^n$, under the assumption of a GMM to be

$$L(\boldsymbol{\theta}) = \frac{1}{n} \sum_{i=1}^{n} \log \sum_{y=1}^{q} \pi_y \phi\left(\mathbf{x}_n; \boldsymbol{\mu}_y, \frac{\lambda_y^2}{2}\mathbf{I}\right). \tag{3.7}$$

We then seek to obtain the ML estimator $\hat{\boldsymbol{\theta}}_n$, which can be defined as an appropriate root of the score equation $\nabla L(\boldsymbol{\theta}) = 0$. Here, we cannot define the ML estimator purely as the maximizer of (3.7) since the objective function is highly multimodal and lacks identifiability under permutation of the mixture components (cf. [42]).

A stochastic version of the ML estimation problem is to maximize

$$l(\boldsymbol{\theta}) = \mathbb{E}_{\mathbf{X}}\left[l(\boldsymbol{\theta}; \mathbf{X})\right] \tag{3.8}$$

instead, where $l(\boldsymbol{\theta}; \mathbf{x}) = \log f(\mathbf{x}; \boldsymbol{\theta})$, $f(\mathbf{x}; \boldsymbol{\theta})$ is of form (3.6), and $\mathbf{X}$ arises as a uniform draw from a very large finite population of random variables, where each member of the population is itself drawn from a distribution that can be characterized by a PDF of form (3.6) and the parameter vector $\boldsymbol{\theta}_0$. Here, $\mathbb{E}_{\mathbf{X}}(\cdot)$ denotes the expectation with respect to the DGP of $\mathbf{X}$. In the same way that the optimization of (3.1) corresponds to finding a root to (3.2), the problem of maximizing (3.8) corresponds to finding a root of the equation system

$$\mathbf{s}(\boldsymbol{\theta}) \equiv \mathbb{E}_{\mathbf{X}}\left[\nabla l(\boldsymbol{\theta}; \mathbf{X})\right] = 0. \tag{3.9}$$

Unfortunately, solving for the roots of (3.9) is made difficult due to the restrictions on the parameter space of $\boldsymbol{\theta}$. That is, although $\boldsymbol{\mu}_y$ is unrestricted in $\mathbb{R}^p$, $\boldsymbol{\pi}^T = (\pi_1, \ldots, \pi_g)$ is restricted by the conditions that $\pi_y > 0$ and $\sum_{y=1}^{q} \pi_y = 1$, and $\lambda_y > 0$, for each $y \in [q]$. The parameter map that allows for simplification of the root finding process is Set $\pi_y = \exp(\pi_y^*) \Big/ \sum_{j=1}^{q} \exp(\pi_y^*)$ for $y \in [q-1]$ and $\pi_q^* = 0$. Further set $\lambda_y^* = \log(\lambda_y)$ and $\boldsymbol{\mu}_y^* = \boldsymbol{\mu}_y$ (for consistency of notation), for each $y \in [q]$. The parameter vector $\boldsymbol{\theta}^*$, which contains the components $\pi_y^* \in \mathbb{R}$, $\boldsymbol{\mu}_y^* \in \mathbb{R}^p$, and $\lambda_y^* \in \mathbb{R}>$, $(y \in [q])$ maps one-to-one between the space of real vectors in $\mathbb{R}^{q(2+p)-1}$ and the restricted space of the original parameterization $\boldsymbol{\theta}$. We can now consider the simpler problem of obtaining a root to the equation system

$$\mathbf{s}^{*}\left(\boldsymbol{\theta}^{*}\right)\equiv\mathbb{E}_{\mathbf{X}}\left[\nabla^{*}l(\boldsymbol{\theta};\mathbf{X})\right]=0 \tag{3.10}$$

instead, where ∇^{*} is taken to mean partial differentiation with respect to the alternative parameterization $\boldsymbol{\theta}^{*}$.

We can write the components of $\nabla^{*}l(\boldsymbol{\theta};\mathbf{x})$ with respect to π_{y}^{*} as

$$\nabla_{\pi_{y}^{*}}^{*}l(\boldsymbol{\theta};\mathbf{x})=\frac{\pi_{y}\phi\left(\mathbf{x};\boldsymbol{\mu}_{y},\dfrac{\lambda_{y}^{2}}{2}\mathbf{I}\right)}{f(\mathbf{x};\boldsymbol{\theta})}-\pi_{y},$$

For $y\in\left[q-1\right]$, and with respect to $\boldsymbol{\mu}_{y}^{*}$ and λ_{y}^{*} as

$$\nabla_{\mu_{y}^{*}}^{*}l(\boldsymbol{\theta};\mathbf{x})=\frac{\pi_{y}\phi\left(\mathbf{x};\boldsymbol{\mu}_{y},\dfrac{\lambda_{y}^{2}}{2}\mathbf{I}\right)}{f(\mathbf{x};\boldsymbol{\theta})}\frac{2}{\lambda_{y}^{2}}\left(\mathbf{x}-\boldsymbol{\mu}_{y}\right),$$

and

$$\nabla_{\lambda_{y}^{*}}^{*}l(\boldsymbol{\theta};\mathbf{x})=\frac{\pi_{y}\phi\left(\mathbf{x};\boldsymbol{\mu}_{y},\dfrac{\lambda_{y}^{2}}{2}\mathbf{I}\right)}{f(\mathbf{x};\boldsymbol{\theta})}\left[\frac{2}{\lambda_{y}^{2}}\left(\mathbf{x}-\boldsymbol{\mu}_{\lambda}\right)^{\top}\left(\mathbf{x}-\boldsymbol{\mu}_{\lambda}\right)-p\right],$$

for $y\in[q]$. Given a stream of data $\mathbf{X}^{n}$, we can apply scheme (3.3) for solving (3.10) to obtain the SAA

$$\boldsymbol{\theta}^{*(i+1)}=\boldsymbol{\theta}^{*(i)}+\gamma_{i}\nabla^{*}l\left(\boldsymbol{\theta}^{(i)};\mathbf{X}_{i+1}\right), \tag{3.11}$$

which can then be made concrete upon substitution of a realized sample $\mathbf{x}^{n}$ in place of $\mathbf{X}^{n}$.

For a well-chosen sequence of gain factors $\left\{\gamma_{i}\right\}_{i=1}^{n}$, the SAA algorithm that is defined by Eq. (3.11) can be shown to satisfy the regularity conditions of Theorem 1 (i.e., conditions (C1) and (C2) are fulfilled). Thus, the conclusion of Theorem 1 applies to the SAA sequence of parameters that is generated via Eq. (3.11).

3.5 Simulation Results

The SAA algorithm described in Section 3.4 is implemented in the *R* statistical programming language [10], with particularly computationally intensive loops programmed in *C* and integrated into the core program via the *Rcpp* package of [43]. The implementation can be freely obtained at https://github.com/andrewthomasjones/

SAGMM. All computations were conducted on a MacBook Pro 15-inch laptop with a 2.2 GHz Intel Core i7 processor, 16 GB of 1600 MHz DDR3 memory, and a 500 GB SSD. Computational times that are reported are obtained via the *proc. time()* function. GMM-based clusterings are obtained using MAP rule (3.5).

3.5.1 Practical Considerations

Although the SAA for fitting GMMs from Section 3.4 is theoretically sound, there are some minor issues that require resolution in order for it to yield successful and consistent outcomes. First, we require a choice for the sequence of gain factors $\{\gamma_i\}_{i=1}^n$ that fulfill assumptions (B1)–(B3). In [18], the authors choose a sequence of the form $\gamma_i = \gamma_0 i_0 / \max\{i_0, i\}$, for $i \in \mathbb{N}$, where $\gamma_0, i_0 > 0$. Via some preliminary experimentation, we have found that such sequences were not successful in our applications.

In [44], the so-called search-then-converge sequence was suggested for SAA and similar algorithms. The suggested sequence of gain factors $\{\gamma_i\}_{i=1}^n$ have the form

$$\gamma_i = \frac{\gamma_0}{1 + i/i_0},$$

where $\gamma_0, i_0 > 0$. In all of our applications, we utilize the search-then-converge sequence with the setting of γ_0 and i_0, which is to be discussed in the sequel. It is simple to check that search-then-converge sequences satisfy assumptions (B1)–(B3).

Next, we must bring to attention the problem of setting the initial parameter vector $\boldsymbol{\theta}^{(0)}$. Considering the closeness of the method of clustering via spherical-covariance GMMs to the method of k-means (as discussed in Section 3.1), we propose a k-means initialization using a small proportion of the overall stream of the data, which we will call the burn-in.

Suppose that the total length n of the data stream is known and that we can partition n into two components, the burn-in n_0 and the remainder $n_1 = n - n_0$. Here, we shall define the burn-in b to be proportional to the total size of n. That is, define $n_0 = n/b$, where $b \in \mathbb{N} \setminus \{1\}$ is the burn-in ratio and $\cdot$ is the floor operator.

Using the burn-in sample of n_0 observations, we then run a k-means algorithm (here we use the *kmeans()* function in R) to search for $k = q$ centers. These centers are then used as initial values $\boldsymbol{\mu}_y^0 \left(i \in [q]\right)$. $\pi_y^0 \left(y \in [q]\right)$ is then obtained as the proportion of the burn-in sample that the k-means algorithm assigns to each of the centers. Initial covariance parameter values $\left(\lambda_1^0\right)^2 = \cdots = \left(\lambda_g^0\right)^2$ are taken to be equal to the maximum diagonal sample covariance element that is obtained from the sample covariance matrix over the n_0 burn-in observations. The method of k-means initialization is standard in the mixture modeling literature and has been reported in key references, such as [12]. Upon selecting a burn-in ratio b and computing $n_0 = n/b$, we have found success in utilizing a hybrid search-then-converge sequence, where $\gamma_i = \log n/n$ for $i \in [n_0]$, and $\gamma_i = \gamma_0/(1+i/i_0)$ for $i \in [n] \setminus [n_0]$, with $\gamma_0 = \log n / n$ and $i_0 = n_1$. For the remainder of the paper, we utilize the initialization scheme and gain factors that are described above.

3.5.2 Simulating Gaussian Mixture Models

In order to ease the burden of exposition, we have chosen to utilize an off-the-shelf package for the simulation of data from GMMs for our numerical simulations. The chosen package to be used is the *MixSimR* package of [45] that was developed for the explicit purpose of generating GMMs for assessing the performances of competing clustering algorithms.

We utilize the core *MixSim()* function from the package, which allows for the generation of n observations from a p-dimensional q-component GMM with variable parameters that are controlled to adhere to some properties. First, we set the Gaussian components of the GMMs to each be spherical in nature (so as to conform with our spherical covariance clustering methodology). Secondly, the mixture proportions are set to be generated randomly such that the smallest possible $\pi_y \left(y \in [q] \right)$ is no less than $0.5/q$. Lastly, the *MixSim()* function allows for setting of a closeness parameter $\bar{\omega}$ that controls the probabilistic overlap between the generated Gaussian components. The definition of $\bar{\omega}$ and its control methodology are laborious and we refer the interested reader to [45] for details. We choose to set $\bar{\omega} \in \{0.01, 0.1\}$.

Along with our choices for $\bar{\omega}$ above, we also select $b \in \{5, 10\}$, $n \in \{10^4, 10^5\}$, $p \in \{5, 10\}$, and $q \in \{5, 10\}$. This results in a total of 16 unique simulation scenarios, where the SAA is implemented with the two different values of b that we had chosen above. Aside from the feature vectors that are generated from the *MixSim()* function, we also retain the labels that indicate the subpopulation mixture component from which each observation arises.

3.5.3 Comparisons

For each scenario, we repeat the simulation ten times and compute the average time taken using the *proc.time()* function from R. Additionally, we assess the quality of the GMM clusterings via the well-known and popularly used adjusted-Rand index (ARI) of [46], for comparison of the obtained clusterings to the true subpopulation labels. The ARI is a measurement that takes value between -1 and 1. A value of 0 or lower indicates a poor clustering performance, whereas a value close to 1 indicates a high-quality clustering.

For comparisons, we assess the performance of the SAA-fitted GMM clusterings against those of the k-means algorithm implemented via the *kmeans()* function in the R with all default settings, except that we allow the algorithm to restart ten times. We note that this is a batch algorithm and we should expect it to perform better than our stream-based algorithm, since it is allowed to utilize the information from all of the data, simultaneously. We also compare our methodology to the *DSC_CluStream()* function from the *streamMOAR* package [47], which is a port of the two-stage stream *k*-means algorithm of [23], from [48]. We make a final note that we do not compare our algorithm to any batch GMM methods as they are generally significantly slower and thus are not applicable in our scenarios.

3.5.4 Results

The average timing results and the ARI results for the three tested algorithms are reported in Table 3.1. We observe that the SAA for fitting GMMs is the fastest among the three algorithms in all but two scenarios. Between the two configurations for the burn-in ratio b, we find that $b = 10$ is faster than $b = 5$. On average, the algorithm implemented with $b = 10$ requires approximately 88% the time of the $b = 5$ implementation. Furthermore, and as expected, we also find that all algorithms increase in computational time with increases in d, g, and n.

With regards to ARI, the SAA-fitted GMM outperforms or matches the performance of the two comparison algorithms in all but three of the simulation scenarios. This is particularly surprising when comparing to the batch *k*-means algorithm, since it is not required to learn the clustering in a streamed manner but is able to

Table 3.1 Average (over Ten Repetition) Computation Time (in Seconds) and ARI Results for the SAA-Fitted GMM Algorithm, the Batch *k*-Means Algorithm, and the Stream *k*-Means Algorithm of [23] for Each Simulation Scenario

D	q	N	$\bar{\omega}$	SAA (b = 5)	SAA (b = 10)	Batch k-Means	Stream k-Means
Time (s)							
5	5	1.00E+04	0.01	0.21	**0.18**	0.22	1.05
5	5	1.00E+04	0.1	0.21	**0.18**	0.30	0.99
5	5	1.00E+05	0.01	2.24	**1.77**	3.41	10.61
5	5	1.00E+05	0.1	2.36	**1.84**	5.24	10.35
5	10	1.00E+04	0.01	0.36	0.34	**0.30**	1.06
5	10	1.00E+04	0.1	0.37	**0.34**	0.49	0.98
5	10	1.00E+05	0.01	3.82	**3.54**	4.53	10.09
5	10	1.00E+05	0.1	4.14	**3.63**	7.04	9.91
10	5	1.00E+04	0.01	0.34	**0.30**	0.34	1.78
10	5	1.00E+04	0.1	0.35	**0.30**	0.45	1.72

(Continued)

Table 3.1 (*Continued*) Average (over Ten Repetition) Computation Time (in Seconds) and ARI Results for the SAA-Fitted GMM Algorithm, the Batch *k*-Means Algorithm, and the Stream *k*-Means Algorithm of [23] for Each Simulation Scenario

D	q	N	$\bar{\omega}$	SAA (b = 5)	SAA (b = 10)	Batch k-Means	Stream k-Means
10	5	1.00E+05	0.01	3.45	**3.07**	4.84	18.29
10	5	1.00E+05	0.1	3.77	**3.14**	6.96	16.73
10	10	1.00E+04	0.01	0.61	0.56	**0.47**	1.85
10	10	1.00E+04	0.1	0.64	**0.58**	0.77	1.65
10	10	1.00E+05	0.01	6.58	**5.79**	6.72	17.97
10	10	1.00E+05	0.1	6.89	**6.17**	12.27	15.54
ARI							
5	5	1.00E+04	0.01	0.87	0.83	**0.93**	**0.93**
5	5	1.00E+04	0.1	**0.59**	**0.59**	0.57	0.51
5	5	1.00E+05	0.01	0.82	0.86	**0.92**	0.84
5	5	1.00E+05	0.1	0.53	**0.60**	0.52	0.47
5	10	1.00E+04	0.01	0.84	**0.91**	0.87	0.78
5	10	1.00E+04	0.1	**0.50**	**0.50**	0.46	0.38
5	10	1.00E+05	0.01	**0.88**	0.87	0.86	0.76
5	10	1.00E+05	0.1	0.49	**0.52**	0.48	0.41
10	5	1.00E+04	0.01	0.82	**0.92**	0.89	0.79
10	5	1.00E+04	0.1	0.50	0.56	**0.59**	0.31
10	5	1.00E+05	0.01	**0.93**	0.92	0.92	0.87
10	5	1.00E+05	0.1	0.42	**0.50**	**0.50**	0.27
10	10	1.00E+04	0.01	0.88	**0.90**	0.86	0.73
10	10	1.00E+04	0.1	**0.52**	0.32	0.47	0.17
10	10	1.00E+05	0.01	**0.92**	0.90	0.88	0.79
10	10	1.00E+05	0.1	0.43	**0.44**	**0.44**	0.22

Note: The bold values indicate the minimum computational time out of the four methods that were assessed.

construct the clustering from all of the data, simultaneously. Also interesting is the fact that the GMM clustering outperforms the stream k-means clustering from the *DSC_CluStream()* function in all but one of the problems. This is an excellent outcome considering that the *DSC_CluStream()* function represents one of the state-of-the-art algorithms for clustering streamed data. Lastly, we note that there appears to be little predictable pattern regarding the setting of b with regard to the performance outcome of the SAA-fitted GMM algorithm. As such, we can recommend that $b = 10$ be used when choosing between 5 and 10, since it requires lesser amount of data in order to initialize the algorithm.

3.6 MNIST Application

The MNIST dataset is a famous and publicly available machine learning dataset that can be obtained from [27]. The dataset $\mathbf{z}^n$ consists of $n = 70{,}000$ handwritten images of digits $y_i \left(i \in [n] \right)$ between 0 and 9 (coded as $y \in [10]$ for a total of $q = 10$ classes), each rendered as a 28×28-pixel image of intensities $\mathbf{x}^i$, taking values between 0 and 255. The numbers of images of digits in the dataset between 0 and 9 (in order) are 6903, 7877, 6990, 7141, 6824, 6313, 6876, 7293, 6825, and 6958.

We utilize the SAA algorithm for GMM-based clustering to cluster the MNIST data using the feature vectors $\mathbf{x}^n$ without knowledge of the digit labels $\mathbf{y}^n$. We then utilize the labels $\mathbf{y}^n$ in order to assess the quality of the clustering outcome via the ARI, as we had done in Section 3.5. We further compare the GMM clustering to those obtained via the the *kmeans()* function in the R as well as the *DSC_CluStream()* function, in order to gain some insight into how our method benchmarks against a standard batch methodology and a state-of-the-art streamed data clustering algorithm. Clustering performances are once again measured with the ARI statistic and computation times are measured using the *proc. time()* function.

3.6.1 Data Preprocessing

In the original format, each feature vector $\mathbf{x}_i$ is $p = 28^2 = 784$ dimensional. Upon inspection of the data, many of the pixels, or features, take value zero for all $i \in [n]$. As such, we can remove these zero features in order to decrease the dimensionality of the data dramatically. Using the R data processing package *caret* [49], we can remove these features by using the *nearZeroVar()* function.

Upon removal of the zero features, we are left with $p^{(1)} = 250$ dimensional feature vectors $\left\{ \mathbf{x}_i^{(1)} \right\}_{i=1}^n$. For each coordinate $k \in \left[p^{(1)} \right]$ of the feature vector $\mathbf{x}_i^{(1)}$ (denoted as $x_{ik}^{(1)}$), we take the logarithm transformation $x_{ik}^{(2)} = \log \left(x_{ik}^{(1)} + 1 \right)$, in order to mitigate the large spread on the original intensity scale. A principal component analysis (PCA; see, for instance, [50]) is then conducted and the first five and ten principal components are used to form the reduced-dimensional datasets $\mathbf{x}^n_{[5]} = \left\{ \mathbf{x}^{[5]}_i \right\}^n_{i=1}$ and $\mathbf{x}^n_{[10]} = \left\{ \mathbf{x}^{[10]}_i \right\}^n_{i=1}$.

3.6.2 Results

Using the PCA reduced-dimensional datasets $\mathbf{x}^n_{[5]}$ and $\mathbf{x}^n_{[10]}$, we then perform clustering using the GMM fitted by SAA with burn-in ratios set to $b \in \{5, 10\}$ and $q \in \{10, 20\}$. Here, we perform analysis for $q = 20$ in order to capture the potential of heterogeneity within the digit subpopulations. For example, some sevens may be crossed, whereas others are not. Along with the GMM clusterings, we also perform clustering using the *kmeans()* and the *DSC_CluStream()* functions in *R*, for the same values of q and PCA reduced data $\mathbf{x}^n_{[5]}$ and $\mathbf{x}^n_{[10]}$. Each clustering method and combination of settings is repeated ten times. The average timing and ARI results are presented in Table 3.2.

From Table 3.2, we observe that the SAA for fitting GMMs is the fastest among the compared methods in every scenario (when implemented with $b = 10$). Furthermore, the GMM clusterings were able to match the performance of the batch *k*-means algorithm with respect to ARI performance in all but one scenario. This is a good result considering that the algorithm can be fitted iteratively and does not require the entire dataset simultaneously.

Table 3.2 Average (over Ten Repetition) Computation Time (in Seconds) and ARI Results for the SAA-Fitted GMM Algorithm, the Batch *k*-Means Algorithm, and the Stream *k*-Means Algorithm of [23] for Clustering of the MNIST Data

Principal Components	Q	SAA (b = 5)	SAA (b = 10)	Batch k-Means	Stream k-Means
Time (s)					
5	10	2.66	**2.29**	3.78	7.70
5	20	5.07	**4.53**	6.93	8.17
10	10	4.44	**3.99**	5.78	13.70
10	20	8.54	**7.76**	8.46	13.87
ARI					
5	10	**0.30**	**0.30**	**0.30**	**0.30**
5	20	**0.28**	**0.28**	**0.28**	0.27
10	10	0.40	0.38	**0.41**	0.34
10	20	**0.36**	**0.36**	**0.36**	0.33

Note: The bold values indicate the minimum computational time out of the four methods that were assessed.

3.7 Conclusions

The big data context, which can be characterized by the three Vs, is a prevalent setting for modern data analysis. Here, the Vs stand for variety, velocity, and volume, and modern algorithms that operate with big data are required to be able to cope with all three of these data characteristics.

In this chapter, we presented an algorithm for conducting model-based clustering, which utilizes an SAA to fit heterogeneous spherical-covariance GMMs. The SAA framework allows the GMMs to be fitted to very large datasets that arrive to the analyst in a stream and, thus, the algorithm is suitable in the big data context. The clusterings produced by our algorithm can be directly comparable to other streamed *k*-means algorithms such as that of [23].

We provided a brief introduction of the SAA framework for algorithm construction and derived the algorithm for the ML estimation of GMMs within the discussed framework. The derived algorithm can be proved convergent due to the known results of [18].

To demonstrate the SAA algorithm GMM-based clustering, we perform a set of numerical simulations and apply the algorithm to cluster the well-known MNIST dataset. In both cases, the SAA-fitted GMM algorithm compared very favorably against the state-of-the-art stream *k*-means algorithm of [23] as well as the traditional batch *k*-means algorithm, in terms of both clustering performance and computation time.

The positive assessment of the algorithm leads to numerous avenues for future study. For example, we can restrict the algorithm to fitted homogeneous Gaussian components with equal component probabilities in order to produce a "soft" *k*-means algorithm in the sense of [20]. Alternatively, we can expand upon the current work and utilize the matrix derivative expressions of [51] in order to produce an SAA algorithm for estimating heterogeneous non-spherical GMMs. Both of these directions are potentially highly impactful and require further attention and investigation.

References

1. G.J. McLachlan and K.E. Basford, *Mixture Models: Inference and Applications to Clustering*. New York: Marcel Dekker, 1988.
2. B.S. Everitt, S. Landau, M. Leese, and D. Stahl, *Cluster Analysis*. Chichester: Wiley, 2011.
3. K. Pearson, Contributions to the theory of mathematical evolution, *Philosophical Transactions of the Royal Society of London A*, vol. 185, pp. 71–110, 1894.
4. J.D. Banfield and A.E. Raftery, Model-based Gaussian and non-Gaussian clustering, *Biometrics*, vol. 49, pp. 803–821, 1993.
5. C. Fraley and A.E. Raftery, Model-based clustering, discriminant analysis, and density estimation, *Journal of the American Statistical Association*, vol. 97, pp. 611–631, 2002.
6. C. Fraley and A.E. Raftery, MCLUST: Software for model-based cluster analysis, *Journal of Classification*, vol. 16, pp. 297–306, 1999.

7. C. Fraley and A.E. Raftery, Enhanced model-based clustering, density estimation, and discriminant analysis software: MCLUST, *Journal of Classification,* vol. 20, pp. 263–286, 2003.

8. C. Fraley and A.E. Raftery, Model-based methods of classification: Using the mclust software in chemometrics, *Journal of Statistical Software,* vol. 18, pp. 1–13, 2007.

9. L. Scrucca, M. Fop, T.B. Murphy, and A.E. Raftery, mclust 5: Clustering, classification and density estimation using Gaussian finite mixture models, *R Journal,* vol. 8, pp. 289–317, 2016.

10. R Core Team, *R: A Language* and *Environment* for *Statistical Computing.* Vienna: R Foundation for Statistical Computing, 2016.

11. A.P. Dempster, N.M. Laird, and D.B. Rubin, Maximum likelihood from incomplete data via the EM algorithm, *Journal of the Royal Statistical Society Series B,* vol. 39, pp. 1–38, 1977.

12. G.J. McLachlan and D. Peel, *Finite Mixture Models.* New York: Wiley, 2000.

13. J.K. Jain and R.C. Dubes, *Algorithms for Clustering Data.* Englewood Cliffs: Prentice Hall, 1988.

14. L. Kaufman and P.J. Rousseeuw, *Finding Groups in Data: An Introduction to Cluster Analysis.* New York: Wiley, 1990.

15. A.K. Jain, M.N. Murty, and P.J. Flynn, Data clustering: A review, *ACM Computing Surveys,* vol. 31, pp. 264–323, 1999.

16. C. Hennig, M. Meila, F. Murtagh, and R. Rocci, Eds., *Handbook of Cluster Analysis.* Boca Raton: CRC Press, 2016.

17. A. McAfee, E. Brynjolfsson, and T.H. Davenport, Big data: The management revolution, *Harvard Business Review,* vol. 90, pp. 60–68, 2012.

18. J. Zhang and F. Liang, Convergence of stochastic approximation algorithms under irregular conditions, *StatisticaNeerlandica,* vol. 62, pp. 393–403, 2008.

19. F. Liang and J. Zhang, Estimating the false discovery rate using the stochastic approximation algorithm, *Biometrika,* vol. 95, pp. 961–977, 2008.

20. W.H. Press, S.A. Teukolsky, W.T. Vetterling, and B.P. Flannery, *Numerical Recipes: The Art of Scientific Computing.* Cambridge: Cambridge University Press, 2007.

21. J.A. Hartigan and M.A. Wong, Algorithm AS 136: A k-means clustering algorithm, *Journal of the Royal Statistical Society Series C,* vol. 28, pp. 100–108, 1979.

22. L. Bottou and Y. Bengio, Convergence properties of the k-means algorithms, In *Advances in Neural Information Processing Systems,* 1994.

23. C.C. Aggarwal, J. Han, J. Wang, and P.S. Yu, A framework for clustering evolving data streams, In *Proceedings of the 29th VLDB Conference,* 2003.

24. N. Ailon, R. Jaiswal, and C. Monteleoni, Streaming k-means approximation, In *Advances in Neural Information Processing Systems,* 2009.

25. D. Sculley, Web-scale k-means clustering, In *Proceedings of the 19th International Conference on World Wide Web,* 2010.

26. M. Shindler, A. Wong, and A.W. Meyerson, Fast and accurate k-means for large datasets, In *Advances in Neural Information Processing Systems,* 2011.

27. Y. LeCun, The MNIST Database of Handwritten Digits. 1998.

28. H. Robbins and S. Monro, A stochastic approximation method, *Annals of Mathematical Statistics,* vol. 22, pp. 400–407, 1951.

29. J. Kiefer and J. Wolfowitz, Stochastic approximation of a regression function, *Annals of Mathematical Statistics,* vol. 23, pp. 462–466, 1952.

30. H.F. Chen, *Stochastic Approximation and Its Applications.* London: Kluwer, 2002.

31. H.J. Kushner and G. Yin, *Stochastic Approximation and Recursive Algorithms and Applications.* New York: Springer, 2003.
32. M. Chau and M.C. Fu, An Overview of Stochastic Approximation, In *Handbook of Simulated Optimization*, M.C. Fu, Ed. New York: Springer, 2015, pp. 149–178.
33. F.H. Clarke, *Optimization and Nonsmooth Analysis.* SIAM, 1990.
34. J.-P. Baudry, Estimation and model selection for model-based clustering with the conditional classification likelihood, *Electronic Journal of Statistics,* vol. 9, pp. 1041–1077, 2015.
35. G. Schwarz, Estimating the dimensions of a model, *Annals of Statistics,* vol. 6, pp. 461–464, 1978.
36. C. Maugis and B. Michel, A non asymptotic penalized criterion for Gaussian model selection, *ESAIM: Probability and Statistics,* vol. 15, pp. 41–68, 2011.
37. P. Massart, *Concentration Inequalities and Model Selection.* New York: Springer, 2007.
38. J.-P. Baudry, C. Maugis, and B. Michel, Slope heuristic: Overview and implementation, *Statistics and Computing,* vol. 22, pp. 455–470, 2012.
39. B. Mirkin, Choosing the number of clusters, *WIREs Data Mining and Knowledge Discovery,* vol. 252–260, 2011.
40. G.J. McLachlan and S. Rathnayake, On the number of components in a Gaussian mixture model, *WIREs Data Mining and Knowledge Discovery,* vol. 4, pp. 341–355, 2014.
41. H. White, Maximum likelihood estimation of misspecified models, *Econometrica*, vol. 50, pp. 1–25, 1982.
42. D.M. Titterington, A.F.M. Smith, and U.E. Makov, *Statistical Analysis of Finite Mixture Distributions. New York: Wiley, 1985.*
43. D. Eddelbuettel, *Seamless R and C++ Integration with Rcpp.* New York: Springer, 2013.
44. C. Darken and J. Moody, Note on learning rate schedules for stochastic optimization, In *Advances in Neural Information Processing,* 1991.
45. V. Melnykov and I. Melnykov, Initializing the EM algorithm in Gaussian mixture models with an unknown number of components, *Computational Statistics and Data Analysis,* vol. 56, pp. 1381–1395, 2012.
46. L. Hubert and P. Arabie, Comparing partitions, *Journal of Classification,* vol. 2, pp. 193–218, 1985.
47. M. Hahsler, M. Bolanos, and J. Forrest, streamMOA: Interface for MOA Stream Clustering Algorithms. 2015.
48. A. Bifet, G. Holmes, R. Kirkby, and B. Pfahringer, MOA: Massive online analysis, *Journal of Machine Learning Research,* vol. 11, pp. 1601–1604, 2010.
49. M. Kuhn, Building predictive models in R using the caret package, *Journal of Statistical Software,* vol. 28, pp. 1–26, 2008.
50. I.T. Jolliffe, *Principal Component Analysis.* New York: Springer, 2002.
51. O. Boldea and J.R. Magnus, Maximum likelihood estimation of the multivariate normal mixture model, *Journal of the American Statistical Association,* vol. 104, pp. 1539–1549, 2009.

Chapter 4

Information Retrieval Methods for Big Data Analytics on Text

Abhay Kumar Bhadani and Ankur Narang

Yatra Online Pvt. Ltd

Contents

4.1 Introduction to Information Retrieval

Information retrieval is one of the most important topics as it has a wide range of applications in the real world, from retrieving documents, aggregating similar news articles to recommending articles, and so on. IR has varied meanings that can differ from retrieving textual data from a vast amount of text stored in an unstructured format to retrieving information from a well-structured database. However, in this chapter, we focus on different approaches to retrieve text document in some order from a vast pool of unstructured textual data.

Text classification is a part of IR activities, where the algorithm tries to tag each document in the text with a relevant class. Some of the classic examples of text classification are understanding sentiment and email classification for promotion, social, primary, spam, and so on. In this digital era, millions of digital contents are being created every moment from different sources. With such a pace, it is almost impossible to perform any sort of solid analysis with just human effort. Rather, it would require a huge amount of time along with human effort to assign them to different matching categories, such as spam and non-spam, social, and primary. Text classification algorithms under the NLP umbrella come to our rescue here.

According to Wikipedia, "IR is the science of searching for information in a document, searching for documents themselves, and also searching for metadata that describes data, and for databases of texts, images or sounds" [1].

However, to be precise and to stick to the context of IR systems from text document extraction, IR can be defined as "retrieving relevant textual information from a vast pool of unstructured text data stored in digital format on a computer system" [2].

Though IR has its presence in the early 1940s, it started to seek attention only with the advent of search engines, which can be accessed via the Internet. The most prominent search engines that help in retrieving relevant documents today are Google Search and Bing. However, Archie was the first commercial web search engine that existed in 1993, which was followed by many others, such as Altavista, Yahoo search, Google search, and Bing.

IR has many applications ranging from web search, searching emails, recommending similar jobs, finding similar users, understanding trends, search polarity, determining sentiments, and so on. However, despite rapid advancement in search engines, there are numerous challenges that still exist which have the potential to improve the quality of results and determine the document order in the fastest possible manner. These challenges are increasing day by day as a huge amount of text is getting generated in various forms, such as blogs, digitization of libraries, comments, and posts on social networks.

Recently, models developed on neural networks have become increasingly popular [3–5]. We will discuss different models that are based on neural networks as well as linear models to understand its effectiveness in building IR systems.

One of the critical parts of IR lies in fetching relevant documents by capturing the intent of the search phrase, based on which results can be retrieved and displayed. In this chapter, we address some of the concerns related to capturing the intent of the user and developing a context-based information retrieval system.

4.2 Vector Space Models

As we all know, computers are good at computation, hence the first step lies in representing any information (be it text, image, speech, or anything) in a numeric format or precisely in a vector format. Thus, vector plays an important role in addressing this basic requirement. We can represent any piece of information in a vector format. Once we represent the desired information in the form of vectors, we can apply different vector arithmetic operations for the retrieval task.

Vector space model (VSM) is defined as a statistical model for representing the text document in a vector format that can be used for IR tasks [2]. In the simplest form, a VSM may consist of information regarding the number of terms occurring in a corpus. A corpus is a collection of large text documents and the importance of words that each document contains [6]. However, by using advanced word embedding approaches, complex and compact information (Word2Vec [7], GloVe [8], FastText [9], etc.) can be stored in a vector format to represent different words and their contexts.

4.2.1 Document-Term Matrix

Document-term matrix is a numerical representation of terms present in a corpus in a vector format. A corpus can have multiple paragraphs. Here, one document represents one paragraph. A paragraph is a sequential collection of terms (or words) in some order, which conveys some meaning. The corpus can be a collection of documents in any of the languages (such as English, French, German, Hindi, and Chinese).

A document-term matrix is thus a representation of the document that can be used for analyzing the text. Each row in the matrix represents a document (i.e., a paragraph). Thus, the size of the matrix would be the number of documents in a corpus and the frequency of unique terms (i.e., vocabulary) in the corpus [2,6,10]. Since each document may not cover most of the words, the document-term matrix is highly sparse.

Let us consider a simple example to illustrate the concept. Suppose we have a corpus consisting of three sentences:

"The quick brown fox jumps over the lazy dog."
"The fox was red but dog was lazy."
"The dog was brown, and the fox was red."

The abovementioned sentences are broken down into three separate documents. Here, we have just one sentence in one paragraph, but a paragraph can also have more than one sentence.

doc1: "The quick brown fox jumps over the lazy dog."
doc2: "The fox was red but dog was lazy."
doc3: "The dog was brown, and the fox was red."

The document-term matrix for the above corpus would look like Table 4.1.

Now, we have a document-term matrix for each document. Thus, we can also say that now we have a vector representation for each document. The length of the vector is equal to the size of the vocabulary in the corpus. In our example, the size of vocabulary is 11, which is also the length of the vector for representing each document.

Let's assume that we have these example sentences stored in the underlying database, which will be used to serve the search request raised by a query phrase. Let us say that the query is "fox jumps over brown dog."

First, the query will be converted to an equivalent vector of size 11 (Table 4.2). Now, the task is to retrieve relevant documents based on some similarity score for the given query.

Table 4.1 Document-Term Matrix

	The	quick	brown	fox	jumps	over	lazy	dog	was	red	and
doc1	2	1	1	1	1	1	1	1	0	0	0
doc2	2	0	0	1	0	0	1	1	2	1	1
doc3	2	0	1	1	0	0	0	1	2	1	1

Table 4.2 Document-Term Matrix for Query: "fox jumps over brown dog"

	The	*quick*	*brown*	*fox*	*jumps*	*over*	*lazy*	*dog*	*was*	*red*	*and*
query	0	0	1	1	1	1	0	1	0	0	0

In order to perform this operation, we are required to use distance metrics that will help in deciding the order of the documents retrieved, based on the relevance of the searched phrase.

4.2.2 Distance Metrics

In this section, we will introduce the concepts related to commonly referred distance metrics in text data. In the distance-based methods, similarity or dissimilarity are conceptualized as the distance between two sentences. It means that if the two sentences are similar, then it is likely to have less distance, whereas if the sentences are not at all related, then we can expect their distance to be bit higher. Though there are different distance metrics that can be referred in the literature, we are limiting ourselves to Euclidean distance, Jaccard similarity, Mahanalobis distance, cosine similarity, and Word Mover's Distance as they are used in computing the dissimilarity between the text documents.

4.2.2.1 Euclidean Distance

The Euclidean distance is the straight-line distance between two points in Euclidean space. Mathematically, it is written as

$$Eucledian(x, y) = \sqrt{\sum_{i=0}^{n-1} |x_i - y_i|^2} \tag{4.1}$$

where x and y are two vectors used for computing the Euclidean distance.

4.2.2.2 Mahalanobis Distance

Mahalanobis distance is a statistical measure, which is better in performance compared with other statistical measures, such as Euclidean distance and Manhattan distance. It is computed by obtaining the correlation among the various dimensions or features for the problem under study. Thus, it is useful for addressing classification as well as clustering problems [11]. Mahalanobis distance accounts for the fact that the variances in each direction for a feature vector are different. It also takes into consideration the covariance between the features. And, further, if the covariance matrix is equal to the identity matrix, then the Mahalanobis distance is like computing the Euclidean distance between two vectors.

The Euclidean and Mahalanobis distance compute the magnitude of the feature vector and, thus, portrays similar objects closer in a variable space. Mathematically, the Mahalanobis distance is defined as follows:

$$\sqrt{(X_i - X_j)^T \sum^{-1} (X_i - X_j)} \tag{4.2}$$

where X_i and X_j are the vector representations for i and j cases, whereas Σ is the group variance–covariance matrix.

4.2.2.3 Jaccard Index

The Jaccard similarity index (also termed as Jaccard similarity coefficient) performs a comparison between the members of two sets to evaluate which members are common and which are distinct. The similarity between two sets ranges between 0 and 1. The closer it is to 1, the more similar are the two populations. The beauty of Jaccard similarity is that it is easier to interpret; however, with small samples sizes or missing values, the results may not be reliable, thus showing an extremely sensitive behavior. Mathematically, it is represented as

$$J(X,Y) = |X \cap Y| / |X \cup Y| \tag{4.3}$$

where X and Y are the two different sets for comparison and compute the similarity.

Let's say we have two sentences: (A) "The quick brown fox jumps over the lazy dog." and (B) "The fox was red but dog was lazy."

These sentences can be represented using the following set notations:

```
A = {"The", "quick", "brown", "fox", "jumps", "over", "lazy",
     "dog"}

B = {"The", "fox", "was", "red", "but", "dog", "lazy"}
```

Then the Jaccard similarity index will be the following:

```
J(A,B) = |{"The", "fox", "dog", "lazy"}| / |{"The", "quick",
          "brown", "fox", "jumps", "over", "lazy", "dog", "was",
          "red", "but"}|
       = 4/11
       = 0.36
```

4.2.2.4 Cosine Similarity

Cosine similarity computes the normalized dot product of two vectors of equal length. It helps to find the cosine of the angle between the two vectors. The mathematical notation for the cosine similarity is given as Equation 4.4, and the extended notation is given in Equation 4.5.

The cosine of $0°$ is 1 (it also means that there is no difference between the two vectors and hence 0, which means the similarity between the two vectors computes to 1), and it is less than 1 for any other angle. If the distance is closer to 1, the terms are somewhat closer or similar in nature. On the other hand, if the distance is closer to 0 (i.e., the two vectors are at $90°$), it indicates that the terms are not related. Thus, cosine similarity is a judgment of orientation and does not focus on magnitude.

$$\cos(x, y) = \frac{x.y}{\| x \| \| y \|} \tag{4.4}$$

$$\cos(x, y) = \frac{\sum_{i=0}^{n-1} x_i y_i}{\sqrt{\sum_{i=0}^{n-1} (x_i)^2} \sqrt{\sum_{i=0}^{n-1} (y_i)^2}} \tag{4.5}$$

It is particularly used in positive space and the outcome is bounded within [0, 1]. One of the primary reasons for the popularity of cosine similarity is that it can be evaluated very efficiently, especially if the vectors are sparse in nature.

4.2.2.5 Word Mover's Distance

A critical success factor for any application lies in the metric that is used for comparing the results and carrying out a benchmark analysis. It acts as a valuable building block. In NLP applications, cosine similarity works well, if bag-of-words representation is used. However, when we want to compare different documents (or sentences) having similar meaning, cosine similarity with BOW representation may not work in the real world. Thus, it becomes important to decide on the similarity metrics judiciously while building a solution that may require comparing or clustering similar documents. Ideally, a metric should have the capability to capture semantically related information.

Usually, one measures the distance between two word2vec vectors using the cosine distance, which measures the angle between vectors. WMD, on the other hand, uses the Euclidean distance. The Euclidean distance between two vectors might be large because their lengths differ, but the cosine distance is small because the angle between them is small; we can mitigate some of this by normalizing the vectors. Two similar documents will have a high similarity score and a small distance; two very different documents will have low similarity score and a large distance. Document lengths have a high impact on the running time of WMD. WMD is a method that allows us to assess the "distance" between two documents in a meaningful way, even when they have no words in common [12,13]. It uses word2vec/fastText vector embeddings of words.

4.2.3 Term Frequency–Inverse Document Frequency

In the previous section, we discussed term-frequency (TF) approach to create the vectors for each document. However, it has certain limitations, which will be discussed here. We will also discuss some corrective measures that would help in improving the IR algorithm.

As a preprocessing step, we suggest removing stop words. Stop words are those words that do not contribute much to the query string. A few examples are: the, is, that, had, has, have, he, she, her, etc. Thus, these stop words won't be part of the vector any more. After this, we will improve the weights of the vector by increasing the importance of those words which occur infrequently. The infrequently occurring terms across the collection is a measure of its importance. This step is known as inverse document frequency (IDF). We can say that the importance of a term is inversely proportional to the frequency of the occurrence of the term as given in the following equation:

$$idf_t = \log\left(1 + \frac{N}{n_t}\right) \tag{4.6}$$

where

N is the number of documents in the corpus
n_t is the number of documents containing the term t

TF–IDF is a way to compute the vector representation for each document by considering both TF matrix and IDF matrix [10]. One of the simplest ways is to multiply TF with IDF matrix. However, many other variants of the TF–IDF scheme have been studied.

The IDF matrix for the corpus is shown in Table 4.3.
The TF–IDF matrix is presented in Table 4.4.

Table 4.3   IDF Matrix

	The	quick	brown	fox	jumps	over	lazy	dog	was	red	and
IDF$_t$	0.301	0.602	0.398	0.301	0.602	0.602	0.398	0.301	0.398	0.398	0.602

Table 4.4 TF–IDF Matrix

	The	quick	brown	fox	jumps	over	lazy	dog	was	red	and
doc1	0.602	0.602	0.398	0.301	0.602	0.602	0.398	0.301	0.000	0.000	0.000
doc2	0.602	0.000	0.000	0.301	0.000	0.000	0.398	0.301	0.796	0.398	0.602
doc3	0.602	0.000	0.398	0.301	0.000	0.000	0.000	0.301	0.796	0.398	0.602
query	0.000	0.000	0.398	0.301	0.602	0.602	0.000	0.301	0.000	0.000	0.000

4.3 Information Retrieval Approaches

In this section, we will discuss different algorithms that are used for IR tasks. But before we proceed further, we will first discuss *n*-grams. An *n*-gram is a continuous sequence of words occurring together in a given order in a sentence or speech. The value of *n* decides how many times these *n*-sequences of words occur together in a corpus. If the value of *n* is 1, we typically call it 1-gram or unigram; similarly, if *n* is 2, we call it bigram; if *n* is 3, it is called trigram; and so on. An *n*-gram model is a probabilistic model that is used in understanding the languages, which can help in predicting the next sequence of words or the missing words in a sentence. The value of n determines the accuracy of prediction. However, if the value of n increases the size of vocabulary increases as well as the storage and processing time. Unigram model stores the word vocabulary list, whereas bigrams or trigrams will store vocabulary with two or three words and also store their frequency count. We normally use a variant of *n*-gram model to find word embedding for the word(s).

One of the most popular applications of *n*-gram models is in detecting plagiarism. However, the major limitations of *n*-gram word model lie in the fact that it is unable to predict the new word that is not yet seen by the model, i.e., the word was not present in the corpus, while it was being trained.

4.3.1 Latent Semantic Analysis

Latent semantic analysis (LSA), also known as latent semantic indexing (LSI), helps in analyzing documents so that the underlying meaning or concepts of those documents can be found [14]. LSA was proposed by [15] for processing tasks related to NLP. Ideally, each word should have a single meaning and concept, in which case LSA's work would have been to describe each concept by one word; however, it is not the case. It has been observed that a single word carries different meanings when used in different contexts in almost all the languages. This creates a certain level of ambiguity that obscures the concepts and makes it hard for people to understand the meaning. In the English language, there are around 13 million estimated tokens; unfortunately, most of them are not completely unrelated, for example, hotel and motel. Not only that, some of them convey different meanings depending on the context of usage. For example, the word "bank" when used together with the names of rivers means a place beside the river, whereas if it is used with respect to loans, credit cards, exchange rates, and mortgage, then probably it means a financial institution. Now, we explain some of the basic differences between frequently used terms, such as latent semantic analysis (LSA), latent semantic indexing (LSI), and singular value decomposition (SVD).

SVD is a topic from standard linear algebra and statistics, which helps in reducing the dimension of a matrix based on eigenvalues [16]. LSI is an application of

SVD for information retrieval tasks. LSA is a special case where LSI is applied to natural language processing and principal component analysis is a statistical technique that is an application of SVD.

LSA approach makes three claims: that semantic information can be captured from a co-occurrence matrix of a document; one of the essential parts of this approach is dimensionality reduction; and any documents or words can be represented as a point in a Euclidean space. It is a class of statistical models in which the semantic properties of words and documents are expressed in terms of probabilistic topics.

4.3.2 word2vec

As the name itself suggests, word2vec is a technique that converts words to vector representation. Primarily, there are two approaches to compute the vectors: (a) continuous bag-of-words (CBOW) and (b) skip-gram model.

As we know, n-grams are a sequence of words occurring in an order. Though it is logical to think of a sequence of words, however it has been shown that skip-grams work equally good while computing the word embeddings. Skip-grams or more specifically skip-n-grams consider the subsequence of words that may occur, at most, within some k-neighborhood distance.

The probabilistic feedforward neural network language model proposed by Vincent et al. [17] is the basis for designing word2vec [18]. It consists of input layers, projection, hidden, and output layers. The N previous words are encoded using 1-of-S coding, where S is the size of the vocabulary. The input layer is further projected to a layer P that has dimensionality $N * D$, using a distributed projection matrix. At a given time, only N inputs are active; hence, the composition of the projection layer is a relatively computationally efficient operation.

4.3.2.1 CBOW Model

CBOW architecture is very similar to probabilistic feed forward neural network language model [19], but in CBOW, the nonlinear hidden layer has been eliminated and the projection layer shares all words; thus, all words get projected into the same position. This architecture is known as a bag-of-words (BOW) model as the order in which words occur does not affect the projection layer.

In this model, the middle or missing words are predicted, provided k words occurring before and k words occurring after the middle word are provided to the model. As a result, it tries to predict the middle word. In a simple form, we can say the task of BOW (or, precisely, CBOW as it is continuous in nature) model is to predict the middle word, given the context words. An illustrative diagram of CBOW is shown on the left side of Figure 4.1.

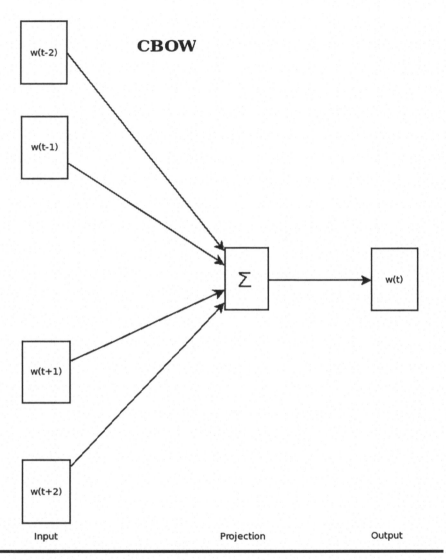

Figure 4.1   CBOW model.

4.3.2.2 Skip-Gram Model

In the skip-gram model, we are given a corpus of words w and their contexts c. So, we can model this phenomenon with conditional probabilities, i.e., $p(w|c)$ and then try to compute the probabilities for the predicted word. We also need to understand that the prediction lies on the appropriateness of tuned parameters or hyperparameters, which is normally denoted by θ. So, to be precise, the conditional probability equation is represented as $p(w|c; \theta)$.

$$\arg\frac{\max}{\theta} \prod_{(w,c)\in S} p(c \mid w;\theta) \tag{4.7}$$

Here, S is the set of possible words and context pairs that is built from the corpus.

The concept behind skip-gram is to train a model in the context of each word, such that similar words end up having similar embeddings. The skip-gram model in word2vec uses neural networks to estimate the hyper parameters θ by adjusting the weights using backward-propagation. It models the conditional probability $p(w|c; \theta)$ that uses soft-max classifier in the last layer of the neural networks.

$$p(c \mid w;\theta) = \frac{e^{v_c \cdot v_w}}{\sum_{c' \in C} e^{v_{c'} \cdot v_w}} \tag{4.8}$$

where $(v_c, v_w) \in R^d$ are vector representations for c and w, respectively, and C is the set of all available contexts. The parameters θ are v_{ci}, v_{wi} for $w \in V, c \in C, I \in 1, 2,...,$ d (a total of $|C|*|V|*d$ parameters).

While defining context in a sentence having n words $w_1,...,w_n$, contexts of a word w_i come from a window of size k in the neighborhood of the word: $C(w) = w_{i-k,...,}w_{i-1}, w_{i+1,...,}w_{i+k,}$ where k is a parameter.

At this point, we are ready to fine-tune the parameters such that the product (4.4) is maximized. This product operation can be converted to summation if we apply log on both sides for easier computation. An illustrative diagram of the skip-gram model is shown on the right side of Figure 4.2.

Overall, word2vec treats each word in the corpus like an atomic entity and generates word-embedding for each word and context words. Thus, the smallest unit in word2vec is a word. The main limitation of this approach is that it fails to generate or classify words that do not exist in the corpus.

In Section 4.3.2, we will see how fastText overcomes this limitation by using n-gram character as its basic unit for creating the word embeddings.

4.3.3 fastText

fastText is one of the recent advances in the area of NLP, which helps to generate word embeddings, very similar to what word2vec does [9]. It is an open-source library created by Facebook for carrying out their NLP activities, such as word embeddings or text classification. However, the beauty of fastText lies in the fact that it takes several orders of magnitude less time to train a model. fastText takes less than ten minutes to train a model using a standard multicore CPU and can classify 312K classes in less than a minute for half a million sentences.

Its performance is comparable and even better in few cases than deep learning approaches, such as word2vec and GloVe, in terms of accuracy, but it is many orders of magnitude faster for training and evaluation. Thus, it helps in reducing

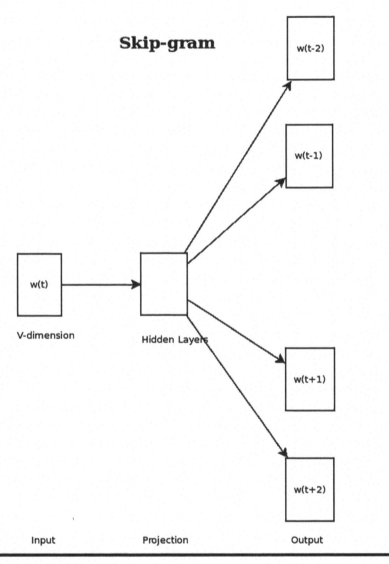

Figure 4.2   Skip-gram model.

the training time. The basic unit for fastText is character *n*-gram, whereas the basic unit for word2vec is word or *n*-gram word.

It represents a text by a low-dimensional vector, which is an aggregation of words appearing in the text. It treats each word as a composition of *n*-gram characters. For example, we want to understand how *orange* is treated by fastText using *n*-gram character. Here, there are two hyper-parameters that need to be set initially (i.e., *n*-gram min and *n*-gram max). Let's say *n-gram min* is 3 and *n-gram max* is 7. Then, *orange* will be represented as follows:

```
<or, ora, oran, orang, orange, orange>,
ran, rang, range, range>,
ang, ange, ange>,
nge, nge>,
ge>
```

The beauty of this approach lies in the fact that it generates a decent word embeddings for words that occur rarely. This happens due to the fact that the character *n*-grams used to construct the words share the vector representation of different words. Hence, it is likely that the embeddings can still be acceptable.

This approach of character *n*-grams also helps in constructing words that were not seen previously in the corpus. Thus, out-of-vocabulary problems are handled using this approach.

In spite of some good points, it also comes with a price. Since it trains the model on a character level or a character *n*-gram level, it ends up taking more time to generate word embeddings compared to word2vec. So, we must be selecting the hyper-parameters carefully, as the values of min and max have direct impact on this time. One of the limitations of fastText is that it works better on small datasets.

4.4 Walk-Through of IR: An Illustrative Example

In this section, we will discuss two examples illustrating the concepts related to different distance metrics on a text corpus.

Example 1

Let us consider the discussed example again.

> doc1: "The quick brown fox jumps over the lazy dog."
> doc2: "The fox was red but dog was lazy."
> doc3: "The dog was brown, and the fox was red."

We have learned the two basic and most popular distance metrics (Euclidean and cosine) that can handle vector arithmetic and one advanced metric WMD. Now, we will compute the scores and document retrieval order using Euclidean and cosine metrics. Further, we will show a detailed example to show WMD.

The search query is: "fox jumps over brown dog"

Here, we discussed how to compute and retrieve documents, given a query string using two approaches in Tables 4.5 and 4.6.

However, there are certain limitations with this approach. The document vector representation we explained, is also popularly called BOW vector representation.

Table 4.5   Euclidean Distance Computation and Retrieval Order

Document	Euclidean Distance	Order
doc1	2.4494897428	1
doc2	3.7416573868	3
doc3	3.4641016151	2

Table 4.6   Cosine Computation and Retrieval Order

Document	Cosine Similarity	Order
doc1	0.6741998625	1
doc2	0.2581988897	3
doc3	0.3872983346	2

In BOW, the basic assumptions about the data are that the order of words is not important, but only the term frequency matters. So, we can say, BOW is a collection of unordered list of terms. One of the major limitations of this approach is that it does not capture the context. It may fail to detect the difference between a valid positive sentence and, maybe, a negative sentence composed of the same set of words, or even sarcasm may go undetected. For Example:

"The quick brown fox jumps over the lazy dog" is, in this context, identical to the document "The lazy brown dog jumps over the quick fox." It is so because both the sentences have the same vector representation (i.e., BOW representation).

It may be a good fit if we intend to find similarity in the topics, something like grouping political news, sports news, scientific news, and so on. Now, we will again compute both the metrics based on TF–IDF matrix (refer Table 4.4) to see if there are any differences.

We see that the document retrieval order does not change in Tables 4.7 and 4.8, in this particular case. But, if we have a large corpus, then TF–IDF works better compared to the document-term matrix. It is so because it penalizes frequently occurring words and gives more weight for those words whose frequency is less.

Table 4.7   Euclidean Distance Computation and Retrieval Order Based on TF–IDF

Document	Euclidean Distance	Order
doc1	0.1324138712	1
doc2	1.9478555502	3
doc3	1.5957805672	2

Table 4.8   Cosine Computation and Retrieval Order Based on TF–IDF

Document	Cosine Similarity	Order
doc1	0.7392715831	1
doc2	0.1437187361	3
doc3	0.2692925425	2

Example 2

Now, we will take another example shown on a real dataset of Amazon's book reviews. It is a rich dataset and comprises of real reviews written by several customers based on their experience. Few researchers have used this dataset to address some real challenges, such as answering product related queries and recommending products [20,21] The dataset can be downloaded from [19]. It consists of the following fields.

■ reviewerID: unique identification of the reviewer
■ asin: unique product ID
■ reviewerName: name of the reviewing customer
■ helpful: helpfulness rating of the review, e.g., 2/3
■ reviewText: text of the review
■ overall: rating of the product
■ summary: summary of the review
■ unixReviewTime: time of the review (Unix time)
■ reviewTime: time of the review (raw)

In our case, we extracted "asin" and "reviewText" columns for training our model. Word embedding is an approach where the words (in any language, i.e., English, Chinese, French, Hindi, etc.) are represented using dense vectors and still maintain their relative meaning. We can also say that the word embedding is a continuous vector space where semantically related words are mapped to nearby points. It is an enhanced way of representing the words in a dense vector format as compared with BOW (document-term matrix), which is sparse representation. Dense vector representation of textual data is usually achieved using neural networks having certain hidden nodes trained over the underlying corpus. Once the model is trained, it can be reused again and again for multiple purposes. The usage can vary from finding synonyms, finding dissimilar words, machine translation, and sentence generation to name a few.

A word embedding ($W: words \to R^n$) is a representation technique of mapping words in some language to high-dimensional vectors (perhaps 100–300 dimensions) by training a neural network.

For simplicity, we have trained our model having ten dimensions (though it may not be desirable). The dense vector representation of a few initial words from the review corpus that is trained using word2vec-CBOW approach is shown in Table 4.9.

Table 4.9 Dense Word Vector Representation Having Ten Dimensions Generated Using word2vec

book	-0.17	-0.96	0.48	4.78	0.18	0.58	-0.14	-1.44	-0.56	2.17
read	-0.96	-1.13	0.53	4.97	-0.72	1.57	1.52	-0.10	-1.68	4.78
story	0.21	0.52	-2.28	3.11	0.93	2.44	-2.88	-2.36	0.69	0.56
one	1.13	-1.10	-0.24	2.58	-0.47	0.46	-0.09	0.69	-0.80	2.28
like	0.73	-0.21	-0.46	1.70	1.51	-0.57	0.20	0.25	-3.70	1.57
characters	1.14	0.58	-2.40	3.17	2.59	1.62	-6.31	-2.91	0.08	0.17
books	-0.11	-2.24	1.65	3.82	1.01	0.90	-0.24	-1.66	-0.14	4.49
would	-0.45	1.31	1.85	3.90	0.03	-1.85	-1.48	-0.30	-1.78	2.53
good	-0.71	0.23	-1.32	3.41	0.63	1.03	0.40	-1.42	-2.34	3.17
reading	-1.65	-0.52	2.02	6.05	-1.03	1.76	0.52	0.09	-0.86	2.38
could	-0.72	0.84	1.69	6.37	1.05	1.08	-3.81	0.62	0.01	1.61
really	0.74	0.17	-0.95	4.69	1.59	-0.62	-1.61	-0.93	-1.98	1.72
rest	1.74	-3.95	-0.76	5.12	0.62	1.48	0.93	-0.23	-2.20	0.44
great	-0.37	0.11	-2.73	3.17	-0.09	2.67	0.30	-1.50	-0.64	4.01
love	2.08	0.96	-4.09	2.02	-1.96	-1.46	-1.34	-1.51	-1.13	3.30

Table 4.10   Document Retrieval by Word Mover's Distance

WMD	Document
0.0	(QUERY:) good and easy reading having fantastic romantic, motivational story
2.8175	This is a good story and story and easy read. I am a Grisham fan and this did not disappoint.
2.9357	Awesome book I was very impressed with the story the plot was good it made me cry hf oe nf pdd awww ggtt vgvbh cvcvg dfrw shyev
3.0640	This was a wonderful book, it was an easy read with a great story. I am happy to own this book.
3.1404	It's a book definitely for relaxation. The courtroom description is fantastic. Nice easy reading. Enjoyed it very much.
8.8928	A favorite. can't wait for the movie

We will illustrate an example, which has been trained using word2vec on Amazon's book reviews dataset. It learns the word embeddings based on the words used in a sentence, i.e., reviews. word2vec has two different implementations: the CBOW model and the skip-gram model. Algorithmically, both these models work similarly, except that CBOW predicts target words (e.g., "mat") from source context words ("the cat sits on the"), whereas the skip-gram does the inverse and predicts source context words from the target words.

Query string: "good fantastic romantic, jealous, motivational"

Results of the queried string are shown in Table 4.10.

It can be clearly observed that the WMD of the query string is 0.0, whereas sentences that have closely related meaning have low scores. However, if the sentences are not related then the distance is farther as we can see in case of the last line "a favorite. can't wait for the movie".

Apart from information retrieval tasks, these word embeddings can also help us in finding similar words or find odd words from a given set of words.

For example, if "book" is related to "kindle," so "children" is related to ????

```
result = model.most_similar(positive=[`book', `children'],
                     negative=[`kindle'], topn=5)
print(result)

[(`teenagers', 0.8260207772254944), (`age',
0.8220992684364319),
(`normal', 0.8047794699668884), (`girls',
0.8042588233947754),
(`older', 0.8039965629577637)]
Similarly, we can find out odd words out, i.e., which word
   is least related:
result = model.doesnt_match("motivational fabulous bad
   good".split())
print(result)
```

```
motivational

result = model.doesnt_match("notes book author players
    reviews".split())
print(result)
players

result = model.doesnt_match("author men women children".
split())
print(result)
author
```

The results presented here are dependent on the trained corpus, and we may expect a few changes in the results as the corpus changes. The quality of results is likely to improve with the increase in the size of the dataset.

4.5 Applications

NLP is a special branch that falls under a broad application of artificial intelligence. It has many implications for the ways that people and computers have started interacting. NLP has the power to become an important technology that has the potential to bridge the gap between human communication and digital data. A few applications that are very useful and are yet to mature are enlisted in Sections 4.5.1–4.5.8.

4.5.1 Sentiment Extraction

Sentiment extraction is helpful in several ways, such as understanding the market sentiment for a particular political party or a company. Many people refer to Glassdoor reviews or Google reviews before they plan to join a new organization. Similarly, people read product reviews before buying a product or read restaurant reviews before choosing the restaurant for birthday parties.

4.5.2 Text Categorization/Spam Detection

The goal of text categorization is to classify the topic or theme of a document. One of the important applications is to classify news in different sections, such as sports, politics, financial news, and country-specific. Emails can be classified as spam, social, promotional emails, important, and so on.

4.5.3 Translation to Other Languages

Translation is the problem of converting a source text written in a particular language to a desired language. It is considered to be an important application of NLP and has huge application in real life. It is almost impossible to know all possible languages in the world, but anyone can visit or meet people during their course of interaction. Often, it becomes difficult to communicate if both the parties don't understand the same languages. Machine translation can act as a rescue application that can help them to communicate without much problem.

4.5.4 Automated Q&A and Chatbots

Chatbots are important applications that may help in answering the questions asked by a human, especially, if it is a routine question. However, it would be interesting to design such an application that is smart enough to replace a human expertise.

4.5.5 Text Summarization

Document summarization is an application where a brief description is created from the original, typically large document. Some examples of document summarization may include assigning a suitable title for the document, predicting the author or organization from where the article might have been published, generating abstract automatically from a large text article, and so on.

4.5.6 Resume Short Listing

Resume/CV matching for a particular job is one of the most important and critical applications for most organizations. It may also be used to predict the behavior of the candidate and so on. Gathering details from different formats of CVs to correct spots is still an application that most of the companies would like to have. However, it is still a distant dream while this book gets written.

4.5.7 Replacing Medical Codes from Patient's Prescription

Medical codes (commonly referred to as the International Classification of Disease [ICD]) are a standard set of codes that are used by the insurance agencies to cross-verify the procedures followed by the physicians or hospitals while serving a patient during his/her visit. Accordingly, payments are released, if the procedures followed lie under the policy. Converting patient's prescriptions to medically coded documents requires human interference, in spite of the fact that these are a standard set of practice that is followed in a standard way. Placing correct medical codes at the right place is a challenging task, even for humans, and it still suffers from errors leading to declination of the payment. Developing such solutions is the need for processing huge amount of patient's prescriptions.

4.5.8 Writing Automatically/Text Generation/Poetry

Text generation is one of the ambitious projects that are being researched upon. Writing or generating correct and meaningful sentences in a particular language is still a far-sighted dream. However, deep learning in NLP has proved to be quite helpful.

4.6 Conclusions

In this chapter, we discussed the basics of vector space model and its need for mining textual data for extracting meaningful insights in terms of information retrieval, classification, or sentiment analysis. We introduced some basic concepts related to the vector space model and how words are represented for deriving word embeddings. Different distance metrics have been discussed which are used frequently. We discussed different approaches such as TF–IDF, word2vec, and fastText for representing the words in dense vector notation. Toward the end of the chapter, several applications of NLP and text analysis along with relevant examples were discussed. After reading this chapter, the readers must have become aware of the nuances of text mining and handling textual data.

References

1. Wikipedia. Information retrieval. https://en.wikipedia.org/wiki/Information_retrieval. Accessed on 15th Feb, 2018.
2. C.D. Manning, P. Raghavan, and H. Schütze. *Introduction to Information Retrieval*. Cambridge University Press, New York, 2008.
3. A. Conneau, H. Schwenk, L. Barrault, and Y. Lecun. Very deep convolutional networks for natural language processing. *arXiv preprint*, 2016.
4. Y. Kim. Convolutional neural networks for sentence classification. In *EMNLP*, 2014.
5. X. Zhang and Y. LeCun. Text understanding from scratch. *arXiv preprint*, 2015.
6. D.M. Blei, A.Y. Ng, and M.I. Jordan. Latent dirichlet allocation. *The Journal of machine Learning Research*, 3:993–1022, 2003.
7. T. Mikolov, I. Sutskever, K. Chen, Greg S. Corrado, and J. Dean. Distributed representations of words and phrases and their compositionality. In C.J.C. Burges, L. Bottou, M. Welling, Z. Ghahramani, and K.Q. Weinberger, editors, *Advances in Neural Information Processing Systems*, 26, pp. 3111–3119. Curran Associates, Inc., Lake Tahoe, NV, 2013.
8. J. Pennington, R. Socher, and C.D. Manning. Glove: Global vectors for word representation. In *Empirical Methods in Natural Language Processing (EMNLP)*, pp. 1532–1543, 2014.
9. A. Joulin, E. Grave, P. Bojanowski, and T. Mikolov. Bag of tricks for efficient text classification. *CoRR*, abs/1607.01759, 2016.
10. G. Salton and M.J. McGill. *Introduction to Modern Information Retrieval*. McGraw-Hill, Inc., New York, 1986.
11. G. Taguchi and R. Jugulum. *The MahalanobisTaguchi Strategy: A Pattern Technology System*. John Wiley and Sons, Somerset, NJ, 2002.
12. M.J. Kusner, Y. Sun, N.I. Kolkin, and K.Q. Weinberger. From word embeddings to document distances. In *Proceedings of the 32nd International Conference on International Conference on Machine Learning - Volume 37*, ICML'15, pp. 957–966. JMLR.org, 2015.

13. E. Levina and P.J. Bickel. The earth mover's distance is the mallows distance: Some insights from statistics. In *ICCV*, pp. 251–256, 2001.

14. S. Deerwester, S.T. Dumais, G.W. Furnas, T.K. Landauer, and R. Harshman. Indexing by latent semantic analysis. *Journal of the American Society for Information Science*, 41(6):391–407, 1990.

15. J.R. Bellegarda. Latent semantic mapping [information retrieval]. *IEEE Signal Processing Magazine*, 22(5):70–80, 2005.

16. D. Kalman. *A Singularly Valuable Decomposition: The SVD of a Matrix*. The American University, Washington, DC, 2002.

17. P. Vincent. Y. Bengio, and R. Ducharme. A neural probabilistic language model. *Journal of Machine Learning Research*, 3:1137–1155, 2003.

18. T. Mikolov, K. Chen, G. Corrado, and J. Dean. Efficient estimation of word representations in vector space. *CoRR*, abs/1301.3781, 2013.

19. Amazon. Amazon product data. http://snap.stanford.edu/data/amazon/productGraph/categoryFiles/ reviews_Books_5.json.gz, 2016.

20. J. McAuley and A. Yang. Addressing complex and subjective product-related queries with customer reviews. In *Proceedings of the 25th International Conference on World Wide Web*, WWW '16, pp. 625–635, Republic and Canton of Geneva, Switzerland, 2016. International World Wide Web Conferences Steering Committee.

21. R. He and J. McAuley. Ups and downs: Modeling the visual evolution of fashion trends with one-class collaborative filtering. In *Proceedings of the 25th International Conference on World Wide Web*, WWW '16, pp. 507–517, Republic and Canton of Geneva, Switzerland, 2016. International World Wide Web Conferences Steering Committee.

Chapter 5

Big Graph Analytics

Ahsanur Rahman and Tamanna Motahar

North South University

Contents

5.1 Introduction

Nowadays, people, devices, processes, and other entities are much more connected with each other than in any other time of history. This connectivity stems from the popularity of online social networks (such as Facebook, Twitter, Google+, and LinkedIn), mobile communication networks, online forums, collaboration networks (such as Stack Overflow, Quora, Ubuntu Forums, Academia.edu, and Mendeley), wireless sensor networks, World Wide Web (WWW), and many other networks. These networks often contain billions of entities (vertices) and/or connections (edges) and as such have been aptly named as large-scale graphs [1] or simply, *big graphs* [2,3]. An example of a big graph is the Twitter network which contains more than 40 million users and more than a billion edges (leader–follower relations) [4].

Big graphs may have other characteristics other than their huge sizes. Specifically, big graphs can be characterized by the three *V*'s of big data[1]: *volume, variety*, and *velocity* [5]. A big graph (i) must have high *volume, i.e.,* it must contain numerous[2] vertices and edges, (ii) it may contain a *variety* of vertices/edges (e.g., we can form a big graph using Facebook data consisting of undirected edges representing friendship relations, directed edges representing who follows whose status updates, undirected edges representing connections among the persons in the same Facebook group, directed edges representing who liked/shared whose status, etc.), and (iii) it may have high *velocity, i.e.,* it may change its topology with time (from now on, we will call such graphs *big dynamic graphs*, whereas graphs that don't change with time will be called *big static graphs*). Note that while high volume is a necessary feature of big graphs, having a high variety or velocity is not required for a network to be called a big graph.[3]

5.1.1 Motivation and Challenges of Big Graph Analytics

Analysis of big graphs has many applications, such as product recommendation, data cleaning, plagiarism detection, and traffic route planning [6]. However, the characteristics of big graphs (discussed previously) pose significant computational challenges in storing and analyzing them. Specifically, it is impossible to fit these graphs entirely into a typical RAM. Moreover, analyzing them with a single processor is often practically infeasible. These issues are even harder to cope with while dealing with big dynamic graphs or graphs containing different types of vertices/edges. Therefore, a traditional, simple sequential computational model is not suitable for analyzing big graphs.

5.1.2 Frameworks for Big Graph Analytics

A number of computational frameworks/platforms have been proposed in the literature to tackle the challenges of big graph mining. These frameworks enable the programmers to implement parallel graph mining algorithms without worrying about the low-level details related to parallel processing, such as how the graph should be partitioned into different processors or worker machines, how the processes should communicate with each other, and how/whether to synchronize the execution of the parallel processes. These abstractions provided by the big graph frameworks simplify the task of the programmers.

These frameworks can broadly be classified into different categories based on (i) whether they are distributed or are single-machine systems and (ii) whether they are designed for static or dynamic graphs. In this chapter, we will discuss about these categories and subcategories of big graph frameworks and compare them. We will highlight their relative advantages and disadvantages and discuss which use cases are best suited for each type of framework. We will also briefly review some popular big graph platforms and discuss how to implement some important graph algorithms in these frameworks. Section 5.1.3 highlights the detailed organization of the rest of this chapter.

5.1.3 Organization and Goal of This Chapter

In Section 5.2, we will explore some notable distributed frameworks that are capable of analyzing big static graphs. In Section 5.3, we will briefly discuss about single-machine frameworks that have been designed to analyze big static graphs. Sections 5.4 and 5.5 are dedicated, respectively, to the discussions on distributed and single-machine frameworks designed to process big dynamic graphs. We will draw conclusions in Section 5.6.

Note that this chapter is intended to serve as a quick beginner's guide on understanding, using, and comparing big graph frameworks. Our ultimate goal is to enable the reader to evaluate different types of frameworks and determine which ones are best suited for his/her needs. Therefore, we don't intend to discuss in details how these frameworks are implemented. For a more detailed discussion of these frameworks, please read the book written by Yan et al. [7].

5.2 Distributed Frameworks for Analyzing Big Static Graphs

Distributed systems are obvious choices for analyzing big graphs due to the difficulty in processing/storing them in a single machine (unless the machine is very powerful). As a result, a number of distributed frameworks have been designed for processing big graphs. In this section, we will discuss such frameworks. This section will occupy a major part of this chapter because most research on big graph analytics was done on these types of frameworks. We divide these frameworks into the following types based on their working principles: (i) vertex-centric frameworks, (ii) block-centric frameworks, (iii) subgraph-centric frameworks, (iv) matrix-based frameworks, and (v) DBMS (database management system)-based frameworks. We dedicate separate sections to each of these types of frameworks as discussed next.

5.2.1 Vertex-Centric Frameworks

Vertex-centric frameworks enforce the programmers to "think like a vertex" (TLAV).[4] Specifically, programmers define a user-defined function (UDF),[5] which is to be executed on each vertex using only the "local data" available to that vertex, *i.e.,* data about itself and its adjacent vertices/edges. These programs are executed for a certain number of iterations or until a predefined convergence criterion is satisfied. These programs typically communicate with each other via message passing or by accessing a shared memory. Thus, it is possible to execute these functions in parallel, thereby yielding high scalability.

As an example, we illustrate the procedure (Algorithm 1) of Pregel [1], the pioneer vertex-centric graph processing framework. Pregel allows the programmers to define a function to initialize the vertices (*init* function in line 2 of Algorithm 1) as well as a UDF (*compute* function in line 5). It takes three inputs: a graph, maximum number of iterations, and a set of vertices (called the *active vertices*[6]) upon which the UDF will be executed in the first iteration. After initializing the vertices, Pregel iteratively executes the *compute* function on the set of active vertices (lines 4 and 5). While running the *compute* function, an active vertex may send messages to its neighbors. At the end of each superstep, all the vertices which received some message(s) form the new set of active vertices, upon which the *compute* UDF is run in the next iteration. The program terminates when no vertex receives any message in a superstep or when the number of iterations crosses the given threshold (line 3).

Algorithm 1: Pregel (*G, MaxIteration, A*)

Inputs: $G = (V, E)$: the input graph whose set of vertices is V and set of edges is E
      MaxIteration: maximum number of iterations (set it to ∞ if not needed),
      A: initial set of active vertices.

1. **foreach** $v \in V$ **do**
2. $v.init()$
3. **while** *numIteration* $\leq$ *MaxIteration AND* $A \neq \emptyset$ **do**
4.   **foreach** $v \in A$ **do in parallel**
5. $v.compute()$
6. $A \leftarrow$ *set of vertices which received message(s) in this superstep*

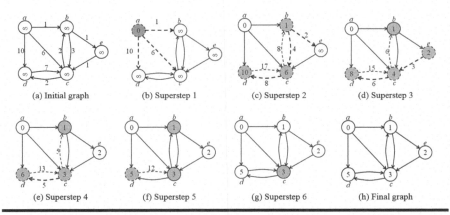

(a) Initial graph   (b) Superstep 1   (c) Superstep 2   (d) Superstep 3

(e) Superstep 4   (f) Superstep 5   (g) Superstep 6   (h) Final graph

Figure 5.1 **Illustration of how shortest paths from vertex *a* to other vertices are computed in Pregel. Active vertices are shown in gray shade, active vertices that send messages are shown as dashed circles, messages from one vertex to another are shown as dashed arcs, and thick dashed arcs represent messages which cause their end vertices to update their current values in the next superstep. The value beside each edge in the initial graph (inset [a]) indicates its weight, whereas the value beside a dashed arc in the other insets [b–f] indicates a message sent by a vertex to its out-neighbors.**

We will now explain how the *compute()* UDF of Pregel can be defined (Algorithm 2) to calculate single-source shortest paths (SSSPs, in short) in a graph (Figure 5.1). Just like Dijkstra's algorithm, we set the initial value of each vertex to ∞. Then a message containing the value zero is sent to the source vertex (vertex *a* in Figure 5.1) so that it becomes an active vertex and as such the *compute* UDF is executed on it in the next (*i.e.*, first) iteration. During the execution of the *compute* UDF, an active vertex checks if the smallest of its received messages is less than its current value (line 1 of Algorithm 2), and if so, it replaces its current value by the smallest received message and then sends a message (containing the sum of its new value and the edge weight) to each of its out-neighbors (lines 2–4 of Algorithm 2). Upon completion of the *compute()* UDF, the active vertex is always automatically deactivated in Pregel unless it receives a new message.

Each superstep of Algorithm 1 calls this function (line 5 of Algorithm 1) on each of the current active vertices, which causes updates of their states (Figure 5.1b–g). This process terminates when there is no active vertex left. The values of the vertices in the final graph give their SSSP distances (Figure 5.1h).

Algorithm 2: compute()   ▷ for computing SSSP

Data: *v.incoimgMessages*: list of incoming messages of vertex *v*
     v.value: current value of vertex *v*
     v.outNeighbors: list of out-neighbors of vertex *v*

1. **if** $v.value <$ min $(v.incoimgMessages)$ **then**
2. $v.value \leftarrow$ min $(v.incoimgMessages)$
3. **foreach** $u \in v.outNeighbors$ **do**
4. $v.send$ $(u, v.value + weight$ $(v,u))$

Connected components (CCs) of an undirected graph can be computed in a similar manner. Different algorithms are available for computing CCs. Here we will discuss how the HashMin algorithm [8] can be implemented in Pregel to compute CCs. At first, all the vertices are made active and each of them has its ID as its initial value (by appropriately defining the *init* function of line 1 of Algorithm 1). The compute function for computing CCs is identical to Algorithm 2 except in line 4, an active vertex broadcasts only its own value to its neighbors. In each superstep, each active vertex sets its value to the smallest of all its incoming messages (lines 1 and 2 of Algorithm 2). Thus, after sufficient number of iterations, the value of each vertex becomes the smallest vertex ID in its CC, which also serves as the ID of that CC. In other words, when the framework stops its execution, each vertex knows which CC it belongs to (Figure 5.2).

Note that this algorithm is quite slow. Its inefficiency stems from the fact that only neighboring vertices are allowed to communicate. Thus, it will take a lot of time to settle the values of vertices in a CC with large diameter (e.g., a long chain). However, unlike some other frameworks (such as *GraphLab* [9]), Pregel allows communication between two vertices as long as the sender vertex knows the ID of the receiver. Faster algorithms have been designed to compute CCs that exploit this facility [8].

5.2.1.1 Classification of Vertex-Centric Frameworks

Vertex-centric frameworks can be classified in different ways based on (i) whether the execution of the UDFs are synchronized or not, (ii) how the vertices

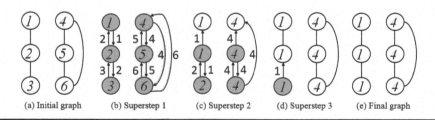

(a) Initial graph   (b) Superstep 1   (c) Superstep 2   (d) Superstep 3   (e) Final graph

Figure 5.2 Computation of CCs of a graph using HashMin algorithm [8]. Active vertices are shown in gray color, messages from one vertex to another are shown as directed edges (arcs), and their associated messages are shown beside those. The value inside each vertex represents its current value (equal to its ID in the initial graph). In insets (b–d), undirected edges are shown between two neighboring vertices only when no communication is happening between them.

communicate with each other, (iii) how the graph is partitioned among worker machines, and (iv) which type of programming model is used in this framework. We will briefly discuss these classifications as well as their relative advantages and disadvantages below. For a more detailed discussion of these classifications, please read the review paper written by Mccune et al. [10].

5.2.1.1.1 Partitioning Graph

Distributed vertex-centric frameworks typically partition the input graph first and then assign those partitions to different worker machines[7] before the actual execution of the framework starts. For example, Pregel uses a hash function to determine the worker machine to which a vertex will be assigned. It also allows the user to replace this default partitioning algorithm by an algorithm of his/ her choice [1]. Different algorithms can be used to partition the graph. Among them, hash-based algorithms and range-based algorithms (which assign a range of vertex IDs to a certain worker) are the simplest to implement and they are the fastest to execute as well. However, a lot of edges may be present between the partitions generated by these algorithms. As a result, the number of messages passed between worker machines (during the actual execution) can potentially be very high, which may hamper the total efficiency of the framework. This issue can be solved by employing more advanced partitioning algorithms that try to minimize the number of edges between partitions. Although rigorous partitioning algorithms (such as METIS [11]) can reduce the communication cost during actual execution, they also incur a huge preprocessing time, especially for big graphs. Another disadvantage of these algorithms is that unlike hashing-based methods (which can be used to quickly compute the ID of the worker machine that will process a query vertex), these algorithms make it difficult for a message-sender (active vertex) to find the location of a message-receiver. Distributed hash tables or some other mechanisms can be used to solve this problem, but those come with additional communication overhead [12].

A lot of research has been going on that attempt to design better partitioning algorithms. These algorithms can be classified into two categories: distributed heuristics and streaming algorithms. The goal of distributed heuristics [13,14] is to detect communities efficiently using distributed label propagation algorithm [15]. Communities are good candidates for graph partitions because communities tend to have few edges between them. Streaming partitioning algorithms, on the other hand, attempt to assign each vertex to a worker at a constant time. For example, LDG [16], a prominent streaming partitioning algorithm, puts a vertex to a partition that contains most of its neighbors. Streaming algorithms are typically implemented on top of the graph loader so that vertices are partitioned while the graph is loaded from the file-system to the main memories.

So far, we have discussed about algorithms for partitioning vertices among workers, which is used as a preprocessing step in most vertex-centric frameworks.

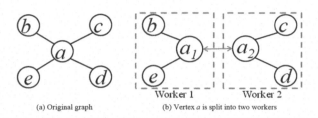

(a) Original graph   (b) Vertex *a* is split into two workers

Figure 5.3 Illustration of vertex-cut partitioning of a graph. Here, vertex *a* is split into two mirror vertices: a_1 and a_2, which are assigned to two different workers. a_1 does not need to know that *c* and *d* are also its neighbors. Similarly, a_2 does not need to know that *b* and *d* are its neighbors. As a result, only a partial adjacency information of vertex *a* can be stored in each worker, which reduces resource requirement of worker machines. The bi-directed edge between a_1 and a_2 indicates the communication between them to achieve synchronization.

However, partitioning vertices may cause the problem of load imbalance due to the skewed degree distribution of real-world networks. Specifically, real graphs often follow power-law degree distribution, *i.e.,* only a few vertices in these graphs have very high degrees (such vertices are called *hubs*), whereas most vertices tend to have moderate or low degrees. Thus, partitioning of vertices may yield some partitions containing the hubs. Processing these partitions typically requires more resources than processing other partitions[8] does; thus, working loads of different workers becomes imbalanced (this is called the *load imbalance* problem) [17].

Vertex-cut algorithms attempt to solve this problem by partitioning edges[9] among the workers. Specifically, the data of a vertex (e.g., its adjacency list/matrix) is split into multiple workers (Figure 5.3). This approach has been found to reduce load imbalance [7] and therefore decrease the communication cost [10]. However, this approach does not come without price. To be able to use vertex-cut partitioning, a framework must adopt some mechanism (via message passing, for example) to synchronize these workers, *i.e.,* whenever the vertex data is changed in a worker, this update must be reflected into its mirrors. Some frameworks that use vertex-cut partitioning[10] are PowerGraph [18], PowerLyra [19], and GraphX [20].

Even if we use a good partitioning algorithm before the actual execution of the framework, load imbalance may still occur after some iterations of the framework because the number of active vertices in a worker may be drastically different from that in another worker. In order to solve this issue, Mizan [12], GPS [21], and some other frameworks migrate active vertices from one worker to another during the execution of the framework. This strategy is called *dynamic repartitioning* [10].

5.2.1.1.2 Communication among UDFs

Two most common methods used by vertex-centric frameworks for inter-process communication are (i) message passing and (ii) shared memory. In message passing systems, one process communicates with another by sending messages to it, whereas in shared memory systems, processes communicate with each other by reading/ writing to a memory shared by all of them (Figure 5.4).

Message passing systems are very common among distributed vertex-centric frameworks. If both the sender and the receiver vertices are processed by the same worker, then the messages are directly delivered to the recipient vertices. However, if sender and receiver vertices are in different machines, then the message is sent to the worker that possesses the recipient. Typically, these messages are sent in batches, *i.e.,* the sender worker stores its messages in an outgoing message buffer until the number of messages in that buffer exceeds a threshold, at which point all the messages are sent to their recipient workers. Sending messages in batches reduces communication overhead [22]. Moreover, it allows a worker to group messages by their destinations[11] and to send each such group-message in one go (instead of sending multiple messages). This technique reduces network traffic and therefore improves the network throughput [23]. Similarly, a buffer is also used in the

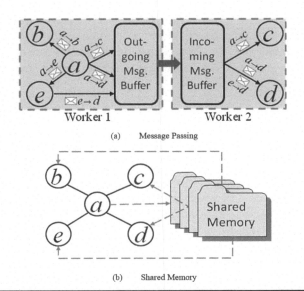

(a) Message Passing

(b) Shared Memory

Figure 5.4 **Two ways of communication among the UDFs running on the vertices of the graph of Figure 5.3(a) are illustrated. (a) In message passing system, a process sends a message to another process, which activates the second process. Here, process *a* is sending messages to processes *b*, *c*, *d*, and *e*. Each arc indicates a message and the big arrow represents a batch message from worker 1 to worker 2. Incoming message buffer of worker 1 and outgoing message buffer of worker 2 are not shown for simplicity. (b) In the shared memory system, a process (here process *a*) writes its state to a shared memory, which are later read by some other processes (here processes *b*, *c*, *d*, and *e*). Here, solid lines represent edges in the graph and dashed gray lines represent read/write operations on shared memory.**

receiver side to store the incoming messages temporarily before they are delivered to the corresponding receivers and are subsequently processed by the UDF running on the recipient vertices.

In a shared memory system, processes do not have to deal with messages because they communicate with each other by accessing a shared memory, as if they are running in a single machine. In reality, the shared memory is distributed across different machines. Since the data of the same vertex are either split (in case of vertex-cut partitioning used by PowerGraph, for example.) or copied (in case of ordinary partitioning used by GraphLab, for example.) among different workers, ensuring data consistency among them is a big challenge for shared memory systems. For this purpose, GraphLab uses pipelined distributed locking [24], whereas PowerGraph uses parallel Chandy-Misra locking [25]. Both these approaches ensure consistency via inter-machine communication.

Another challenge for shared memory frameworks is to handle *race conditions* that may arise when the same memory location is accessed by multiple processes. In such a case, memory consistency is typically ensured via mutual exclusions, *i.e.,* by ordering the memory accesses of processes in such a way that no two processes work on the same memory location at the same time. In other words, shared memory systems ensure that the schedule of memory accesses by the processors has an equivalent sequential schedule. Such a schedule is called a *serializable schedule* [10].

5.2.1.1.3 Execution of UDFs

Pregel and many other vertex-centric frameworks mimic bulk synchronous parallel (BSP) [26] execution model, which synchronizes the execution of concurrently running programs. For example, in each superstep of Pregel, the UDF is executed on all the active vertices. After its execution is finished in all the active vertices, they are allowed to send messages to each other. When all the messages are passed and no vertex remains active (this is ensured by a layer called *synchronization barrier*), the next superstep begins. Thus, in each superstep, each vertex knows the current values of its in-neighbors. This kind of execution is called *synchronous execution* [10]. To our knowledge, most vertex-centric frameworks follow this execution model.

While synchronous frameworks are conceptually simple, they may cause significant wastage of resources because no vertex can start the next round of execution until all the processes finish. However, it is unlikely that all processes will take similar amounts of time unless the workload is evenly distributed, which is very difficult to ensure. Some frameworks tried to solve this issue by providing the option to execute asynchronously. Specifically, in *asynchronous execution*, one vertex does not wait for another vertex to finish its execution. Vertex execution order is determined by a scheduler, which dynamically maintains vertex schedule. Once the execution of a UDF is finished on a vertex, computing resources become free and the next vertex in the schedule starts executing its UDF immediately [10].

By getting rid of the synchronization barrier, asynchronous systems avoid the bottleneck encountered by the synchronous models. As a result, asynchronous platforms often converge faster than their synchronous counterparts when loads are imbalanced. For example, Lu et al. [27] found that in case of large diameter graphs, HashMin algorithm runs faster in the asynchronous mode than in the synchronous execution mode of GraphLab [9]. However, synchronous mode outperforms its asynchronous counterpart when a small diameter graph is used. Because, in that case, the communication overhead of asynchronous mode undercuts the efficiency achieved from faster convergence. Besides, it is harder to design asynchronous systems because of the added complexity for designing the scheduler and for ensuring data consistency [10]. Also, due to the unrestricted nature of the schedule, such frameworks do not ensure that execution of certain algorithms (e.g., PageRank) will always give us the same result—which is clearly undesirable in many applications [7].

Hybrid systems combine the best of both synchronous and asynchronous systems. These systems intelligently switch between synchronous and asynchronous modes in an attempt to ensure little idle time, low latency,[12] and high efficiency. A mode-switcher module is used which decides when to switch modes. Typically, this module is initially trained on multiple instances to make decisions about later instances or it takes decision based on the execution profiles of the UDFs [28].

Table 5.1 shows the classification of some notable big graph frameworks based on their execution modes and methods of communication.

5.2.1.1.4 Programming Model

Different frameworks adopt different programming models depending on their mode of execution, communication, and/or other design choices. For example,

Table 5.1 Classification of Vertex-Centric Frameworks Based on How the UDFs Communicate with Each Other and Whether Their Executions Are Synchronized or Not

Execution Communication	Synchronous	Asynchronous	Hybrid
Message Passing	Pregel [1], GPS [21], Pregel+ [17], Giraph [29], Mizan [12]	Maiter [30], GiraphUC [31], MOCgraph* [32], GiraphAsync [33]	PowerSwitch [28], GraphHP [34], Hieroglyph [35]
Shared Memory	GiraphX [36]	GraphLab* [9], PowerGraph* [18], PowerLyra* [19]	–

The frameworks marked by asterisks (*) support both synchronous and asynchronous modes of execution.

Table 5.2 Classification of Vertex-Centric Frameworks Based on Their Programming Models

Programming Model	Frameworks Using This Model
Single phase	Pregel, Giraph, Pregel+, GPS, MOCgraph, Mizan
Scatter–gather	X-Stream
GAS	PowerGraph, PowerLyra, PowerSwitch

Pregel adopts a single phase model, *i.e.*, in each iteration, only one UDF, namely, the *compute()* function, is executed on active vertices. Giraph, MOCgraph, Mizan, and so on (see Table 5.2) also adopt similar strategies.

X-Stream adopts a programming model consisting of two phases: (i) *scatter*: in this phase, an active vertex broadcasts its values to some other vertices (typically, its neighbors) and (ii) *gather*: in this phase, an active vertex collects data from the adjacent vertices and then uses them to update its own value. Such a model is typically used by frameworks which read/write edge values [37].

PowerGraph, PowerLyra, and PowerSwitch use a programming model consisting of three phases: (i) *gather*, (ii) *apply*, and (iii) *scatter*. The meanings of gather and scatter phases remain the same as that of X-Stream; the apply phase combines the data gathered in the previous phase. Such a programming model is called gather–apply–scatter or *GAS model*, in short. Briefly, in each iteration of such a model, an active vertex *gathers* data from its neighboring vertices and/or edges, aggregates those data to update its own value (*apply* phase), and then *scatters* this updated value across its neighbors [18].

5.2.2 Block-Centric Frameworks

Vertex-centric frameworks like Pregel try to achieve extreme parallelism, even among the processes running on the vertices within the same worker. This goal comes at the cost of high communication overhead. To solve this problem some systems adopt sequential execution of the vertices within the same worker while keeping execution of worker processes parallel. Following Yan et al. [7], we will call them block-centric frameworks. In this section, we will discuss two such frameworks: BLOGEL [38] and Giraph++ [39].

5.2.2.1 BLOGEL

BLOGEL considers the problem of skewed degree distribution where a few nodes have very high degrees and most others have low/moderate degrees. BLOGEL supports three types of tasks: (i) computation on vertices, (ii) partitioning graph, and (iii) computation on blocks. In the first two tasks, the message receiver (called the worker vertex), $\in \Gamma v$,[13] is identified by hashing $id(u)$ when a vertex v sends message to its neighbor. On the other hand, in block-centric tasks, the vertices are divided into blocks by a partitioning algorithm at first. These blocks are then executed by the B-workers (in block-centric computation, a worker is called a B-worker). The block of a vertex v is denoted by $block(v)$ and the worker of a block B is denoted by $worker(B)$. An ID is then assigned to a vertex v represented as a triplet: $trip(v) = \{id(v), block(v), worker(v)\}$. A B-worker will be able to get the worker and the block of vertex v using its ID. A block B can reach any of its vertices. Also, a block can send message to any other block B while $worker(B)$ is available. Similarly, it can send message to any vertex v if $worker(v)$ is available. Each B-worker has two message buffers: one is to receive/send messages to/from vertices and the other is for block level messaging. A combiner is used to combine these two which is associated with each buffer.

BLOGEL provides numerous predefined partitioning algorithms. It also supports user-defined partitioners. While partitioning, each vertex v is assigned to a block, denoted by $block(v)$. After partitioning, each block B is assigned to a worker, denoted by $worker(B)$, in such a way that load imbalance is minimized. The steps followed for assigning workers to blocks are given below:

Step 1: At first, each partitioner divides the group of vertices into blocks and sends the master the number of vertices of each block. The master collects these numbers from the partitioners and uses these to compute an aggregated number of vertices in blocks.

Step 2: Using a greedy algorithm, the master then computes the workload and broadcasts the block-to-worker assignment to each block.

Step 3: According to the received assignment, each partitioner selects its worker from its vertices and transmits this to all workers.

BLOGEL can be applied to solve different graph problems, such as for computing PageRank of vertices. It has been found that PageRank runs faster (especially on web-graphs[14]) in BLOGEL than in Pregel because the former benefits from initializing PageRank values using the information of its blocks. In Blogel, calculation of PageRank value is done in two steps. The first step is done in the block mode and, in this step, each block B calculates the local PageRank of each vertex in B from the single-machine PageRank algorithm. Then the BlockRank is computed by combining all the PageRank results using vertex-centric PageRank algorithm, and therefore, a weight is assigned to all outgoing edges. Then the BlockRank is dispersed to outgoing neighbors in proportion to the assigned edge weights. Finally, in the second step, the standard PageRank algorithm is applied for the total graph using the current BlockRank.

5.2.2.2 GIRAPH++

GIRAPH++ is a distributed graph processing platform, which exposes the partition structure to the programmers so that they can exploit it via asynchronous communication within the partition. It has been found that this technique makes it more flexible and more efficient than the corresponding vertex-centric frameworks because it has less communication overhead.

In this model, the graph is divided into multiple subgraphs. The vertices within each subgraph are called *internal vertices*. The neighbors of internal vertices outside the subgraph are called *boundary vertices*. Thus, internal vertices can be in only one subgraph, but boundary vertices can be in more than one subgraph. A partition has access to all the information of its internal vertices, but it knows only the vertex numbers of its boundary vertices. In GIRAPH++ boundary, vertices can only send messages to the primary copies of the internal vertices since communication among the internal vertices are cheap and spontaneous. State changes of boundary vertices have to wait for the next superstep, while internal vertices can change their states at any point of time. The internal vertices can be active or inactive, whereas boundary vertices do not have such states.

Algorithm 3 shows how PageRank can be implemented in GIRAPH++. Here each vertex has two components/fields: (i) its current PageRank score (*v.pr* in Algorithm 3) and (ii) the iterative updates of its PageRank score computed from other vertices within its partition, which is called its delta value (*v.delta* in Algorithm 3). Initially, these fields are initialized (lines 1–4 of Algorithm 3) with zeros (except that the delta values of active internal vertices are initialized with *(1-d)*, where *d* is the damping factor). Then these two fields of all active internal vertices are iteratively updated and all their neighbors' delta values are updated accordingly (lines 5–10). Finally, delta values of all the boundary vertices are reset (lines 11 and 12).

Algorithm 3: PageRank _GIRAPH++(*G, MaxIteration, A, d*)

Inputs: $G = (V,E)$: the input graph whose set of vertices is V and set of edges is E
      MaxIteration: maximum number of iterations (set it to ∞ if not needed)
      A: set of active internal vertices
      B: set of boundary vertices
      d: damping factor (typically, 0.85)
Data: *v.pr*: page rank value of vertex *v*
      v.delta: current delta value of vertex *v*
      v.incomingMessages: list of incoming messages of vertex *v*
      v.numOutGoingEdges: number of outgoing edges incident upon *v*
      v.neighbors: list of neighbors of *v*

1. **if** *superstep > MaxIteration* **then** exit
2. **if** *superstep* = 0 **then**
3.   **foreach** *v* in *V* **do** *v.pr = 0, v.delta = 0*

4.   **foreach** $v \in A$ **do** $v.delta = v.delta + (1-d)$
5. **foreach** $v \in A$ **do**
6. $v.delta{+}{=} \displaystyle\sum v.incomingMessages$
7.   **if** $v.delta > 0$ **then**
8. $v.pr{+} = v.delta$
9. $u = d{*}v.delta/v.numOutGoingEdges$
10.   **foreach** $w \in v.neighbors$ **do** $w.delta{+} = u$
11. **foreach** $v \in B$ **do**
12.   **if** $v.delta > 0$ **then** send $v.delta$ to v and set $v.delta$ to zero

---

5.2.3 Subgraph-Centric Frameworks

Although many graph problems can be solved by "thinking like a vertex," many problems cannot be solved via a TLAV framework. For example, computing local clustering coefficient of a vertex requires the information of the whole subgraph induced by that vertex as well as by its neighbors. To solve such problems, some frameworks (such as NScale [40] and Arabesque [41]) propose to "think like a subgraph", *i.e.,* they ask the programmers to write UDFs on subgraphs, instead of vertices. We will discuss one such framework here, namely, NScale.

5.2.3.1 NScale

NScale [40] is a Hadoop-based big graph framework, which allows distributed processing of subgraphs in the cloud. It provides three special features: (i) subgraph-centric computation on a graph, (ii) computation on selected subgraphs, and (iii) space-efficient packing of subgraphs into memory.

In this framework, the programmer needs to specify (i) the subgraphs in which the user is interested and (ii) an UDF that will be executed on these subgraphs. The UDF is written using a graph API called BluePrints. The NScale execution engine ensures that the UDF has access to only its corresponding subgraph. It also allows the users to select a subgraph formed by the k-hop neighborhood of a vertex filtered by some given properties of the nodes and edges. Thus, the user can choose any desired subgraph with special attributes (e.g., subgraphs formed by vertices annotated with certain hashtags). Then the selected subgraph will entirely reside in a single machine to be processed.

NScale has two major components:

1. **GEP (graph extraction and packing module)**: It extracts the relevant subgraphs, decides the optimum number of machines that will process these subgraphs and distributes the workload in a balanced fashion.
2. **Distributed execution engine**: It executes the UDFs on subgraphs of interest.

In the GEP module, Map Reduce jobs are executed depending on the size of the graph and sizes of the machines. This module follows the following steps.

First step: In this map step, the GEP module reads the graph and finds out the query vertices. It also filters the vertices and edges that do not match with the purpose/interest of the user and evaluates the space necessary according to the graph structure and weights. There are a few cases to consider here.

> *Case 1*: If a single machine can contain the filtered graph, then all the vertices, their weights, and their incident edges are sent to the reducer that constructs the subgraph and applies the packing algorithm to map each vertex to a partition.
>
> *Case 2*: If a single machine cannot contain the filtered graph, then a distributed process completes both subgraph extraction and packing. The steps of this process depend on the radius of the subgraph of interest.

Second step: It is the packing stage where the extracted subgraphs are packed into minimum possible number of partitions. A standard bin packing algorithm is used to find the minimum number of partitions.

The distributed engine provides different execution modes: (i) the vector bitmap mode allows parallel execution on subgraph-centric UDFs, (ii) the batch bitmap mode decreases memory consumption but increases execution time, and (iii) the single-bit bitmap mode decreases space requirement, but it allows only serial execution of UDFs.

NScale, like many other distributed graph frameworks, uses the bulk synchronous protocol (BSP) to support iterative processes. However, unlike the original BSP model, messages within a subgraph are transferred using shared memory, which reduces communication overhead. Only messages between subgraphs are transmitted via a barrier synchronization step to confirm the completion of message exchange among the subgraphs.

5.2.4 Matrix-Based Frameworks

Some frameworks such as Hama [42], PEGUSUS [43], GBASE [44], and System ML [45] represent the graph as a matrix (e.g., the adjacency matrix) and translate different graph computations into matrix operations. Some of these frameworks require the programmers to think of graphs as matrices, while others still rely upon traditional programming models, thereby hiding the underlying matrix calculations. We call both these types of frameworks matrix-based frameworks. In this section, we will discuss one such framework, namely, PEGUSUS, to give the reader an idea about such frameworks.

5.2.4.1 PEGUSUS

PEGUSUS is a peta-scale graph framework that can be used to quickly process a big static graph. It is implemented on the Hadoop platform. The main primitive of PEGUSUS is GIM-V (generalized iterative matrix-vector multiplication), which provides a way to process computations on a graph via efficient matrix vector multiplications.

Suppose M is an $n \times n$ adjacency matrix of a graph and v is a vector of size is n.

So, their product is $v' = M \times v = \sum_{j=1}^{n} m_{i,j} v_j$ where $m_{i,j}$ is the (i, j) th element in the

M matrix. Then v' can be computed using the following UDFs:

a. *combine2()*: computes $x_i = m_{i,j} \times v_j$
b. *combineAll()*: computes the sum of the results obtained from Combine2 $(x_1, x_2, \ldots x_n)$. Let this sum be v_{new}.
c. *assign():* decides the next value of v_i based on the current value of v_i and the value of v_{new}

These steps can be customized to implement different convenient algorithms, such as PageRank, Random Walk with Restart, CCs, and diameter approximation. For example, PageRank algorithm can be implemented using GIM-V in the following way.

The eigenvector equation of PageRank algorithm is $p = (dE^T + (1 - d)U)p$. Here, p is the PageRank vector of size n, where n is the number of vertices, d is the damping factor (typically, has a value around 0.85), E is the row-normalized adjacency matrix, and U is a matrix each of whose elements is equal to $1/n$. The current PageRank vector is denoted by p^{curr}, and the next PageRank vector is denoted by p^{next}. So, the eigenvector equation becomes $p^{next} = (dE^T + (1 - d)U)p^{curr}$. The GIM-V calculation can be directly applied to PageRank. First, a column-normalized matrix M is constructed by taking the transpose of E, and then the following operations are executed to compute PageRank scores.

Combine$(m_{i,j}, v_j)$: return $c \times m_{i,j} \times v_j$

CombineAll$(x_1, x_2, \ldots x_n)$: return $\dfrac{(1-d)}{n} + \sum_{j=1}^{n} x_j$

Assign(v_i, v_{new}): $v_i = v_{new}$

One iteration of GIM-V takes $O(V + E)$ space and $O\left(\dfrac{V+E}{M} \log \dfrac{V+E}{M}\right)$ time. The main contribution of PEGUSUS is to provide a highly scalable and efficient tool to process large scale graphs, such as "Yahoo" and other web graphs. Moreover, the authors of PEGUSUS applied different optimization techniques and found that the best combination of these optimizers makes it five times faster than its non-optimized version. Among these optimization techniques are performing GIM-V on sub-matrices/blocks instead of individual elements, clustering edges, and reducing number of iterations via multiplication of diagonal sub-matrices with their corresponding vectors.

5.2.5 DBMS-Based Frameworks

Several frameworks, such as Pregelix [46], DG-SPARQL [47], and GraphX [20], depend on DBMSs and their operations to store and analyze big graphs. These frameworks attempt to bring the fruits of long research on the storage and query optimization techniques in the area of DBMSs to the area of big graph analysis. Typically, these types of frameworks use some kind of database as their back end engines. For example, Pregelix uses traditional relational database, whereas DG-SPARQL uses graph database in the back end. In the next two subsections, we will discuss about these two frameworks.

5.2.5.1 Pregelix

Pregelix [46] is a big graph analytics system that uses an iterative dataflow approach. It transformed the Pregel programming model into a set of database operations. To reconstruct the execution of Pregel states, Pregelix uses a set of nested relations shown in Table 5.3.

Here, each instance of *Vertex* relation is read as an input and constitutes a row of this relation. Each vertex has three attributes: vertexID, halt, value, and neighbors. The value and neighbors are user defined that represent its current state and list of neighbors. Vertices whose *halt* value is *False* are considered to be active. The *Msg* relation represents the messages sent to an instance of *Vertex* whose ID is destinationID and whose received message is denoted by payload. GS relation holds the global state of execution of an UDF. The aggregate attribute of this relation represents an aggregated value over all iterations and the superstep denotes the current iteration count. If *halt* = *True* in this relation, then the program terminates.

Pregelix has been implemented on top of Hyracks platform, a data-parallel engine capable of processing big data. Pregelix first loads the graph (*i.e.*, the *Vertex* relation) from a distributed file system to Hyracks, partitions it using the vertexIDs, and then dispatches these partitions to Hyracks for processing them in parallel. The partitioning can be done by a user defined partitioning function. After finishing the full process (determined by the attributes of the *GS* relation), the partitioned vertex relation is scanned and dumped back to the file system. During execution, the message-passing behavior of Pregel is achieved via joining *Vertex* and *Msg* relations. On the other hand, different UDFs of Pregel are written by

Table 5.3 Nested Relational Schema of Pregel State

Relation	Schema
Vertex	(vertexID, halt, value, neighbors)
Msg	(destinationID, payload)
GS	(halt, aggregate, superstep)

the programmers as database queries, which may in turn affect the relations of Table 5.3. For example, the *compute* UDF may affect the relations in the following way in a superstep: it may change some attributes of its corresponding Vertex tuple, it may add/update the list of outgoing messages in *Msg* relation, it may change the attributes of *GS* relation, or it may mutate the graph (via adding/deleting tuples from *Vertex* relation).

5.2.5.2 DG-SPARQL

DG-SPARQL [47] is a distributed graph database management system. Graph databases store the graph data as entities (vertex) and relationships (edges). Each vertex in a graph database stores a list of relationship records that signify its relationships to other vertices. These relationship records are organized by type and direction and may hold additional attributes. Whenever a *JOIN* operation is executed, the database just uses this list and directly accesses its neighbors, which eliminates the need for an expensive search or match computation that are done in traditional relational databases. As a result, graph databases often outperform relational databases in terms of efficiency. Graph databases also allow the user to perform different graph queries including subgraph matching queries, path algebras, regular path queries, and reachability queries. Queries in a graph database are written using a graph query language, such as OpenCypher, SPARQL, GRAPQL, or Gremlin.[15] For example, DG-SPARQL uses a version of SPARQL as a query language.

DG-SPARQL is a distributed implementation of G-SPARQL [48], which is a centralized graph DBMS. Following G-SPARQL, DG-SPARQL provides a hybrid storage system in which the structure of a big attributed graph resides in the distributed memory and the graph data resides in a relational database whose replicas are contained in each node. This hybrid approach allows DG-SPARQL to execute part of the query using fast in-memory graph traversal algorithms. The rest of the query is executed in RDBMS via SQL as usual. It also optimizes the query processing by (i) using a divide and conquer algorithm that splits the query plan into some manageable chunks and (ii) cleverly selecting the appropriate number of database nodes based on a cost model. It allows the user to search the graph based on both the structural properties and the attributes of the vertices/edges of the graph. Specifically, the following types of structural queries can be processed in DG-SPARQL: (i) *reachability query*: check if any path exists between two vertices, (ii) *shortest path query*: find the shortest path between two vertices, and (iii) *pattern matching queries*: search for the incidences of subgraphs based on patterns in a big graph.

Figure 5.5 shows an attributed graph representing a student database which contains information (age) about some students, courses, degrees, departments, and the interrelations among them. Figure 5.6 shows a sample query on this graph database, which searches for all pairs of students (A, B) such that A's age is at least 22 years and A is senior to B. In this code, line 3 represents the requirement that A must be senior to B, lines 4 and 5 represent the filtering condition that the age

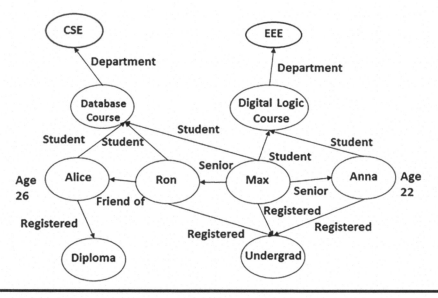

Figure 5.5   A sample attributed graph of student database.

```
1   SELECT ?Name1 ?Name2
2   WHERE {?A @label ?Name1.      ?B @label
    ?Name2.
3   ?A Senior ?B.
4   ?A @age  ? age.
5   FILTER(?age >=22).
6   FilterPath (Length (??E2, <=5)) .}
```

Figure 5.6   A sample DG-SPARQL query on the graph database shown in Figure 5.5.

of A must be at least 22, and line 6 is used to filter out any possible paths between vertices within a five-hop distance.

5.3 Single-Machine Frameworks for Analyzing Big Static Graphs

Although distributed systems are natural choices to process big graphs, a number of single-machine systems have been proposed in the literature that can efficiently handle big graphs. These systems are usually built on a powerful machine with enough memory as well as high computational and storage capacity. These frameworks do not incur any network communication overhead, which gives them an extra advantage over their distributed counterparts. Among these frameworks, Ligra [49], GraphChi [50], X-Stream [37], FlashGraph [51], GraphMat [52], and GRACE [53] are some of the well-known ones. Ligra uses a fast implementation of BFS [54] to encode traversal-based graph algorithms. Both GraphChi and X-Stream use edge-centric GAS programming model and provide out-of-core execution of graph algorithms by loading a graph into the memory, one partition at a time. FlashGraph keeps vertex data in the memory and edge data in SSDs. In order to decrease I/O cost, it only accesses those edge data that are required by the algorithm and are not already available in the cache. Grace is an asynchronous block-centric graph framework that can process graphs efficiently when they fit into the main memory.

In this section, we will discuss about one single-machine framework, namely, GraphMat, in greater details. GraphMat [52] is a single-machine multicore static graph framework that achieves good multicore scalability with 1.1–1.7 times speed up as compared to other notable distributed frameworks. It is implemented based on a generalized sparse matrix vector multiplication (SPMV) scheme that is similar to the GIM-V technique of PEGUSUS. However, GraphMat has two distinctions/advantages over PEGUSUS: (i) unlike PEGUSUS, it does not suffer from network communication overhead, and (ii) it does not expose the matrix calculations to the user/programmer; rather its front end is based on the popular GAS programming model of vertex-centric frameworks—which makes it easy for the programmers to make a transition from vertex-centric frameworks to GraphMat.

In the back end, GraphMat uses SPMV that exploits the optimization techniques developed over the last few decades for manipulating sparse matrices in order to do efficient computations on matrix representations of graphs. Thus, GraphMat combines the best features of "both worlds": expressiveness of vertex-centric GAS model and efficiency of optimized algorithms for sparse matrix computation.

Specifically, GraphMat is built on the idea that many vertex-centric iterative processes can be transformed into some matrix vector operations. For example, for an unweighted graph, multiplying the transpose of its adjacency matrix with a vector of all ones yields a vector of vertex in-degrees (Figure 5.7). Similarly, vertex out-degrees can be obtained by multiplying the adjacency matrix with an all one vector.

GraphMat programming model has four functions that the programmer/user needs to define: *send_message()*, *process_message()*, *reduce()*, and *apply()*. The first and last UDFs are analogous to the *scatter()* and *apply()* UDFs of the GAS model, respectively. On the other hand, the second and third UDFs together mimic the *gather()* UDF of GAS model. From the programmer's point of view (front end), these UDFs work in the following way. At first, each vertex is initialized and some of them are activated. The *send_message()* function is called on each active vertex, which produces a message based on the value of that vertex. The *process_message()* function reads the incoming messages along with the information of the edge through which it came and then processes them to compute a processed message. The *reduce()* function combines all the processed messages received by a vertex to

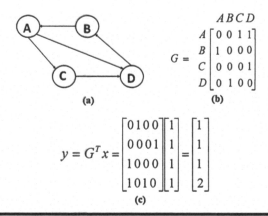

Figure 5.7 (a) A graph, (b) its adjacency matrix, and (c) in-degree calculation via SPMV.

compute a single value. The *apply()* function uses this value to decide whether/how the vertex data should be updated.

However, in the back end, these functions use SPMV to achieve the goal. Specifically, *send_message()* UDF creates a sparse vector representing the active vertices. The tasks of *process_message()* and *reduce()* UDFs are accomplished via an operation (typically, multiplication) on this vector and the adjacency matrix of the input graph. Finally, *apply()* does the same thing as the *apply()* UDF of GAS model.

5.4 Distributed Frameworks for Analyzing Big Dynamic Graphs

Unlike static graphs, dynamic graphs change their topologies over time. In other words, they have different topologies at different time points.[16] Each of these time point-specific topologies is a static graph itself which is called a *snapshot*. Thus, dynamic graphs can be considered as a sequence of snapshots [55].

There are two types of dynamic graphs: (i) *temporal/historical/time-varying graphs*, whose entire history (*i.e.*, sequence of topologies at all time points) of topological changes is already known to the user when s/he analyzes them, and (ii) *streaming graphs*, which are continuously being updated as we analyze them [7]. Both types of graphs raise some interesting questions, which are somewhat different from the questions asked about static graphs, e.g., how rumors/diseases spread in dynamic networks [56], which edges/links are important for disease/rumor propagation [57], how to compute "time-respecting" shortest paths [56] or node-disjoint paths [58] in dynamic networks, how to detect evolving communities [59], how PageRank scores (or some centrality measures) of vertices change with time, how to classify vertices of dynamic networks [60], etc.

In general, two types of analyses can be done on dynamic graphs: (i) *point-in-time analysis*—which analyzes a specific snapshot to answer some questions about it (e.g., what are the highest degree vertices in the Facebook friendship graph on Dec 30, 2017?) and (ii) *time-range analysis*—which analyzes graphs in a time range to answer some questions related to their dynamic nature (e.g., which non-hubs became hubs[17] in Facebook friendship graph between Jan 1, 2010, and Jan 1, 2017?). While traditional big static graph frameworks can still be used for point-in-time analysis, time-range analysis requires special purpose frameworks.

Note that although both temporal and streaming graphs raise similar research questions, answering them often requires one to apply distinct techniques. In general, graph frameworks should be designed specifically to store and analyze any of these types of dynamic graphs. In the next two subsections we will discuss some notable frameworks that can handle each of these types of dynamic graphs.

5.4.1 Frameworks for Analyzing Temporal Graphs

Till now a few frameworks have been proposed in literature that can process big temporal graphs. We will discuss two of them in this section: DeltaGraph [55] and Chronos [61]. These frameworks focus on solving different problems related to temporal graphs as discussed below.

5.4.1.1 DeltaGraph

DeltaGraph is a distributed graph database system designed to support *snapshot queries* in a big dynamic graph. Specifically, it supports two types of queries: (i) *single-point snapshot query*—which is used to search for the snapshot/graph of a given time point (e.g., "retrieve the subgraph induced by the vertices *a*, *b*, and *c* on Jan 2, 2018") and (ii) *multipoint snapshot query*—which is used to search for all the snapshots between a range of time points (e.g. "retrieve all the subgraphs induced by the vertices *a*, *b*, and *c* between Jan 2, 2018 and Jun 13, 2018"). To process queries in an efficient manner, it maintains an in-memory index in the form of a rooted directed acyclic graph (DAG). The root of this DAG is an empty graph, the lowest level vertices of this DAG represent[18] snapshots, and internal nodes typically represent the intersection graph[19] of its children. An edge between a parent and a child in this DAG is associated with the information about the difference (called *delta*) between the graphs represented by the parent and child. Thus, the graph corresponding to a node of this DAG can be formed by applying the deltas across all the edges from the root to that node. A weight is assigned to each such edge (parent–child relation) which captures the cost of reading its associated delta and applying that on the parent graph to form the child graph. Thus, single point snapshot queries can be efficiently answered by computing the shortest path from the root of this DAG to one of its leaves, which correspond to the given time point. Similarly, multipoint snapshot queries can be answered by first finding the leaves that fall under the given time range and then computing a Steiner tree that connects those leaves to the root.

5.4.1.2 Chronos

Chronos has been designed to efficiently store and analyze big dynamic graphs. It partitions the vertices of the input dynamic graph and then assigns each of these partitions along with the entire history of vertex-states in that partition to a worker machine. Han et al. [61] noticed that partitioning vertices in this fashion yields much better performance than partitioning snapshots. Partitioning this way allows Chronos to execute UDFs on each vertex across all the snapshots in a batch. This strategy also allows Chronos to do *incremental computations* (doing a computation on a snapshot utilizing the results of that computation done on a previous snapshot;e.g., computing the SSSP distances in the first snapshot, using these results to update SSSP distances in the second snapshot, then using these results to update SSSP distances in the second snapshot, and so on) efficiently. Chronos also allows one to store and use deltas of consecutive snapshots to achieve greater efficiency in incremental computation. It can be implemented both in a single powerful machine and in a distributed system.

5.4.2 Frameworks for Analyzing Streaming Graphs

Although analysis of temporal graphs gives valuable insights, we are often interested in analyzing the most recent graph in real time. For example, Facebook may want to recommend friends and ads to users based on the up-to-date friendship and/or follower–followee network. Streaming graph frameworks are the best choice for such applications. So far, a number of frameworks have been specifically designed to store, update, and/or analyze streaming graphs. Some frameworks of this class are GraphTau [62], Kineograph [63], GraphInc [64], TIDE [65], DISTINGER [66], and BLADYG [67]. GraphTau is a framework built on Apache Spark that achieves efficient and fault tolerant processing of streaming graphs via several optimization techniques. Kineograph implements two layers: the storage layer is responsible for storing and updating graphs in real time and the computation layer is responsible for processing the recently generated graph (by the storage layer) efficiently. GraphInc is a Pregel-based framework designed to handle real-time incremental analysis of streaming graphs. TIDE computes the probability of an edge to be present in the current graph using a user-defined function and uses that to generate the most recent graph from one or more previous snapshots. DISTINGER is a distributed implementation of STINGER [68], a single-machine framework discussed in the next section. BLADYG is a block-centric framework adapted to handle streaming graphs in a distributed setting.

5.5 Single-Machine Frameworks for Analyzing Big Dynamic Graphs

Although distributed systems are obvious choices for developing frameworks for big dynamic graphs, a few single-machine frameworks have shown their capabilities of storing and/or processing such graphs in powerful machines. Here we will discuss three such frameworks: LLAMA, SLOTH [69], and STINGER [68] as representatives of this class of frameworks.

5.5.1 LLAMA and SLOTH

LLAMA is a single-machine framework designed to efficiently perform whole graph analysis on systems that receive incremental graph updates in a steady rate. LLAMA allows both in-memory and out-of-core execution of graph algorithms. Since most graph algorithms do not change the graph itself, many frameworks use a compact immutable/read-only data structure (called *compressed sparse row* or CSR, in short) to represent graphs. While CSR is highly space efficient, it is neither suitable for static graphs (due to its immutability) nor does it provide a way to store graphs in a persistent storage. Mutable data structures allow a framework to handle dynamic graphs. On the other hand, storing snapshots in a persistent storage allows a platform to perform out-of-core execution as well as enables the user to process the same snapshot multiple times. The author of LLAMA attempted to achieve these two goals in order to store and process large dynamic graphs efficiently. To achieve persistency, the author designed an on-disk graph representation that closely mimics the CSR format. He achieved mutability by adding multi-versioned array support to CSR. Specifically, LLAMA uses a large multi-versioned array (LAMA) data structure (called the vertex table) to store vertex information. For versioning of this array, LLAMA uses a software copy-on-write technique. It also uses an array of edge records (called an edge table) to store the information of the edges added/deleted in each snapshot. Vertex table contains pointers to the edge table which are used to determine the adjacency list of each vertex. LLAMA was able to decrease the reading cost by using this augmented CSR representation while allowing the programmer to process dynamic graphs. It also decreases the writing cost by using a buffer that temporally stores newly added/deleted edges before updating the snapshot in the storage. The author of LLAMA also built SLOTH—a sliding-window framework based on LLAMA, which reduces space requirement by storing only the most recent k snapshots (k is the window size) and deleting the older ones.

5.5.2 STINGER

STINGER (Spatio-Temporal Interaction Networks and Graphs Extensible Representation) is a single-machine framework that supports storing and analyzing streaming graph updates that may come in a nonsteady rate and as such may not have temporal resolution. STINGER maintains a single in-memory representation of the most recent snapshot. For this purpose, it uses a modified version of the CSR data structure to store graphs. This data structure combines the ideas of both CSR and adjacency list. Specifically, it stores the record of the neighbors of each vertex as a list of arrays. When a neighbor gets deleted, a negative value is placed in its cell—which creates a "hole" in that place. When a new neighbor is added, its record is placed in a hole; if no hole is present, a new array is created to place it and the new array is linked with the existing arrays of neighbors. Thus, STINGER is able to update the graph (edge insertions/deletions) efficiently. To achieve high parallelism, STINGER runs graph-reader processes (called by the graph algorithm running in this framework) along with graph-updater processes in parallel. The authors of STINGER reasoned that in a big graph, the probability of conflict between graph readers and graph updaters will be very low. However, this may cause inconsistencies since different passes of a reader process may read different information. STINGER tolerates such inconsistencies because it assumes that the current graph is already an approximate representation of the concerned real-world network, in which case, these inconsistencies will not affect the result significantly.

5.6 Conclusions

In this chapter, we have explored different categories of frameworks that are capable of analyzing big graphs, discussed their features, and highlighted their advantages/disadvantages. We also briefly discussed about some notable frameworks. We hope that this discussion will help the reader to get an idea about the evolution of research in this area. Specifically, the very first framework for processing big static graphs was Pregel. It is a vertex-centric distributed framework, which is conceptually easy to design and understand. However, it may suffer from high idle time due to its strict adherence to the BSP model even at the vertex level. To solve this issue, block-centric frameworks were proposed. However, both these types of frameworks force the programmer to write operations from a vertex-centric point of view, which makes it difficult to encode graph algorithms that require the programmer to think like a subgraph (e.g., algorithms for computing dense clusters). Subgraph-centric, matrix-based, and DBMS-based frameworks offer different solutions to this problem. While many of these frameworks are designed as distributed systems, rapid decrease in costs of high-configuration workstations encouraged many researchers to develop single-machine frameworks of similar/superior capabilities. Also, currently the focus of this line of research is shifting more and more towards processing dynamic graphs since they better represent real-world networks than their static counterparts.

Notes

1 Because big graph is really a type of big data.
2 We could not find any standard lower bound of graph size that has been used to define big graphs. However, most papers on big graphs discuss about graphs with at least millions, and most often, billions of vertices/edges.
3 We have found in the literature that whenever a graph has high volume it is considered to be a big graph, even if it does not have a high volume/velocity.
4 Vertex-centric frameworks are also known as *vertex-oriented* or *TLAV* frameworks.
5 In TLAV frameworks, this function is also called a *vertex program kernel* or simply, a *vertex program*.
6 A vertex upon which the UDF is run is called an *active vertex*.
7 To keep our discussion simple, previously (in Section 5.2.1) we have discussed two Pregel algorithms in such a way that it may seem to the reader that each vertex is assigned to only one processor. However, in reality, a big graph contains billions of nodes and as such multiple vertices may be assigned to the same worker.
8 Because hubs need to communicate with many more vertices than other vertices, since it has too many neighbors as compared to others.
9 This approach is called vertex-cut partitioning because it "cuts/splits" the data of some vertices into different machines that contain their incident edges.
10 Since these frameworks assign edges (instead of vertices) to workers and/or requires the programmer to define some UDFs for processing edges, they are sometimes called edge-centric frameworks [38]. However, we consider them to be vertex-centric frameworks, just like Yan et al. [7] and Mccune et al. [10] did, because these frameworks require the programmer to define some vertex-centric UDFs, *i.e.*, functions for processing vertices (just like other vertex-centric frameworks).
11 This may happen when multiple vertices are assigned to the same worker and some of those vertices want to send messages to the same recipient. For example, vertices *a* and *e* in Figure 5.4(a) tries to send messages to vertex *d*.
12 The time required to finish communication between two machines in the network.
13 Γv is the set of adjacent vertices of v.
14 The authors of BLOGEL construct a web-graph by considering each webpage as a vertex and put an edge between two webpages if one contains a link to another. They also grouped all vertices in a block that have the same host name.
15 https://react-etc.net/entry/graph-query-languages-graphql-opencypher-gremlin-and-sparql.
16 Typically, time is considered to be a discrete variable in big graph analysis [7].
17 Vertices with very high (statistically significant) degrees are called hubs.
18 Each leaf of this DAG represents a snapshot; none of them actually contains a graph. Graphs are partitioned into different workers, as usual.
19 Internal nodes can represent some other graph (other than intersection graph) formed from the graphs of its children.

References

1. G. Malewicz, M. H. Austern, A. J. C. Bik, J. C. Dehnert, I. Horn, N. Leiser, and G. Czajkowski, "Pregel: a system for large-scale graph processing," In *Proceedings of the 2010 International Conference on Management of Data—SIGMOD '10*, 2010, p. 135.

2. A. Cuzzocrea and I.-Y. Song, "Big graph analytics: The State of the Art and Future Research Agenda," In *Proceedings of the 17th International Workshop on Data Warehousing and OLAP—DOLAP '14*, 2014, pp. 99–101.
3. U. Kang and C. Faloutsos, Big graph mining: Algorithms and discoveries, ACM SIGKDD Explor. Newsl., vol. 14, no. 2, ACM, p. 29, 30-Apr-2013.
4. A.R. Benson, D.F. Gleich, and J. Leskovec, Higher-order organization of complex networks, *Science*, vol. 353, no. 6295, pp. 163–166, Jul. 2016.
5. P. Zikopoulos and C. Eaton, *Understanding Big Data: Analytics for Enterprise Class Hadoop and Streaming Data*, New York: McGraw-Hill Osborne Media, 2011.
6. S. Ma, J. Li, C. Hu, X. Lin, and J. Huai, Big graph search: Challenges and techniques, *Front. Comput. Sci.*, vol. 10, no. 3, pp. 387–398, Jun. 2016.
7. D. Yan, Y. Bu, Y. Tian, and A. Deshpande, Big graph analytics platforms, *Found. Trends Databases*, vol. 7, no. 1–2, pp. 1–195, 2017.
8. D. Yan, J. Cheng, K. Xing, Y. Lu, W. Ng, and Y. Bu, Pregel algorithms for graph connectivity problems with performance guarantees, *Proc. VLDB Endow.*, vol. 7, no. 14, pp. 1821–1832, Oct. 2014.
9. Y. Low, D. Bickson, J. Gonzalez, C. Guestrin, A. Kyrola, and J.M. Hellerstein, Distributed GraphLab: A framework for machine learning and data mining in the cloud, *Proc. VLDB Endow.*, vol. 5, no. 8, pp. 716–727, Apr. 2012.
10. R.R. McCune, T. Weninger, and G. Madey, "Thinking Like a Vertex: a Survey of Vertex-Centric Frameworks for Distributed Graph Processing," vol. 48, no. 2, 2015.
11. G. Karypis and V. Kumar, A fast and high quality multilevel scheme for partitioning irregular graphs, *SIAM J. Sci. Comput.*, vol. 20, no. 1, pp. 359–392, Jan. 1998.
12. Z. Khayyat, K. Awara, A. Alonazi, H. Jamjoom, D. Williams, and P. Kalnis, "Mizan: a system for dynamic load balancing in large-scale graph processing," In *Proceedings of the 8th ACM European Conference on Computer Systems—EuroSys '13*, 2013, p. 169.
13. G.M. Slota, K. Madduri, and S. Rajamanickam, "PuLP: Scalable multi-objective multi-constraint partitioning for small-world networks," In 2014 *IEEE International Conference on Big Data (Big Data)*, 2014, pp. 481–490.
14. L. Wang, Y. Xiao, B. Shao, and H. Wang, "How to partition a billion-node graph," In 2014 *IEEE 30th International Conference on Data Engineering*, 2014, pp. 568–579.
15. U.N. Raghavan, R. Albert, and S. Kumara, Near linear time algorithm to detect community structures in large-scale networks, *Phys. Rev. E*, vol. 76, no. 3, p. 36106, Sep. 2007.
16. I. Stanton and G. Kliot, "Streaming graph partitioning for large distributed graphs," In *Proceedings of the 18th ACM SIGKDD International Conference on Knowledge Discovery and Data Mining—KDD '12*, 2012, p. 1222.
17. D. Yan, J. Cheng, Y. Lu, and W. Ng, "Effective techniques for message reduction and load balancing in distributed graph computation," In *Proceedings of the 24th International Conference on World Wide Web—WWW '15*, 2015, pp. 1307–1317.
18. J.E. Gonzalez, Y. Low, H. Gu, D. Bickson, and C. Guestrin, "PowerGraph: distributed graph-parallel computation on natural graphs," In *10th USENIX conference on Operating Systems Design and Implementation (OSDI)*, 2012, pp. 17–30.
19. R. Chen, J. Shi, Y. Chen, and H. Chen, "PowerLyra: differentiated graph computation and partitioning on skewed graphs," In *Proceedings of the Tenth European Conference on Computer Systems—EuroSys '15*, 2015, pp. 1–15.
20. J.E. Gonzalez, R.S. Xin, A. Dave, D. Crankshaw, M.J. Franklin, and I. Stoica, "GraphX: graph processing in a distributed dataflow framework," In *11th USENIX Symposium on Operating Systems Design and Implementation (OSDI)*, 2014, pp. 598–613.

21. S. Salihoglu and J. Widom, "GPS: a graph processing system," In *Proceedings of the 25th International Conference on Scientific and Statistical Database Management—SSDBM*, 2013, p. 1.
22. J.D. Cavanaugh, "Protocol Overhead in IP/ATM Networks," 1994.
23. A. Lulli, "Distributed Graph Processing: Algorithms And Applications," 2017.
24. E.W. Dijkstra, Hierarchical ordering of sequential processes, In *The Origin of Concurrent Programming*, edited by P.B. Hansen, New York: Springer, 1971, pp. 198–227.
25. K.M. Chandy and J. Misra, The drinking philosophers problem, *ACM Trans. Program. Lang. Syst.*, vol. 6, no. 4, pp. 632–646, Oct. 1984.
26. L.G. Valiant and L.G., A bridging model for parallel computation, *Commun. ACM,* vol. 33, no. 8, pp. 103–111, Aug. 1990.
27. Y. Lu, J. Cheng, D. Yan, and H. Wu, Large-scale distributed graph computing systems, *Proc. VLDB Endow.*, vol. 8, no. 3, pp. 281–292, Nov. 2014.
28. C. Xie, R. Chen, H. Guan, B. Zang, and H. Chen, "SYNC or ASYNC: time to fuse for distributed graph-parallel computation," In *Proceedings of the 20th ACM SIGPLAN Symposium on Principles and Practice of Parallel Programming—PPoPP* 2015, 2015, vol. 50, no. 8, pp. 194–204.
29. A. Ching, S. Edunov, M. Kabiljo, D. Logothetis, and S. Muthukrishnan, One trillion edges: Graph processing at Facebook-scale, *Proc. VLDB Endow.*, vol. 8, no. 12, pp. 1804–1815, Aug. 2015.
30. Y. Zhang, Q. Gao, L. Gao, and C. Wang, Maiter: An asynchronous graph processing framework for delta-based accumulative iterative computation, *IEEE Trans. Parallel Distrib. Syst.*, vol. 25, no. 8, pp. 2091–2100, Aug. 2014.
31. M. Han and K. Daudjee, Giraph unchained, *Proc. VLDB Endow.*, vol. 8, no. 9, pp. 950–961, May 2015.
32. C. Zhou, J. Gao, B. Sun, and J.X. Yu, MOCgraph: Scalable distributed graph processing using message online computing, *Proc. VLDB Endow.*, vol. 8, no. 4, pp. 377–388, Dec. 2014.
33. Y. Liu, C. Zhou, J. Gao, and Z. Fan, "GiraphAsync: supporting online and offline graph processing via adaptive asynchronous message processing," In *Proceedings of the 25th ACM International on Conference on Information and Knowledge Management—CIKM '16*, 2016, pp. 479–488.
34. Q. Chen, S. Bai, Z. Li, Z. Gou, B. Suo, and W. Pan, "GraphHP: A Hybrid Platform for Iterative Graph Processing," 2017.
35. X. Ju, H. Jamjoom, and K.G. Shin, Hieroglyph: Locally-sufficient graph processing via compute-sync-merge, *Proc. ACM Meas. Anal. Comput. Syst.*, vol. 1, no. 1, p. 9, 2017.
36. S. Tasci and M. Demirbas, "Giraphx: parallel yet serializable large-scale graph processing," In *Proceedings of the 19th international conference on Parallel Processing*, Springer-Verlag, 2013, pp. 458–469.
37. A. Roy, I. Mihailovic, and W. Zwaenepoel, "X-Stream: Edge-centric graph processing using streaming partitions," In *Proceedings of the Twenty-Fourth ACM Symposium on Operating Systems Principles—SOSP '13*, 2013, pp. 472–488.
38. D. Yan, J. Cheng, Y. Lu, and W. Ng, "Blogel: A block-centric framework for distributed computation on real-world graphs," *Proc. VLDB Endow.*, vol. 7, no. 14, pp. 1981–1992, Oct. 2014.
39. Y. Tian, A. Balmin, S.A. Corsten, S. Tatikonda, and J. McPherson, From think like a vertex to think like a graph, *Proc. VLDB Endow.*, vol. 7, no. 3, pp. 193–204, 2013.
40. A. Quamar, A. Deshpande, and J. Lin, NScale: Neighborhood-centric large-scale graph analytics in the cloud, *VLDB J.*, vol. 25, no. 2, pp. 125–150, 2016.

41. C.H.C. Teixeira, A.J. Fonseca, M. Serafini, G. Siganos, M.J. Zaki, and A. Aboulnaga, "Arabesque: a system for distributed graph mining," In *Proceedings of the 25th Symposium on Operating Systems Principles—SOSP '15*, 2015, pp. 425–440.

42. S. Seo, E.J. Yoon, J. Kim, S. Jin, J.-S. Kim, and S. Maeng, "HAMA: an efficient matrix computation with the mapreduce framework," In 2010 *IEEE Second International Conference on Cloud Computing Technology and Science*, 2010, pp. 721–726.

43. U. Kang, C.E. Tsourakakis, and C. Faloutsos, "PEGASUS: a peta-scale graph mining system implementation and observations," In 2009 *Ninth IEEE International Conference on Data Mining*, 2009, pp. 229–238.

44. U. Kang, H. Tong, J. Sun, C.-Y. Lin, and C. Faloutsos, "GBASE: a scalable and general graph management system," In *Proceedings of the 17th ACM SIGKDD International Conference on Knowledge Discovery and Data Mining—KDD '11*, 2011, p. 1091.

45. M. Boehm, M.W. Dusenberry, D. Eriksson, A.V. Evfimievski, F.M. Manshadi, N. Pansare, B. Reinwald, F.R. Reiss, P. Sen, A.C. Surve, and S. Tatikonda, SystemML: Declarative machine learning on spark, *Proc. VLDB Endow.*, vol. 9, no. 13, pp. 1425–1436, Sep. 2016.

46. Y. Bu, V. Borkar, J. Jia, M.J. Carey, and T. Condie, Pregelix: Big(ger) graph analytics on a dataflow engine, *Proc. VLDB Endow.*, vol. 8, no. 2, 2015.

47. O. Batarfi, R. Elshawi, A. Fayoumi, A. Barnawi, and S. Sakr, A distributed query execution engine of big attributed graphs, *Springerplus*, vol. 5, no. 1, p. 665, 2016.

48. S. Sakr, S. Elnikety, and Y. He, "G-SPARQL: a hybrid engine for querying large attributed graphs," In *Proceedings of the 21st ACM International Conference on Information and Knowledge Management—CIKM '12*, 2012, p. 335.

49. J. Shun, G.E. Blelloch, J. Shun, and G.E. Blelloch, "Ligra: a lightweight graph processing framework for shared memory," In *Proceedings of the 18th ACM SIGPLAN Symposium on Principles and Practice of Parallel Programming—PPoPP '13*, 2013, vol. 48, no. 8, p. 135.

50. A. Kyrola, G. Blelloch, and C. Guestrin, "GraphChi: large-scale graph computation on just a PC," In *Proceedings of the 10th USENIX Conference on Operating Systems Design and Implementation*, 2012, pp. 31–46.

51. D. Zheng, D. Mhembere, R. Burns, J. Vogelstein, C.E. Priebe, and A.S. Szalay, "FlashGraph: processing billion-node graphs on an array of commodity SSDs," In *13th USENIX Conference on File and Storage Technologies (FAST '15)*, 2015, pp. 45–58.

52. N. Sundaram, N. Satish, M. M. A. Patwary, S. R. Dulloor, M. J. Anderson, S. G. Vadlamudi, D. Das and P. Dubey, GraphMat: High performance graph analytics made productive, *Proc. VLDB Endow.*, vol. 8, no. 11, pp. 1214–1225, Jul. 2015.

53. G. Wang, W. Xie, A. Demers, and J. Gehrke, "Asynchronous large-scale graph processing made easy," In *6 th Biennial Conference on Innovative Data Systems Research (CIDR'13)*, 2013.

54. J.K. Hollingsworth, K. ACM Digital Library., D. Sigarch., and S. I. G. on H. P. C. ACM Special Interest Group on High Performance Computing, "Direction-optimizing breadth-first search," In *Proceedings of the International Conference on High Performance Computing, Networking, Storage and Analysis*, 2012, p. 1161.

55. U. Khurana and A. Deshpande, "Efficient snapshot retrieval over historical graph data," In 2013 *IEEE 29th International Conference on Data Engineering (ICDE)*, 2013, pp. 997–1008.

56. D. Kempe, J. Kleinberg, and A. Kumar, "Connectivity and inference problems for temporal networks," In *Proceedings of the thirty-second annual ACM symposium on Theory of computing—STOC '00*, 2000, pp. 504–513.

57. M. Karsai, N. Perra, and A. Vespignani, Time varying networks and the weakness of strong ties, *Sci. Rep.*, vol. 4, no. 1, p. 4001, May 2015.

58. H. Wu, J. Cheng, S. Huang, Y. Ke, Y. Lu, and Y. Xu, Path problems in temporal graphs, *Proc. VLDB Endow.*, vol. 7, no. 9, pp. 721–732, May 2014.
59. S.-Y. Chan, P. Hui, and K. Xu, "Community detection of time-varying mobile social networks," In *International Conference on Complex Sciences*, 2009, pp. 1154–1159.
60. C. Aggarwal and K. Subbian, Evolutionary network analysis, *ACM Comput. Surv.*, vol. 47, no. 1, pp. 1–36, May 2014.
61. W. Hant, Y. Miao, K. Li, M. Wu, F. Yang, K. Zhou, V. Prabhakaran, W. Chen, and E. Chen, "Chronos," In *Proceedings of the Ninth European Conference on Computer Systems—EuroSys '14*, 2014, pp. 1–14.
62. A.P. Iyer, L.E. Li, T. Das, and I. Stoica, "Time-evolving graph processing at scale," In *Proceedings of the Fourth International Workshop on Graph Data Management Experiences and Systems—GRADES '16*, 2016, pp. 1–6.
63. R. Cheng, J. Hong, A. Kyrola, Y. Miao, X. Weng, M. Wu, F. Yang, L. Zhou, F. Zhao, and E. Chen, "Kineograph: taking the pulse of a fast-changing and connected world," In *Proceedings of the 7th ACM European Conference on Computer Systems—EuroSys '12*, 2012, p. 85.
64. Z. Cai, D. Logothetis, and G. Siganos, "Facilitating real-time graph mining," In *CloudDB*, 2012.
65. W. Xie, Y. Tian, Y. Sismanis, A. Balmin, and P.J. Haas, "Dynamic interaction graphs with probabilistic edge decay," In *31st International Conference on Data Engineering (ICDE)*, 2015, pp. 1143–1154.
66. G. Feng, X. Meng, and K. Ammar, "DISTINGER: A distributed graph data structure for massive dynamic graph processing," In 2015 *IEEE International Conference on Big Data (Big Data)*, 2015, pp. 1814–1822.
67. S. Aridhi, A. Montresor, and Y. Velegrakis, "BLADYG: A novel block-centric framework for the analysis of large dynamic graphs," In *Proceedings of the ACM Workshop on High Performance Graph Processing—HPGP '16*, 2016, pp. 39–42.
68. D. Ediger, J. Riedy, D.A. Bader, and H. Meyerhenke, Computational graph analytics for massive streaming data, In *Large Scale Network-Centric Distributed Systems*, edited by H. Sarbazi-Azad , A.Y. Zomaya, Hoboken, NJ: John Wiley & Sons, Inc., 2013, pp. 619–648.
69. P. Macko and Peter, "LLAMA: A Persistent, Mutable Representation for Graphs," *Doctoral dissertation*, Harvard University, 2015.

DATA ANALYTICS TECHNIQUES

Chapter 6

Transition from Relational Database to Big Data and Analytics

Santoshi Kumari and C. Narendra Babu

M. S. Ramaiah University of Applied Sciences

Contents

6.1 Introduction

The term big data was invented to represent large data generated continuously with the advancement in digital technology, smart devices, and cheap hardware resources. Enterprises, businesses, and government sectors producing a large amount of valuable information need to be processed to make better decisions and improve their performance [1]. Processing a huge amount of unstructured data is difficult using relational data management technologies. Efficient tools and technologies are required to process such large-scale and complex data. Several tools such as Google's Map Reduce [2], Spark [3], and Mahout [4,5] were developed to overcome the limitations of traditional methods.

Understanding the fundamental principles and properties [6] of big data system is essential for building robust and scalable tools and technologies. Various frameworks and tools such as Hadoop, Spark, Cassandra [7], ZooKeeper [8], HBase, and MLlib [9] are introduced for batch processing, stream processing, and graph processing of large-scale data.

6.1.1 Background, Motivation, and Aim

The data generated from social media, sensor-equipped smart device, Internet of Things (IoT), E-business, and research centers is spiking every day with an increase in complexity [10]. This huge amount of data generated essentially requires new technology to store, process, and analyze the data to discover hidden insights for better decisions. Parallel processing is one such technique of big data system that achieves significant efficiency in processing terabytes and petabytes of complex data.

The key features of the emerging database systems for advanced analytics have been a boundless motivation to take a look into big data processing frameworks, like Hadoop [11,12] and Spark. A thoughtful review on the development of new systems to overcome the drawbacks of traditional analytical methods for large data is taken into account. To develop a generalized system for processing large dataset, the Lambda Architecture [6] provides three layers of architecture structure, which in turn helps to understand the basic requirement for processing and analyzing large data in batch, stream, and real time.

This chapter aims to present interpretations on the drawbacks of traditional methods for processing big data, the characteristics and challenges of big data, the properties of big data analytics, and the tools and technologies for processing big data. There are several benefits of big data analytics [13] in various areas, such as finance and marketing, government, and health care.

6.1.2 Chapter Organization

This chapter is organized as follows: Section 6.2 provides a review on the transition from relational database to big data and the difference between relational data and big data. Section 6.3 elaborates on the evolution of big data, the basic principles and properties of big data, and the generalized framework for big data systems. Section 6.4 describes big data analytics, the necessity of big data analytics, and the challenges in big data analytics. Lastly, tools and technologies for big data processing are discussed in Section 6.5. Conclusion and future work are presented in Section 6.6.

6.2 Transition from Relational Database to Big Data

This topic provides an overview of the transition from the relational database system to the big data system. Starting with the evolution of relational database management system (RDBMS) and its introduction, it outlines the characteristics of relational database systems, traditional tools, and the drawbacks of the tools in handling unstructured large data.

A later part provides a brief introduction to big data and an understanding on different types of data formats. Finally, it concludes with comparisons between RDBMS and big data in terms of performance evaluation parameters, such as scalability, efficiency, storage and management, and size and schema.

6.2.1 Relational Database

In 1970, E. F. Codd [14] introduced a new approach for calculating and manipulating data in relational database format. Since then, RDBMS has been implemented and used for more than four decades, satisfying the business needs. It is a traditional method for managing structured data in which rows and columns are used to store the data in the form of tables and each table has a unique primary key.

The key characteristics of relational database are to support ACID (atomicity, consistency, isolation, and durability) property [15] that guarantees consistency in handling all the transactions. RDBMS includes a relational database and a schema to manage, store, query, and retrieve the dataset. The RDBMS maintains data integrity through the following characteristics:

1. Tuple and attribute orders are not important.
2. Each entity is unique.
3. Each cell in the table contains a single value.
4. An attribute should contain all the values of the same data space.
5. In a database, table names and attributed names should be unique. But two different tables can have similar attribute names.
6. SQL (Structured Query Language) is used for administrative operations, which include data definition language (DDL), data manipulation language (DML), and data access layer (DAL).

Data warehouses and data marts are the key methods for managing the structured datasets. A data warehouse integrates data from multiple data sources that are used for storing, analyzing, and reporting, whereas a data mart is used to access the data stored in a data warehouse so that data is filtered and processed. Preprocessed data is given as an input for data mining and online analytical processing to find new values to solve various business problems. The two ways to store data in a data warehouse are as follows:

- **Dimension table**—To uniquely identify each dimension record (row), it maintains a primary key, and it is associated with a fact table. Using primary key data from the fact table, the associated data is filtered and grouped into slices and dices to get various combinations of attributes and results.
- **Normalization**—Normalization splits the data into entities to create several tables in a relational database. It has a property of duplicating data within the database and often results in the creation of additional tables. The tables are classified based on data categories, such as data on employee, finance, business, and department.

There are several challenges faced by today's enterprises, organizations, and government sectors due to some limitations of the traditional database system which are as follows:

- Real-time business decision is difficult using the traditional database system due to the complexity of processing and analysis of real-time unstructured data.
- Difficult to extract, manage, and analyze the data islands, such as data from a personal digital assistant (PDA) (mobiles, tablets) and other computing devices.
- Traditional data models are nonscalable for large amounts of complex data.
- Data management cost increases exponentially with the increase of data and complexity.

Hence, big data analytics, tools, and technologies were introduced to overcome the limitations of traditional database systems for managing complex data generated rapidly in various formats characterized by [16] volume, velocity, variability, and variety.

6.2.2 Introduction to Big Data

The term big data emerged to describe complex unstructured data generated from click streams, transaction histories, sensors, and PDAs. Big data technologies find new opportunities to make quick and better decisions from large complex data at less cost.

Big data is characterized mainly by four V's [16,17], which are described by identifying the drawbacks of traditional methods as follows:

- **Volume:** Large data is generated continuously so that traditional methods fail to manage it.
- **Velocity:** Data is generated at a very high frequency which traditional methods are incapable of processing it.

■ **Variety**: Data is generated in different formats such as audio, videos, log files, and transaction history from various sources, which no longer fits traditional structures.

■ **Veracity**: Large amount of unorganized data is generated, such as tweets, comments with hash tags, abbreviations, and conversational text and speeches.

In order to address the above characteristics of big data, several new technologies such as Not only SQL (NoSQL), Hadoop, and Spark were developed.

■ **NoSQL database**: NoSQL [18,19] database is a schema-less database used to store and manage unstructured data, where the management layer is separated from the storage layer. The management layer provides assurance of data integrity.

NoSQL provides high performance scalable data storage with low-level access to a data management layer, so that data management tasks are handled at the application layer. Advantage of NoSQL is that the structure of the data is modified at the application layer without making any changes to the original data in the tables.

■ **Parallel processing:** Many processors (300 or more in number) work in loosely coupled or shared nothing architecture. Independent processors with their own operating systems and memories work parallelly on different parts of the program to improve the processing speed of the tasks and memory utilization. Communication between tasks takes place through messaging interface.

■ **Distributed file system (DFS)**: DFS allows multiple users working on different machines to share files, memories, and other resources. Based on access lists on both servers and clients, the client nodes get restricted access to the file systems, but not to the whole block of storage. However, it is again dependent on the protocol.

■ **Hadoop:** It is a fundamental framework for managing big data on which many analytical tasks and stream computing are carried out. Apache Hadoop [20] allows distributed processing of huge datasets over multiple clusters of commodity hardware. It provides a high degree of fault tolerance with horizontal scaling from a single to thousands of machines.

■ **Data-intensive computing:** Data parallel approach is used in parallel computing application to process big data [21]. This is based on the principle of association of data and programs to perform computation.

6.2.3 Relational Data vs. Big Data

Table 6.1 highlights some of the key differences between RDBMS and big data systems.

Table 6.1 Difference between Relational Data and Big Data

Sl. No	RDBMS	Big Data
Description	Structured data is split into many tables containing rows and column. Tables are interrelated. A foreign key stored in one of the columns is used to refer the interrelated tables.	Unstructured data files are spared across many clusters where distributed file system handles data redundancy. Hadoop on DFS supports many application interfaces for processing large-scale data.
Properties	RDBMS is characterized by ACID properties.	Big data is characterized by four V's: volume, velocity, verity, and veracity.
Data supported	Supports only structured data.	Supports structured, semistructured, and unstructured data.
Data size	Terabytes	Petabytes
Database management	SQL database: It deals with a structured data table; hence, data is stored at a single node and it requires fixed table schemas.	NoSQL: It deals with unstructured data record; hence, data is stored across multiple nodes and no fixed schema is required.
Scalable	Vertical scaling: The database is scaled by increasing server and hardware powers. Building bigger servers to scale up is expensive.	Horizontal scaling: More machines are added to a pool of resources to scale up the database.
Maintaining	Maintaining RDBMS systems is expensive and requires a skilled resource.	Require less maintenance. Many features such as auto-repair, data redundancy, and easy data distribution are supported.

(Continued)

Table 6.1 (*Continued*)   Difference between Relational Data and Big Data

Sl. No	RDBMS	Big Data
Schema	Fixed schema: SQL database is schema oriented. Data is stored in the form of tables containing rows and columns with a unique primary key so that the format of data cannot be changed at any time.	Dynamic schema: NoSQL database is schema-less. Data format or data model can be changed dynamically, without making any changes to application.
Management and storage	Relational database combines both data storage and management layers.	NoSQL database separates data management from data storage.

6.3 Evolution of Big Data

In 1989, British computer scientist Tim Berners-Lee introduced the hypertext system to share information between computers across the world, and eventually the World Wide Web (WWW) was invented. As more and more systems are connected to the Internet, huge amounts of data are generated.

In 2001, Doug Laney [17], an analyst at Gartner, presented a paper "3D Data Management: Controlling Data Volume, Velocity and Variety." It defines commonly accepted characteristics of increasing data. With the introduction of Web 2.0 in 2004, numerous devices were connected to the Internet and also many web-based applications were hosted, which led to the explosion of data. Later, Roger Mougalas invented the term "big data" in 2005 to define a huge volume of complex data generated at high speed.

To manage this large-scale complex data, a new tool called Hadoop was introduced by Yahoo in the same year. To perform large-scale distributed computing, a Map Reduce software concept was introduced by Oracle in 2004. Initially, Hadoop was built on top of Google Map Reduce to index WWW. Later, Hadoop was made available as an open source, and it is in use by many organizations to manage their increasing data.

Currently, the importance of big data technology is increasing in various fields, such as health care, business, government, sports, finance, and security for making better decisions and cost-effective and process improvements. For example, financial trading like investments in stock market and purchase and sale of shares is dependent on big data analytics. Big data analytics using real-time traffic data collected from sensors, Global Positioning System (GPS), and social media help in optimizing traffic flow and predicting weather condition.

6.3.1 Facts and Predictions about the Data Generated

According to "A Comprehensive List of Big Data Statistics" (Big data statistics, 2012), August 1, 2012, a list of big data generated from various sectors, such as business, market, education, and social media, is given as follows:

1. Data generated in every 2 days is equal to data generated from the beginning of time until 2003.
2. Over 90% of all the data in the world was produced in the past 2 years.
3. By 2020, the amount of digital information generated is expected to grow from 3.2 ZB today to 40 ZB. Data generated by industries gets doubled in every 1.2 years.
4. Every minute, 200,000 photos are uploaded on Facebook, 204 million emails are sent, 1.8 million likes are shared on Facebook, and 278,000 tweets are posted, and around 40,000 search queries are served by Google every second.
5. In YouTube, every minute, around 100 hours of video are uploaded and it would take 15 years to watch all the videos uploaded in a single day.
6. Thirty billion pieces of information are exchanged between Facebook users every day.
7. Every minute, around 570 new websites are hosted into existence.
8. Around 12 TB of tweets is analyzed every day to measure "sentiment."
9. An 81% increase in data over the mobile network had been observed per month from 2012 to 2014.

6.3.2 Applications of Big Data

Applications of big data technology making significant differences in a wide range of areas are discussed below.

1. **Understanding and aiming customers:** Understanding the necessities and the requirements of customers is one of the important factors for many business entities to improve their business. Big data applications play an important role in understanding the customers, their behaviors, and their inclinations by analyzing the behaviors and sentiments of the customers from previously collected large data. In order to get a more comprehensive picture of their customers, many companies are keen to increase their datasets with social media data, browser logs, as well as text analytics and sensor data. Nowadays, using big data, e-business giants such as Flipkart and Amazon are able to predict what products are on demand and can be sold, and they can suggest similar products to the customers. Similarly, telecom companies are now able to better understand the customer expectations and can make better decisions. Exit polls of elections are more predictive using big data analytics [22].

2. **Understanding and improving business practices**: Big data helps in boosting the business processes [23]. Analytics on social media data, search histories on web sites, and weather forecasts help retailers in adjusting their stocks. GPS systems and sensor-equipped vehicles are used to track the delivery of goods, and analysis of live traffic data helps in finding the shortest path. Most importantly, customer feedback on social media helps to improve the business processes.

3. **Health care:** A large amount of patient medical history help in understanding the symptoms and in predicting possible diseases and solutions [24,25]. Better prediction on a disease pattern enables to provide better treatments. For example, a success factor of in vitro fertilization treatment can be predicted by the analysis of multiple attributes of N number of patient records. The risk factors in a patient's treatment can be identified by analyzing conditions such as blood pressure levels, asthma, diabetes, genetics, and previous records. Future judgments in medicine would not be limited to small samples, instead it would include a huge set of records.

4. **Sports:** IBM SlamTracker tool used for video analytics in tennis tournaments works on big data analytics. The performance of players in football and baseball games can be tracked and predicted based on the analysis of historical data and sensor technology in sports equipment. Big data analysis and visualization can help players a lot to improve their performance, for example, a cricket player can improve his/her bowling skills by understanding what kind of shots are played by the opponent.

5. **Science and research:** Current potentials of big data analytics are transforming science and research technology. For example, CERN, the Swiss nuclear physics lab data center, has 65,000 processors. It generates huge amounts of data by experimenting on the discovery of universe coverts and analyzes 30 PB of data on many distributed computers across 150 data centers. This data is used in many other research areas to compute new insights.

6. **Optimizing machine and device performance:** A large data used to train machines and devices with the help of artificial intelligence and machine learning makes better and smarter devices without human involvement. The more the training data, the more accurate and smarter the device. For example, Google's self-driving car uses data captured from sensors, cameras, and GPS systems to analyze the traffic movement and for safe driving without human intervention.

7. **Security and law enforcement:** Big data analytics is used by many developed countries such as the United States, the United Kingdom, Japan, and Singapore to advance security and law enforcement. For example, the National Security Agency in the United States and National Computer Systems in Singapore use big data analytics to track and avoid terrorist activities.

8. **Smart cities:** Big data analytics [26] help optimize traffic flow by predicting weather using real-time traffic data collected from sensors, GPS, and social media. Analysis of data from tweets, comments, blogs and end-user feedback helps in building better transportation systems and hence in making better decisions for building smarter cities and a smarter planet.

9. **Financial operation:** Big data analytics plays an important role in making financial decisions and improving financial operations. Understanding costumer requirements and inclinations helps to provide best services, such as insurance, credit, and loan facilities. Further financial operation process improvements can be made based on the analysis of feedbacks. Nowadays, most of the financial trading such as investments in stock market and purchase and sale of shares is dependent on big data analytics.

6.3.3 Fundamental Principle and Properties of Big Data

Before we dive into big data tools and technologies, it is necessary to understand the basic principle and properties of big data. It is also essential to know the complexity and scalability issues of traditional data systems in managing large data as discussed previously. To overcome the issues of traditional methods, several open-source tools are developed, such as Hadoop, MongoDB, Cassandra, HBase, and MLlib. Theses system scale to huge set of data processing and management. On the other hand, to design and understand a robust and scalable system for big data processing, it is essential to know the basic principle and properties of big data.

6.3.3.1 Issues with Traditional Architecture for Big Data Processing

There are many issues with the traditional systems to deal with increasing complex data. Some major challenges are identified and discussed as follows:

1. **Architecture was not completely fault tolerant**: As the number of machines increases, it is more likely that a machine would go down as it is not horizontally scalable. Manual interventions are required such as managing queue failures and setting replicas to keep the applications running.

2. **Distributed nature of data**: Data is scattered in pieces on many clusters, and the complexity is increased at the application layer to select the appropriate data and process it. Applications must be aware of the data to be modified or must inspect the scattered pieces over the clusters and process it and then merge the result to present the final result.

3. **Insufficient backup and unavoidable mistakes in software**: Complexities are pushed to the application layer with the introduction of big data technology. As the complexity of system increases, the possibility of making mistakes

will also increase. Systems must be built robust enough to avoid or handle human mistakes and limit damages. In addition, a database should be aware of its distributed nature. It is more time consuming to manage distributed processes.

The big data system scalability and complexity issues of traditional systems are addressed and resolved in a systematic approach.

- First, replication and fragmentation are managed by the distributed nature of database and distributed computation methods. Furthermore, systems are scaled up by adding more machines to the existing systems to cope with increasing data.
- Second, database systems should be immutable to design systems in different ways to manage and process large-scale data, so that making changes to the original data does not destroy the valuable data.

To manage a large amount of data, many large-scale computation systems, such as Hadoop and Spark, and database systems, such as HBase and Cassandra, were introduced. Hadoop has high computation latency for batch processing large-scale data in parallel, whereas database Cassandra offers a much more limited data mode to achieve their scalability.

The database systems are not human fault tolerant as they are alterable. Consequently, every system has its own pros and cons. To address these arbitrary issues, systems must be developed in combination with one another with least possible complexity.

6.3.3.2 *Fundamental Principle for Scalable Database System*

To build scalable database systems [6], primarily we need to understand "what does a data system do?" Basically, database systems are used to store and retrieve information. Instead of limiting it to storage, new generation database systems must be able to process large amounts of complex data and extract meaningful information to take better decisions in less time.

In general, a data system must answer queries by executing a function that takes the entire dataset as an input. It is defined as

$$Query = function \ (on \ all \ data)$$

To implement the above arbitrary function on random dataset with small latency, Lambda Architecture provides some general steps for developing scalable big data systems. Hence, it becomes essential to understand the elementary properties of big data systems to develop scalable systems.

6.3.3.3 Properties of Big Data System

1. **Fault tolerant and reliable:** Systems must be robust enough to tolerate faults and manage their work when one or two machines are down. The main challenge of distributed systems is to "do the right thing." Database systems should be able to handle complications such as randomly changing data in distributed database, replication of data, and concurrency so that we can drive around the systems and make the systems recalculate the original systems immutably. The system must be tolerant to handle human errors [27].

2. **Minimal latency for reads and update:** Several applications read and update the database. Some applications need updates to be transmitted immediately. Without compromising on the speed and robustness of the systems, database systems should be able to satisfy low latency reads and updates for applications.

3. **High scalability and performance:** Increasing the data size would increase the load; however, this should not affect the performance of the system. Scalability and performance of the system are achieved by adding more machines with an increased processing capacity. To handle increasing data and load, systems are horizontally scaled over all the layers of the system stack.

4. **Support for a wide range of applications:** A system should support a diverse range of applications. To achieve this, systems are built with many combinations and are generalized to support a wide range of applications. Applications such as financial management systems, hospital management, social media analytics, scientific applications, and social networking require big data systems to manage their data and values [28].

5. **Compatible system with low cost:** Systems should be extensible by adding new functionalities at low cost to support a wide range of applications. In such cases, old data is required to relocate in new formats. Systems must be easily compatible to support past data with minimal upgrading cost for supporting a wide range of applications.

6. **Random queries on a large dataset:** Executing random queries on a large dataset is very important to discover and learn interesting insights from the data. To find new business insights, applications require random mining and querying on datasets.

7. **Scalable system with minimal maintenance:** The number of machines added to scale should not increase the maintenance. Choosing a module with small implementation complexity is key to reduced maintenance. The more complex the system is, the more likely it is that something will go wrong, hence requiring more debugging and tuning of the system. Minimum maintenance is obtained by keeping a system simple. Keeping processes up, fixing

errors, and running efficiently when machines are scaled are the important factors to be considered for developing systems.

8. **Easy to restore:** Systems must be able to provide the basic necessary information to restore the data when something goes wrong. It should have enough information replicas saved on distributed nodes to easily compute and restore the original data by utilizing saved replicas.

6.3.4 Generalized Framework for Big Data Processing

Based on the abovementioned basic principle and properties of big data, Lambda Architecture provides [6] some general steps for implementing an arbitrary function on a random dataset in real time. The challenges of big data processing are framed into a three generalized layer architecture to produce a result with small latency. The three layers of the framework are storage layer, knowledge discovery layer, and speed layer, as shown in Figure 6.1.

It is redundant to run a query on the whole dataset to get the result, considering the general equation "query = function (on all data)." It takes a large amount of resources and hence is expensive. However, the data can be processed efficiently using the layered architecture shown in Figure 6.1.

6.3.4.1 Storage and Precomputation Layer

According to the basic principle of data processing, the storage layer precomputes the function on the whole data and stores the results in a number of batches and indexes them. Subsequent queries use the precomputed data, instead of preprocessing whole dataset again. Hence, this layer helps to get the results quickly by giving a precomputed view of data.

Precomputed view gets outdated whenever new data is collected in the data store (Hadoop DFS [HDFS]) and hence the queries. To resolve this problem, the *batch layer* (*MAP REDUCE*) [2] precomputes its view on the main dataset after a particular time period. It is a high latency operation as it executes a function on the entire dataset at periodic intervals.

This layer has two tasks: to store an absolute persistently increasing master dataset and to execute a random query on that dataset. It is simple to use as parallel computation across the clusters and to manage varying sizes of datasets at the precomputation layer.

6.3.4.2 Knowledge Discovery Layer (Serving Layer)

It saves and stores precomputed views for extracting valuable information by efficiently querying the precomputed view. The basic function of the serving layer is to update the precomputed views from the distributed database and make them

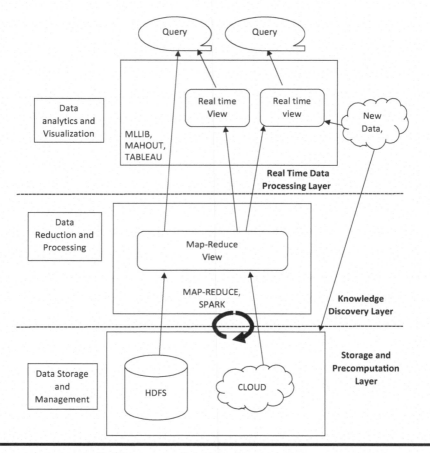

Figure 6.1   Generalized framework for big data processing.

available for knowledge discovery. Finally, it periodically refreshes the precomputed views to update new datasets.

It requires storage layer updates and random reads. It does not support arbitrary writes as it increases the complexity in the database. Hence, it makes the database systems simple, robust, easy to configure, and easy to operate, for example, HBase and Cassandra.

All the desired properties of big data systems are accomplished at the storage and serving layers, except low latency. Hence, the next real-time data processing layer resolves the problem of low-latency updates.

6.3.4.3 Real-Time Data Processing Layer (Speed Layer)

The purpose of this layer is to increase the computation speed so that arbitrary data in real time is computed by arbitrary functions. Finally, the issues that are needed to be addressed in present and future research work is real time data processing and computation [29]. Instead of precomputing the data from the storage layer, real-time views are updated with new data that gets generated, eventually achieving the highest possible latency.

This layer provides solutions for datasets generated in real time to improve latency, whereas the storage layer produces precomputed views on the entire dataset. Datasets that are no longer essential in real-time processing are removed, the results are temporarily saved, and the complexity is pushed to the application layer. Hence, the real-time data processing layer is more complex than the storage and serving layers.

Finally, valuable results are obtained by joining the results from the precomputed views and real-time views. Hence, future research work would be focused on bringing together the batch and real-time views to produce new and valuable insights and to make better decisions. It requires advanced machine learning and analytical techniques to improve the computational speed with maximum accuracy for continuously changing random datasets.

A generalized flexible architecture with distinct components focused on specific purposes leads to more acceptable performance. Applications must be robust enough to precompute values, corrupted values, and results by eventually executing the computation on whole datasets to relocate or fix problems.

6.4 Big Data Analytics

Advancement in electronics and communication technology leads to increased digitization of the world, such as IoT, social media, and sensor networks. It results in massive amounts of data eruption every day. The capability to analyze such large volumes of data brings in a new age of invention [16]. "Big data is a collection of large, dynamic, and complex datasets. New innovative and scalable tools are required to deal with it. Analytics refers to processing and extracting meaningful data, which could help in making better predictions and decisions." There are many advantages of big data analytics and many challenges as well.

6.4.1 Big Data Characteristics and Related Challenges

The three basic characteristics—volume, velocity, and variety—as shown in Figure 6.2 are used to define the nature of big data [17].

6.4.1.1 Volume

A large amount of unstructured data is generated and archived compared to traditional data. This data is generated continuously from various sources, such as system logs, sensor data, click streams, transaction-based data, email communications,

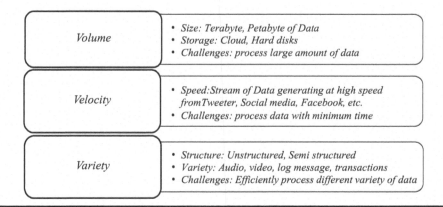

Figure 6.2 Big data characteristics and related challenges.

housekeeping data, and social media. The amount of data is increasing [10] to a level that the traditional database management and computation systems are incapable of handling it. The solution based on data warehouse may not be capable of analyzing and processing huge data due to the lack of a parallel processing design. So, increasing volume is one of the biggest challenges as it requires a new level of scalability for storage and analysis.

6.4.1.2 Velocity

The amount of data increased is exponential to the increase of IoTs, sensor-equipped devices, e-business, and social media. The data generated continuously at high speed makes it challenging to process and analyze it. It is essential to device an algorithm to get quick results from streaming data. For example, online interactions and real-time applications require high rate of analysis.

6.4.1.3 Variety

A variety of data is generated from various sources in different structures, such as text, video, audio, images, and log files. A combination of structured, unstructured, and semistructured data is not supported by the relational database system. Hence, this requires modified storage and processing methods for manipulation of heterogeneous data.

6.4.2 Why Big Data Analytics?

Big data analytics refers to the analysis of large unstructured data to extract the knowledge hidden in every single bit of data for making better decisions and predictions. It is essential to discover new values from past unused data and predict a better future.

Many large-scale organizations and enterprises require big data tools and technologies to analyze their past history and customer information to understand customer needs, in order to improve their business and finally to make better decisions and predictions to survive in the competitive era. They also need [16] robust big data analytics tools and technologies to make new innovations, process improvements, monitoring, security, and many other functions. The analytical methods used to handle big data in different areas are listed in Sections 6.4.2.1–6.4.2.5.

6.4.2.1 Text Analytics

The process of mining valuable and meaningful information from text data is called text analytics. Some of the examples of text data are mail threads, chat conversations, reviews, comments, tweets, feedbacks, financial statements, and log records. Text analytics comprise natural language processing, statistical analysis [29,30], machine learning [32], and computational linguistics. Meaningful abstracts are extracted from large-scale text data by applying many text mining and analytical methods. Text analytics is basically used for question answering, information extraction, sentiment analysis, and text summarization. Text analytics is very essential in analyzing social media data [31] such as tweets and Facebook comments to understand peoples' sentiments and events happening in real time.

6.4.2.2 Audio Analytics

Audio analytics refers to the extraction of valuable and meaningful information from audio data. It is most commonly used in call centers and health care services for improving skills and services provided by call centers and also for improving patient treatments and health-care services. It is also essential in customer relationship management to understand the customers and improve the quality of products and facilities to satisfy their needs and to maintain their relationships.

6.4.2.3 Video Analytics

Video analytics refers to extracting valuable data by tracking and analyzing the video streams. It is used in key application areas, such as marketing and operations management. Analyzing video streams of sports such as tennis and cricket helps to improve the performance of the sports person.

6.4.2.4 Social Media Analytics

Social media channels contain huge volume of structured and unstructured data, which help to identify recent trends and changes in the market by analytics. Real-time analysis of social media is essential to identify events happening around the world, to understand the sentiments of the people toward particular issues, people interest for particular products, and so on. Many organizations are trying to improve their markets by analyzing social media data, such as people behavior, sentiments, and opinions. According to [33], social media are categorized as follows:

1. Social news: Reddit, Digg
2. Wiki: Wikihow, Wikipedia
3. Social networks: LinkedIn, Facebook
4. Microblogs: Tumblr, Twitter
5. Sharing Media: YouTube, Instagram

6.4.2.5 Predictive Analytics

Predictive analytics is used to make predictions on future events based on the analysis of current and historical data. According to [33,30], statistical methods form the base for predictive analysis.

Making use of in-memory data analytics, big data tools have improved the performance of data query notably. Big data analytics is not just about making better decisions but also about real-time processing that motivates businesses to derive new values and improve performance and profit rates from insights gained.

Big data beats RDBMS in several ways including robust backups, recovery, faster search algorithms, overall scalability, and low-latency reads and writes.

6.4.3 Challenges in Big Data Analytics

Capturing the data generated at high speed from various sources, storing huge data, querying, distributing, analyzing, and visualization are the major challenges of a big data system. Data incompleteness and inconsistency, scalability, timeliness, and data security are the challenges [34] in analyzing the large data of big data systems. The primary step in big data analytics is to clean and preprocess raw data to get quality information. However, efficient access, analysis, and visualization would still remain big challenges for future research work. Some of the challenges in each phase of big data analytics are discussed in Sections 6.4.3.1–6.4.3.5.

6.4.3.1 Collect and Store Data

The enterprise storage designs, such as direct-attached storage (DAS), storage area network (SAN), and network-attached storage (NAS), were usually used for collecting and storing data. In large-scale distributed systems, some drawbacks and limitations of all these existing storage structures are observed.

On highly scalable computing clusters, concurrency and throughput for each server are essential for the applications, but current systems lack these features. Improving data access is a way to improve the data intensive computing performance [21]. Data access needs to be improved by including the replication of data, distribution of data, relocation of data, and parallel access.

6.4.3.2 Data Management

The traditional methods of managing structured data includes two important parts. One is a schema to store the dataset and another is a relational database for data retrieval. Data warehouse and data marts are the two standard approaches for managing large-scale structured datasets. SQL is used to perform operations on relational structured data. Data warehouse is used to store, analyze, and report the outcomes to users. Access and analysis of the data obtained from a warehouse is enabled by a data mart.

> To overcome the rigidity of normalized RDBMS schemas, big data system accepts NoSQL. NOSQL is a method to manage and store unstructured and non-relational data, also known as "Not Only SQL" [19], for example, HBase database.
>
> Since SQL is simpler and is a reliable query language, many big data analytical platforms, such as SQL stream, Impala, and Cloudera, still use SQL in their database systems.
>
> NoSQL employs many approaches to store and manage unstructured data. Data storage and management are controlled independent to each other to improve the scalability of data storage and low-level access mechanism in data management. However, the schema-free structure of NoSQL database allows applications to dynamically change the structures of tables and data are not needed to rewrite. Apache Cassandra [7] is the most popular NoSQL database used by many businesses, such as Twitter, LinkedIn, and Netflix. Updating the developments and deployments of applications, NoSQL provides very flexible methods and is also used for data modeling.

6.4.3.3 Data Analysis

According to Moore's law, to cope with increasing data size, researchers gave more attention to speeding up the analysis algorithms. As the data size increases significantly faster than the CPU speed, there is a remarkable change in processor technology, even though processors are doubling the clock cycle frequency. It is essential to develop on-line, sampling, and multi-resolution analysis means. On the other hand, development of parallel computing is required with increasing numbers of cores in processors. Large clusters of processors, distributed computing, and cloud computing are developed fast to aggregate several different workloads.

In real-time applications like navigation, social networks, finance, biomedicine, astronomy, intelligent transport systems, and IoT, speed is the top priority. It is still a big challenge to be addressed for stream processing by giving quick and appropriate replies when large amounts of data need to be processed in a short span of time.

6.4.3.3.1 Algorithms for Big Data Analysis

In big data analysis, data mining algorithms play a dynamic role in determining the cost of computation, requirement of memory, and accuracy of final results. Problems associated with large data generation have been appearing since the last decade. Fan and Bifet defined [35] the terms big data and big data mining for representing large datasets and knowledge extraction methods from large data, respectively. Many machine learning algorithms play a major role in solving big data analysis tasks. Data mining, machine learning algorithms, and their importance in big data analytics are described as follows:

1. **Clustering algorithms:** In data clustering, many challenges are emerging in addressing the characteristics of big data. One of the important issues that need to be addressed in big data clustering is how to reduce the data complexity. Big data clustering is divided into two groups [36]: (i) single-machine clustering using sampling and dimension reduction solutions and (ii) multiple-machine clustering using parallel and Map Reduce solutions [37]. Using sampling and dimension reduction methods, complexity and memory space required for data analytical processes will be reduced.

   Inappropriate data and dimensions are discarded before data analysis process starts. To reduce the data size for data analysis processes, data sampling is used, and for reducing the whole dataset, dimension reduction is used.

   To perform the clustering process in parallel, CloudVista [38] uses cloud computing. It is a common solution for clustering big data. To handle large-scale data, CloudVista uses balanced iterative reducing and clustering using hierarchies (BRICH) and sampling methods.

2. **Classification algorithms:** Many researchers are working toward developing new classification algorithms for big data mining and transforming traditional classification algorithms for parallel computing. Classification [39] algorithms are designed in such a way that they take input data from distributed data sources and use various sets of learners to process them. Tekin et al. presented "classify or send for classification" as a novel classification algorithm.

   In the distributed data classification method, the input data should be processed in two different ways by each learner. One performs classification functions, whereas the other forwards the input data to another labeled learner. Big data classification problem improves the accuracy using these kinds of solutions.

   For example, to perform big data classification, Rebentrost et al. [40] defined a quantum-based support vector machine and showed that with $O(\log NM)$ time complexity the proposed classification algorithm can be implemented, where M represents the amount of training dataset and N is the number of dimensions.

3. **Association rules and sequential pattern mining algorithms:** The early methods of pattern mining were tried to analyze the transaction data of large shopping malls. At the beginning, many researches tried to use frequent pattern mining methods for processing big datasets. FP-tree (frequent-pattern tree) [41] uses the tree structure to reduce the computation time of association rule mining. Further, Map Reduce method was used in the frequent pattern mining algorithms to improve its performance [42,43]. Big data analysis using the Map Reduce model significantly improves the performance of these methods compared to old-style frequent pattern mining algorithms running on a single machine.

4. **Machine learning algorithms for big data:** Machine learning algorithms [44,45] typically work as the "search" algorithms for required solutions and are used for different mining and analysis problems compared to data mining methods. To find a fairly accurate solution for the optimization problem, machine learning algorithms are used. For example, machine learning algorithms and genetic algorithms can also be used to resolve the frequent pattern mining problems as they are used to solve the clustering problems. Improving the performance of the other parts of knowledge discovery in databases (KDD), the potential of machine learning is used as input operators feature reduction.

The consequences indicate that machine learning algorithms have become the essential parts of big data analytics. Subsequently, many statistical methods, data mining algorithms, data processing solutions, graphical user interfaces, and several descriptive tools also play major role in big data platforms.

6.4.3.4 Security for Big Data

To improve data security, data protection laws are implemented by several developed and developing countries. Intellectual property protection, financial information protection, personal privacy protection, and commercial secrets are major security issues. Data security is difficult as large amounts of data are generated due to the digitization in various sectors. Hence, the big data security challenges in many applications to protect the increasing distributed nature of big data need to be addressed in future research work. It is even more complex to identify the threats that can intensify the problems from anywhere in the big data network.

6.4.3.5 Visualization of Data

Information hidden in large and complex datasets can easily be conveyed in both functionality and visual forms. The challenges in data visualization [46] are to represent facts more instinctively and effectively by using distinct patterns, graphs, and visualization techniques. For valuable data analysis, information should be abstracted in some schematic form from complex datasets, and it should include variables or attributes for the units of information.

To extract and understand the hidden insights from the data, e-commerce companies, such as eBay and Amazon, use big data visualization tools, such as Tableau [47]. This tool helps to convert large complex datasets into interactive results and intuitive pictures. For example, data about thousands of customers, goods sold, feedback, and their inclinations. However, there are many challenges in the current visualization tools, such as scalability, functionalities, and response time that can be addressed in future work.

6.5 Tools and Technologies for Big Data Processing

The extensive changes in big data technologies come with remarkable challenges, with the need of innovative methods and techniques of big data analytics. Many new methods and techniques are developed by data scientists to capture, store, manage, process, analyze, and visualize the big data. Multidisciplinary methods such as statistics, math, machine learning, and data mining [48,49] are applied to unearth most valuable pieces from big data. This topic is followed by a brief discussion on some of the important tools and technologies developed for processing big data.

There are three classifications on which the current technologies are built: batch processing, stream processing, and interactive analysis tools and technologies. Most batch processing technologies, such as Map Reduce [2] and Dryad [50], are based on Hadoop. Storm and S4 [51] are examples of stream processing tools usually used for real-time analytics for streaming data. The third category is interactive analysis where the data analytics is done interactively with the user inputs. The user can interact in real time and can review, compare, and analyze the data in graphic or tabular form or both at a time. Examples of interactive analysis tools are Google's Dremel [52] and Apache Drill. Tools of each category are discussed in the following Sections 6.5.1–6.5.5.

Hadoop was developed by Yahoo for large-scale computation, and later it was taken over by the Apache Foundation. The framework was based on the Google's Map Reduce system and Google File System [53]. The initial version of Hadoop lacks the capability to access and process the huge volume of data with the commodity hardware in a distributed environment. To make the computation layer more robust, it is separated from storage layers. The storage layer, named Hadoop distributed file system (HDFS), is capable of storing huge amounts of unstructured data in large clusters of commodity hardware, and the Map Reduce computation structure is built on top of the HDFS for data parallel applications. A complete

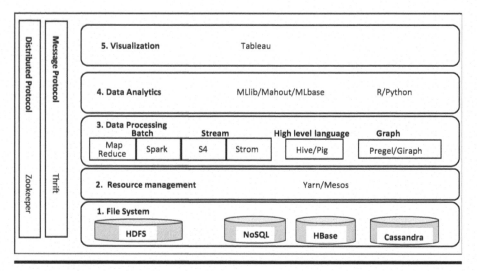

Figure 6.3   Hadoop stack.

stack of big data tools was built on Hadoop by Apache to support different applications as shown in Figure 6.3. The later version of Hadoop is called Apache YARN in which a new layer, called resource management layer, is added for efficient utilization of resources in clusters of big data.

There are five layers in big data systems (Figure 6.3). Distributed file storage is the bottom layer for storing large distributed data, above which there is a cluster resource management layer. The purpose of this layer is to manage large clusters of hardware resources and to allow the upper layers to utilize the resources efficiently. The data stored in distributed file systems are processed by the data processing layer as batch, stream, or graph processing. Preprocessed data is fed to the data analytic layer to analyze and extract more valuable information. To represent valuable results, high-level abstractions are built in the visualization layer.

6.5.1 Tools

6.5.1.1 Thrift

Thrift is a scalable cross-language services library and code generation tool set to support scalable back-end services. Its major goal is to provide efficient and reliable communication across different programming languages by selecting portions of each language that require the most modification into a common library and finally implementing them in each language. Thrift [54] supports many languages such as Haskell, Java, C++, Perl, C#, Ruby, Cocoa, Python, D, Delphi, Erlang, OCaml, PHP, and Smalltalk.

6.5.1.2 *ZooKeeper*

Yahoo developed a distributed coordination system called ZooKeeper [8], and later, it was taken over by the Apache Software Foundation. To coordinate the distributed applications, it offers an integrated service. ZooKeeper provides the following support for distributed coordination:

- **Sequential consistency**: Client updates are made in an orderly manner as they are sent.
- **Atomicity**: All the updates should be complete. No partial updates are allowed.
- **Single system**: Distributed ZooKeeper system has a single system image for clients.
- **Reliability**: The updates are more persistent and more reliable.

The capabilities of ZooKeeper can be used by applications to build functions with higher level of controls, such as read/write maintainable locks, queues, hurdles, and leader.

6.5.1.3 *Hadoop DFS*

HDFS is a hierarchical file system consisting [55] of directories and files similar to a UNIX file system. Users can perform all the administrative and manipulation operations such as create, delete, copy, save, and move files to the HDFS as in a normal UNIX system.

HDFS architecture: HDFS architecture consists of two units: a single name node and multiple data nodes. Name node is a local file system responsible for managing the file system namespace and tracks. Edit log keeps track of the logs and updates whenever changes are made to the file system. Additionally, it keeps track of all the blocks in the file system assigned to data nodes and mapping of blocks to data nodes.

Name nodes are replicated for fault tolerance. To manage a large number of files, file systems are divided into a number of blocks and are saved on data nodes. The operations on files and directories such as opening, closing, and renaming are performed by the name node. Mapping of blocks to data nodes is tracked by the name node. The client directly communicates to the data nodes by obtaining a list of files from the name node to read a file.

Block report is used to manage the copies of files. A separate file is created for each block stored in the local file system by the data node. It also creates directories for dividing the files belonging to different applications.

Fault tolerance in HDFS: HDFS replicates the files into blocks and keeps them in different data nodes for fault tolerance. The name node uses the replicated copy of blocks to process the requested data chunk if any data node goes down.

6.5.2 Resource Management

Clusters of commodity servers are cost-efficient solutions for intensive scientific computations and are used for running large Internet services. The issues of traditional resource management for Hadoop and Storm are described in two aspects: First, a system that runs Hadoop or Storm should be commodity hardware. Second, Hadoop requires a lot of configurations and scheduling to support fine-grained tasks.

To address these issues of traditional resource management system, new tools such as YARN [56] and Mesos [57] are introduced.

- **YARN:** It offers a resource management structure in cluster for better resource utilization. Before introducing YARN into the Hadoop framework, the cluster is partitioned to share the resources and different frameworks are run on these partitions. But this was not a promising way of efficient resource utilization. Hence, YARN was introduced in Hadoop V2.0 to handle diverse computational frameworks on the same cluster.
- **Mesos:** It is another cluster resource manager that supports processing frameworks such as Hadoop, Spark, Storm, and Hypertable run on shared cluster environments.

The abovementioned two resource management approaches are compared in terms of their design and scheduling work.

Mesos first finds free and available resources and then calls the application scheduler. This model includes a two-level scheduler with pluggable scheduling algorithms and is called a non-monolithic model. Mesos supports an unlimited number of scheduling algorithms, thus allowing thousands of schedulers to run as multi-tenants on the same cluster. Each structure has the flexibility of deciding the algorithms that are used to schedule the tasks to be run.

However, in Apache YARN, when a job request arrives, it tries to approximate the available resource and schedules the job accordingly in a monolithic model. YARN is improved for scheduling Hadoop jobs, typically batch jobs, with a long running time. It does not handle DFSs or database services. Combining the new algorithms, the scheduling program allows YARN to handle different types of workloads.

6.5.3 NoSQL Database: Unstructured Data Management

NoSQL database is used to manage unstructured, complex, nested, and hierarchical data structures [18,19]. As relational database systems are no longer capable of handling the unstructured data or they need a lot of manipulations, it is not a good solution for big data analytics. There is a dramatic change in the requirements of database management with the evolution of interactive web applications and smartphone applications. The need of high-performance data computing, availability, and scalability is fulfilled by the NoSQL database. It is a schema-less design and does not need to follow any format like the tables in a relation database.

6.5.3.1 Apache HBase

HBase is stimulated by the Google Bigtable application [4]. It is built on HDFS and is a multidimensional, distributed, column-oriented data storage method. It provides faster access to records and updates for the data tables. It uses HDFS to store the data and ZooKeeper framework for distributed coordination. Row key, column key, and a timestamp are used for distributed index mapping in the HBase multidimensional data model. The row keys are used for organizing the mapping. Each row has its unique key, and a set of columns and number of columns are added dynamically to the column families.

6.5.3.2 Apache Cassandra

Apache Cassandra [7] was developed by Facebook and is based on a peer-to-peer distributed key-value store construct. Cassandra is a row-oriented data model where all nodes are treated as equal. Cassandra is suitable for real-time applications where a large data needs to be handled with a faster random access.

Three orthogonal properties called consistency, availability, and partition tolerance (CAP) [58] are considered to develop distributed applications. It is difficult to satisfy all three properties together to have tolerable latency for the operations, according to the CAP theorem. By loosening the value of strong consistency to subsequent consistency, Cassandra satisfies two properties, high availability and partition acceptance. Cassandra uses partitioning and replication similar to the Amazon Dynamo database model.

Architecture: Cassandra data model is based on the design of Google Bigtable. The data model is partitioned into a number of rows, and each row contains a number of columns. Similar to SQL, Cassandra offers a query language CQL (Cassandra Query language). Tables are designed to hold duplicates of the data, but CQL does not support join operations. For faster access to data values, Cassandra present indexes on columns.

6.5.4 Data Processing

Basic data processing frameworks are divided into batch mode, stream mode, or graph processing and interactive analysis mode based on their processing methods and speed. The resource managers, Mesos and YARN, manage these runtime systems in clusters at the lower layers. Unstructured data from HDFS as well as structured data from NoSQL are used as an input to these systems. Output of these structures are redirected to these storage layers or cached for performing analytics and visualization on it.

6.5.4.1 Batch Processing

Batch processing is suitable for processing large amounts of data stored in batches. Hadoop Map Reduce is a basic model introduced to process huge amounts of data in batch. However, it is not suitable for all kinds of batch processing tasks such as iterative processing. To overcome some of these disadvantages, new processing models, Spark and Apache Hama, are presented.

1. **Hadoop**

   Hadoop is a distributed processing framework to processes big datasets over groups of computers [16] using simple programming models. It is planned and designed for scale-up from single servers to thousands of machines. The role of each computer is to provide storage and local computation, instead of depending on hardware, to provide high-availability. Machine learning libraries are designed and modified to handle failures at the application layer, hence providing an extensive service on top of the clusters.

   Hadoop framework was introduced and published by Google, illustrating its method to manage and process a large data. Afterward, Hadoop is the typical structure for storing, processing, and analyzing terabytes to exabyte of data. As Doug Cutting started developing Hadoop, the framework got its name "Hadoop" from his son's toy elephant.

   Yahoo is a main contributor to Hadoop advancement. Using 10,000-core Hadoop clusters, by 2008, Yahoo's web search engine index was generated. It was developed to run on local hardware, and without any system intervention, it can scale up and down. Three important functions of Hadoop framework are storage, resource management, and processing.

   – **Hadoop Map Reduce (prior to version 2.0):** Hadoop Map Reduce structure consists of three main components: HDFS, job tracker (master), and task tracker (slave). HDFS is used to store and share the data among Map Reduce jobs computational tasks. First, the job tracker reads the input data from the HDFS and splits it into partitions to run map tasks on each input partition, and the intermediate results are stored in the local file system. Second, reduce tasks read the intermediate results from map tasks and run the reduced code on it. The results of the reduce phase are saved in HDFS.

   – **Hadoop Map Reduce Version 2.0:** A new version of Map Reduce introduces the resource allocation and scheduling tool, Apache YARN [59]. Task tracker is replaced by YARN node managers. To keep track of the finished jobs, job history server is a new added feature to the architecture.

Initially, clients request YARN for the resources required for their jobs. The resource manager assigns a place to execute the master task on jobs.

- **Hadoop characteristics:**
    1. **Fault tolerant:** The Hadoop cluster is highly prone to failures as thousands of nodes are running on the commodity hardware. However, data redundancy and data replication are implied to achieve fault tolerance.
    2. **Redundancy of data:** Hadoop divides data into many blocks and stores them across two or more data nodes to improve the redundancy. The master node preserves information of these nodes and data mapping.
    3. **To scale up and scale down:** The distributed nature of Hadoop file system allows Hadoop to scale up and scale down by adding or deleting the number of nodes required in the cluster.
    4. **Computations moved to data:** Queries are computed on data nodes locally and the results are obtained by combining them in parallel to avoid the overhead of bringing the data to the computational environment.

2. Spark

Spark was built on top of HDFS as an open-source project [60] by the University of Berkley to address the issues of Hadoop Map Reduce. The objective of the system is to support iterative computation and increase the speed of distributed parallel processing to overcome the limitations of Hadoop Map Reduce.

In-memory fault-tolerant data structure, resilient distributed datasets (RDDs), was introduced by [61,62] the Berkeley University for efficient data sharing across parallel computations. It supports batch, iterative, interactive, and streaming in the same runtime with significantly high performance. It also allows applications to scaled up and scale down with efficient sharing of data. Spark differs from Hadoop by supporting simple *join* and *group-by* basic operations.

Spark with RDDs runs applications with 100 times faster in memory and 10 times faster on disk compared to Hadoop Map Reduce.

Spark overcomes some of the limitations of Hadoop as follows:

1. **Iterative algorithms:** Spark allows applications and users to explicitly cache data by calling the cache () operation, so that subsequent queries can use intermediate results stored at the cache and provide dramatic improvements in time and memory utilization.
2. **Streaming data:** Spark offers an application programming interface to process the streaming data. It also gives an opportunity to design methods to process real-time streaming data with minimum latency.

3. **Reuse intermediate results:** Instead of saving output to the disk every time, it is cached to reuse for other computations, thus reducing the time. RDDs are fault tolerant as they record the modifications and use them to rebuild a lost copy of dataset rather than the actual data. If any slice of RDD crashes, it stores sufficient information for recomputation and recovery without demanding costly replication.
4. Unlike Hadoop, Spark is not only limited to iterative Map and Reduce tasks that need an implicit group-by. Further, map phase should need serialization and disk I/O call in each iteration. RDDs are basically in-memory cache aids to avoid frequent serialization and I/O overhead.

6.5.4.2 Distributed Stream Processing

Apache Storm [63] and Apache S4 [51] are the two main distributed stream processing tools. Twitter built Apache Storm and Yahoo developed S4 "Simple Scalable Streaming System" for real-time stream processing.

1. **Storm**
   Storm is an open-source distributed real-time computation framework, dedicated to stream processing. It offers a fault-tolerant mechanism to execute computation on an event as it runs into a system.
   Using Apache Storm, it is easy to process real-time streaming [63] data. It has many useful applications, such as real-time analytics, online machine learning, continuous computation, distributed RPC (remote procedure call), and ETL (extract, transform, and load). Storm is easy to set up and operate. It is also scalable and fault tolerant. Storm typically does not run on top of Hadoop clusters, and it uses Apache ZooKeeper and its own master worker processes to manage topologies.
2. **S4**
   S4 offers a modest programing model [51] for programmers and offers an ease and efficient automated distributed execution, for example, automatic load balancing. On the other hand, in Storm, the programmer should take care of load balancing, adjusting size of the buffer, and the level of parallelism for getting optimum performance.

6.5.4.3 Graph Processing

The earlier method of graph processing on top of Map Reduce was inefficient as it took entire graphs as input and processed them and then wrote the complete updated graph into the disk. Pregel [64], Giraph [65], and many other systems are developed for efficient graph processing and to overcome the limitations of Map Reduce.

1. **Pregel**

   Pregel was constructed on the bulk synchronous parallel model (BSP) [64] as a graph processing parallel system. In the BSP model, a set of processors that are interconnected by a communication network follow a different set of computation threads in which individual processors are armed with a fast local memory. The platform based on the BSP model consists of the following three important mechanisms:
   - Trained system for processing local memory transactions (i.e., processors)
   - Efficient networks for communication between these systems
   - A hardware support for synchronization between the systems

2. **Apache Giraph**

   Giraph is developed on top of Apache Hadoop for graph processing. Giraph is built on Pregel for distributed processing of a graph [65]. Pregel is built on top of Apache Hadoop, and it runs into map tasks of Map Reduce. To coordinate between its tasks, Pregel uses Apache ZooKeeper, and for inter-node communications, it uses Netty. A set of vertices and edges are used to represent a graph in Giraph. Vertices perform computational tasks and connections are represented by edges. Compared to Giraph, Pregel is used for very large-scale graph processing.

6.5.4.4 High-Level Languages for Data Processing

To retrieve the information from huge amounts of data stored in HDFS and NoSQL database, small batch jobs were used by programmers. The high-level languages enable programmers to easily access the data stored in HDFS or NoSQL database. Pig and Hive are examples of high-level languages for data processing.

1. **PIG**

   It is a procedure-oriented high-level programming language developed by Yahoo for scripting Hadoop Map Reduce jobs. The language is also called Pig Latin. Data pipelines are represented in a more usual way as it is a procedure-oriented language. Due to its procedural nature PIG is suitable for iterative data processing, data pipeline applications, and transformation jobs, and is best suited for processing unstructured data.

   A major advantage of PIG [66] compared to a declarative language is that one can have control and check the operations performed over the data. In declarative languages, programmers must have a good knowledge of the algorithms and data operations and should also have knowledge on query optimizer to choose the appropriate query to process the data.

2. **Hive**

   Hive [67] is developed on Hadoop as a high-level language to perform analytics on big data. It supports large amounts of structured data processing. It offers a method to map a structure of the data stored in HDFS and query it by using a query language such as HiveQL. Like SQL in RDBMS, HiveQL is a query language for Hadoop systems to query large-scale structured data. The queries are sometimes compiled to Map Reduce jobs to read the data. Whereas simple queries are run directly without map reduce to read the data from HDFS. To maintain the metadata about tables, Hive uses RDBMS tables. In JDBC, Hive JDBC drivers are used to access the tables created by Hive, making them available for a rich set of operations supported by Java.

6.5.5 Data Analytics at the Speed Layer

Standard data analytical methods are developed using machine learning and data mining algorithms for specific applications [4,44,68]. Advancing these methods is necessary for optimizing the performance of analytical tasks for large-scale data. Machine learning libraries are built to archive different machine learning algorithms to apply for different applications on the speed layer.

1. **Mahout**
   Mahout is a set of machine learning algorithm library [4] built on Hadoop Map Reduce to support various analytical tasks. It also aims to include various algorithms for machine learning on different distributed systems. Mahout library includes several algorithms for various tasks as shown in Table 6.2.
2. **MLlib**
   It is a machine learning library developed on Spark [9,68] that consists of a set of machine learning algorithms, as shown in Table 6.3, for classification and clustering, regression analysis, and collaborative filtering.

   A summary of the chapter on relational data and big data analytical methods and technologies is presented in Table 6.4 and Figure 6.4. An overview of characteristics and tools and technologies for managing structured and unstructured data is represented in the form of a flowchart to easily understand the overview of bog data tools and technologies. It also shows the

Table 6.2 Algorithms in Mahout

Algorithms	Task
Naive Bayes, neural networks, boosting, logistic regression	Classification
Hierarchical clustering, canopy clustering, *k*-means, fuzzy *k*-means, spectral clustering, minimum hash clustering, top-down clustering, mean shift clustering	Clustering
Frequent item mining	Pattern mining

Table 6.3   Algorithms of MLlib

Algorithms	Task
Logistic regression, linear support vector machines	Binary classifications
Linear regression, L1 (lasso) regression, L2 (ridge) regularized	Regression
k-means	Clustering
Alternating least squares	Collaborative filtering

area of applications for which big data technology and relational database are suitable.

6.6   Future Work and Conclusion

6.6.1   Future Work on Real-Time Data Analytics

In earlier days, producing a result by processing petabyte of data in an hour was a challenging task. Nowadays, technological progresses have made it possible to see the results in a minute. Advancement of data analytics and computational intelligence made it possible to think about questions and get answers in a fraction of seconds.

Introduction of big data technology improves and supports data-driven decision-making from large-scale data. However, applications of big data analytics are currently bound by significant latency. Many of the above big data technologies need to advance toward real-time analytics. The challenging task is to find results on time or in a fraction of seconds. The challenges further intensify when data is related with other data.

The focus of big data analytics so far is to collect previously unused data, store it in a database, and manage, preprocess, and analyze the data to find new insights. However, the main objective of real-time big data analytics [29] is to process and analyze continuously generating, randomly changing, streaming data. It will be challenging to store all the data and events and get answers within a fraction of seconds. Therefore, real-time big data analytics systems should process data by sampling events without losing any valuable information from the data.

Fast processing and analysis for making quick decisions is important for real-time big data analytics. So, future research work in this direction will give better predictions and actionable decisions in real time. Real-time analytics of big data finds its application in numerous areas including finance, health care, fraud detection, finance industry, and social media.

Table 6.4 Relational and Big Data Tools and Technologies

Data	Characteristics	Storage and Management	Tools	Data Processing	Analytics	Visualization	Application
Relational data (structured data)	Atomicity, consistency, isolation, and durability [14]	DBMS, data warehouse, data mart	SQL	On-line transaction processing (OLTP), On-line analytical processing (OLAP)	Data mining, clustering, classification	Graph, chart	Employee details management, hospital management, insurance company
Big data (unstructured data)	Volume, velocity, veracity, verity [17]	HDFS (DFS)	NoSQL [19] HBase [4] Cassandra [7]	Batch: Hadoop Map reduce [2] Spark [60]	Mathematic: Statistics, Fundamental Mathematics	Tableau (Jason Brooks, 2016) R TOOL PYTHON	Social media computing, health care, government, finance, business, and enterprise
		Coordinator: ZooKeeper Thrift		Stream: S4 Storm	Data analysis: Data mining Machine learning; MLlib Mahout neural networks		Text analytics, web analytics, stream analytics, predictive analytics

(Continued)

Table 6.4 (Continued) Relational and Big Data Tools and Technologies

Data	Characteristics	Storage and Management	Tools	Data Processing	Analytics	Visualization	Application
		Resource management: (job scheduling) YARN Mesos		Graph: Giraph Pregel			
				High-level languages: Pig Hive			

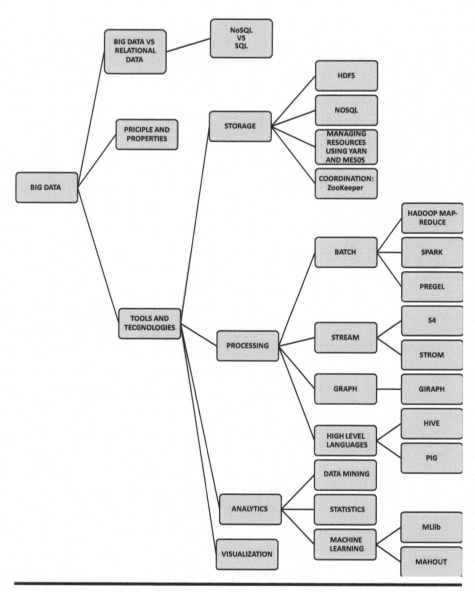

Figure 6.4 Flow chart of big data analytical tools and technologies.

6.6.2 *Conclusion*

Enormous amounts of data are generated with increasing speed in different formats due to digitization around the world. Big data technology will definitely enter every domain, enterprise, and organization. Traditional database management system fails to scale for growing data needs such as multiple partitioning and parallelizing abilities. It is also incapable of storing, managing, and analyzing unstructured data generated from different sources such as sensors, smart applications, wearable technologies, smartphones, and social networking websites. Evolution of big data analytics and tools and technologies made it possible to efficiently handle huge unstructured growing data. One of the most popular open source frameworks, Hadoop, is a generally recognized system for large-scale data analytics. It is mainly known and accepted for support in large-scale distributed parallel computing of clusters, and is cost-effective, fault tolerant, reliable, and provides highly scalable support for processing and managing terabyte to petabyte of data. However, it is not suitable for real-time data analytics. To overcome the incapability of this earlier version of Hadoop system for real-time analytics, a new framework was introduced, known as Spark. To support real-time analytics, Spark with RDDs gives results in a fraction of seconds. Several areas such as business, social media, government, health care, and security are implementing big data technologies to gain knowledge from previously unused data to make better decisions and predictions. In the future, it will be motivating to overcome the drawbacks of the Spark and Hadoop systems and work toward real-time analytics. The challenges in batch processing and stream processing analytical systems also need to be addressed in the future work.

References

1. McKinsey & Company. "Big Data: The Next Frontier for Innovation, Competition, and Productivity." *McKinsey Global Institute*, p. 156, June 2011.
2. J. Dean and S. Ghemawat. "MapReduce." *Communications of the ACM*, vol. 51, no. 1, p. 107, January 2008.
3. "Apache Spark™—Lightning-Fast Cluster Computing." http://spark.apache.org/ (Accessed January 25, 2017).
4. A. Duque Barrachina and A. O'Driscoll. "A Big Data Methodology for Categorising Technical Support Requests using Hadoop and Mahout." *Journal of Big Data*, vol. 1, p. 1, 2014.
5. F. Aronsson. "Large Scale Cluster Analysis with Hadoop and Mahout." February 2015.
6. N. Marz and J. Warren. "Big Data—Principles and Best Practices of Scalable Realtime Data Systems." *Harvard Business Review*, vol. 37, pp. 1–303, 2013.
7. L. Avinash and P. Malik. "Cassandra: A Decentralized Structured Storage System." *ACM SIGOPS Operating Systems Review*, pp. 1–6, 2010.
8. F. Junqueira and B. Reed. *ZooKeeper: Distributed Process Coordination*. O'Reilly Media, Inc., 2013.
9. X. Meng, J. Bradley, S. Street, S. Francisco, E. Sparks, U. C. Berkeley, S. Hall, S. Street, S. Francisco, D. Xin, R. Xin, M. J. Franklin, U. C. Berkeley, and S. Hall. "MLlib: Machine Learning in Apache Spark." *Journal of Machine Learning Research*, vol. 17, pp. 1–7, 2016.
10. C. Lynch. "Big Data: How Do Your Data Grow?" Nature, 2008.
11. "Welcome to Apache™ Hadoop®!" http://hadoop.apache.org/ (Accessed January 25, 2017).
12. T. White. *Hadoop: The Definitive Guide.* O'Reilly Media, Inc., 2012.

13. K. Mayer-Schönberger, V. and Cukier. *Big Data*: A *Revolution* that *Will Transform How We Live, Work,* and *Think.* Boston, MA: Houghton Mifflin Harcourt, 2013.
14. E. F. Codd. "A relational Model of Data for Large Shared Data Banks." *Communications of the ACM*, vol. 26, no. 6, pp. 64–69, 1983.
15. T. Haerder and A. Reuter. "Principles of Transaction-Oriented Database Recovery." *ACM Computing Surveys*, vol. 15, no. 4, pp. 287–317, 1983.
16. P. Zikopoulos and C. Eaton. *Understanding Big Data: Analytics for Enterprise Class Hadoop and Streaming Data.* McGraw-Hill Osborne Media, 2011.
17. D. Laney. "META Delta." *Application Delivery Strategies*, vol. 949, p. 4, 2001.
18. R. Cattell. "Scalable SQL and NoSQL Data Stores." *ACM SIGMOD Record*, vol. 39, no. 4, p. 12, May 2011.
19. J. Han, E. Haihong, G. Le, and J. Du. "Survey on NoSQL Database." In *2011 6th* International Conference on Pervasive Computing and Applications (ICPCA), Port Elizabeth, South Africa, 2011.
20. D. Borthakur. "The Hadoop Distributed File System: Architecture and Design." Hadoop Project Website, 2007.
21. G. Bell, T. Hey, and A. Szalay. "Beyond the Data Deluge." *Science*, vol. 323, pp. 1297–1298, 2009.
22. E. Al Nuaimi, H. Al Neyadi, N. Mohamed, and J. Al-jaroodi. "Applications of Big Data to Smart Cities." *Journal of Internet Services and Applications*, vol. 6, no. 1, p. 25, 2015.
23. H. Chen, R. Chiang, and V. Storey. "Business Intelligence and Analytics: From Big Data to Big Impact." MIS *Quarterly*, 2012.
24. T. Huang, L. Lan, X. Fang, P. An, J. Min, and F. Wang. "Promises and Challenges of Big Data Computing in Health Sciences." *Big Data Research*, vol. 2, no. 1, pp. 2–11, 2015.
25. W. Raghupathi and V. Raghupathi. "Big Data Analytics in Healthcare: Promise and Potential." *Health Information Science and Systems*, vol. 2, no. 1, p. 3, 2014.
26. S. Kumar and A. Prakash. "Role of Big Data and Analytics in Smart Cities." *International Journal of Science and Research*, vol. 5, no. 2, pp. 12–23, 2016.
27. L. Garber. "Using In-Memory Analytics to Quickly Crunch Big Data." *Computer*, vol. 45, no. 10, pp. 16–18, October 2012.
28. M. Özsu and P. Valduriez. Principles of *Distributed Database Systems.* Springer Science & Business Media, 2011.
29. S. Shahrivari. "Beyond Batch Processing: Towards Real-Time and Streaming Big Data." *Computers*, vol. 3, no. 4, pp. 117–129, 2014.
30. J. Friedman, T. Hastie, and R. Tibshirani. *The Elements of Statistical Learning.* Vol. 1, New York, NY: Springer series in statics, 2001.
31. R. Irfan, C.K. King, D. Grages, S. Ewen, S.U. Khan, S.A. Madani, J. Kolodziej, et al. "A Survey on Text Mining in Social Networks." *The Knowledge Engineering Review*, vol. 30, no. 2, pp. 157–170, 2015.
32. R. Bekkerman, M. Bilenko, and J. Langford. *Scaling Up Machine Learning: Parallel and Distributed Approaches.* Cambridge: Cambridge University Press, 2011.
33. A. Gandomi and M. Haider. "Beyond the Hype: Big Data Concepts, Methods, and Analytics." *International Journal of Information Management*, vol. 35, no. 2, pp. 137–144, April 2015.
34. J. Ahrens, B. Hendrickson, G. Long, and S. Miller. "Data-intensive Science in the US DOE: Case Studies and Future Challenges." *Computing in Science & Engineering*, vol. 13, no. 6, pp. 14–24, 2011.
35. W. Fan and A. Bifet. "Mining Big Data : Current Status, and Forecast to the Future." *ACM SIGKDD Explorations Newsletter*, vol. 14, no. 2, pp. 1–5, 2013.

36. A. Shirkhorshidi, S. Aghabozorgi, T. Wah, and T. Herawan. "Big Data Clustering: A Review." In *International Conference on Computational Science and Its Applications*, LNCS, vol. 8583. Cham: Springer, 2014.

37. W. Kim. "Parallel Clustering Algorithms: Survey." *Parallel Algorithms*, Spring 2009.

38. H. Xu, Z. Li, S. Guo, and K. Chen. "Cloudvista: Interactive and Economical Visual Cluster Analysis for Big Data in the Cloud." *Journal Proceedings of the VLDB Endowment*, vol. 5, no. 12, pp. 1886–1889, 2012.

39. C. Tekin and M. van der Schaar. "Distributed Online Big Data Classification using Context Information." In *2013 51st Annual Allerton Conference on Communication, Control, and Computing*, Allerton, IL, 2013.

40. P. Rebentrost, M. Mohseni, and S. Lloyd. "Quantum Support Vector Machine for Big Data Classification." *Physical Review Letters*, vol. 113, no. 13, pp. 1–5, 2014.

41. J. Ayres, J. Flannick, J. Gehrke, and T. Yiu. "Sequential Pattern Mining Using a Bitmap Representation." In *Proceedings of the* Eighth *ACM SIGKDD International Conference on Knowledge Discovery and Data Mining*, Edmonton, Canada, 2002.

42. M. Lin, P. Lee, and S. Hsueh. "Apriori-based Frequent Itemset Mining Algorithms on MapReduce." In *Proceedings of the 6th International Conference on Ubiquitous Information Management and Communication*, Kuala Lumpur, Malaysia, 2012.

43. C. Leung and R. MacKinnon. "Reducing the Search Space for Big Data Mining for Interesting Patterns from Uncertain Data." big data (BigData), 2014.

44. T. Kraska, U. C. Berkeley, U. C. Berkeley, R. Griffith, M. J. Franklin, U. C. Berkeley, and U. C. Berkeley. "MLbase : A Distributed Machine-learning System." *CIDR*, vol. 1, pp. 1–2, 2013.

45. M. Mehta, R. Agrawal, and J. Rissanen. "SLIQ: A Fast Scalable Classifier for Data Mining." In *International Conference on Extending Database Technology*, pp. 18–32, Berlin, Heidelberg: Springer, 1996.

46. D. Keim, C. Panse, and M. Sips. "Visual Data Mining in Large Geospatial Point Sets." *IEEE Computer Graphics and Applications*, vol. 24, no. 5, pp. 36–44, 2004.

47. "Data Visualization | Tableau Software." www.tableau.com/stories/topic/data-visualization (Accessed January 25, 2017).

48. A. Di Ciaccio, M. Coli, and J. Ibanez. *Advanced Statistical Methods for the Analysis of Large Data-sets*. Springer Science & Business Media, 2012.

49. X. Wu, V. Kumar, J. Ross Quinlan, J. Ghosh, Q. Yang, H. Motoda, G. J. McLachlan, A. Ng, B. Liu, P. S. Yu, Z.-H. Zhou, M. Steinbach, D. J. Hand, and D. Steinberg. "Top 10 Algorithms in Data Mining," *Knowledge and Information Systems*, vol. 14, no. 1, pp. 1–37, January 2008.

50. M. Isard, M. Budiu, Y. Yu, A. Birrell, and D. Fetterly. "Dryad." In *Proceedings of the 2nd ACM SIGOPS/EuroSys European Conference on Computer Systems 2007—EuroSys'07*, New York, NY, p. 59, 2007.

51. L. Neumeyer, B. Robbins, and A. Nair. "S4: Distributed Stream Computing Platform." Data Mining Workshops, 2010.

52. S. Melnik, A. Gubarev, J. J. Long, G. Romer, S. Shivakumar, M. Tolton, and T. Vassilakis. "Dremel: Interactive Analysis of Web-Scale Datasets." In *36th International Conference on Very Large Data Bases*, pp. 330–339, 2010.

53. S. Ghemawat, H. Gobioff, and S. Leung. "Google_File_System." Vol. 37, no. 5. ACM, 2003.

54. M. Slee, A. Agarwal, and M. Kwiatkowski. "Thrift : Scalable Cross-Language Services Implementation." *Facebook White Paper*, vol. 5, no. 8, 2007.

55. K. Shvachko, H. Kuang, S. Radia, and R. Chansler. "The Hadoop Distributed File System." In *2010 IEEE 26th Symposium on Mass Storage Systems and Technologies (MSST 2010)(MSST)*, Incline Village, NV, pp. 1–10, 2010.

56. V. Vavilapalli, A. Murthy, and C. Douglas. "Apache Hadoop Yarn: Yet Another Resource Negotiator." In *Proceedings of the 4th annual Symposium on Cloud Computing, SoCC'13*, Santa Clara, CA, 2013.

57. B. Hindman, A. Konwinski, M. Zaharia, and A. Ghodsi. "Mesos: A Platform for Fine-Grained Resource Sharing in the Data Center." In *NSDI'11 Proceedings of the 8th USENIX Conference on Networked Systems Design and Implementation*, Boston, MA, 2011.

58. S. Gilbert and N. Lynch. "Perspectives on the CAP Theorem." *Computer*, vol. 45, no. 2, pp. 30–36, 2012.

59. V. K. Vavilapalli, S. Seth, B. Saha, C. Curino, O. O'Malley, S. Radia, B. Reed, E. Baldeschwieler, A. C. Murthy, C. Douglas, S. Agarwal, M. Konar, R. Evans, T. Graves, J. Lowe, and H. Shah. "Apache Hadoop YARN." In *Proceedings of the 4th Annual Symposium on Cloud Computing—SOCC'13*, pp. 1–16, New York, NY, 2013.

60. M. Zaharia, M. Chowdhury, M. J. Franklin, S. Shenker, and I. Stoica. "Spark : Cluster Computing with Working Sets." In *HotCloud'10 Proceedings of the 2nd USENIX Conference on Hot Topics in Cloud Computing*, p. 10, Boston, MA, 2010.

61. M. Zaharia, M. Chowdhury, T. Das, and A. Dave. "Resilient Distributed Datasets: A Fault-tolerant Abstraction for In-memory Cluster Computing." In *NSDI'12 Proceedings of the 9th USENIX Conference on Networked Systems Design and Implementation*, p. 2, San Jose, CA, 2012.

62. M. Zaharia. "An Architecture for Fast and General Data Processing on Large Clusters." *Berkeley Technical Report*, p. 128, 2014.

63. T. da Silva Morais. "Survey on Frameworks for Distributed Computing: Hadoop, Spark and Storm." *Proceedings of the 10th Doctoral Symposium in Informatics Engineering—DSIE'15*, vol. 15, pp. 95–105, 2015.

64. G. Malewicz, M. Austern, A. Bik, and J. Dehnert. "Pregel: A System for Large-scale Graph Processing." In *Conference: SPAA 2009: Proceedings of the 21st Annual ACM Symposium on Parallelism in Algorithms and Architectures*, Calgary, Alberta, Canada, August 11–13, 2009.

65. O. Batarfi, R. El Shawi, A. G. Fayoumi, R. Nouri, S.-M.-R. Beheshti, A. Barnawi, and S. Sakr. "Large Scale Graph Processing Systems: Survey and an Experimental Evaluation." *Cluster Computing*, vol. 18, no. 3, pp. 1189–1213, September 2015.

66. C. Olston, B. Reed, U. Srivastava, R. Kumar, and A. Tomkins. "Pig latin." In *Proceedings of the 2008 ACM SIGMOD International Conference on Management of Data—SIGMOD'08*, Vancouver, p. 1099, 2008.

67. A. Thusoo, J. Sen Sarma, N. Jain, Z. Shao, P. Chakka, S. Anthony, H. Liu, P. Wyckoff, and R. Murthy. "Hive." *Proceedings of the VLDB Endowment*, vol. 2, no. 2, pp. 1626–1629, August 2009.

68. X. Meng, J. Bradley, B. Yavuz, E. Sparks, S. Venkataraman, D. Liu, J. Freeman, D. Tsai, M. Amde, S. Owen, D. Xin, R. Xin, M. J. Franklin, R. Zadeh, M. Zaharia, and A. Talwalkar. "MLlib: Machine Learning in Apache Spark." *Journal of Machine Learning Research*, vol. 17, pp. 1–7, 2015.

Chapter 7

Big Graph Analytics: Techniques, Tools, Challenges, and Applications

Dhananjay Kumar Singh
National Institute of Technology, Durgapur

Pijush Kanti Dutta Pramanik and Prasenjit Choudhury
National Institute of Technology, Durgapur

Contents

7.1 Introduction

The attainment of Google has made the phrase "to Google" synonymous with the search for anything. The success mantra behind Google's dominance as a search engine is its ability to exploit the direct and indirect connections among the humongous amounts of data. Google has adopted the graph-centric approach to represent and model the relationships between documents and has used graph analysis techniques to understand their semantics and contexts and find out relevant information. The more vast and diverse data it can explore, the more relevant information can be extracted. With the explosion of the digital world, the amount of digital data originated from varied sources is increasing colossally. In today's world, the devices, processes, people, and other entities are becoming more connected than ever before. As the number of data sources increases, it is vital that we define the underlying relationships between them. Social media, sensors, surveillance intelligence, industrial control systems, and connected devices have become visibly important in the data-procurement scenario. With this explosive increase of global data, the term "big data" was coined and mainly used to describe huge datasets that are generated from numerous heterogeneous sources [1]. Mining and analyzing these data helps us to get an in-depth knowledge of the hidden values that bring new opportunities for discovering new values. As the variety and volume of our data increase, more sophisticated methods are required to unveil the valuable information hidden in it.

Although big data generated from diverse sources might appear to be discrete and isolated on the surface, they are all nodes of a bigger network that binds them through complex relationships. The modern big data increasingly appears in the form of large-scale complex graphs/networks. Some of the examples of massive complex networks include the World Wide Web, the physical Internet, phone networks, online social networks (OSNs), and biological networks. In addition to their big sizes, these graphs/networks are transient, noisy, and dynamic. They also conform to most of the popular V's (e.g., volume, velocity, variety) that define big data. Hence, these large-scale graph-structured data are referred to as the "big graph."

The term "graph analytics" refers exactly to the study and analysis of data that can be transformed into big graph representations.

Graph analytics is a fast-growing field in both big data mining and visualization community that is utilized for numerous multidisciplinary and high-impact applications, such as network security, finance, and health care. Even though the analysis of unstructured collections of multidimensional points has already been addressed in the past by several methods, graph analytic technologies form a rather recent trend and they pose many challenges, concerning not only the performance of the data mining algorithms that promote knowledge discovery through algorithmic computation but also the production of effective graph visualizations in order to enhance human perception.

Graph analytics is all about modeling, storing, retrieving, and performance analysis of graph-structured data by applying a combination of statistical, graph theoretic, and graph database techniques. These techniques enable us to understand the structure of a large network and how it changes in different conditions, identify clusters/modules or closely interacting subgroups inside the graphs, find subgraphs that are similar to a given pattern, or find paths between the pairs of entities that satisfy different constraints.

The main purpose of graph analytics is to analyze graph-structured data to find the answers to questions (e.g., Who are the most influential people in a community? What are the important infrastructure nodes in the Internet or urban networks?) for better practical actions and decision-making.

Thus, graph analytics can be used to model all sorts of relationships and processes in a wide range of applications. For instance, they can reveal the patterns across varying datasets that signal at the beginning of cyberattacks.

Graph techniques can also identify the root (cause) of surrounding or bigger events, i.e., they can help in finding the most influential people in social media. Alternatively, graph analytics can help in the identification of communities that revolve around a certain theme, i.e., it helps in detecting patterns in communication that might indicate a threat to national defense by identifying the groups of people who have been communicating about terrorist events, something security agencies and/or authorities might be interested in.

Throughout the history of computation, graph analytics has always been an interesting topic for researchers, but due to the big data movement, which has seen an increased use of the advanced analytics on huge volumes of semistructured or unstructured data, the research on big graph processing has also attracted the attention of the computer science fraternity in recent years.

In the modern digital ecosystem, the need for differently advanced graph analytics to make out something of the big data becomes more than essential as the sources, types, and the amount of data continue to expand. In this respect, the contextual impact of data and the impact of graph analytics technologies on organizations seeking to discover the cause, effect, interrelation, and the influence of events on business outcomes need to be defined. In this way, big graph analytics are not only able to identify the key insights in the big data but also able to visualize them. Moreover, they can detect correlations of the findings and determine their nature and their significance within the given environment. New tools and algorithms need to be developed regularly to help the business stakeholders optimize their key business processes and open new opportunities.

The rest of the chapter is organized as follows: Section 7.2 examines the bigness of the graph and how graphs are related to big data. To store big graph data, we need special databases. This section also mentions some popular graph databases. Section 7.3 defines and explains big graph analytics. Section 7.4 mentions different big graph analytics approaches while categorizing different frameworks for each approach. Sections 7.5 and 7.6 discuss different techniques and algorithms used in graph analytics. Section 7.7 mentions the issues and challenges involved in big graph analytics. Section 7.8 identifies a number of such application areas for big graph analytics. Section 7.9 concludes the chapter.

7.2 Graph + Big Data = Big Graph

Graphs are widely used structures that aid in representing networks consisting of nodes and their interconnections called edges. They could be exploited to describe paths in a city, circuit networks like telephone and computer ones or even social networks, whereby each node is a structure and contains information such as person name, date of birth, and address. It, thus, becomes apparent that data used in a wide range of applications can be intuitively formulated into a graph, providing a holistic view of the correlations that an entity participates in and extending to both visualization and analytics fields.

Generally, the complex interactions, relationships, and interdependencies between the objects are naturally modeled as graphs. Graph is the best method to store and query the complex interconnected data. To represent the data in a wide range of application domains (e.g., computational biology, knowledge bases, social science, computer networks, astronomy, telecommunications, protein networks, semantic web, bioinformatics applications, and much more), graphs are used. To model different types of relations and processes in biological, social, physical, and information systems, graphs can be used. For example, in computer science, massive graphs are used to represent networks of communication, computational devices, data organization, and computation flow.

Though graph structures have been used since the early days of computer science [2], the importance of graphs has been rejuvenated with the emergence of big data, e.g., recommender systems, consumer web [3], social graphs, etc. The big data is often represented graphically and is referred to as big graph because graphical modeling helps in understanding the relationships among big data that are really complex and diverse in nature. Considering the overgrown data size, constructing proper queries for information retrieval has become difficult, time consuming, and sometimes ineffective. The graph has a big role to play in information retrieval in the big data era. The connected data, in a grand fashion, will be able to express its semantics and context, independently and automatically [4]. Our ability to understand and utilize big graphs will lead us beyond mere information retrieval. Proper big graph analysis unearths the answers that might otherwise go unquestioned explicitly.

7.2.1 The Scale of Big Graph: How Big Is Big Graph?

One of the examples of a massive graph is the web graph. Recently, Google estimated roughly that the total number of web pages exceeds one trillion and the WWW experimental graphs contain more than 20 billion pages and 160 billion hyperlinks [5]. Another example of a large-scale graph is social networks. In 2012, reportedly, the Facebook network contained more than thousands of millions of users (nodes) and more than 140 billion friendship relationships (edges) [5]. As of the third quarter of 2017, monthly active Facebook users has reached up to 2.07 billion [6]. In the

LinkedIn network, very nearly 8 million users (nodes) and 60 million friendship relationships (edges) exist. The latest estimate states that the user count reached 500 million [7]. And in the semantic web network, DBpedia ontology contains nearly 4 million objects (nodes) and almost 400 million facts (edges) [5].

7.2.2 V's of Big Graph

Big data is often defined by the famous five V's: volume, variety, velocity, value, and veracity. Similarly, big graph may also be described using some of these V's as well. The following four V's more appropriately define big graphs.

Volume: The volume represents the size of the graph in terms of the number of nodes and edges. As the volume of graph increases, the analysis gets difficult. Data-to-analysis time is too high if the volume of the graph is big [8].

Velocity: The velocity is the rate at which the graphs increase in size and complexity (in large graphs, the streaming edges). These streaming edges make graph analytics very difficult. The continuous stream of edges does not fit in the memory. And this makes it difficult to compute a metric, e.g., the shortest distance between two nodes and counting of strongly connected groups [8].

Variety: There are different sources and types of data that are combined to form the graphs. The graphs data are often created through integration, e.g., XML/ JSON, relational, document, and graph-structured data [8]. The different types of large graphs may have different meanings that can make the things more complex if they are combined. Some examples are citation networks, social networks, protein–protein interaction networks, ontologies, and linked data/semantic web.

Valence: Valence refers to the degree of connectedness or interdependence. If the valence is high, then the data elements are strongly related. In graph analytics, this relatedness is significantly exploited. In some cases, as the time valence increases, the average distance between the arbitrary node pairs decreases and the parts of massive graph become denser [8].

7.2.3 Graph Databases

Legacy relational database management systems (RDBMSs) have been successfully utilized to store, manage, and retrieve data for a long time. But the emergence of big data has exposed the weakness of RDBMSs in handling relationships between a huge number of heterogeneous data points semantically, which is absolutely necessary to generate unforeseen insight from various data sources. Their tabular data models and rigid schemas make it difficult to add connections that are new and/or diverse in nature [9]. As the relationships between data points are more important than the isolated data points, to leverage those data relationships, different DBMS approaches are needed, which prioritize storing the relationship between the data rather than the data itself. Graph databases do exactly the same. A graph database is a database that uses graph structures to represent and store data. The relationships between data (nodes) are represented through the directed edges of the graph. Storing big data using graph database is like having a mini web inside our big data applications. To crawl through that web, one can set off from a logical starting point and fan out through the edges until the goal is attained. Graph databases not only store the relationships between the data points effectively, but they are also flexible in adding new and diverse kinds of relationships or in adapting a data model to new business requirements [9]. A graph database is more appropriate for dealing with complex, densely connected, and semistructured data. Some of the popular graph databases are discussed briefly as follows:

Neo4j (Neo Technology): Neo4j [10], the world's leading graph database, is a high-performance, scalable, and robust database that is appropriate for enterprise deployment. The features of Neo4j are high-speed querying through traversals, scales to trillions of nodes and relationships, declarative graph query language, and so on.

DEX: DEX [11] is a high-performance graph database querying system. For temporary graphs, DEX includes best integrity model. DEX makes the graph querying possible in various networks, e.g., pattern recognition, link analysis, keyword search, and social network analysis.

InfoGrid: InfoGrid [12] is an open-source web graph database and is being developed in Java. It includes many important software components, which make the buildup of web applications on a graph very easy.

InfiniteGraph: InfiniteGraph [13] is a scalable, cross-platform, and distributed graph database. It is able to manage very complex relationships which require multiple hops and are designed to yield very high throughput. InfiniteGraph provides very high performance in terms of the query and also allows graph-wise indexes on multiple key fields.

HyperGraphDB: HyperGraphDB [14] is an open-source graph database based on generalized hypergraphs. It is a transactional, embedded graph database designed as a universal data model. HyperGraphDB is used in the modeling of the graph data for very complex, large-scale knowledge representation applications, e.g., natural language processing, artificial intelligence, bioinformatics, and so on.

Titan: Titan [15] is a very highly scalable graph database for querying and storing graphs having billions of vertices and trillions of edges. In real time, Titan supports a large number of concurrent users executing the complex graph traversals. It gives very fast responses to very complex queries and also provides various important features, such as support for the global graph data analytics using Apache Giraph integration.

Table 7.1 compares the properties of the abovementioned graph databases.

Table 7.1 Comparison of Different Graph Databases

Name	Language	Type	Features	Weakness	Strength
Neo4j	Java	Transactional	Native graph storage and processing	Does not support sharding	ACID-compliant transactional database
Dex	C++	Bitmap-based	Allows for integration of multiple data sources	Integrity constraint preservation	High-performance and scalable
InfoGrid	Java	Web graph	Data integration, Data referencing	Linkage description language	Combine data integration with knowledge discovery process
InfiniteGraph	Java	Distributed	Cloud-enabled, cross-platform, scalable, etc.	Loosely synchronized batch loader	Designed to handle the very high throughput
HyperGraphDB	Java	Embedded, Transactional	Directed hypergraphs-based open-source data storage mechanism	Reachability	Portable
Titan	Java	Highly scalable	Batch graph processing using Hadoop framework	Dependent on the third-party storage backend	Scaling feature

7.3 Big Graph Analytics

Big graph analytics is an exciting new area for data analytics. In big graph analytics, to model, store, retrieve, and perform analysis, a combination of statistical, graph theoretic, and graph database techniques is applied to the graph-structured data. These techniques are very useful for the researchers to understand the structure of a large network and how it changes in different conditions, e.g., finding subgraphs that are similar to a given pattern, identifying closely interacting subgroups inside a graph, and finding paths between the pairs of entities that satisfy different constraints [16].

7.3.1 Definition

The big graph analytics is essentially an important and effective tool for knowledge discovery in big data. In big graph analytics, the underlying data can be modeled or is natively structured as a set of graphs. Graph analytics leverage graph-structured data to visualize and understand relationships that exist between devices or people in a network. It is used to model the pairwise relationships between objects, people, or nodes in a network. Big graph analytics can uncover insights about the *strengths* and *directions* of the relationships hidden in the big data. Example of strengths of the relationship—*How frequently do individuals or nodes communicate with each other? What other individuals or nodes tend to join that conversation?* Example of directions of the relationship—*Who does typically start the conversation? Is it a two-way conversation or does one always lead? In what situations and how often does the conversation get forwarded to others?*

Big graph analytics defines and strengthens these complex relationships by using mathematical concepts of graph theory. Graph analytics can help to answer the questions—*What is the maximum number of friends an individual has? How many friends do individuals have on average? How interconnected are the groups of users? Are there isolated groups of individuals who are connected to each other, but not to individuals that are not in their group?*

7.3.2 Relationships: The Basics of Graph Analytics

The OSNs (e.g., LinkedIn, Twitter, and Facebook) are driven by the fundamental concepts of connections and relationships. The Facebook users can use services such as Graph Search to find friends of friends who like the same cricket team or who live in the same city, and based on the mutual connections that two or more unconnected individuals have established, the site frequently suggests "people you may know." LinkedIn emphasizes on helping professionals to increase their social connections. Moreover, the ability to assess and comprehend such relationships is a key component that drives the world of business analytics. The business managers are often interested to know—*Who are the most social influencers?* or *Who has the social power to influence the perspectives of others?*

Consider the important question—*How two or more persons might be connected to social media?* This question may seem simple, but when we look closely it gets complicated. The simplest problem is in looking at how two or more persons may be connected on Facebook. These connections might be friends or friends of friends. Sometimes, two individuals may only get the connection by sharing a few "Likes." This information may be valuable to the business. So, we want to know those specific persons out of the trillion users on Facebook so that we can target those persons directly for online advertisements.

7.4 Big Graph Analytics Approaches

This section discusses different approaches used for big graph analytics as well as the frameworks that follow these approaches. Figure 7.1 shows the classification of different big graph analytics frameworks, while Table 7.2 summarizes and compares the frameworks listed here.

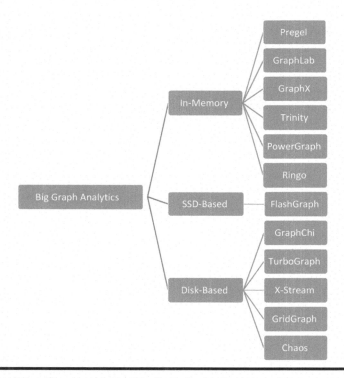

Figure 7.1 Classification of Big Graph Analytics Frameworks.

Table 7.2 Comparison of Different Big Graph Analytics Frameworks

Name	Language	Type	Features	Weakness	Strength
Pregel	C/C++	In-memory scalable graph processing system	Vertex-centric computation	Not suitable for dense graph	Design for sparse graph
Apache Giraph	Java	In-memory graph the processing system	Sharded aggregators, vertex-centric API	To reduce maximum memory usage, it does not have better workload balancing	Message-based communication, global synchronization, and massively parallelizable
GraphLab	C++	Graph-based computation the	Distributed data graph in which the program state is stored as a directed graph	It does not support dynamically evolving graphs	It preserves strong data consistency guarantees
Pregelix	Java	Dataflow-based Pregel-like system	Pregel API with data parallel query evaluation techniques	—	It handles both the in-memory and out-of-core workloads
GraphChi	C++	Disk-based parallel graph engine	PSW method	Limited parallelism, separate steps for I/O processing and CPU processing	To minimize the number of random accesses, it uses PSW method

(Continued)

Table 7.2 (*Continued*) Comparison of Different Big Graph Analytics Frameworks

Name	Language	Type	Features	Weakness	Strength
GraphX	Scala	Distributed	Low-cost fault tolerance, transparent recovery	—	It supports graph parallel abstractions and iterative graph algorithms
PowerGraph	C++	Distributed	GAS decomposition, vertex partitioning	Time-evolving graphs, out-of-core storage, etc.	Highly parallel bulk synchronous Pregel model of computation, asynchronous GraphLab model of computation
TurboGraph	C++	Disk-based parallel graph engine	Pin-and-slide model (implements column view of matrix-vector multiplication)	—	Full parallelism and full overlap of CPU processing and I/O processing
Ringo	C++ and Python	Interactive, large memory multicore machine	Interactive Python interface	—	Powerful operations to construct various types of graphs

7.4.1 In-Memory Big Graph Analytics

The in-memory graph analytics helps to quickly detect patterns, analyze the massive volume of graph data on the fly, and perform their operations very quickly. The advantages of in-memory graph analytics include dramatic performance improvements and cost-effectiveness The prominent big graph analytics frameworks that follow this approach are mentioned as follows:

Pregel: Pregel [17] is a scalable, in-memory, fault-tolerant, graph-parallel distributed analytics engine. It is inspired by the Valiant's bulk synchronous parallel (BSP) model [18]. A C++ application programming interface (API) of Pregel is specifically designed for graph algorithms, challenging researchers to "think like a vertex." In Pregel, at the beginning of a program, the input graph is loaded once and all the operations are performed in-memory [16]. Pregel maintains data locality (to avoid communication overheads) by making sure that computation is performed on the locally stored data.

Apache Giraph: Apache Giraph [19] is an iterative graph-processing platform built for large graphs. It is mostly used to analyze social media data. For example, Yahoo, Facebook, and Twitter are all users of Apache Giraph. These companies are tweaking Giraph to their own purposes. Apache Giraph is the open-source counterpart to Pregel and is developed at Google. Beyond the basic Pregel model, Apache Giraph adds many features, such as the master computation, edge-oriented input, sharded aggregators, and out-of-core computation. For the coordination, checkpointing, and failure recovery schemes, Apache Giraph uses the Apache ZooKeeper. At large scale, for unleashing the potential of structured data, Apache Giraph is the best choice. Facebook uses Apache Giraph to analyze the social graphs formed by the users and their connections.

GraphLab: GraphLab [20] is an asynchronous, in-memory, large-scale graph-parallel distributed analytics engine. Unlike Pregel that works on the BSP model, GraphLab allows the vertices to be processed asynchronously as per the scheduler [16]. Some of the characteristics of GraphLab are automatic fault tolerance, flexibility in expressing arbitrary graph algorithms, and shared memory abstraction (in contrast to Pregel that uses message-passing programming model). GraphLab extends the shared memory concept to the distributed setting by relaxing the scheduling requirements, refining the execution model, and introducing the new distributed data graph, execution engines, and fault tolerance systems.

Ringo: Ringo [21] is an in-memory interactive graph analytics system that combines the high-productivity analysis with fast and scalable execution time [16]. It offers several features:
1. An interactive easy-to-use Python interface.
2. A rich set of over 200 advanced graph operations and algorithms, integration of tables and graph processing, and support for efficient graph construction and transformations between tables and graphs.

3. Object provenance tracking to make it easier for a data scientist to follow multiple data exploration paths in parallel and later to reproduce the analyses.

Trinity: Trinity [22] is a scalable, memory-based distributed graph engine. The main focus of Trinity is to optimize the memory and the communication costs under the consideration that entire graph is divided across the memory cloud. It is mainly designed to support fast graph exploration and efficient parallel graph computations. To support large-scale graphs, Trinity organizes the memories of multiple machines into the globally distributed addressable memory address space. Furthermore, it leverages the graph access patterns in both offline and online computations to optimize the memory and communication costs for better performance. For bridging the data storage and graph model, Trinity provides the support of a language called Trinity Specification Language.

PowerGraph: PowerGraph [23] is a scalable, graph-parallel distributed computation framework written in C++. With PowerGraph, it is possible to emulate both computationally efficient asynchronous GraphLab model of computation as well as the highly parallel bulk synchronous Pregel model of computation [16]. For splitting high-degree vertices, factoring vertex programs over edges, and exposing greater parallelism, PowerGraph uses the gather–apply–scatter (GAS) model of computation. And to effectively place its large-scale graphs in a distributed environment, PowerGraph allows vertex partitioning. PowerGraph uses vertex partitioning and the fast-greedy heuristic collections to reduce the communication costs and the storage of massive distributed power-law graphs.

GraphX: GraphX [24] is a graph analytics engine that supports distributed data flow frameworks, such as Spark. To express the existing graph APIs, GraphX introduces a composable graph abstraction. Its API enables the composition of tabular and graph with unstructured data and permits the same physical data to be viewed both as collections and as a graph without data duplication or movement [16]. GraphX unifies the data-parallel and graph-parallel systems.

7.4.2 SSD-Based Big Graph Analytics

Analyzing massive-scale graphs requires a cluster of machines. So, the aggregate memory exceeds the graph size. This problem can be solved by utilizing commodity solid-state drives (SSDs) with a minimal performance loss. One of the well-known frameworks that follow this approach is FlashGraph.

FlashGraph: FlashGraph [25] is a scalable, semi-external memory graph-processing engine on top of a user-space SSD file system that stores vertex state in the memory and edge lists on the SSDs. To realize both high IOPS (input/output operations per second) and lightweight caching for the SSD arrays on nonuniform memory and the I/O systems, FlashGraph uses SAFS (set-associative file system) and a user-space file system. FlashGraph reduces data access by selectively accessing the edge lists required by the graph algorithms from SSDs. It conservatively merges I/O requests to reduce the CPU consumption and to increase the I/O throughput. To express the wide range of graph algorithms and their optimizations, FlashGraph provides a concise and flexible programming interface.

7.4.3 Disk-Based Big Graph Analytics

Analyzing massive-scale graphs such as biological networks, social networks, and chemical compounds is a very challenging task. Many distributed graph analytics engines analyze the massive-scale graphs efficiently but incur overheads of efficient graph partitioning and distribution of graph over a cluster of machines. Distributed graph processing also requires cluster management and fault tolerance. In order to overcome these problems, many disk-based graph processing systems are proposed. Some of them are mentioned as follows:

GraphChi: GraphChi [26] is a disk-based graph processing system for computing efficiently on large-scale graphs. It can execute a number of advanced machine learning, data mining, and graph mining algorithms on graphs having billions of edges. GraphChi first gathers the data from neighbors by reading the edge values, then computes and applies the new values to the vertices, and then scatters the new data to the neighbors by writing the values on edges [16]. If random I/O accesses are reduced by using the Parallel Sliding Windows (PSW), GraphChi is able to process the large-scale graphs in a reasonable time.

X-Stream: X-Stream [27] is an edge-centric graph processing system for analytics on massive graphs. To utilize the sequential streaming bandwidth of storage medium, X-Stream uses the streaming partitions [16]. X-Stream exposes the familiar scatter–gather programming model, but it works on the concept of streaming data from storage. It is similar to the systems such as Pregel [5] and PowerGraph [10].

TurboGraph: TurboGraph [28] is a disk-based parallel graph processing system that processes massive graphs very efficiently. It exploits (i) the full parallelism (including the Flash SSD I/O parallelism and the multicore parallelism) and (ii) the full overlap of I/O processing and CPU processing as much as possible [16]. TurboGraph can restrict the computation to just a subset of vertices utilizing two types of threads (execution threads and callback threads) by interpreting the matrix vector multiplication column view.

Chaos: Chaos [29] is a scalable graph processing engine designed for analytics on massive graphs using the small clusters. Using three synergistic techniques— (i) streaming partitions, (ii) flat storage, and (iii) work stealing—Chaos achieves the computational load balance, the sequential storage access, and the I/O load balance. In order to achieve sequential access to the storage, Chaos uses the streaming partitions, but parallelizes the execution of the streaming partitions.

GridGraph: GridGraph [30] is a massive graph processing system build on a single machine using the two-level hierarchical partitioning. In this graph processing system, large graphs are broken into one-dimensional partitioned vertex chunks and two-dimensional partitioned edge blocks [16].

7.4.4 Other Big Graph Analytics Frameworks

Recently, different approaches based on dataflow method, shared memory, and multicore machines have received a significant attention for processing and analysis of large-scale graphs. A couple of well-known big graph analytics frameworks that are based on dataflow and shared-memory concept are mentioned below.

Pregelix: Pregelix [31] is a dataflow-based graph analytics engine which is designed to handle both the in-memory and the out-of-core workloads. It is an open-source Pregel-like system that sustains multiuser workloads. To support the large-scale graph analytics, Pregelix combines the Pregel API with data-parallel query evaluation techniques. It leads to an effective and transparent out-of-core support, throughput, scalability, and also increased physical flexibility and software simplicity.

Ligra: Ligra [32] is a lightweight, shared-memory programming model for parallel or multicore machines. Based on the user-provided threshold, Ligra switches between the push-based and pull-based operators automatically.

7.5 Graph Analytic Techniques

7.5.1 Centrality Analysis

Centrality analysis enables the identification of relevancy to find the most important vertices within a graph. It detects and characterizes the most significant nodes in a network with respect to the specific analysis problem. For example, it addresses the question—*Who is the most important or central person in this network?*

7.5.1.1 Degree Centrality

In the real-world interactions, we often consider people with more connections to be more important. A degree centrality is a simple centrality measure which counts, e.g., *How many neighbors does a node have?* There are two types of degree centrality measures:

1. **In-degree:** It is the number of predecessor nodes or the number of incoming links.
2. **Out-degree:** It is the number of successor nodes or the number of outgoing links.

Since the in-links are given by other nodes in the network, typically we are interested in the in-degree, while the out-links are determined by the node itself.

7.5.1.2 Eigenvector Centrality

By incorporating the importance of the neighbors, eigenvector centrality tries to generalize degree centrality. Eigenvector centrality is defined for both the directed graphs as well as the undirected graphs. To keep track of neighbors, we can use the adjacency matrix A of a graph. The eigenvector centrality is defined as

$$c_e(v_i) = \frac{1}{\lambda} \sum_{j=1}^{n} A_{j,\,i} c_e(v_i)$$

where $c_e(v_i)$ denote the eigenvector centrality of node v_i, λ is some fixed constant, and A denotes the adjacency matrix of the graph, to keep track of the neighbors, assuming $c_e = \left(c_e(v_i),\, c_e(v_i),..,\, c_e(v_i)\right)^T$ is the centrality vector for all the nodes.

7.5.1.3 Katz Centrality

A potential problem with eigenvector centrality is that it works well only if the graph is (strongly) connected. In this case, by adding the bias term to the centrality value, the problem can be rectified. For all the nodes, irrespective of the network topology, the bias β is added to the centrality values. The Katz centrality measure [33] is formulated as

$$C_{Katz}(v_i) = \alpha \sum_{j=1} A_{j,\,i}\, C_{Katz}(v_j) + \beta$$

where α is a constant. The bias term β avoids the zero centrality values.

7.5.1.4 PageRank Centrality

A major problem with Katz centrality arises when a node with high centrality is connected to many nodes and then all these nodes get high centrality. In many cases, however, this is not so significant if a node is only one among the many that are linked. To solve this problem, one can divide the passed centrality value by the number of outgoing links (out-degree) from that node such that each connected neighbor from the source node gets a fraction of the source node's centrality. The PageRank centrality [34] of a node v_i is defined as

$$C_p(v_i) = \alpha \sum_{j=1}^{n} A_{j,\,i}\, \frac{C_p(v_j)}{d_j^{out}} + \beta$$

where, $c_p(v_i)$ denote the PageRank centrality of node v_i, and d_j^{out} is nonzero.

7.5.1.5 Closeness Centrality

Closeness centrality [35] is a centrality measure that measures the mean distance from one vertex to the other vertices. The concept of closeness centrality is that the more the central nodes , the more quickly they can reach the other nodes. The closeness of a node v is defined as

$$closeness\ (v) = \frac{1}{\sum_{i \neq v} d_{vi}}$$

where i and v belong to the set of vertices of the graphs (networks).

7.5.1.6 Betweenness Centrality

It measures the number of shortest paths in which a vertex is in sequence of vertices in the path. For a node v_i, the betweenness centrality [36] is defined as the number of shortest paths between other nodes that pass through node v_i.

$$C_b(v_i) = \sum_{s \neq t \neq v_i} \frac{\sigma_{st}(v_i)}{\sigma_{st}}$$

where σ_{st} denotes the number of shortest paths from node s to t, and $\sigma_{st}(v_i)$ denotes the number of shortest paths from s to t that pass through v_i.

Betweenness centrality needs to be normalized to be comparable across networks.

7.5.2 Path Analysis

Path analysis is used to identify and explore all the connections between a pair of nodes. For example, in the graph, path analysis can be used to determine the shortest distance between two nodes. Route optimization is an obvious use case that is particularly applicable to supply, logistics, distribution chains, and traffic optimization for smart cities.

7.5.3 Community Analysis

In general, a community is formed by individuals in such a way that the individuals within the group interact with each other more often than with those outside the group. The distance-based and density-based analyses are used to find the groups of frequently interacting people. Community analysis plays an important role in understanding the issues in sociology and biology.

7.5.4 Connectivity Analysis

In a graph, how nodes are connected with each other is defined by connectivity. To determine weakness in utility networks, such as power grid, connectivity analysis can be used. Another example where connectivity analysis is used is in the comparison of connectivity across the networks.

7.6 Algorithms for Big Graph Analytics

7.6.1 PageRank

PageRank [37] is an algorithm for measuring the importance of website pages. In the Google search engine, PageRank is used to rank the websites. Some of the applications of PageRank are in recommendation systems, OSNs, and the natural science to study the relationships between proteins and ecological networks.

7.6.2 Connected Component

In a graph, the connected component is the maximal subgraph in which all the vertices are connected with each other. A graph can be made of many connected components. Consider a social network that is made up of two or more groups of friends in which none of the individuals from one group knows any individuals from the other groups and vice versa. Each group of friends represents different components because the members of one group are not connected with the members of the other groups.

7.6.3 Distributed Minimum Spanning Tree

For a weighted, undirected graph, minimum spanning tree is a spanning tree (a subset of the graph having all vertices with the minimum number of edges) with minimum weight. The input graph of a distributed minimum spanning tree algorithm (DMST) does not need to be connected, but it must be undirected. The DMST [38] produces the minimum spanning forest for the unconnected graph.

7.6.4 Graph Search

A graph is basically a collection of nodes where each node might point to the other nodes. The graphs can be directed like one-way streets or can be undirected like two-way streets in the city. Suppose we want to go through this graph, and specifically suppose we want to do something, like figure out if there is a path from one node to another. There are two common ways of doing this:

1. **Breadth-first search (BFS):** The BFS is a level-by-level graph traversal algorithm that performs searching on unweighted, undirected graph from the given start vertex and assigns the distance to each vertex.
2. **Depth-first search (DFS):** The DFS is typically a recursive graph traversal algorithm that explores as deeply as possible using one neighbor before backtracking to other neighbors. DFS does not go through all the edges. The vertices and edges, which depth first search has visited, form a tree (graph spanning tree).

7.6.5 Clustering

Clustering is a task of grouping the set of nodes that have denser relations among each other in comparison with the rest of the network. Based on the characteristics of objects, the bunch of objects is placed in one group that has high intra-cluster similarity and low inter-cluster similarity. Clustering is used in many applications, such as data or text mining, statistics, image processing, and machine learning.

7.7 Issues and Challenges of Big Graph Analytics

To solve large-scale graph problems, much research remains to be done in parallel graph processing [39]. There are many properties of graph problems that present significant challenges for efficient parallelism. A brief discussion on the issues and challenges that must be addressed for effective big graph analytics is given in Sections 7.7.1–7.7.5.

7.7.1 High-Degree Vertex

Graphs having high-degree vertices are very common, e.g., in OSNs, a very popular person (e.g., Prime Minister of India: Narendra Modi) is connected to many other persons; in text analysis we have a popular word that appears in many documents; and so on. These types of graphs are computationally challenging and difficult to partition.

7.7.2 Sparseness

In real-world graphs, most vertices have relatively few neighbors, whereas a few have many neighbors. For example, in the Twitter follower graph, some people have more than 50 million followers [40] (e.g., President of the United States: Donald J. Trump), whereas a normal user just has a hundred followers or even lesser. More computation, synchronization, and communication are required to split the sparse graphs.

7.7.3 Data-Driven Computations

The graph computation algorithms are in most cases completely data driven. In these algorithms, if the structure of graph computations is not known a priori, then the parallelism based on the partitioning of the computation can be difficult to express.

7.7.4 Unstructured Problems

In general, data in graph problems are unstructured and irregular in nature. While parallelizing the graph problems, the irregular structure of the graph problem data makes it difficult to extract the parallelism by partitioning the graph problem data [16].

7.7.5 In-Memory Challenge

The size of natural graphs is massive in nature, and it does not fit in a single memory. To reduce the response time, the graph data should reside in the RAM, instead of the hard disk drive (HHD) or SSD.

7.7.6 Communication Overhead

The high-degree vertices (like more popular people on Twitter) lead to communication overheads. At present, high-degree vertices are in the billions, but in the future, it will be in the trillions and beyond.

7.7.7 Load Balancing

Many of the natural graphs have followed the power law of the degree distribution. It means that most of the vertices are connected to a small number of vertices and only those small number of vertices are connected to a larger number of other vertices. When we analyze such graphs, there is a need to pay extra attention to the load balancing.

7.8 Applications of Big Graph Analytics

There are many potential applications of big graph analytics such as the following:

- Conducting research in bioinformatics including disease pathologies, medical research, and analysis of the biochemical pathways and chemical structure identification.
- Applying influencer analysis in social network communities.
- Spotting instances of both internal and external frauds, which applies to fraudulent activities in telecommunications, applications and claims of fraud in insurance, benefits fraud in government, and fraudulent transactions and applications in banking and financial services companies.

■ Detecting financial crimes such as money laundering.
■ Maintaining quality of service in grid networked services (e.g., identifying weaknesses in water grids, power grids, and network quality of service in transportation networks).
■ Preventing crime and performing counterterrorism.
■ Optimizing routes in highways, railways, and airlines.
■ Package routings for better logistics in manufacturing industries and retail.
■ Online map applications (e.g., Google maps) to compute driving direction.
■ For root cause analysis in networking and information technology.
■ Recommending suitable products for the online buyers.

Basically, the predominant uses of graph analytics are in those areas that require addressing relationship-based problems. Some of the prominent applications of big graph analytics are briefly discussed in Sections 7.8.1–7.8.7.

7.8.1 Social Network Analysis

Large graphs are heavily employed in the OSNs (e.g., Facebook, Twitter, LinkedIn, etc.). The fundamental task in OSNs (e.g., LinkedIn, Twitter, Facebook, etc.) is relationship analysis. In the social networks, relationship analysis is involved in finding the paths between users (nodes). A graph offers various types of relationships that are important for the social networks. From one application to another application, the properties and the characteristics of massive graphs vary significantly. For example, in Twitter, the follower–following relationship graphs are directed graphs having users as their vertices.

7.8.2 Behavior Analytics

In social media, individuals exhibit different behaviors that can be categorized into individual and collective behaviors. Individual behavior is the behavior that an individual targets toward

1. Another individual (which is known as the individual–individual behavior).
2. An entity (which is called the individual–entity behavior).
3. A community (which is known as the individual–community behavior).

Collective behavior is the behavior when a group of individuals having or not having any coordination act in an aligned manner.

7.8.3 Biological Networks

Interactions arise naturally in biology. Genes produce proteins, proteins regulate the functions of other proteins, cells transmit signals to other cells, etc. All these interactions can be assembled into the graphs where each node represents the biological entity and each edge represents associations or interactions between entities.

7.8.4 Recommendation Systems

Graph-based recommendation systems help many companies to personalize content, services, and products by leveraging the multitude of connections. One popular example of recommendations is the friend recommendations in the OSNs.

7.8.5 Smart Cities

Nowadays, cities have various interacting networks, such as mobile-to-mobile and broadband Internet Protocol networks, power networks, and sewage and water networks. Graph analytics is used for planning the smart hubs, energy-optimal routing, estimating the congestion patterns, etc.

7.8.6 Geospatial Data and Logistics

Graphs can be used to represent many scenarios; maps are one of them. If we think about maps, we can also think about geospatial and logistics applications. The geospatial applications that can take advantages of graph databases range from calculating the routes between locations in the networks, such as the road networks, railway networks, or airline networks, or logistical network, to spatial operations, such as calculating the intersection between two or more regions, finding the center of a region, and finding all points of interest in a bounded area.

eBay, one concrete example of graph analysis being used in logistics, provides a service based on graphs that are used to compute quick delivery of goods between sellers and buyers.

Let us consider a highly simplified scenario. A parcel needs to be delivered and the delivery man needs to deliver it at the earliest time possible. So, he should choose the fastest route to the customer's doorstep from the delivery center.

We can solve this problem by representing the streets (between the delivery center and the customer) as a graph. Hence the intersections or road junctions are represented as nodes of the graph and the lanes connecting the junctions are represented as edges of the graph.

So, now finding the fastest route is essentially a matter of weighted shortest path calculation. We calculate it by keeping in mind the two attributes of the relationship:

1. Distance (actual distance between the intersections).
2. Coverability (depends on a lot of factors, such as traffic, road condition, and terrain).

7.8.7 Insurance Fraud Detection

According to Shanghai Institutes for International Studies (SIIS) report, about 10% of all the insurance claims are fraudulent, and in the United States, almost $80 billion is spent annually [41] in fraudulent claims. The insurance fraud is definitely an issue that needs to be addressed.

The insurance fraud can be perpetrated by either the buyer or the seller. Buyer fraud happens when a buyer consciously and intentionally exaggerates or invents the loss to get more receive or coverage money for damages. Few examples are faking accidents, postdated life insurance, false medical history, and murder for proceeds. Seller fraud happens when a seller of a policy hijacks usual processes to make as large a profit as possible. Some examples include fee churning, premium diversion, and many more.

To detect and prevent this type of fraud, there are many traditional methods, such as identifying the outliers, calculating the statistical parameters, duplicate testing using date validation systems, and identifying gaps in sequential data. To catch most of the casual (single fraudsters) offenders, these are the best methods, but highly advanced fraud rings use generally well-planned methods, i.e., traditional methods are unable to detect advanced fraud rings. In this scenario, graph analytics plays a significant role.

7.9 Conclusions

In this chapter, we have presented an overview of big graph and big graph analytics. We have understood the importance of graph in big data analytics. As big data is growing even bigger, traditional database techniques are turning out to be ineffective in generating innovative insights needed for the organizations to be competitive. Storing big data graphically ensures prioritizing relationships between data over the data that automatically reflects the semantics of the data connections. This has helped data analysts to expose new knowledge, thus helping organizations to take innovative business decisions. Big graph analytics may be used for a variety of analytical purposes, such as identifying notable persons in OSNs, spotting fraudulent acts in financial networks, and analyzing consumers' buying patterns in order to consider better marketing strategies. Familiar DBMSs are incapable of coping with the expectations from big data. Graph databases are required to store big graph data. It gives responses to complex queries in a few milliseconds. Many such graph databases are emerging in the market, Neo4j being one of them. Different approaches for big graph analytics such as in-memory, SSD-based, and disk-based are adopted by different big graph analytics frameworks. Several techniques (e.g., centrality analysis, path analysis, community analysis, and connectivity analysis) and algorithms (e.g., PageRank, clustering, etc.) are used in big graph analytics. Big graph analytics is extremely helpful in industries, such as online business solution, health care, online media, financial sector, social network, communication, and retail. Though big graph has a lot of promises, some hitches such as sparseness, high-degree vertex, and load balancing are to be taken care of.

References

1. M. V. Rijmenam. *Think Bigger: Developing a Successful Big data Strategy for Your Business.* Amacom, 2014.
2. H. Motoda. "What Can We Do with Graph-Structured Data?—A Data Mining Perspective." In *19th Australian Joint Conference on Artificial Intelligence, Hobart, Australia*, 2006.
3. R. Valdes. "The Competitive Dynamics of the Consumer Web: Five Graphs Deliver a Sustainable Advantage." July 13, 2012. Available: www.gartner.com/doc/2081316/ competitive-dynamics-consumer-web-graphs (Accessed December 27, 2017).
4. R. Marsten. "Is Graph Theory Key to Understanding Big data?" March 2014. Available: www.wired.com/insights/2014/03/graph-theory-key-understanding-big-data/ (Accessed December 4, 2017).
5. S. Sakr. "Processing Large-scale Graph Data: A Guide to Current Technology." June 10, 2013. Available: www.ibm.com/developerworks/library/os-giraph/ (Accessed December 30, 2017).
6. "Number of Monthly Active Facebook Users Worldwide as of 3rd Quarter 2017 (in millions)." Statista, 2017. Available: www.statista.com/statistics/264810/number-of-monthly-active-facebook-users-worldwide/ (Accessed December 30, 2017).
7. B. Darrow. "LinkedIn Claims Half a Billion Users." Fortune, April 24, 2017. Available: http://fortune.com/2017/04/24/linkedin-users/ (Accessed December 30, 2017).
8. R. Kumar. "Graph Analytics." February 16, 2016. Available: www.ranjankumar.in/ graph-analytics/ (Accessed August 2, 2017).
9. J. Webber. "The Top 5 Use Cases of Graph Databases: Unlocking New Possibilities with Connected Data." Neo4j, 2015.
10. "Neo4j Graph Database." Neo Technology. Available: https://neo4j.com.
11. N. Martínez-Bazan, V. Muntés-Mulero, S. Gómez-Villamor, J. Nin, M.-A. Sánchez-Martínez and J.-L. Larriba-Pey. "Dex: High-performance Exploration on Large Graphs for Information Retrieval." In *6th ACM Conference on Information and Knowledge Management (CIKM '07)*, Lisbon, Portugal, 2007.
12. N. Giannadakis, A. Rowe, M. Ghanem and Y.-k. Guo. "InfoGrid: Providing Information Integration for Knowledge Discovery." *Information Sciences*, vol. 155, no. 3–4, pp. 199–226, 2003.
13. "InfiniteGraph," Objectivity, Inc. Available: www.objectivity.com/products/infinitegraph/ (Accessed January 27, 2018).
14. B. Iordanov. "HyperGraphDB: A Generalized Graph Database." In *International Conference on Web-age Information Management (WAIM'10)*, Jiuzhaigou Valley, China, 2010.
15. "Titan: Distributed Graph Database." Available: http://titan.thinkaurelius.com/ (Accessed January 27, 2018).
16. D. K. Singh and R. Patgiri. "Big Graph: Tools, Techniques, Issues, Challenges and Future Directions." In *Sixth International Conference on Advances in Computing and Information Technology (ACITY 2016)*, Chennai, India, 2016.
17. G. Malewicz, M. H. Austern, A. J. Bik, J. C. Dehnert, I. Horn, N. Leiser and G. Czajkowski. "Pregel: A System for Large-scale Graph Processing." In *ACM SIGMOD International Conference on Management of Data (SIGMOD'10)*, New York, 2010.
18. L. G. Valiant. "A Bridging Model for Parallel Computation." *Communications of ACM*, vol. 33, no. 8, pp. 103–111, August 1990.
19. "Welcome to Apache Giraph!" The Apache Software Foundation, October 24, 2016. Available: http://giraph.apache.org/ (Accessed January 27, 2018).

20. Y. Low, D. Bickson, J. Gonzalez, C. Guestrin, A. Kyrola and J. M. Hellerstein. "Distributed GraphLab: A Framework for Machine Learning and Data Mining in the Cloud." *VLDB Endowment*, vol. 5, no. 8, pp. 716–727, April 2012.
21. Y. Perez, R. Sosič, A. Banerjee, R. Puttagunta, M. Raison, P. Shah and J. Leskovec. "Ringo: Interactive Graph Analytics on Big-Memory Machines." In *ACM SIGMOD International Conference on Management of Data (SIGMOD'15)*, New York, 2015.
22. B. Shao, H. Wang and Y. Li. "Trinity: A Distributed Graph Engine on a Memory Cloud." In *ACM SIGMOD International Conference on Management of Data (SIGMOD'13)*, New York, NY, 2013.
23. J. E. Gonzalez, Y. Low, H. Gu, D. Bickson and C. Guestrin. "PowerGraph: Distributed Graph-Parallel Computation on Natural Graphs." In *10th USENIX Conference on Operating System Design and Implementation (OSDI'12)*, Berkeley, CA, 2012.
24. J. E. Gonzalez, R. S. Xin, A. Dave, D. Crankshaw, M. J. Franklin and I. Stoica. "GraphX: Graph Processing in a Distributed Dataflow Framework." In *11th USENIX Conference on Operating Systems Design and Implementation (OSDI'14)*, Berkeley, CA, 2014.
25. D. Zheng, D. Mhembere, R. Burns, J. Vogelstein, C. E. Priebe and A. S. Szalay. "FlashGraph: Processing Billion-Node Graphs on an Array of Commodity SSDs." In *13th USENIX Conference on File and Storage Technologies (FAST'15)*, Berkeley, CA, 2015.
26. A. Kyrola, G. Blelloch and C. Guestrin. "GraphChi: Large-Scale Graph Computation on Just a PC." In *10th USENIX Conference on Operating Systems Design and Implementation (OSDI'12)*, Berkeley, CA, 2012.
27. A. Roy, I. Mihailovic and W. Zwaenepoel. "X-Stream: Edge-centric Graph Processing using Streaming Partitions." In *24th ACM Symposium on Operating Systems Principles (SOSP '13)*, New York, 2013.
28. W.-S. Han, S. Lee, K. Park, J.-H. Lee, M.-S. Kim, J. Kim and H. Yu. "TurboGraph: A Fast Parallel Graph Engine Handling Billion-scale Graphs in a Single PC." In *19th ACM SIGKDD International Conference on Knowledge Discovery and Data Mining (KDD'13)*, New York, 2013.
29. A. Roy, L. Bindschaedler, J. Malicevic and W. Zwaenepoel. "Chaos: Scale-out Graph Processing from Secondary Storage." In *25th Symposium on Operating Systems Principles (SOSP'15)*, New York, 2015.
30. X. Zhu, W. Han and W. Chen. "GridGraph: Large-Scale Graph Processing on a Single Machine Using 2-Level Hierarchical Partitioning." In 2015 *USENIX Conference on Usenix Annual Technical Conference (USENIX ATC'15)*, Berkeley, CA, 2015.
31. Y. Bu, V. Borkar, J. Jia, M. J. Carey and T. Condie. "Pregelix: Big(ger) Graph Analytics on a Dataflow Engine." *VLDB Endowment*, vol. 8, no. 2, pp. 161–172, October 2014.
32. J. Shun and G. E. Blelloch. "Ligra: A Lightweight Graph Processing Framework for Shared Memory." In *18th ACM SIGPLAN Symposium on Principles and Practice of Parallel Programming (PPoPP'13)*, Shenzhen, China, 2013.
33. L. Katz. "A New Status Index Derived from Sociometric Analysis." *Psychometrika*, vol. 18, no. 1, pp. 39–43, 1953.
34. S. Brin and L. Page. "The Anatomy of a Large-scale Hypertextual Web Search Engine." *Computer Networks and ISDN Systems*, vol. 30, no. 1–7, pp. 107–117, April 1, 1998.
35. G. Sabidussi. "The Centrality Index of a Graph." *Psychometrika*, vol. 31, no. 4, pp. 581–603, 1966.
36. L. C. Freenan. "A Set of Measures of Centrality Based on Betweenness." *Sociometry*, vol. 40, no. 1, pp. 35–41, 1977.

37. L. Page, S. Brin, R. Motwani and T. Winograd. "The PageRank Citation Ranking: Bringing Order to the Web." In *7th International World Wide Web Conference*, Brisbane, Australia, 1998.
38. R. G. Gallager, P. A. Humblet and P. M. Spira. "A Distributed Algorithm for Minimum-Weight Spanning Trees." *ACM Transactions on Programming Languages and Systems,* vol. 5, no. 1, pp. 66–77, 1983.
39. A. Lumsdaine, D. Gregor, B. Hendrickson and J. Berry. "Challenges in Parallel Graph Processing." *Parallel Processing Letters*, vol. 17, no. 1, pp. 5–20, 2007.
40. "Twitter: Most Followers." Available: http://friendorfollow.com/twitter/most-followers/ (Accessed August 16, 2017).
41. Sparsity Technologies. "Graph Database Use Case: Insurance Fraud Detection." May 12, 2015. Available: http://sparsity-technologies.com/blog/graph-database-use-case-insurance-fraud-detection/ (Accessed January 27, 2018).

Chapter 8

Application of Game Theory for Big Data Analytics

Mohammad Muhtady Muhaisin
Huawei Technologies Bangladesh Limited

Taseef Rahman
Axway Inc.

Contents

8.1 Introduction

In today's technology-driven world, data is being produced at an astronomical rate. As a matter of fact, more than 85% of the data in the world today has been created in the past 2 years. Also, experts suggest a 4,300% increase in annual data production by 2020 [1]. This staggering amount of data generated every second, which is to be processed and analyzed, has given rise to the domain of big data. Expounded as the data that requires processing beyond the conventional methods, big data size is an ever-varying factor. Added to that, with the fear of being left behind, many business entities today are becoming data-rich, but with very poor data insight. They are storing data that they have no idea what to do with, without extracting meaningful information from it. Furthermore, these stored data have a finite life span as after some time they become outdated. As a result, novel tools are being deployed to extract valuable information from this ocean of data collected and stored.

Rowly et al. [2] distinguished between knowledge and wisdom by formulating data, information, knowledge, understanding, and wisdom (DIKUW) hierarchy represented in Figure 8.1. Game theory is a branch of mathematics that helps gain "wisdom" by finding an optimal solution for a given situation when "rational" decision makers are at play. Big data explosion has paved the path for implementing the game theory features in this domain because the game theory system theoretically becomes more accurate with each iteration as it collects data in every stage. To make sense of the huge chunk of data at hand, game theory data science might turn

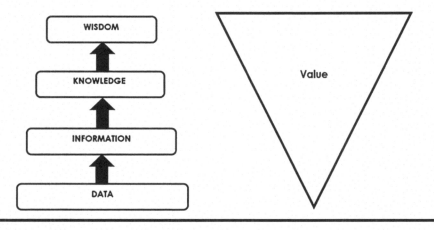

Figure 8.1   DIKUW hierarchy [2].

out to be an auxiliary concept that data analysts can deploy to forecast and devise effective data-driven decisions under strategic circumstances. Game theory has the potential to supersede the intuitive evaluation of big data analysis with quantifiable data-driven decision-making.

When implemented, "rational" independent players participating in the game always try to maximize their own profit. Whether a player gains a profit is decided by the success of that particular step or action [3].

Modern game theory began with an idea regarding the existence of mixed-strategy equilibria in two-person zero-sum games and its proof by John von Neumann. The evolutionary game theory, on the other hand, comes into play when more than two players are involved [4]. Then the best strategy to be chosen may depend upon the strategies used by other players [5]. It also takes into account not only the outcomes of various competing strategies but also the frequencies with which those various strategies are found in the populace.

Recently, the application of game theory in various facets of big data analytics has gained traction due to its ability to converge fast into optimality. To name a few, game theory is used to set up pricing mechanisms in decentralized transactions, in incentivizing cooperative behavior in crowdsourcing platforms, in intrusion detection in cybersecurity platforms, and in devising data exchange protocols among Internet of Things (IoT) devices. Besides, game theory is emerging as the perfect tool to address the V factors of big data analytics—velocity, volume, value, variety, and veracity.

The major contributions of this chapter are as follows:

- An overview of the classical game theory and evolutionary game theory.
- A review of the recent implementations of those games in various big data domains.
- Discussion on the future challenges that are to be addressed by applying game theory mechanisms.

Thus, readers will be able to get a lucid idea about the basics of game theory, with the scopes of application of game theory and evolutionary game theory in big data analytics discussed in various sections of this chapter.

8.1.1 Chapter Roadmap

The chapter is organized as follows: Section 8.2 focuses on briefing the readers on the basics of classical and evolutionary game theory and on some technical terms frequently used in the chapter. After that, Section 8.3 aims at reviewing the literature on the application of game-theoretic approaches in multiple facets of big data, followed by Section 8.4 that sheds light on the challenges to be addressed. Lastly, Section 8.5 concludes the chapter.

8.2 Basics of Classical and Evolutionary Game Theory

Game theory has a wide field of applications ranging from economics to computer science and biology. Application of game theory in critical decision-making processes has been proven to be quite effective. In Section 8.2.1, various types of games are discussed with respect to the number of players involved, payoffs, and preferred strategies.

8.2.1 Classical Game Theory

Game theory is a branch of applied mathematics that provides tools for analyzing situations in which parties, called players, make decisions that are interdependent. This interdependence causes each player to consider the possible decisions, or strategies, of other players while formulating his/her own strategy. A solution to a game describes the optimal decisions of the players, who may have similar, opposed, or mixed interests and the outcomes that may result from these decisions.

It has been over a decade that game theory is being used as an attractive mechanism to solve numerous problems in wireless networking and, in recent times, in the IoT network, cloud security platforms, crowdsourcing, etc. The so-called game consists of a set of players, a set of strategies for each player, and a set of corresponding utility functions or payoffs. Let the parameters assigned to each of the n nodes in a game be $H = [O, T, V]$ where H is a particular type of game and $O = [o_1, o_2, \ldots, o_n]$ is a finite set of nodes. Then $T = [T_1, T_2, \ldots, T_n]$ is the set of corresponding strategies of sensor node i represented by $T_i[i = 1, 2, \ldots, n]$ and $V = [v_1, v_2, \ldots, v_n]$ is the set of respective payoff functions of node i represented by $v_i[i = 1, 2, \ldots, n]$. This v_i is the value of the utility that each of the nodes receives at the end of each round of the game.

Each node always aims to maximize its own payoff and thus acts selfish. The focus is always to formulate the payoff functions so that the maximum output is obtained by the node i in choosing a strategy S_i against other strategies of $n - 1$ nodes. The strategies $t = t_i, t_{-i}$ are called strategy combinations where t_i is the particular strategy chosen by node i and t_{-i} is the particular strategy chosen by the other nodes in the game. The strategy combinations, i.e., s, should always aim at reaching the nash equilibrium that defines a steady-state condition in a game of two or more players. More on nash equilibrium will discussed in later sections.

8.2.2 Evolutionary Game Theory

Evolutionary game theory also assumes that the survival of a node is proportional to the payoff of the strategy that the nodes select. It is to be noticed that as the nodes have mutual dependency on each other, the strategy distribution of nodes determines their superiority. Now, if we consider there are k strategies that are to be chosen by two players, i.e., nodes, then a $k * k$ payoff matrix is obtained, $A = [a_{ij}]$, which represents all possible strategy pairs of these two players. $A_{ij}, (i, j = 1, 2, 3, ...k)$ denotes the payoff of strategy i while competing with strategy i against strategy j.

Let $x_i (i = 1, 2, ...k)$ denote the ratio or relative frequency of each strategy [6,7]. All x_i sum up to 1, i.e.,

$$\sum_{i=1}^{n} x_i = 1 \tag{8.1}$$

The expected payoff f_i of strategy i is given by

$$f_i = \sum_{j=1}^{n} x_j a_{ij} \tag{8.2}$$

The average payoff of the nodes becomes

$$\varphi = \sum_{i=1}^{n} x_i f_i \tag{8.3}$$

From these equations, we can find the standard replicator equations.

$$x_i' = x_i (f_i - \varphi), \ i = 1, 2, 3 ..., n \tag{8.4}$$

where the superscript stands for time derivation. Equation 8.4 represents that the number of players selecting strategy i increases with the relative difference between the expected payoff of strategy i and the average payoff of all the strategies. This equation only stands for an infinitely large and well-mixed population where every node can equally play games with all the other nodes. Now, if we want to consider the evolutionary game dynamics on a k-regular graph [8], the modified payoff matrix would become $A' = [a_{ij}']$. This modified matrix is the sum of the original $n * n$ payoff matrix, $A = [a_{ij}]$ and a $n * x$ modifier matrix $M = [m_{ij}]$ where m_{ij} describes the local competition between strategies i and j. Now, the expected payoff g_i for the local competition of strategy i is defined as

$$g_i = \sum_{j=1}^{n} x_j m_{ij} \tag{8.5}$$

It has to be noted that the average payoff of the local competition of strategy i sums to zero.

$$\sum_{i=1}^{n} x_i g_i = 0 \tag{8.6}$$

So, the average payoff ψ of the population on graph will be

$$\Psi = \sum_{i=1}^{n} x_i \left(f_i + g_i \right) = \sum_{i=1}^{n} x_i f_i \tag{8.7}$$

If x_i is used to denote the frequency of strategy i on a k-regular graph, then the replicator equation on graph can be written as

$$x_i' = x_i \left(f_i + g_i - \Psi \right), \; i = 1, 2, 3, \ldots, n \tag{8.8}$$

8.2.3 Nash Equilibrium

For an N finite set of networking nodes, T_i are all the possible strategies where i represents the player and $T = (t_1, t_2, \ldots t_3)$ is the set of strategies for each player and T_{-i} is the strategy profile T without agent i's strategy [9]. In relation to that, $V_i(T)$ is the payoff for a node i if the strategy profile is T. T_i is the best response to T_{-i} if $V_i(t_i, T_{-i} > V_i(t_i', T_{-i}))$ for every strategy t_i' available to agent i where $(t_i, T_{-i} = (t_1, \ldots, t_{i-1}, t_i', t_{i+1}, \ldots, t_n))$. This set of strategies $t = (t_1, \ldots, t_n)$ can be termed as nash equilibrium, when for every i, t_i is the best response to T_i, which means no node can do better by unilaterally changing its strategy. Every game with a finite set of participants/players is bound to have at least one nash equilibrium. For the game to reach an equilibrium, each node has to identify its optimal strategy in response to the strategies of the other players and all the nodes have to play with their optimal strategies simultaneously.

8.2.4 Pareto Efficiency

Pareto efficiency, another important criterion of game theory, is defined as a situation where there is no way for a node to choose a different strategy and get benefited without making other nodes worse off [3]. A strategy profile T Pareto dominates a set of strategies T' if no player ends up with a worse payoff with T than with T'. Mathematically put, $V_i(T) \geq V_i(T')$ for all i and at least one player gets a better payoff with T than with T', i.e., $V_i(T) \geq V_i(T')$ for at least one i.

8.2.5 Repeated Game

In repeated games, a set of players will play the game repeatedly with the same strategy, taking into consideration the history of the past behavior. For better understanding, let us consider a repeated prisoner's dilemma game.

It is a strategic game in which a player, in this case a prisoner, is unaware of the other player's action and chooses its action simultaneously and independently. The strategy chosen by a player and the corresponding payoff has been provided in Table 8.1. Each of the players, i.e., prisoners, aims to reduce their sentences [10].

Table 8.1   Prisoner's Dilemma

	Cooperate	Defect
Cooperate	2, 2	10, 0
Defect	0, 10	4, 4

If cooperation is present, then both of them will remain silent and each will be sentenced to 1 year in prison. In case they defect, i.e., both confess, then each will be sentenced for 3 years. If only one of them confesses, then she/he will be freed, while the other will end up with 4 years' incarceration. Although it will be beneficial for both the prisoners to cooperate, i.e., not confessing to the crime, but as each has an incentive to get freed, in isolation both players will defect leading to a unique nash equilibrium (defect, defect) of the game in case of a non-repeated game. But if the players repeatedly take into account the past outcomes, then the mutual desirable outcome will be to cooperate, which will ensure a long-term gain but a short-term loss.

8.2.6 Bayesian Game

In games of complete information, the players know not only their own preferences, but also the preferences of the other players as well. But in many situations, however, there is likely to be considerable uncertainty on the part of each player regarding the preferences of his or her opponents. To incorporate this possibility, Bayesian games or games of incomplete information is introduced. In Bayesian games, each player can be one of a certain number of types. Each player knows his/her own type but cannot observe the type of the other players directly, which influences each player's payoff.

In the Battle of Sexes, suppose there are two players—player 1 and player 2. They have different preferences on whether to watch ballet or football. But player 1 does not know whether player 2 wishes to meet or wishes to avoid player 1. Therefore, this situation is of "incomplete information." We represent this by considering that player 2 has two different types, one type that wishes to meet player 1 and the other that wishes to avoid him. More explicitly, suppose that these two types have probability 1/2 each (Tables 8.2).

Table 8.2   Bayesian Game

	B	F
Cooperate	5, 2	0, 0
Defect	0, 0	2, 5

Then the game takes the form of one of the following two with probability 1/2. Crucially, player 2 knows which game it is (she knows the state of the world), but player 1 does not. Most importantly, from player 1's point of view, player 2 has two possible types (or equivalently, the world has two possible states each with probability 1/2 and only player 2 knows the actual state). Let us consider the following strategy profile $(C, (C, F))$, which means that player 1 will play C, i.e., ballet, while in state 1, player 2 will also play F (when she wants to meet player 1) and in state 2, player 2 will play F, i.e., football (when she wants to avoid player 1). Clearly, given the play of B by player 1, the strategy of player 2 is the best response. Let us now check if player 1 is also playing the best response. Since both states are equally likely, the expected payoff of player 1 is

$$E[C,(C,F)] = 1/2*2 + 1/2*0 = 1 \tag{8.9}$$

If, instead, he deviates and plays F, his expected payoff is 1.

$$E[F,(C,F)] = 1/2*0 + 1/2*1 = 2 \tag{8.10}$$

Therefore, the strategy profile $(C, (C,F))$ is a (Bayesian) nash equilibrium.

Interestingly, meeting at football, which is the preferable outcome for player 2 is no longer a nash equilibrium. Why not? Suppose that the two players will meet at football when they want to meet. Then the relevant strategy profile is $(F, (F,C))$ and

$$E[F,(F,C)] = 1/2*1 + 1/2*0 = 2 \tag{8.11}$$

If, instead, player 1 deviates and plays C, his expected payoff is

$$E[C,(F,C)] = 1/2*0 + 1/2*2 = 1 \tag{8.12}$$

8.2.7 Chicken Game

Let us understand the chicken game with a quintessential scenario. Let us say that there are two cars (players) heading toward each other. If the players continue on the same path, they bump into each other; if one swerves out of the way and the other does not, then that player "loses" and is labeled as the *chicken*, while the second, implicitly braver player, wins.

The payoff matrix is mentioned in Table 8.3. In the table, (−2, 2) and (2, −2) are two pure nash equilibria because if either of the players deviates from their current strategies in these two cases, then they would end up with more negative payoffs. But the same cannot be said for (−100, 100) and (0, 0) because deviating from these

Table 8.3 Chicken Game

	Keep Going	*Swerve*
Keep going	−100, −100	2, −2
Swerve	−2, 2	0, 0

strategies would yield a higher payoff for each individual. So, they can be ruled out from being equilibria stages.

8.2.8 Tit-for-Tat Game

Tit for tat is a game theory with a payoff matrix similar to that of prisoner's dilemma. It is relevant to a problem called the iterated prisoner's dilemma. This strategy can be implemented in games involving repeated moves. A player using this strategy will first cooperate, then replicate an opponent's previous action. If the opponent had been cooperative, the player would have been cooperative and vice versa.

This strategy states that a person is more successful in game theory if he/she is cooperative with another person. The idea is that if a person rewards another with good behavior, according to this theory, then he/she reciprocates with good behavior. This strategy is based on the concept of forgiveness (retaliation). When faced with a dilemma, an individual cooperates only when the other person has an immediate history of cooperating and does not cooperate when the counterparty previously defaulted.

8.2.9 Stackelberg Game

The original Stackelberg game is an asymmetric duopoly. Player 1 takes on the role of leader, while player 2 takes on the role of follower. It is a two-period model where in the first period the leader chooses its strategy. This decision is irreversible and cannot be changed in the second period. The leader might emerge in a game because of historical precedence, size, reputation, innovation, information, and so forth. In the second period, the follower chooses its strategy after observing the strategy chosen by the leader (the strategy chosen by the follower must, therefore, be along its reaction function).

There are some variations of this game. If both players are followers, then you have a Cournot game. If both players believe themselves to be the leaders, then neither will be successful at following the strategy above. This is a leader–leader game, and it will lead to a Stackelberg disequilibrium. The leader–leader model will require both parties to start with incorrect assumptions about each other, and it will lead to nonoptimal output in the market.

In a multistage game, as rational players, the players will revise their expectations. As a result, either one will take the role of follower or a player will exit the market, providing with the remaining leader a monopoly.

8.2.10 Potential Game

A potential game is one where the incentives of all the players to change their strategies can be expressed using one global function called potential function. Two types of potential games are the ordinal and cardinal potential games. In cardinal games, the difference in individual payoffs for each player obtained by individually changing one's strategy only must have the same value as the difference in values for the potential function. In ordinal games, only the signs of the differences have to be the same.

The potential function is a useful tool to analyze equilibrium properties of games, since the incentives of all players are mapped into one function, and the set of pure nash equilibria can be determined by finding the local optima of the potential function. Convergence and finite-time convergence of an iterated game toward a nash equilibrium can also be understood by studying the potential function.

8.3 Game-Theoretic Application in Big Data Analytics

Gathered knowledge from big data analysis can be used to form regulations to which a particular game can stick to. Inversely, game theory has the capability to improve the understanding of rules that govern big data analytics. In a game, players can be tempted to perform with the potential of high reward to aid the process of data aggregation. In this section, we are going to review how game-theoretic approaches have been implemented in big data analytics.

At present, the field of geoscience and remote sensing generates a huge amount of data. The decision makers have to sort out the conflicting and redundant data from this data pool to take the right course of action. Game theory plays a vital role in decision-making in this field, particularly in solving the problems of feature selection and automated ground cover classification. Lori Mann Bruce [11], in this work, focuses on the application of the game-theoretic approach in spectral band selection while utilizing hyperspectral imagery. All the players, i.e., band groups in this game who are inclined to maximize individual payoffs, might undermine the overall system payoff. That is why the author applies the principle of Pareto-efficient nash equilibrium. He demonstrates that when the proposed hyperspectral band grouping using game theory is implemented in multi-classifier decision fusion system, the overall accuracy rises to 77% in comparison with 63% and 58% produced by uniform partitioning and Bhattacharyya distance and spectral band correlation, respectively.

Liu et al. [12] model the interaction between the customers and the hotel industry as a noncooperative two-stage bargain game. The customers around the world look for the best hotel to stay and receive the highest cost performance. Here, first, the necessity of the customers and hotel managements have been analyzed, followed by sorting out the decision factors that affect the chosen policies by the customers. Then analyzing the interactions between the clients and the hotel operators based on big data, the modeled game has been simulated. The results supported by Monte Carlo simulation infer that the proposed game with big data generates the best output because the two-stage game provides the customer with an extra chance to choose and the hotel with an extra chance to accept the price. The outcome infers that this novel method can reduce the price for the customers to select a hotel at a lower price with lesser failure rate, thus benefiting the hotel operators as well.

Lancelot et al. [13] address the problem of joint policy correlation (JPC) in the multi-agent reinforcement learning mechanism. A new algorithm is put forward that allows independent learners to measure the extent of correlation of policies, which in turn helps in visualizing the acuteness of the overfitting problem. This novel algorithm is capable of immensely lessening JPC while participating in the partially observable coordination games. Furthermore, it generates a defense mechanism utilizing the decision-making approach of other participating players in a competitive imperfect information game.

Map Reduce, a framework developed by Google, processes big data from distributed servers and runs several responsibilities in parallel to each other. Till today, Map Reduce applications have been bottlenecked by various limitations, e.g., execution time and capacity allocation. Gianniti et al. [14] focus on establishing novel capacity allocation techniques for ensuring more robust performance among private clouds. Game-theoretic approach leading to a generalized nash equilibrium solves the problem of joint admission control, which in turn helps improve capacity allocation of multi-class Hadoop clusters (Table 8.4).

The explosion of online services and the resultant big data containing personal information of the users have resulted in assigning intrinsic economic values to these personal data. Chessa et al. [15] put forward a game-theoretic mechanism termed as public good game, which is capable of quantifying the worth of revealing personal data. Selecting the cooperative game appropriate for the model, the authors quantify the value of personal data using core and Shapley values. Also, while implementing network games, it is inferred that creating more links among neighbors helps them increase the value of their personal data. This in turn provides higher incentives that benefit all as they also ascertain a stable network.

Jiang et al. [16] proposed the application of game theory in detecting communities in dynamic social networks. Every day people are getting more involved with each other on social networks, which has led to the generation of big data in this domain. Game theory, being the tool for extracting valuable information from these complex relations in networks, has been used in this work in the form of a noncooperative game. Here, each rational independent node is able to switch, join,

Table 8.4 Applications of Game Theory in Big Data Analytics

Reference	Objective
Lori Mann Bruce [11]	To select spectral bands utilizing hyperspectral imagery
Liu et al. [12]	To design a hotel–customer transaction with lower price and lesser failure rate
Lancelot et al. [13]	To address a joint policy correlation problem in the multiagent reinforcement learning mechanism
Gianniti et al. [14]	To ensure the robust cloud performance with the novel capacity allocation technique.
Chessa et al. [15]	To quantify the value of personal data used in online services
Jiang et al. [16]	To detecting communities in dynamic social networks
Tao et al. [17]	To analyze the behavior of protocols in big data domain
Zheng et al. [18]	To maximizing the data transmission rate in wireless sensor networks
Pillai et al. [19]	To devise a resource allocation mechanism for virtual machines of cloud system
Chung et al. [20]	To introduce rationality by using Q-learning in intrusion detectors.
Kaur et al. [21]	To evaluating the automated employee performance using IoT monitoring devices
Tosh et al. [22]	To promote cyber security information sharing to raise security infrastructure
Zhang et al. [23]	To introduce an incentive mechanism among workers on a crowdsourcing platform
Hoh et al. [25]	To implement a data authentication mechanism on a crowdsourcing platform
Wang Yi [26]	To efficiently integrate decision-making with data mining
Wu et al. [27]	To formulate privacy level hierarchy among datasets
Zheng et al. [28]	To propose a novel incentive mechanism for data controllers in WCN

(Continued)

Table 8.4 (*Continued*) Applications of Game Theory in Big Data Analytics

Reference	Objective
Kargupta et al. [29]	To solve the problem of PPDM using game theory considering non-ideal behavior from each party
Wang et al. [30]	To apply data mining on manufacturing data with rules derived from game theory
Miyaji et al. [31]	To model a game-theoretic protocol for PPDM
Peng et al. [32]	To discuss two types of incentive mechanism: crowdsourcer-centric model and user-centric model
Luo et al. [33]	To model heterogeneous crowdsourcing with the assumption that each worker's probabilistic knowledge is different
Wang et al. [34]	To devise a twofold incentive mechanism for smartphone users in a crowdsourcing platform
Kumar et al. [35]	To discuss a strategy selection process in VCPS using a stochastic coalition game
Pouryazdan et al. [36]	To ensure truthfulness among users of a mobile crowdsensing system

or leave a community independently after evaluating certain factors like participation degree in the existing community and the strength of friendship in it. The utility function has been designed as the difference between gain function and loss function described in the chapter. Finally, the obtained local nash equilibrium shows that each individual can find their suited communities effectively.

Tao et al. [17] address the challenges concerning the exchange of information among the protocols of IoT, big data, and cloud computing. An extensive imperfect information game-based model is designed to analyze the behavior of the participating protocols. The fairness properties and the rationality of the players are selected as the payoff and an exchange protocol game is designed in such a way that only one player is allowed to take the action at a certain stage. This work further compares the proposed model with Buttyan's model and shows that the proposed model strictly contains the Buttyan's by attaining a subgame perfect equilibrium. A tree analysis mechanism supported by a linear algorithm is designed to verify the business security properties of cloud computing.

With the emergence of big data domain, it has become necessary to find an efficient approach to optimize this huge amount of data for fast convergence of the data and network size. To achieve that, Zheng et al. [18] model a hierarchical network and a pricing mechanism to formulate the Stackelberg game. The Stackelberg game is chosen because in the designed hierarchy the agents (network operators) of the network help the leader (ISP) in attaining its objective. Moreover, the fast and smooth linear convergence is independent of the network size as the objective functions have been designed as convex functions. This ensures the model's proper functioning in big data networks. Lastly, this work verifies the designed pricing framework's fast convergence in a virtualized wireless network where the agents always aim to maximize the total data transmission rate by allocating the maximum resource possible.

Pillai et al. [19] in their work apply the uncertainty principle of game theory to design a resource allocation mechanism among the virtual machines of a cloud system. To cope with the surge in demand for infrastructure-as-a-service of cloud platform, the distributed virtual machines need to form a coalition among themselves. This work shows that the coalition and uncertainty-oriented model is better suited for optimal resource allocation and utilization that is capable of attaining a lower task completion time in comparison with the existing systems.

In modeling security games, the efficiency of machine learning application has been tested previously where a huge amount of historical data was fed to the machine learning system. As a result, the system becomes sensitive to the attacks which only has relevance to previous attacks as per the historical data. Chung et al. [20] introduce rationality by using Q-learning approach which reinforces the decision-making model by adapting to newer intrusion patterns by analyzing the previous iterations. As a result, this novel approach is better suited in taking necessary actions to maximize the payoff of the security system administration against newer attacks.

Kaur et al. [21] propose an automated employee performance evaluation using IoT-based monitoring devices. The authors implement a game-theoretic approach while checking the performance appraisal to ensure unbiased evaluation. In the designed model, employees get rewards for positive performance and vice versa. Prior to applying game theory for making the decision, data is mined from the IoT devices using colocation mining. Performance comparison carried out in this work infers that implementation of game-theoretic approach reduces the execution time for the system significantly in comparison to the other decision-making processes, such as fuzzy systems or Bayesian model. The equilibrium obtained shows that the strategy of rewarding the employees ensures better performance from them, which helps in attaining a stable business environment.

Tosh et al. [22] propound the concept of establishing a structure called cyber information exchange (CYBEX) with a view to promote mutual security information sharing for improving security infrastructure of the funds. As the funds will always have a tendency to dominate the market, the competition among them will always be noncooperative. But the authors devise a mechanism based on the distributed noncooperative game model to impose a self-enforcement mechanism, which maximizes the participation from the firms in sharing their security information and also maximizes the CYBEX incentive for its sustenance in the market.

Capable of reaching an evolutionary stable strategy (ESS), deploying evolutionary game theory works as the perfect learning heuristic for the firms while learning to update their strategy at each stage, based on the feedback from the previous iterations.

Zhang et al. [23] model a repeated game to formulate incentive protocols among workers and requesters on a crowdsourcing platform. The proposed model erases the drawbacks of existing pricing schemes, such as currency inflation and free-riding [24]. Choosing a flat-rate pricing scheme and designing the transaction as an asymmetric gift-giving game, the authors formulate the repeated game to ensure revenue maximization of the website owner. This model relies on a reputation-based reward and punishment scheme that provides generous incentive to the workers on ex ante basis. Simulation analysis displays an equilibrium closer to Pareto-efficient outcome as a result of using intrinsic parameters (reward, patience, cost) and the workers' attributes in devising an incentive protocol.

TruCentive, a crowdsourced parking information-providing platform, was proposed by Hoh et al. [25]. This platform utilizes a three-stage incentive mechanism to ensure authentic data from an unreliable mobile using crowd. The incentive protocol uses game theory analysis and ensures that the users are providing accurate parking information instead of lying as the game-theoretic model is set with a reward parameter where reselling gain is more than lying and refund policy. This protects the platform from malicious participants by reducing high volume of useless false data.

Yi [26], in this paper, presents a framework that integrates data mining and game theory by adapting to an innovative approach. This approach involves representing gained knowledge as a set of rules. These rules can be used for decision-making or strategy selection process. Here, the general framework that combines data mining and game theory consists of four steps: data selection, data preprocessing, data mining, and, finally, strategy selection. The mining process is further divided into three separate steps, namely, classification, clustering, and association, to provide the aspects that would define the combination process.

Maximizing data utility compromises privacy constraints and vice versa. Also, the privacy level of some datasets can be influenced by the privacy parameters of its neighbors other than itself. So, Wu et al. [27] seek to formulate a correlated privacy game after measuring the influence of correlated datasets, utility of data, and value of privacy to seek the trade-off between utility and privacy. This game consists of a finite set of players, a finite strategy space, and a payoff function. The conditions for obtaining nash equilibrium and the price of anarchy are also considered while analyzing the aforementioned game.

A rapid increase in the rate of data generation in wireless communication networks (WCNs) is not possible to be handled only by the controllers in WCNs. But agents have their own tasks and they need to be incentivized. This paper [28] addresses this incentivization problem by forming it as a hierarchical game between agents and controllers, which can also be used as an incentivization mechanism so that controllers can ask agents to help in their respective tasks. Here, previous issues in the case of applying game theory in wireless big data processing, namely, convergence conditions, convergence speed, and scalability, are also discussed.

In real-life applications of privacy-preserving distributed data mining (PPDM), where multiple parties are involved, every party does not always behave according to the protocols. Kargupta et al. [29] intend to solve this problem by forming a game where each party tries to optimize its benefit, assuming a nonideal behavior from each party. It presents a case study in the form of equilibrium analysis of secure sum computation as an example. Furthermore, to achieve an optimal solution, a distributed penalty function mechanism is discussed to help achieve equilibrium without any collusion between the parties involved.

To address the difficulty of applying game theory in manufacturing engineering, Wang et al. [30] discuss a new approach that amalgamates game theory and data mining to utilize real-life manufacturing datasets. It divides an iterative process called game mining into six stages with an aim to provide a general framework. Alongside discussing the game behavior and levels and addressing the drawbacks of game theory, it utilizes mining algorithm based on the work of association and dynamic mining to achieve the desired goal.

Owing to the need to preserve privacy, there have been various adversaries modeled till now, namely, semi-honest, malicious, and covert. But game theory gives us the scope to assume that each party acts in its own interest. So, this paper [31] discusses a protocol involving two parties in light of game theory. Here, verifiable random functions are used as cryptographic algorithms underlying the protocol. It is also shown that it satisfies nash equilibrium and stability conditions.

Smartphone users can be used by crowdsourcers on the condition of receiving enough rewards for participation. So, this paper [32] visualizes a noncooperative dynamic game consisting of multiple mobile crowdsourcers and a crowd of smartphone users to study the interrelationship between them. The game is later evolved to a repeated game to consider joint acts between the crowdsourcers. The problems related to the amount of reward for smartphone users, interaction with the market, and stability of the market are also discussed.

Luo et al. [33] model heterogeneous crowdsourcing with a view that each worker's probabilistic knowledge is different. Here, an incentive mechanism is designed in an incomplete information scenario using an auction-based framework. In the process, they also discuss strategy autonomy, i.e., the phenomenon of workers behaving the same in a heterogeneous setting as they would in a homogeneous setting. Later, they obtain accurate solutions for achieving equilibrium despite assuming an unorthodox setting.

Realizing the great potential of smartphone users as a medium of crowdsensing, Wang et al. [34] discuss two types of incentive mechanisms: crowdsourcer-centric model and user-centric model. In the crowdsourcer-centric model, crowdsourcer is the leader and vice versa for the user-centric model. For the first case, the conditions for Stackelberg equilibrium are considered. For the latter case, an auction-based incentive mechanism is discussed which is quite effective. Subsequently, evaluations and validations of implementation and verification of these models are also discussed.

Kumar et al. [35] in this work propose a strategy selection process in Vehicular Cyber-Physical Systems (VCPS) using a stochastic coalition game where vehicles are assumed as players. Some predefined strategies help learning automata to aggregate data from the environment which are placed in the vehicles. At any given moment, the player with the highest payoff is permitted to make a move to maintain stability when considered against the actions of all the players. Later, it is also shown to have better performances in particular cases, e.g., duration of clustering and maintenance cost where the proposed scheme is applied.

To ensure the voters' truthfulness in a mobile crowdsensing system, they need to be incentivized. Pouryazdan et al. [36] in this paper suggest a game-theoretic recruitment system consisting of three phases: user recruitment, collaborative decision-making, and badge rewarding. Here, the incentivizing mechanism is based on the subgame perfect equilibrium and gamification techniques and adopts a method called social network-aided trustworthiness assurance and a consequent badge reward. Later, successful resistance against users with low quality data contribution are also demonstrated via simulation.

8.4 Limitations and Future Work

In spite of a stark rise in the implementation of game theory to make big data analysis more efficient, there remain a lot of limitations to be addressed (Figure 8.2). For example,

- In modeling cybersecurity solution designs using game theory, there remains an incompleteness/imperfectness in the information of the player participating in the game. As a result, imperfect information stochastic games are in play in many cases that have to go through a lot of iterations in learning phases to accurately predict the outcome. There lies a big challenge in reducing the number of iterations while learning from a big data pool with reinforcement learning to solve partially observable stochastic games.
- While applying the Q-learning method in adapting to malicious attacks, the accuracy of the system depends on the completeness of the attack models that are used in training the system to take rational decisions. Limitations still remain in covering undefined actions or states as well as in fixing the reward metrics for successful attack detection.
- Application of game theory in cybersecurity still lacks scalability. Limitation in considering the states of the systems as finite can be alleviated by involving an infinite state assumption which will aid in making the model more realistic.
- At present, the utility and payoff functions of the security models are employed depending on ad-hoc strategies. Implementation of big data analytics in fine-tuning the payoff and utility functions is yet to be explored.

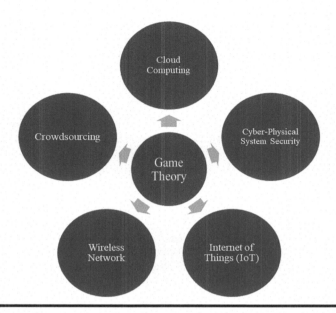

Figure 8.2   Emerging fields of application of game theory in big data domain.

- While applied in marketing measurement, game theory falls short in giving an accurate analysis if the participating players behave "irrationally." There is still a lot of work to be done assuming variable behavior from decision makers to make game theory compatible for application in this field.
- In the crowdsourcing domain, a situation similar to Designers Dilemma arises with the application of game theory. In the practical situation, one player's decision-making process is affected by that of others, which can affect the overall game process. This presents a significant challenge as it might result in particular situations giving different outcome than anticipated.

8.5 Conclusion

There is obviously a shift in the progress of decision making processes where previously time consuming, inefficient models were built for ensuring accurate estimates and judgments. Reality was simulated using data-driven models accumulated from big data pool. Strategic decision-making from a huge amount of data is a research area with far-reaching implications/effects. In summary, the concept of game theory is not a core part of traditional data science, rather a tool that can analyze a huge amount of data with meaningful visualizations and quantifiable data-driven decision-making. This chapter has synopsized game-theoretic applications in the field of big data analytics. Application of game theory is already being used in making the decision-making process more rationalized in an interactive context and with the potential to contribute further.

References

1. Bernard Marr. "Big data overload: Why most companies can't deal with the data explosion." *Forbes*, April 28, 2016. Available: www.forbes.com/sites/bernardmarr/2016/04/28/big-data-overload-most-companies-cant-deal-with-the-data-explosion/#312d21ce6b0d. (Accessed February 7, 2018).
2. Jennifer Rowley. "The wisdom hierarchy: Representations of the DIKW hierarchy." *Journal of Information Science 33*, no. 2 (2007): 163–180.
3. Drew Fudenberg and Jean Tirole. *Game Theory*. Mit Press: Cambridge, MA, 1991.
4. Peter D. Taylor and Leo B. Jonker. "Evolutionary stable strategies and game dynamics." *Mathematical Biosciences* 40 (1978): 97–98.
5. Erez Lieberman, Christoph Hauert, and Martin A. Nowak. "Evolutionary dynamics on graphs." *Nature* 433, no. 7023 (2005): 312–316.
6. Hisashi Ohtsuki and Martin A. Nowak. "The replicator equation on graphs." *Journal of Theoretical Biology* 243, no. 1 (2006): 86–97.
7. K. Habibul Kabir, Masahiro Sasabe, and Tetsuya Takine. "Evolutionary game theoretic approach to self-organized data aggregation in delay tolerant networks." *IEICE Transactions on Communications* 93, no. 3 (2010): 490–500.
8. K. HabibulKabir, Masahiro Sasabe, and Tetsuya Takine. "Design and analysis of self-organized data aggregation using evolutionary Game Theory in delay tolerant networks." In *The Third IEEE WoWMoM Workshop on Autonomic and Opportunistic Communications*, 2010.
9. John Nash. "Non-cooperative games." *Annals of Mathematics* 54, no. 2 (1951): 286–295.
10. Ramona Trestian, Olga Ormond, and Gabriel-Miro Muntean. "Theory-based network selection: Solutions and challenges." *IEEE Communications Surveys and Tutorials* 14, no. 4 (2012): 1212–1231.
11. Lori Mann Bruce. "Game theory applied to big data analytics in geosciences and remote sensing." In 2013 *IEEE International on Geoscience and Remote Sensing Symposium (IGARSS)*. IEEE, 2013.
12. Shasha Liu, et al. "Game theoretic approach of a novel decision policy for customers based on big data." *Electronic Commerce Research* 18, no. 2 (2018): 225–240.
13. Marc Lanctot, et al. "A unified game-theoretic approach to multiagent reinforcement learning." In *Proceedings of the Conference on Advances in Neural Information Processing Systems (NIPS)*, Long Beach, CA, 2017.
14. Eugenio Gianniti, et al. "A game-theoretic approach for runtime capacity allocation in MapReduce." In *Proceedings of the 17th IEEE/ACM International Symposium on Cluster, Cloud and Grid Computing*. IEEE Press, 2017.
15. Loiseau Chessa, et al. "A cooperative game-theoretic approach to quantify the value of personal data in networks." (2017). Doi:10.1145/3106723.3106732.
16. Fei Jiang and Jin Xu. "Dynamic community detection based on game theory in social networks." In 2015 *IEEE International Conference on Big Data (Big Data)*. IEEE, 2015.
17. Xiuting Tao, et al. "A game-theoretic model and analysis of data exchange protocols for internet of things in clouds." *Future Generation Computer Systems* 76 (2017): 582–589.
18. Zijie Zheng, Lingyang Song, and Zhu Han. "Bridging the gap between Big Data and Game Theory: A general hierarchical pricing framework." In 2017 *IEEE International Conference on Communications (ICC)*. IEEE, 2017.

19. Parvathy S. Pillai and Shrisha Rao. "Resource allocation in cloud computing using the uncertainty principle of game theory." IEEE Systems Journal 10, no. 2 (2016): 637–648.

20. Keywhan Chung, et al. "Game theory with learning for cyber security monitoring." In *IEEE 17th International Symposium on High Assurance Systems Engineering (HASE)*. IEEE, 2016.

21. Navroop Kaur and Sandeep K. Sood. "A game theoretic approach for an IoT-based automated employee performance evaluation." *IEEE Systems Journal* 11, no. 3 (2017): 1385–1394.

22. Deepak Tosh, et al. "An evolutionary game-theoretic framework for cyber-threat information sharing." *2015 IEEE International Conference on Communications (ICC)*. IEEE, 2015.

23. Yu Zhang and Mihaela van der Schaar. "Reputation-based incentive protocols in crowdsourcing applications." In *INFOCOM*, 2012 *Proceedings IEEE*. IEEE, 2012.

24. M. Feldman, C. Papadimitriou, J. Chuang, and I. Stoica. "Free-riding and Whitewashing in Peer-to-Peer Systems." In *Workshop on Practice & Theory of Incentives in Networked Systems*, 2004.

25. Baik Hoh, et al. "Trucentive: A game-theoretic incentive platform for trustworthy mobile crowdsourcing parking services." In *2012 15th International IEEE Conference on Intelligent Transportation Systems (ITSC)*. IEEE, 2012.

26. Yi Wang. "Integration of data mining with Game Theory." In *Knowledge Enterprise: Intelligent Strategies in Product Design, Manufacturing, and Management, Proceedings of PROLAMAT 2006, IFIP TC5, International Conference*, Shanghai, China, June 15–17, 2006, 275–280.

27. Xiaotong Wu, et al. "Game theory based correlated privacy preserving analysis in big data." *IEEE Transactions on Big Data* (2017). Doi: 10.1109/TBDATA.2017.2701817.

28. Zijie Zheng, et al. "Game theoretic approaches to massive data processing in wireless networks." *Distributed, Parallel, and Cluster Computing* 25, no. 1 (2018): 98–104.

29. Hillol Kargupta, Kamalika Das, and Kun Liu. "Multi-party, privacy-preserving distributed data mining using a game theoretic framework." In *Practice of Knowledge Discovery in Databases*, Vol. 4702, 2007.

30. Yi Wang. "Combining data mining and game theory in manufacturing strategy analysis." *Journal of Intelligent Manufacturing* 18, no. 4 (2007): 505–511.

31. Atsuko Miyaji, and Mohammad Shahriar Rahman. "Privacy-preserving data mining: A game-theoretic approach." In *IFIP Annual Conference on Data and Applications Security and Privacy*. Springer: Berlin, Heidelberg, 2011.

32. Jia Peng, et al. "Behavior dynamics of multiple crowdsourcers in mobile crowdsourcing markets." *IEEE Network* 30, no. 6 (2016): 92–96.

33. Tie Luo, et al. "Incentive mechanism design for heterogeneous crowdsourcing using all-pay contests." *IEEE Transactions on Mobile Computing* 15, no. 9 (2016): 2234–2246.

34. Dejun Yang, et al. "Incentive mechanisms for crowdsensing: Crowdsourcing with smartphones." *Biological Cybernetics* 24, no. 3 (2016): 1732–1744.

35. Neeraj Kumar, et al. "Optimized clustering for data dissemination using stochastic coalition game in vehicular cyber-physical systems." *The Journal of Supercomputing* 71, no. 9 (2015): 3258–3287.

36. Maryam Pouryazdan, et al. "Game-theoretic recruitment of sensing service providers for trustworthy cloud-centric Internet-of-Things (IoT) applications." In *2016 IEEE Globecom Workshops (GC Wkshps)*. IEEE, 2016.

Chapter 9

Project Management for Effective Data Analytics

Munir Ahmad Saeed
UNSW Canberra

Mohiuddin Ahmed
Canberra Institute of Technology

Contents

9.1 Introduction

Over the years, project management (PM) has developed into a discipline in its own right and has received increasing interest from researchers. PM comprises a number of tools and techniques, and if applied effectively, it can lead to the delivery of specified outcomes.

Snyder et al. [1] stated that though stories about the evolution of PM go back to the building of pyramids in Egypt however, modern PM started in the 1950s and the first article on PM appeared in 1958. Snyder stated that in 1960 very few people knew what the project manager was about, but now the project manager is a key member of management teams. Johnson et al. [2] stated that PM did not get any mention in management literature before World War II (WWII). He argues that during the Cold War there were pressures to develop new defense systems swiftly and operational research, systems engineering, and PM because of increasing realization by the scientists, managers, and engineers that conventional methods of management and development were inadequate. From its inception to the early years of evolution, PM was technical and industry specific. Morris et al. [3] highlighted the journey of PM from tools such as Gantt chart, program evaluation and review technique (PERT), and critical path method in the 1950s to work breakdown structure (WBS) and value analysis in the 1960s; resources scheduling, concurrency, and people in the 1970s; technology, procurement, risk, and fast tracking in the 1980s; and philosophy, quality, knowledge management, and Project Management Office in the 1990s and 2000s.

Tracing the technical and institutional factors behind the emergence of PM, Johnson et al. [4] stated that the Manhattan Project, to build a nuclear bomb, was the single most important project of the WWII that was managed by Leslie Groves of army corps of engineers. The Manhattan Project was a significant event in the history of PM for developing a scientific product. From its origins in the military, PM spread to other sectors in the United States. The emergence and development of PM has its roots in the United States, except a little influence from Germany because Von Braun's team was involved in the development of rocket systems. Initially, PM was limited to the military projects that required secrecy; there were only a few influences from other industries in the United States because these industries did not face similar levels of technological challenges, uncertainties, and pressures of rapid development as experienced by the defense projects. Therefore, the management style that emerged in aerospace and computing industries has the signatures of technical and organizational problems of the military [4]. Pollack et al. [5] provided a comprehensive analysis of PM literature from 1962–2012, where it is identified that PM has moved from a technical and industry specific focus to interpersonal issues. The main themes of current research in the PM discipline are environment issues, strategic planning, project knowledge management, business, and innovation [5]. Since PM has played a key role in research and development of new technologies, it will be interesting to explore how PM can assist data analytics as an emerging discipline.

9.1.1 Chapter Roadmap

The rest of the chapter is organized as follows: Section 9.2 discusses the big data projects. In Sections 9.3–9.6, different types of PM methodologies are described in detail and the relationship with data analytics is established. Finally, in Section 9.7, the key insights gained from these methodologies are discussed from the perspective of data analytics. The chapter concludes in Section 9.8.

9.2 Big Data Projects

According to Standish Group CHAOS report 2017 [6], about $250 billion were spent on 175,000 information technology (IT) projects, but only 28% of software projects at small size companies were completed on time and within the budget. Similarly, 31% projects will be cancelled and nearly 53% projects will be 189% over budget. According to the report, the project success rate in medium size companies in the United States is 16%, while larger size companies present a dismal rate of project completion, i.e., merely 9%. The report did not highlight whether the company size has any impact on the project success rate. The results of this report also reflect in big data projects and, according to Informatica [7], data analytics proof of concepts fail to complete on time and within the budget and, consequently, these projects fail to meet the top management expectations. In companies where big data projects are being implemented, only 27% executives consider their data projects to be successful because there are only 13% companies where big data projects are in full-scale production. Since big data projects are less known, therefore there is a need for research to identify the factors behind the failure of big data projects. Informatica identifies some of the factors that lead to the failure of big data proof of concepts such as projects failing to align with the strategic objectives of sponsoring executives, lack of planning and design, scope creep, and ignoring data management. According to Informatica [7], if projects align to top management strategic plans, it guarantees the wholehearted support of organization executives. In order for projects to get executives' support, the projects must align to the organization's strategic objectives by creating value for the organization. Therefore, Informatica argues that it is very important that PM processes are geared toward aligning projects with organizational strategic objectives. Lack of planning and design is another cause for the failure of big data projects. Informatica recommends that big data projects should run for 6 weeks as starting small reduces the risks, but it also emphasizes that early stage planning, architecture, and design are the other key factors in the implementation of big data projects. Though due to its very nature, big data projects cannot have a fully defined architecture and design right from the start, but Informatica states that it is still important to understand the significance of various technical components at the beginning. Scope creep is a major challenge in all project types and in all industries; therefore, big data projects are not exception [8]. In software development projects, the potential for scope creep is higher than in projects of other industries, such as construction. The main reason behind scope creep in software-based projects is the lack of details in design and architecture at the start as mentioned earlier. Informatica states that big data projects are more prone to overlooking the basic principles of data management. If the very data that instigates big data project's proof of concepts is not reliable, then the project will not be able to solve the business problem, which will ultimately lead to failure in fulfilling the expectations of the top management and also failure int creating value for the business. Due to these factors highlighted by Informatica, there are only 13% organizations where big data projects are in full production; therefore, big data project managers are facing a phenomenal task of increasing the success rate of big data projects by addressing the various factors discussed earlier.

In order to improve the success rate of big data projects, we can seek guidance from the mainstream PM. Before we discuss how PM can help big data projects to achieve higher success rates, it would be pertinent to discuss how PM as a discipline is contributing toward the economic activity and helping businesses achieve their strategic objectives and generate value from projects [9].

PM plays an important role as an economic activity globally, and it has been tremendously adopted by various industries, particularly since the 1980s. Projects are important tools in the hands of organizations for achieving their strategic objectives. Therefore, projects have been employed as management tools by various industries. It is important to explore how far projects have been effective as management tools for organizations. Projects have been employed to achieve strategic objectives by various industries since the 1950s, starting with the defense industry in the United States. The important role played by projects as an effective tool can be gaged from the share of projects in the global economic activity. Bredillet et al. [10] stated that globally more than 20% of the economic activity occurs in the form of projects, and in the emerging economies this ratio is more than 30%. Referring to the World Development Indicators, Bredillet et al. stated that out of $48 trillion of the world's gross domestic product, 22% is entirely project based. These statistics indicate the role of PM in value creation at the global level [10].

Since projects were adopted to achieve strategic objectives, the success of projects also became an important issue for practitioners and researchers. According to PM literature, where the success debate started in the 1980s, a project is considered successful if it is completed within the cost, time, and meeting scope specifications, though the success debate has moved further to include stakeholder's satisfaction as another key variable There is an increasing emphasis on value generation from PM and value is not just limited to economic and financial gains but encompasses social, ethical, and ecological value as well. Since 2010 various authors have challenged the classical success criteria of triple constraints (on cost, time, and scope) and argue for assessing project success not on the basis of project outputs rather on the basis of project outcomes. Project outputs are the artifacts or deliverables, whereas project outcomes are goals for which projects are initiated and implemented. Project outcomes lead to value for the organization, which is also known as project benefits. PM literature makes a powerful case for PM as the most effective management tool to implement organizational strategy, achieve strategic objectives, and obtain value for the organization. Big data analytics need to learn from current debates in PM and evaluate its project's success not only on the basis of triple constraints but also on the basis of project outcomes and benefits. In order to ensure project success, the mainstream PM discipline employs various PM frameworks and methodologies, and according to Pearson et al. [11], following are the key PM methodologies:

- PMBOK (Project Management Body of Knowledge)
- PRINCE2 (Projects in Controlled Environment)
- Agile
- ISO 21500:2012

9.3 Project Management Body of Knowledge

Project Management Institute's (PMI) methodology, famously known as PMBOK, is based on a generic project life cycle approach, which can be applied to any industry, project size, and complexity in public and private sectors.

Pearson et al. [11] provided the following features of PMBOK framework:

- PMI's PMBOK provides a generic life cycle approach.
- It can be applied to projects of all sizes and complexities across all industry and government sectors.
- It provides valuable body of knowledge around PM in general.
- It provides understanding of key tools and techniques applied in other methodologies and frameworks, such as PRINCE2®, ISO 21500:2012, and Agile.
- It is based on ten components known as knowledge areas that cover the entire project life cycle

Figure 9.1 shows PMBOK knowledge areas:

- Scope management
- Time management
- Cost management
- Quality management
- Human resources management
- Communications management
- Risk management
- Procurement management
- Governance management
- Integration management

PMBOK comprises five main processes: initiation, planning, execution, monitoring and control, and closing. These processes can be seen in Figure 9.1.

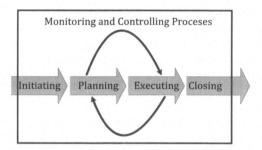

Figure 9.1 PMBOK project management life cycle process. (Adapted from [11].)

Like any effective PM framework, PMBOK provides governance mechanism to keep projects on track and ensure that the project remains aligned to organizational strategies. These are ensured throughout the process of PM, but the framework has some decision gates to make stop or stay on course decisions. However, these decision gates are not provided throughout the project life cycle as in PRINCE2, where such decisions could be made at the end of every project stage. PMBOK stage gates can be seen in Figure 9.2.

PMBOK is a very comprehensive PM standard and a framework, and it has inspired other PM methodologies, such as PRINCE2, Agile, and ISO 21500:2012. PMBOK can be tailored to suit the inherent nature of big data projects, but PMBOK insists on defining project scope and product description during the planning phase, which does not suit the very nature of big data projects that are software based. Therefore, PMBOK can be employed to manage time, cost, quality and risk management, and governance and integration of the project, whereas Agile approach can be applied to develop big data proof of concepts and product development through iterations.

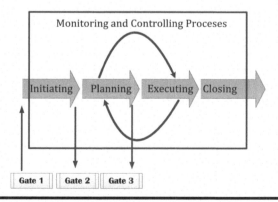

Figure 9.2 PMBOK decision gates. (Adapted from [11].)

9.4 Projects in Controlled Environment 2

PRINCE2 was originally developed by the UK Office of Government Commerce, now the Cabinet Office. This methodology provides a nonproprietary best practice guidance on PM. PRINCE2 is based on stage gates and management by exceptions, as shown in Figure 9.3.

PRINCE2 is predominantly applied in Australia in the public sector by the Commonwealth and state governments. This methodology is based on stage gates where the project governing board can make stop or go-ahead decisions on completion of each stage. This methodology facilitates to ensure that the project remains aligned to organizational strategic objectives and mitigates the issues if the project deviates from organization objectives. PRINCE2 has an intensive reporting mechanism and allows for planning at each stage. It has a comprehensive initiation process, which includes business case in which project objectives are clearly defined and aligned to organizational strategic objectives. Business case also identifies the project product description and provides a mechanism for project review and assesses how far the project has been able to achieve stated objectives and goals, thus leading to business/organizational value. PRINCE 2 has a strong governance mechanism in which the project board performs the role of directing the project.

The project board comprises three main roles: executive, senior user, and senior supplier. The executive owns the business case throughout the project and is

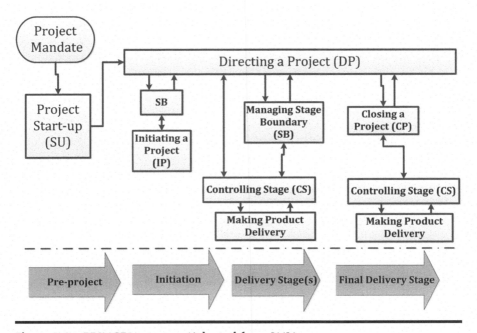

Figure 9.3   PRINCE2 process. (Adapted from [11].)

responsible for overall business assurance of the project. The senior user represents the end users of the product, and therefore specifies the characteristics and features of the project product. The senior supplier represents those who are involved in designing, developing, facilitating, procuring, implementing and, possibly, operating and maintaining project product. The senior supplier role is based on the assumption that project environment is based on the customer/supplier relationship. PRINCE2 is best suited for public sector projects spread over a longer duration with strong governance and reporting mechanisms, whereas big data projects, as stated by Informatica, should not run for more than 6 weeks. Therefore, PRINCE2 does not provide a project framework that can resolve the PM challenges faced by big data projects. Particularly, being software projects, big data projects cannot be initiated with finalized product description that is required by PRINCE2 as the product details may evolve with the project progress. However, PRINCE2 offers a good mechanism for the involvement of key stakeholders in important decision-making at various stages. Big data projects can also learn from PRINCE2 about benefits management to win over the confidence of executives about the value of investment in big data projects.

9.5 Agile

Larson et al. [12] stated that the traditional approaches to PM such as PMBOK are based on comprehensive upfront planning of the entire project, which inherently requires the availability of project product description and demands a high level of predictability to be effective. However, in certain cases, particularly the software development projects, the finite product information is not possible; therefore, the need for a new project methodology was direly felt and Agile endeavored to provide the role of an effective PM methodology. Larson et al. [12] stated some of the following key features of Agile:

- It is based on incremental, iterative development cycles to complete less predictable projects.
- It is best suited for exploratory projects in which product requirements are less known at the start and need to be discovered and new technology needs to be tested.
- As a PM methodology, it focuses on active collaboration between the project team and customer representatives.
- It is based on the continuous design improvement and offers flexibility for later additions and changes in scope; thus, it is based on evolving scope rather than on scope freeze as propounded by PMBOK and PRINCE2.
- It embraces change due to its inherent iterative design, whereas other approaches to PM attempt to minimize changes through effective change control processes.

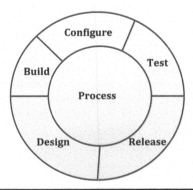

Figure 9.4   Agile process of product development. (Adapted from [12].)

- It promotes continuous, intensive interaction with the stakeholders, particularly customers, compared to other project methodologies.
- Agile project teams are self-regulated and managed compared to conventional project teams.

Figure 9.4 shows the incremental and iterative Agile process of product development.

Larson et al. [12] argued that traditional PM approaches were designed to work in a predictable environment where the project scope is well defined and the technology is stable. On the contrary, Agile is the response to project environment, which are unpredictable and undefined; therefore, agile is more experiential and adaptive of managing projects in unstable and unpredictable circumstances. Agile approach to PM identifies three main roles that play key responsibilities in managing project activities: product owner, self-organizing team, and scrum master. Product owner helps identify the product description and initial features. The product owner has the authority to change product features at the end of each sprint (iteration). Agile project teams, unlike traditional PM teams, are self-managing and the team members decide who is going to do what work, and the team is responsible for the commitments made at the review meetings. The role of a scrum master is quite similar to that of a project manager who facilitates scrum meetings. Scrum meetings are a series of coordinated meetings to manage the development process; in other words, these are project team meetings held on a daily basis.

Though Agile is best suited for software development projects because of its iterative and flexible nature, it does not provide any guidance on the other aspects of PM, such as cost and time management, risk management, quality management, and governance. Larson et al. [12] stated that Agile approach does not address management's top concerns about possible costs and expected timeline for a given project. In many cases, a maximum budget ceiling is identified which is not expected to exceed a certain limit. Agile PM approach faces project integration challenges when various teams are working on different product features. Therefore, to ensure effective integration, processes external to Agile would be necessary.

The Agile approach is also silent on post project implementation activities such as project review, and most of all, it does not guide on benefits management such as how to identify, implement, and realize benefits of software solutions delivered as a project product. It does not seek to direct how an organization can get value by realizing benefits from a big data solution. The fundamental characteristics of Agile are that it facilitates working on project product with initial features, and its iterative nature makes it a strong candidate project approach for big data projects.

9.6 ISO 21500:2012

The ISO 21500:2012 framework has been developed by ISO and it is more of a guidance framework than a full-fledged methodology like the other frameworks discussed previously. It provides a high-level description of various PM processes that can be employed by public or private sector organizations irrespective of the organization size, project size, and complexity. In other methodologies, projects are conceived within the context of portfolios and programs, but ISO 21500:2012 framework sees projects as stand-alone entities; therefore, issues about general management have been addressed only in the context of PM rather than at higher levels, such as programs and portfolios.

This framework considers organizational strategy as the starting point in the PM process, where projects are initiated to exploit opportunities in the light of organizational strategic objectives. Figure 9.5 provides an overview of the ISO 21500:2012 framework.

ISO 21500:2012 has great similarities to the PMBOK framework proffered by PMI in project life cycle. The similarities between the two frameworks can be seen in Table 9.1.

According to Varajaoa et al. [13], ISO 21500:2012 is closely aligned with PMBOK and have almost similar project processes, as can be seen in Table 9.2.

Since there are lot of similarities between ISO 21500:2012 and PMBOK, it is advisable to use PMBOK which is a globally recognized PM standard and which situates projects within the context of programs and portfolios, thus offering effective PM. ISO 21500:2012 framework can be tailored to implement big data projects; however, like PMBOK and PRINCE2 methodologies, ISO 21500:2012 framework also requires scope definition and product description at the planning phase, whereas big data proof of concepts being software projects are started with the basic product features and are finalized as the product gets developed.

However, system development life cycle (SDLC) proposed by Kimball et al. [14] offers a good model, which can be applied to big data projects. Kimball's SDLC model is fundamentally geared toward designing, developing, and deploying data warehousing business intelligence systems. The Kimball model comprises 11 main

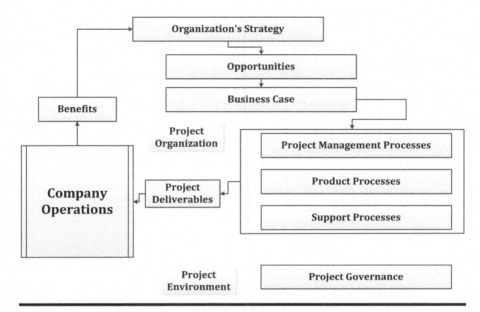

Figure 9.5   ISO 21500:2012 framework. (Adapted from [11].)

Table 9.1   Life Cycle Comparison between PMBOK 2013 and ISO 21500:2012

ISO 21500:2012 Project Life Cycle	PMBOK Project Life Cycle
Initiating	Initiate
Planning	Planning
Implementing	Executing
Controlling	Monitoring and controlling
Closing	Closing

processes, and these are nested in PM context, which makes this model unique. Most of the common SDLCs are predominantly designed for software development, but these overlook the PM aspects in software development. It is possible that such SDLCs either consider PM processes out of the scope of software development or assume that PM processes can be addressed at the organization level. However, the model demonstrates that SDLC can be more effective when implemented in combination with PM processes and PM context.

As can be seen in Figure 9.6, Kimball's model assumes that there exists a PM environment in the organization, where the key PM aspects such as time and cost management, quality and risk management, governance and stakeholders'

Table 9.2 Comparison of ISO 21500:2012 with PMBOK

ISO 21500:2012	PMBOK
Integration	Integration
Scope	Scope
Time	Time
Cost	Cost
Resources	Human resources
Quality	Quality
Risk	Risk
Stakeholders	Stakeholders
Procurement	Procurement
Communication	Communication

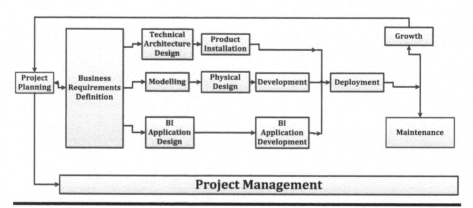

Figure 9.6   Data warehouse SDLCs. (Adapted from [14].)

management are taken care of. Therefore, the Kimball model starts with business requirements definition with the assumption that PM processes have already been completed for a given project. Figure 9.6 shows Kimball's model.

9.7 Key Insights

As mentioned at the start of this chapter, the success rate of IT projects is abysmally low and the project failure rate in bigger organizations is even higher; therefore, big size organizations who are prime beneficiaries of big data projects would also be facing similar low success rates for such projects. Project success is a major issue even in mainstream PM. Although modern project management started in the 1950s, project success started appearing in literature from the 1980s [1,15]. During the early years, project success remained focused on the project delivery within the triple constraints of "on cost," "on time," and "within specifications." As the concept of project success matured gradually, stakeholders' satisfaction was added as another criterion for success. The efforts to identify project success factors continued, and various authors such as Pinto and Slevin [16] identified ten success factors for projects such as project mission, top management support, project schedule plan, client consultation, personnel matters such as human resources and training, technical tasks—adequate technology to support projects, client acceptance, monitoring and feedback, communication, and troubleshooting. Similarly, Freeman and Beale [17] identified seven main elements of project success and stated that the first five have been more frequently mentioned:

- Technical performance
- Efficiency of execution
- Managerial and organizational implications (mainly customer satisfaction)
- Personal growth
- Manufacturability and business performance
- Technical innovation
- Manufacturability and business performance

Dvir and Shanhar [18] investigated the relationship between project planning and project success and argued that planning is central to modern-day PM and a minimum level of planning is required for project success. The authors argue their research found three factors such as "development of functional requirements," "development of technical requirements," and "implementation of PM processes and procedures" have critical roles in project success. The authors identified a positive relationship between the efforts made to determine project goals, functional requirements, and technical specifications of the product and project success, particularly from the end users' perspective. However, the current debate on project success in the mainstream PM literature has extended beyond the execution of the project and it now centers on project benefits realization, which values project outcomes more than project outputs. Since organizations spend precious resources on projects, in return, it is reasonable for them to expect that the intended benefits will flow into the organization. There is a growing realization that benefits accrued by the host organization should be a criterion of project success. Cook-Davies et al. [19] reviewed the six bodies of knowledge in PM and concluded that expected benefits have become the benchmark for stage-gate decision-making and continuous, informal assessment in PM. Zwikael et al. [20] challenged the most commonly used criteria of project success, which is based on project outputs rather than on outcomes, and offered a new framework to evaluate project success in providing project benefits to the organization. The new framework argues for the inclusion of benefits realization phase into the project life cycle. Zwikael et al. [20] defined project benefits as value that is accrued from a project. They also propose to extend the project life cycle to project realization management. The authors support value management (VM) as a management style for projects and argue that if VM is employed proactively, it can help align value system from the start and ensure that a project progresses effectively and efficiently. Zwikael et al. [20] took the project success debate to a new level by arguing to make project outcomes rather than outputs the foundation of project evaluation process. The authors endeavor to modify the conventional view from input–process–output (IPO) to input–transform–outcome (ITO) of project activity. The ITO model developed by the Zwikael and Smyrk gives more importance to project outcomes (ITO) compared to project output (IPO). Zwikael et al. [21] stated that PM literature and relevant PM standards overwhelmingly focus on the need for providing project deliverables within the triple constraints such as time, cost, and specifications, but argued that this focus ignores the significance of project effectiveness in delivering project benefits or value to stakeholders. In light of this discussion, it is fair to say that if big data projects wish to align with the mainstream PM, it should also give due importance to benefits management and realization from its projects. Effective benefits realization would help big data projects win over the executives for more investment as they would see the value accruing to the organization.

As the above discussion on various PM methodologies demonstrates, there is no readymade PM methodology that can be applied to big data projects. Therefore, the viable option with big data projects is that a customized PM methodology be developed which addresses the PM aspects and facilitates the unique nature of big data projects that are basically software projects. Among the methodologies discussed in this chapter, Agile and Kimball's SDLC model come closer to provide solutions to address the PM and software development challenges of big data projects. The most appropriate is Kimball's SDLC model that provides a PM context to the software development of big data projects. However, Kimball's SDLC model needs to be improved with the addition of benefits realization as one of the last processes; the current model terminates the life cycle at growth and maintenance, but it should continue to include benefits realization as the last process. Taking a cue from Zwikael and Smyrk [20], the Kimball model should be geared toward project outcomes rather than outputs.

As highlighted during the discussion of all the main PM methodologies, big data projects can borrow various PM processes to improve the success rate of projects. Unfortunately, none of the major PM methodologies offer a customized readymade solution to big data projects, however where it can adopt Agile process and Kimball's model for software development; it can adopt other important processes as well, such as time and cost management, quality and risk management, project governance, and stakeholders' engagement from PMBOK and PRINCE2. To keep abreast of the current PM practices in various industries, big data projects need to give due importance to benefits management and realization, as in the end every project is initiated and implemented for project outcomes so that benefits and value can flow into the investing organization. For this to happen, big data projects need to adopt program and portfolio management as this will facilitate benefits management throughout the organization. By ensuring that benefits are realized, the managers of big data projects can improve the project success rates and also enhance the confidence of top management in the efficacy and value of big data projects.

9.8 Conclusion

The chapter establishes the relationship between PM and big data analytics. The existing PM methods were developed without considering the impact of big data. However, the increasing amount of data in any project will have to be treated well for effective PM and outcomes. Therefore, in this chapter, we have highlighted the importance of PM for optimized data analytics. We have critically analyzed the state-of-the-art methodologies for PMs and have provided key insights based on the analysis. This chapter will be particularly helpful for project managers who have to deal with large amounts of data and, at the same time, have to look for successful projects.

References

1. Snyder, James R. (1987) www.pmi.org/learning/library/modern-project-management-disciplines-direction-1810, accessed on December 29, 2016.
2. Johnson, Stephen B. (1997) Three Approaches to Big Technology: Operations Research, Systems Engineering, and Project Management. *Technology and Culture*, vol. 38, no. 4, pp. 891–919.
3. Morris, Peter W.G. (2010) Research and the future of project management. *International Journal of Managing Project in Business*, vol. 3, no. 1, pp. 139–146.
4. Johnson, Stephen B. (2013) Technical and Institutional Factors in the Emergence of Project Management. *IJPM*, vol. 31, pp. 670–681.
5. Pollack, Julien and Adler, Daniel (2015) Emerging Trends and Passing Fads in Project Management Research: A Scientometric Analysis of Changes in the Field. *IJPM*, vol. 33, pp. 236–248.
6. Standish Group (2017) CHAOS Report. www.projectsmart.co.uk/white-papers/chaos-report.pdf, accessed on February 25, 2017.
7. Pearson, Neil, Erik W. Larson, and Clifford F. Gray (2013) *Project Management in Practice*. McGraw Hill, Sydney, NSW.
8. Larson, Erik W., Honig, Beverly, Gray, Clifford F., Dantin, Ursala, and Baccarini, David (2014) *Prokect Management: The Managerial Process*. McGrawHill Education, Sydney, NSW.
9. Varajaoa, Joao, Richardo Colomo-Palaciosb, and Helio Silva (2017) ISO 21500:2012 and PMBoK 5 Processes in Information Systems Project Management. *Computer Standards and Interfaces*, vol. 50. pp. 216–222.

Data Analytics*

. Kimball, Ralph, Margy Ross, Warren Thornthwaite, Joy Mundy, and Bob Becker (2008) *The Data Warehouse Lifecycle Toolkit* (2nd ed.). Wiley Publishing, Indianapolis, IN.

11. Ballard, Asbjorn, Iris Tommelein, Per Morten Schiefloe, and Glenn Ballard (2014) Understanding Project Success through Analysis of Project Management Approach. *International Journal of Projects in Business*, vol. 7, no. 4, pp. 638–660.

12. Pinto, Jefrey K. and Dennis P. Slevin (1987) Critical Factors in Successful Projects Implementation. *IEEE Transactions on Engineering Management*, vol. 34, no. 1, pp. 22–27.

13. Freeman, M. and P. Beal (1992) Measuring Project Success. *Project Management Journal*, vol. 23, no. 1, pp. 8–17.

14. Dvir, Don and Aron Shenhar (2003) An Empirical Analysis of the Relationship between Project Planning and Project Success. *IJPM*, vol. 21, no. 2, pp. 89–95.

15. Cooke-Davies, Terry (2000) Towards Improved Management Practice, PhD thesis, Lead Metropolitan University. In Cook-Davies, T. (2002) The Real Success Factors on Projects. *IJPM*, vol. 20, pp. 185–190.

16. Zwikael, Ofer and John Smyrk (2012) A General Framework for Gauging the Performance of Initiatives to Enhanced Organizational Value. *British Journal of Management*, vol. 23, no. 1, pp. 6–22.

17. Zwikael, Ofer (2016) Editorial for IJPM Special Issue on Project Benefit Management. *IJPM*, 34.

18. Turner, Rodney, Frank Anbari, and Christophe Bredillet (2013) Perspectives on Research in Project Management: The Nine Schools. *Global Business Perspectives*, vol. 1, no. 1, pp. 3–28.

19. Informatica (ND). How to Run a Big Data POC in Six Weeks. https://govinsider.asia/wp-content/uploads/docs/[Workbook]%20How%20to%20Run%20a%20Big%20Data%20POC%20in%206%20weeks.pdf, accessed on February 27, 2018.

20. Cao, Longbing (2017) Data Science: Challenges and Directions. *Communications of the ACM*, vol. 60, no. 8. pp. 59–68.

21. Datameer (ND). The Guide to Big Data Analytics. www.datameer.com/pdf/big-data-analytics-ebook.pdf?mkt_tok, accessed on February 25, 2017.

Chapter 10

Blockchain in the Era of Industry 4.0

Md. Mehedi Hassan Onik
Inje University

Mohiuddin Ahmed
Canberra Institute of Technology

Contents

10.1 Introduction

The fourth industrial revolution has begun and this is not going to be like other revolutions. It is not about the steam that powered our factories in the first revolution or the mass production model that dominated the second or even the emergence of computer-driven systems from the third revolution that we are living in today. The fourth industrial revolution or Industry 4.0 is about connectivity and communication. The current digital economy is based on the trust formed between groups of business-minded authorities. Meanwhile, the fourth industrial revolution demands an automated business process with ubiquitous digitization, i.e., a technology that can narrow the gap between human and system. It is an opportunity to radically change the way industry responds to the needs of society. The world is waiting for another industrial revolution, which is capable of automatic machine-to-machine (M2M) communication via a secure and decentralized cyber-physical system (CPS). This exponential challenge must be mobilized by technologies such as blockchain, shared ledger, and cryptocurrency.

The main theme of blockchain is a distributed ledger instead of a traditional centralized system. A closer look at this technology shows the following key characteristics that have opened immense opportunities for Industry 4.0:

- **Decentralized storage:** This will allow any asset or document to be stored in a way that will be public, transparent, and accessible from the network. There will be no centrally controlled database.
- **Public consensus:** Access, transfer, and communication will no more be controlled by any single authority. Any modification will act only after an independent approval from the public.
- **Immutability:** There will be no scope for adjustment or alteration of any information. It will provide a two-layer security system to make business reliable and secure.
- **Increased capacity:** By removing every kind of middleman and approval system, it will provide a cost-effective and faster settlement of any contract, agreement, or approval.

Now, cryptocurrencies are for blockchain, what email was for the Internet in the early 1990s. Digital currency or cryptocurrency is an Internet-based commodity exchanging medium that acts like a bank check, note, and coin. The first usage of blockchain technology, bitcoin (BTC), came in the year 2009. Since then quite a few have been generated. Some superior cryptocurrencies are BTC, ethereum, ripple, BTC cash, litecoin, etc.

Initially, BTC was the only dominant application of blockchain technology, but with further technological achievements, it can be used in other sectors too. Major industries that can utilize the aforementioned properties of blockchain technology are finance and insurance, health and medicine, Internet of Things (IoT), academia, copyright, vehicle sharing, supply chain management, energy management, gambling, government, retail, human resource management, etc. Presently, we have middlemen everywhere, for example, bank for currencies, postal service for product insurance, election commission for election, contract lawyer, court and registry office for land registration, etc. Blockchain can remove these middle parties, secure communication, and build a digital reputation for a trustless secured business. However, there are arguments in the context of technology, standardization, policy, and social adaptability. Although standardization and synchronization for an acceptable blockchain are ongoing, it is important to clear up the upcoming fourth industrial revolution issues such as energy and power consumption, aberrant cryptocurrency value, transaction time and cost, and privacy and regulations.

Blockchain technology has many things to offer, which will surely affect the future industry structure in Industry 4.0. After this revolution, industries can exploit the real digital enterprises, with physical products at the pivot, and decentralized storage, augmented interfaces, and immutable crypto transaction at the end. To underscore the effect of blockchain on Industry 4.0, this chapter lists challenges, scopes, and current status of these technologies in detail. In addition to that, their flaws, effects, and requirements are also pointed out with adequate examples, which can be a good reference point for future study.

10.1.1 Chapter Roadmap

Rest of the chapter is organized as follows: Section 10.2 elaborates the fourth industrial revolution and its components within the scope of Industry 4.0. Section 10.3 contains discussion on blockchain and cryptocurrencies. It also presents the scope of blockchain technology and its correlation with Industry 4.0. In Section 10.4, the impacts of blockchain on diverse industries are highlighted. Section 10.5 highlights the changes that blockchain can bring in the industrial architecture with a potential use case. Finally, Section 10.6 concludes the chapter followed by necessary references.

10.2 Emergence of Industrial Revolutions

As the previous industrial revolution was led by innovations in manufacturing processes and systems, the advancement of Industry 4.0 will be driven by a smart, interconnected, pervasive environment. A well-equipped industry under this

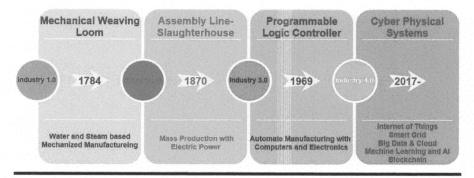

Figure 10.1   Industrial evolution with key developments (Industry 1.0 to Industry 4.0).

revolution will be capable of planning ahead with a clear strategic vision and will be focused on discovering how smart products and processes can be developed. Industry 4.0 will take away isolated silo-driven development, which limits the scopes and values of new projects. Instead, it will move the current industry toward large-scale and proactive integration across their enterprise and among their customer, supply base, and products to ensure that they are aware of every possible opportunity a smart factory has to offer. Under the umbrella of Industry 4.0, a trader understands the value chain from which products are designed, how they are produced, who they are sold for, and how they are purchased. An organization may become radically different in the future with a range of products, services, and processes that we cannot currently predict. We must plan ahead and fight radical changes with integrated radical actions to welcome the new era of the fourth industrial revolution (Industry 4.0). Figure 10.1 shows a gradual change of the industrial revolution from the year 1784 to 2017.

- **Industry 1.0**
  From the beginning of the eighteenth century, for the greater benefit of workers, water and steam-powered machines were invented. Due to industry 1.0, production capabilities maximized, business grew from individual to organization level, and from stakeholders to customers all came under the same platform.
- **Industry 2.0**
  By the beginning of the twentieth century, industries got the taste of electricity and division of labor. By the virtue of electricity, machines had their own power sources, which empowered factories for mass production. In this revolution, workers did only a part of the total job, which increased the overall productivity and efficiency.
- **Industry 3.0**
  The invention of electronic cheapest, integrated circuit, the programmable logic controller (PLC) spawned the development of computerized software

technology to capitalize on the electronic hardware. In the last few decades of the twentieth century, product cost was reduced by replacing operators with low-cost software and transistors. Finally, the manufacturer could move their plant to a cost-effective geographical location for assembly and refabricating, which developed the supply chain management system.

10.2.1 Fourth Industrial Revolution (Industry 4.0)

In the twenty-first century, complexities and requirements in the industries drastically increased. Global manufacturing competition, increasing market volatility, smaller supply chains, and global economic unrest put stakeholders in serious trouble [1]. Existing value creation ways could not fulfil the cost efficiency, stability, and feasibility requirements of the currently overgrown industrialization. Requirements for the competitive market were going higher, and thus, new technologies were also involved manifold, which led us to think of a new industrial revolution. Artificial intelligence allows us to think beyond human capacity; people have started to mine data for policy improvement; smart grid is smoothening the way of using power; IoT has connected every day-to-day life object; big data and cloud computing have reconciled marketing policies and opened up storage bindings; augmented and virtual realities are emerging; 5G is on its way with endless opportunities; robots are being deployed in root-level production; additive manufacturing has already started to produce 3D products; and finally, the shared ledger or blockchain technologies are providing financial independence and security through cryptocurrencies. The combination of all these factors has led us to believe that we need an industrial revolution for an organized impact on manufacturing factories. Now, Industry 4.0 can help these programs reach their fullest potential.

10.2.2 Definition of Industry 4.0

It was 2011 when the declaration "Industrie 4.0" or "fourth industrial revolution" or "Industry 4.0" was first announced publicly by the German manufacturing industry (an association of business and academia) [2]. Later on, in light of this the German federal government announced that "Industrie 4.0" would be an integral part of its "High-Tech Strategy 2020 for Germany" initiative [3]. Thereafter, they formed the "Industrie 4.0 Working Group," which reported their primary recommendations for the fourth industrial revolution back in 2013 [4]. After this, it spread worldwide, for example, "industrial Internet" was proposed by General Electric in 2014 [5]; in the same year, a $2 billion fund was given for research in "Advanced Manufacturing" (President's Council of Advisors on Science and Technology, 2014), and more work has been done on the same path with different names such as "Integrated Industry" [6] and "Smart Industry" [7]. In the United States, Industrial Internet Consortium is working on its improvement.

Industry 4.0 can be defined as an end-to-end digitization and decentralization of all information, and physical assets were the main focus of Industry 4.0. The ultimate goal of this revolution is proposing a digital ecosystem with partners of a supply chain management. Generating, analyzing, and communicating data without any interruption by the third party and introducing new technologies to the manufacturing sector are its final outcomes. An intelligent factory system is where CPS generates a virtual world to communicate through IoT and where transaction is secured by a shared ledger (blockchain).

Since the elements combining Industry 4.0 has not finished yet, it is a gradual process which needs further modification and standardization for adaptation and popularity. Since this trend is still in its infancy, we will mention some widely accepted definitions. According to MacDougall of German Trade and Invest, the definition is as follows:

> Smart industry or 'INDUSTRIE 4.0' refers to the technological evolution of embedded systems to cyber-physical systems. Put simply, INDUSTRIE 4.0 represents the coming fourth industrial revolution on the way to an Internet of Things, Data and Services. Decentralized intelligence helps create intelligent object networking and independent process management, with the interaction of the real and virtual worlds representing a crucial new aspect of the manufacturing and production process. INDUSTRIE 4.0 represents a paradigm shift from "centralized" to "decentralized" production – made possible by technological advances which constitute a reversal of conventional production process logic. Simply put, this means that industrial production machinery no longer simply "processes" the product, but that the product communicates with the machinery to tell it exactly what to do. INDUSTRIE 4.0 connects embedded system production technologies and smart production processes to pave the way to a new technological age which will radically transform industry and production value chains and business models (e.g. "smart factory") [8].

According to Cornelius Baur of McKinsey, the definition of blockchain is as follows:

> Industry 4.0 is the next phase in the digitization of the manufacturing sector, driven by four disruptions: the astonishing rise in data volumes, computational power, and connectivity, especially new low-power wide-area networks; the emergence of analytics and business-intelligence capabilities; new forms of human-machine interaction such as touch interfaces and augmented-reality systems; and improvements in transferring digital instructions to the physical world, such as advanced robotics and 3-D printing [9].

Davies of European Parliament also defined the fourth industrial revolution in 2015 as follows:

> Industry 4.0 is a term applied to a group of rapid transformations in the design, manufacture, operation and service of manufacturing systems and products. The 4.0 designation signifies that this is the world's fourth industrial revolution, the successor to three earlier industrial revolutions that caused quantum leaps in productivity and changed the lives of people throughout the world [10].

Finally, according to Gartner report, Industry 4.0 is defined as follows:

> Industrie 4.0 is a German-government-sponsored vision for advanced manufacturing. The underlying concept of Industrie 4.0 is to connect embedded systems and smart production facilities to generate a digital convergence between industry, business and internal functions and processes. Industrie 4.0 refers to a fourth industrial revolution (following water/steam power, mass production and automation through IT and robotics) and introduces the concept of "cyber-physical systems" to differentiate this new evolutionary phase from the electronic automation that has gone before [11].

Figure 10.2 shows three indispensable characteristics and features that are needed to design the skeleton of Industry 4.0 where decentralization brings autonomous manufacturing and transparent business transactions, technologies assists workers in developing smart products, and compatibility harmonizes devices and sensors for cost efficiency.

10.2.3 Core Components of Industry 4.0

Several catchwords and trends connected with this fourth industrial revolution have been widely researched in several studies and surveys [12–14]. The main

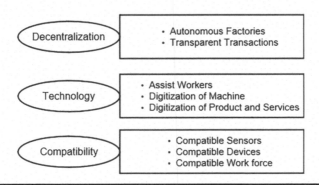

Figure 10.2 Features of Industry 4.0.

components of Industry 4.0 are mentioned in the text that follows (Figure 10.3), though there are other ongoing technologies connected with Industry 4.0.

Manufacturing industries of the fourth industrial revolution will have the abovementioned components (Figure 10.3). A secure CPS is used with cloud computing and big data analysis to improve policies. IoT, Internet of systems (IoS), and additive manufacturing technologies are used to increase the quality and quantity of the product. Training and production systems become more secure and efficient with smart sensors and augmented reality. Finally, blockchain and cryptocurrencies can provide a middleman less, secure, and decentralized transaction facilities. A detailed description of Figure 10.3 is given as follows:

- **Cyber-physical systems**

  Physical and computational elements can be controlled through the Internet via a CPS. These interactions among the machines are dynamic, which change the context to represent a complete system in a digital way. With intelligent embedded sensors, machines will be able to communicate, thus resulting in a smart network for a particular product throughout its supply chain. "Smart anything" is its main concept, which includes everything surrounding us (e.g., cars, buildings, homes, manufacturing, hospitals, factory, grids, and appliances). It is a bridge between the computing and noncomputing devices around us. Lee proposed two main components of CPS: (i) a real-time bidirectional communication for physical and cyber world and (ii) an intelligent data analysis for building an intelligent cyber space [15]. For example, the

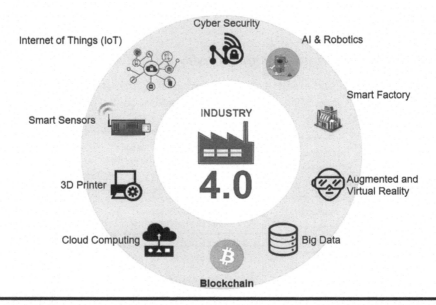

Figure 10.3   Core components of the fourth industrial revolution (Industry 4.0).

Distributed Robotic Laboratory of Massachusetts Institute of Technology developed a group of robots that are responsible for taking care of a tomato garden through navigation, sensors, and wireless technologies.

■ **Internet of Things**

A bidirectional connection between "things" (objects and machines) and the Internet can be the easiest way of expressing IoT. The difference between CPS and IoT is that all IoT devices are CPSs, but all CPSs are not necessarily connected to the Internet and thus are not necessarily IoT devices. Jayavardhana Gubbi categorized the IoT components into three types: (i) hardware (sensors, actuators), (ii) middleware (storage and computing tools), and (iii) application (visualization and interpretation) [16]. The need for time-sensitive networking with dedicated add-ons tailored to fulfil the requirements of automation for IoT was discussed in a study by Wollschlaeger [17]. Industrial IoT is an extended version of IoT, especially evolved for the fourth industrial revolution, for example, the health-care monitoring IoT devices where doctors can remotely monitor patients and store clinical information for future use [18].

■ **Internet of Services**

The technology program AUTONOMIK fürIndustrie 4.0 (in English: AUTONOMICS for Industry 4.0) by the Federal Ministry for Economic Affairs and Energy (BMWi) of Germany introduced "Smart Face" [19]. That was the beginning of the service-oriented architecture. The whole manufacturing section was divided into smaller parts. A server-based application directs the parts production schedule. Another automated machine distributes the workload to complete the whole procedure. Ultimately, a central workflow planning system will be removed by this IoS system. The main idea of IoS is that it turns a simple product into services. A product will automatically evaluate user's expectation and transform itself as a service for more value generation. Several manufacturers have already exploited this. For example, a food-supplying company of the Netherlands analyze patient data from hospitals to decide the meal menu. Another example can be a Tesla car, which automatically upgrades its hardware and software by online ordering.

Sometimes people get confused among IoT, IoS, and CPS. Actually, these three things are completely different based on their applied position, where the Internet is a service and CPS smart production is an application of that service. At the system level, CPS communicates among devices with an infrastructure made by the IoT. Over all, a CPS delivers services like IoS by communication among products through IoT. Figure 10.4 describes the details of CPS, IoT, IoS, and Internet's application position in Industry 4.0.

■ **Smart factory and product**

In a smart factory, a product has an independent production process, which is easily identifiable and locatable. It is not cost efficient currently, but the productivity of the factory increases for smart product supply chain [4]. A smart

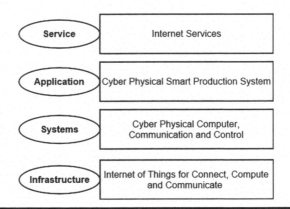

Figure 10.4 Application layer of Industry 4.0 components.

factory must have a feedback and coordination system, implemented on the cloud and analyzed by big data mining [20]. Similarly, a smart product's life cycle is not limited up to its delivery, even after the customer buys a product, its evaluation and service as a product continues. A digital system of customer-specific product variants is the ultimate outcome of this smart product idea. In 2017, Abramovici describes this smart product as "By finishing the manufacturing and delivery phase a cyclic process including the phases of Smart Product use, reconfiguration and remanufacturing begins" [21]. A good example can be the Siemens plant in Germany that claims to be roughly 75% automated, where all the 1,150 employees mostly operate computers and check the process status.

■ **Big data, cloud, and global positioning system (GPS)**
Intelligent big data mining technology provides a range of business-to-business communications that include data supply, cleansing, enrichment, and analysis. It is a cloud-based system offering a secure storage, which facilitates easy access to information. Facilities for location, tracking, and navigation are the three main things offered by the GPS. A self-aware and self-maintained machine proposed by Lee et al. [22] could report pressures, fuel flow rate, temperature, and the rotational speed of the bulldozer to the cloud storage, which then automatically identified the location of the particular vehicle and took necessary action.

■ **Machine-to-machine (M2M) communication**
In an M2M communication, a machine of one working level can communicate with a machine of another working level via wireless or wired media without any human involvement. It is highly linked with the business-to-business (B2B) communication for the formation of the fourth industrial revolution (Industry 4.0). For example, a printer can automatically order a color-supplying ink cartridge supplier machine when it runs out of ink [22].

The development of M2M communication as a new technology is changing the way of B2B communication across the world. A customer acquisition with his/her owner's satisfaction will increase many times in Industry 4.0 with these (M2M and B2B) new technologies.

■ **Augmented reality (AR) and virtual reality (VR)**
Even a few years ago, people used AR and VR for playing and fun purposes only, but currently they are adding a new dimension to Industry 4.0. A matured AR or VR can effectively change the whole idea of the current factory to generate a real smart factory. AR is the technology that combines the physical and real world with computer- and mobile-generated data to bring a virtual object into reality. For example, with "Google glass," a smart factory will be able to train its employees with AR and VR. A training can be more interesting, secure, and cost effective with this technology. Pierdicca also predicted a few applications of AR and VR in Industry 4.0, such as car troubleshooting, shopping, makeup, and game technologies

■ **Additive manufacturing**
Additive manufacturing (AM; 3D printer) is another transformational pillar and innovation accelerator for Industry 4.0. AM is the technology that builds (prints) 3D objects. According to Martha Rehnberg, global value chains will be highly affected due to the extensive use of 3D printers [24]. Product model creation, customization, and spare parts production will be easier with this technology. Plastic, metal, concrete, or, in future, human tissue can also be made with this technology. A use case can be architecture and construction, medical, aeronautics, industrial goods production, electronics, etc.

■ **Artificial intelligence and robotics**
Artificial intelligence and robotics make this industrial revolution more dramatic than what people have predicted before. Robots have started to run in the background. A robot can correlate the previous actions taken by the operator and act accordingly, which grows the company value. Robots are learning the product cycle and involved in a way where they can respond and solve a new problem in continuously changing environments. Two industrial robots arms, robot A (learned from the previous operator of the industry) and robot B (learned from human–robot interaction) were compared where it was proved that a physical human–robot interaction is an improved way of using robots in the context of user experience for Industry 4.0 [25].

10.3 Blockchain and Cryptocurrency

The social network has evolved exponentially in the past few years. Storage and computing power are already having a shared architecture for cloud computing. IoT has connected our devices too. The smart market idea has opened a communication mechanism between businesses. The only thing that was left behind was

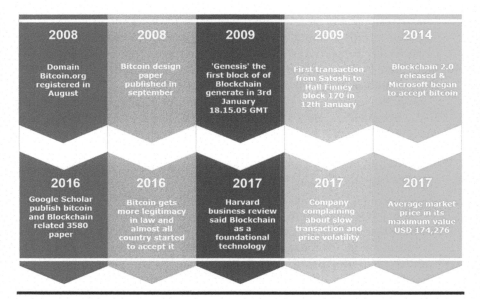

Figure 10.5 Evolution of blockchain and cryptocurrency.

a common, transparent, and shared economy; finally, blockchain filled that space. Companies are facing shared social economy, crowd funding, digital identities, and entrepreneurship. Therefore, stakeholders must welcome blockchain-based transaction for fitting their company to global payment settlement, accounting, or customer loyalty. It was first started in the year 2008 and Satoshi Nakamoto explained about the general idea of the blockchain [26]. The main idea of his BTC white paper was about money transactions between peers without requiring the help of a third party, such as banks or trusted middleman. Instead of trust what was needed was a digital transaction system based on cryptography. It helped to solve the double-spending problem through something called proof of work (POW) through the use of digital wallet. Due to gradual development over time, this technology has become the largest way of solving global economic barrier. As BTC becomes popular worldwide, similar cryptocurrencies are also being developed. Figure 10.5 explains the gradual development of BTC and blockchain over time. It started with the domain registration of bitcoin.org in 2008. The official publication of the blockchain idea publicly happened in the same year. In 2017, BTC and blockchain became mature enough to join as a key technology of Industry 4.0.

10.3.1 Definition of Blockchain

The blockchain is a decentralized ledger of all transactions across a peer-to-peer (P2P) network. Without a central authority and middleman, this technology can confirm the transaction with the approval of an already established and proved group. The blockchain is the base technology on which BTC and other cryptocurrencies are based. Swan mentioned in his book *Blockchain: Blueprint for a New Economy* about two versions of blockchain technology based on its use: version 1.0 was all about currency and version 2.0 reflects smart contract with all other shared ledger use [26]. There are different studies and research trying to introduce and define blockchain and BTC technology from their own viewpoints. According to Robert Hackett of the *Fortune* magazine, "This coding breakthrough—which consists of concatenated blocks of transactions—allows competitors to share a digital ledger across a network of computers without the need for a central authority. No single party has the power to tamper with the records: the math keeps everyone honest" [27]. The blockchain can also allow more advanced transactions other than transferring money with smart contracts [28]. In 1997, Nick Szabo defined backsmart contract as a cryptographic contract. It is a digital protocol to satisfy common contractual conditions such as payment, license, and business deal. A smart contract can reduce transaction costs by removing the trusted intermediaries [29].

Zibin Zheng in 2017 has found four key characters of blockchain technologies: decentralization, persistency, anonymity, and auditability [30]. The International Organization for Standardization (ISO) has also started a technical committee on blockchain in Australia to propose "Standardization of blockchain technologies and distributed ledger technologies."

10.3.2 Components of Blockchain

Major technologies constituting blockchain are shown in Figures 10.6–10.8). Hash function, architecture of a block, and public and private keys in digital signature are discussed as follows:

- **Hash**

  A hash algorithm changes arbitrary data into definite length hash. Generally written as hexadecimal, a slight change in original data results in a significant difference in output hash value by the use of this hash function. It makes falsification difficult that guarantees blockchain data security. Every new block creation or transaction utilizes the calculation of hash value. The hash value calculator that is mostly used is double SHA256 hashing algorithm and this technology was mentioned in this study [31]. An example of hash function is as follows: If an input data in BTC is "2190," after going through a hash function it becomes "e80G1." For the next transaction, if the input data is changed slightly to "2191," after going through a hash function it will generate "2cc6L" as an output. The following scenario shows that in Figure 10.6, 2190 and 2191 are almost similar, but "e80G1" and "2cc6L" are difficult to predict. Blockchain adopts this security mechanism to generate random hash values for data storage and authentication.

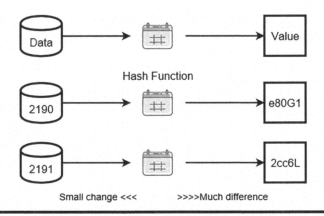

Figure 10.6 The working procedure of hash function.

■ **Block**
Block can be easily defined as a source of information storage for a transaction. A block is thus a permanent store of records that, once written, cannot be altered or removed. If we make a comparison with record kipping common style it's a page of a ledger, we only go to the next page of a ledger when it finishes. Similarly, a block indicates the current transaction, and when the next block is created, it becomes the latest one. Each time a block is "completed," it gives way to the next block in the blockchain. There is no limit to the number for blocks being created; it will continue to grow as long as people use them for transactions. Its parts are header, transaction counter, and block content, which are shown in Figure 10.7. The header contains the basic information about a particular block such as block version, timestamp, nonce, and parent block hash. The basic size of BTC is around 100 bytes per transaction, out of which 80 bytes belongs to the header.

Block header contains the following components as shown in Figure 10.7:

Block Version: It includes the ID, the size of the block, and the version number (the set of rules that a particular block conforms to is also mentioned).
ParentBlock Hash: 2x SHA256 hash of the previous block header, this is how the blockchain is created by pointing to the previous block.
MerkleTree Root Hash: Encodes blockchain data efficiently and securely. It uses double SHA-256. A double hashing is done to generate a tree element.
Timestamp: Used to figure out the mining difficulty re-target. When a node connects to another, it generates a timestamp where 1–2 h delay is normal.
Target Threshold: This is related to mining and how hard it is to successfully mine the block.

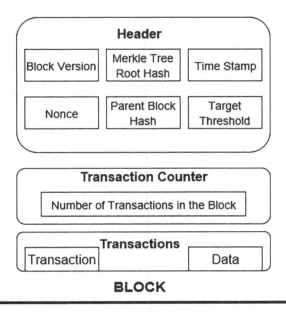

Figure 10.7 Block format (blockchain architecture).

Nonce: It is a random number. It is used for searching a suitable hash, and this is what the miners are looking for.

Transactions Counter: Transaction counter counts the total number of transactions that happen.

Transactions: Transaction value totally depends on the use. Whenever the block transacts, it saves that (data) in this section. It can be BTC transaction, contract records, or business data, etc.

Figure 10.7 represents the aforementioned details of block information graphically where header, transaction counter, and transaction are the three main parts of the block.

■ **Digital signature**

This digital signature was first used by Johnson as the elliptic curve digital signature algorithm (ECDSA) in the year 2000 [32]. A digital signature is a procedure to prove the authenticity of the blockchain transmission. It mainly contains public and private keys to provide a double-layer protection of transaction information. Signing phase and verification phase are the two steps needed for this verification. A private key is reserved for personal transactions, whereas a public key is sent globally for outside security. In the signing part, one encrypts data with the private key and sends the original data-encrypted result, both. In the verification part, the receiver can easily check the validity of

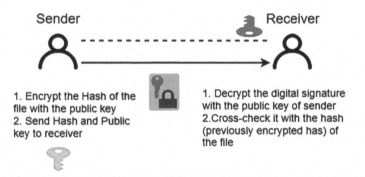

Sender   Receiver

1. Encrypt the Hash of the   1. Decrypt the digital signature
file with the public key   with the public key of sender
2. Send Hash and Public   2.Cross-check it with the hash
key to receiver   (previously encrypted has) of
                                              the file

Figure 10.8 **Digital signature (blockchain architecture).**

the received data with the sender's public key. The sender sends data and hash value, and, on the other hand, the receiver can verify the information that was actually generated from the hash and the private key of the sender. It can be 71–73 bytes long. The private and public keys for BTC are 32 and 33 bytes, respectively. A more detailed elaboration is given in Figure 10.8.

10.3.3 Working Procedure and Algorithm

Generally, a group of people decided to exchange something through a blockchain transaction. First, every user validates each other's ability status. Afterward, if previous transactions are validated, then a new transaction happens and the new block stores new transaction information. A copy of each transaction is saved in every user's node. So, when a new block of transactions is added to the blockchain, the node has to prove that it had done some work to create the new block, and this clarification is done through consensus algorithms such ask POW, proof of stake (POS), proof of activity, proof of burn, practical byzantine fault tolerance (PBFT), Tendermint, etc. In POW, the node in the network calculates the hash value of the block header. The block header contains a nonce and the node (miner) would try to find the correct nonce by changing the nonce frequently to get different hash values until the calculated value is equal to or smaller than a certain given value. And when the node reaches the targeted value, it would broadcast the block to other nodes, and then the other nodes must acknowledge the correctness of the hash value. If the block is valid, other miners would append this new block to their own blockchain. Different consensus algorithms follow their own procedures for consensus finality achievement. As a working procedure of blockchain, we will show how a BTC transaction occurs from the sender to the receiver account with ten steps (Figure 10.9). First of all, the sender node records data and broadcasts it in the network. Second, the receiver node checks the authenticity of the received data; if found correctly, it generates a block. The next step is getting an approval from the miner who executes blockchain algorithms with that block. After that block

Figure 10.9   Step-by-step working procedure of blockchain (BTC).

executed the consensus algorithm and every node with the last block information approved that block, it extends the chain base on this block.

In order for a node in the network to accept the verification of creation of blocks or transactions by other nodes , they must agree with each other on how the system works, so they must find a consensus on that. In the blockchain world, some of the well-known consensus algorithms are (i) PBFT [33], (ii) POW [26], and (iii) POS [34] which is the backbone of Bitshares [35]. The consensus algorithm that collectively uses the trusted sub-networks of a larger network is called ripple [36]. Manu Sporny, in 2017, compared different blockchain-related algorithms and identified the feasibilities and risks in his study [37].

Because the POW requires a huge amount of energy, it has motivated the researchers to find more suitable alternative blockchain protocols. This would eliminate the need of POW by changing the protocol which consumes lesser energy with the same guarantee of work [38]. So, the POS has solved this enormous computation power that is required by the POW. By changing the concept where security levels of the network were not dependent on energy consumption, it provides an energy-saving efficiency and more cost-competitive end-to-end cryptocurrency transactions. POS also requires hashing by the nodes in the network, but it is needed for a limited search space. It is also known as proof of ownership because the verification is done by the one who owns the highest amount of cryptocurrency. There is a belief that the owner having the highest amount will not corrupt the network [30], but there are also others who think otherwise because of the concept "rich gets richer." Although POS helped us to reduce the massive energy consumptions, it has some disadvantages as well, for example, several potential security issues where the coin age might be abused by some malicious nodes helping them to gain significant network weight that leads to a successful double-spending. Another issue related to the coin age is that the honest nodes can be seen abusing the system by staking only on a periodical basis, which can be considered as an unsecured network. In the current system, all the existing components of a POS are predictable enough to allow the precomputation of future POS, wherein (BlackCoin's Proof-of-Stake protocol v2) Vasin [39] illustrated these issues and provided a solution for them. Improved POS also enables more transactions per second and also it is a censorship resistance that prevents maximizing the profit of the members at the expense of nonmembers, and through this improved version, it can recover from netsplits as well as from mass crash failure.

Another group introduced Casper "the Friendly Ghost" for improving the POS [40]. First, there is security-deposit-based security and authentication where the node's "bonded validators" must place a security deposit (bonding) for serving the consensus by producing blocks. Second, gambling on consensus, Casper makes its validators bet a big part of their security deposits on how the consensus process is going to turn out. The consensus process "turns out" according to their bet and the validators have to bet their deposit on how they expect the rest to be betting their deposits as well.

10.3.4 Cryptocurrency

Cryptocurrency is just an application of blockchain technology in real life. It is virtual money for P2P electronic transactions. It started with BTC, and currently, there are more than 900 cryptocurrencies in the market, which will be discussed in detail in later sections. "Announcing the first release of BTC, a new electronic cash system that uses a peer-to-peer network to prevent double-spending. It's completely decentralized with no server or central authority."—Satoshi Nakamoto announced this on January 9, 2009 [26]. A comparison analysis was done by Manu Sporny and Ashiq Anjum in their study stated below, which clearly compares the performances of different crypto coins that vary with situations [37]. According to that study, interplanetary file system (IPFS) and hashgraph performance are better in the context of system availability, scalability, failure tolerance, and latency. On the contrary, BTC, Ethereum, and Blockstack are better in terms of auditability, liveliness, and denial of service, but their performance decreased with higher transactions and verification times. It shows that BTC, Ethereum, and Blockstack spend around 30–60 minutes for achieving consensus. IPFS and Steller are more scalable than other cryptocurrencies. Over 900 cryptocurrencies have been listed up to now [35]. A study by Vigna in 2016 discussed how cryptocurrencies are changing the trends of the age-old economic system and presenting a transparent, shared, and independent transaction system [41].

Every technology evolved with problems and limitations, and with time they got their actual shape for future commanding. Several reports identified the following issues and challenges of blockchain and BTC [30,42]. Common transactions will be impossible in actual business with the current blockchain problems, such ase lack of data modification scope, long approval time, huge power consumption, storage, and security issues. These were identified as flaws of the current blockchain technology in a survey done by the Japan Ministry of Economy, Trade and Industry [43]. They mentioned some security issues such as network cutoff (eclipse attack) and 51% error. 51% error can happen in the current POS protocol where an individual or a group of people getting more than 50% share can control the activity of the chain. More issues like this will be discussed in Section 10.4.

10.4 Blockchain's Impact on Industry 4.0

10.4.1 How Blockchain Supports Industry 4.0

The blockchain is a new technology that is adding a new dimension in the fourth industrial revolution. Over time, industries need a transparent, democratic, decentralized, efficient, and secure architecture, and this is where the blockchain technology comes handy in meeting the goal of the fourth industrial revolution (Industry 4.0). Business is based on trust and the way we interact and exchange commodities is based on trust. Though Internet communication was possible, but it could not provide the trust that is highly needed for business communications. Until the advent of blockchain-based transactions, banks, financial service providers, letter of credit, human intervention, and online marketplaces are used to serve as a third party, but blockchain now allow people to do trade with no prior relationship and trusted third party. This will surely redefine the structure of industries. It allows market participants to trade directly without changing any structure of the company. There are various hybrid models of blockchain depending on the use cases, where they can be both private and public. For example, a gambling company can form a blockchain only with the member of the house, a bank can do so with its customers, and it can also be created for certain local companies to large global companies. Dr. Reinhard Geissbauer of PwC Global Industry 4.0 surveyed between November 2015 and January 2016 with over 2,000 senior executives from 26 countries and found that, on average, a company's operational expenditure will decrease by 3.6% per annum, while efficiency will go up by 4.1% annually by the use of smart manufacturing initiatives [44]. The effect of blockchain on the fourth industrial revolution will be enormous. Research and development, trading, storing, and logistics of companies will be highly affected in Switzerland by the fourth industrial revolution, according to the review [45]. P2P transaction will be more secure and business will be more global. Since blockchain replicated all the business data, this is an open infrastructure that can secure any digital asset.

Uncertainty will be removed from every kind of business and transparency will take that place. Many companies are facing problems in managing different vendors in the horizontal supply chain, where every vendor is having an individual policy and company architecture, which creates a communication gap in business development. Blockchain can remove this barrier easily. With the blockchain, each company can independently monitor and validate other companies without a central authority. From raw material to complete value development, the cycle is open not only to stakeholders but also to the consumers. For example, a car manufacturing company needs to manufacture gear lever, seat belt, steering wheel, windscreen, fuel gauge, temperature gauge, etc. A car manufacturer needs to do business with several other organizations for a successful product development. Now, other organizations may or may not have a similar infrastructure to support the supply chain mechanism of that particular car company. This is where blockchain is offering vertical networking for a smart production system for every organization involved in that product development life cycle. Figure 10.10 clearly shows that blockchain and Industry 4.0 fit each other in several aspects, which makes blockchain a real contender for becoming a member of the fourth industrial revolution.

Blockchain provides a platform for digital transformation of the current industry to adapt to Industry 4.0. This technology is offering the following items to current industry architecture to make it more acceptable and dynamic. The left side of Figure 10.10 shows the needs of Industry 4.0. Autonomy, CPS, P2P

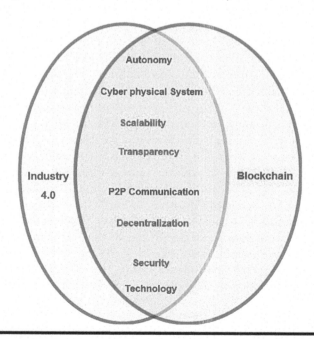

Figure 10.10   Common features between Industry 4.0 and blockchain technology.

communication, and other latest technologies are the requirements of the fourth industrial revolution. On the other hand, the right side reflects the characteristics of the blockchain such as scalability, transparency, decentralization, and secured communication. The abovementioned characteristics of blockchain technology are capable enough of fulfilling the requirements of Industry 4.0.

- **Digital trust**

  From a very lower level of business to the top level, the term that makes a successful completion of the deal is trust. Employees to customers, everyone wants trust without dependencies. Currently, blockchain is there to generate digital trust among the business parties. Juri Mattalia describes that digital trust requires three factors in a system: security, identifiability, and traceability [46]. When we choose to do transactions, we trust that the products and services provided are secure against malware and data abuse. Again, trust must be there regarding the identity of the involved parties. Finally, if, for any circumstance, the contract is not executed, then the contractual right is well preserved for both parties, which is also a kind of trust. Blockchain transaction shelters every party involved in a business-to-business communication. Therefore, in the fourth industrial revolution, digitalized trust will be offered by blockchain technologies.

- **Intelligent data management**

  Data mining, especially big data analysis, has already been deployed in all sectors. In future, manufacturers will use artificial intelligence and neural networking for big data mining in business intelligence development [47]. Business intelligence can transform data into information and that information transfers as knowledge for future use. By virtue of blockchain technology, data will be more secure and reliable. Data manipulation and privacy have been big issues until now, but decentralized databases and a two-layer protection mechanism of blockchain will encourage more data mining. From medical sector to insurance sector, data will more be secure with stakeholders (researchers, customer, public authorities, etc.) participating in the network as blockchain "miners" [48]. So, it is obvious that every kind of industry can deploy blockchain technology for business intelligence development by mining data.

- **Smart ecosystem**

  Companies and organizations along with their suppliers, lead producers, competitors, and other stakeholders form the business ecosystem. Blockchain has a lot to contribute in generating a smart ecosystem for business. P2P and cyber-physical communication protected by blockchain can create a new era of the smart ecosystem that can reduce cost, time, and system loss for Industry 4.0. It brings the concept of "smart contract" [49] that helps to exchange money or anything of value in a transparent and indisputable way. This not only keeps the contract stable but also ensures that it happens successfully and, best of all, it ensures privacy and execution of the agreed terms between the parties.

■ **Digital supply chain (DSC)**

Kari Korpela described the DSC as an integrated business process where an effective connection will be there between parties involved in service, delivery, marketing, and selling [50]. In DSC, product will be trackable throughout the supply chain. This addition of DSC brings transparency in the fourth industrial revolution. In the current DSC transactions, organizations are executing the transactions via a reliable third party, preferably banks, and here comes the need for blockchain that helps in minimizing the need for an unnecessary third-party "bank." One of the blockchain advantages is that it includes a public ledger of the transactions without the need for the transaction party identities. This is because it uses a public key infrastructure to help in notifying the counterparties. Every party involved in an agreement can verify the details of execution. Blockchain can check whether every aspect of the contract has been well maintained, and if not, a party can legally cancel the contract or agreement.

■ **Cybersecurity**

Blockchain saves data in hash functions with timestamps, so it is highly unlikely to be tempered since data once written cannot be overwritten; thus, there is no chance of manipulation. According to Pentagon, blockchain technology can be used as a cybersecurity shield. *The Washington Times* stated that US military sees blockchain technology as a reliable way of maintaining security. American military and security sector can reduce the mega hacking of drone, satellite, and communication media with the help of blockchain technology [51]. The bank's information systems are considered to be one of the most secure systems. Individual banks maintain their interbank communication with highly encrypted data transfer. Transfer of money, settlements, information by banks were trustworthy until recent cyberattacks on the banking sector started growing rapidly. Day by day people are losing their faith on these banks due to corruption and political, technical, and social competition. Security systems like "SWIFT" have also been overcome by cyber attackers. A distributed ledger or a shared database offered by blockchain technology can also be a secure option for banking sector communication. Confidentiality, integrity, and availability of a blockchain service are the three main security challenges for Industry 4.0 as identified in a study by Chhetri [52]. Since blockchain can recode every detail of a transaction, interbank communication improves in the context of data validation, time validation, and identity validation. Since security related issues lose a lot of money for a business and manufacturing industry, blockchain technology can be a good option to secure a business. Hacking and fraudulence cost businesses $400 billion a year. The report also mentioned that global revenues for companies that offer digital security solutions were a total of $2.7 billion in 2015 and are predicted to be more than $4.7 billion in 2020 [53].

10.4.2 Application Domains of Blockchain in Industry 4.0

Blockchain has been widely applied in various application domains. Though BTC and other cryptocurrencies have taken the leading role as applications of blockchain, in future, this can bring a revolution for age-old business ideologies. From finance to health, from insurance to vehicle-sharing start-up, from country governance to office maintenance, from company reputation to patent authentication, every single sector can deploy this technology. An overview of opportunities in blockchain technology is shown in Figure 10.11. We will now highlight a few sectors affected by blockchain.

- **Banking and insurance**

  The banking and financing sector all over the world is keeping eye on blockchain technology. What can the banking sector attain from this? Everything that it was lacking before, for example, a secure transaction approval system, an irreversible information storage, a timestamp-based tracking, etc. Banking giants such as Goldman Sachs, J.P. Morgan, Union Bank of Switzerland, HSBC, Industrial & Commercial Bank of China, Bank of America, Citigroup, Morgan Stanley, Deutsche Bank, Barclays Bank, Ping An Bank, and China Merchants Bank have already established their own blockchain-related research centers for developing their own blockchain-based banking systems.

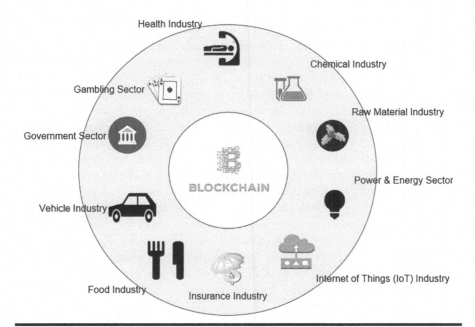

Figure 10.11   Industry influenced by blockchain technology.

For this reason, research industries and software industries have also started developing banking applications to hold this rising market. For example, R3, a US-based software company, has invested $107 million for developing a blockchain or shared ledger-based finance-related application. This company released the second version of "CORDA" software after collaborating with more than 100 banks, layers, and professionals to shape it as the best available banking application [54,55]. According to McKinsey survey in May 2016, half of the bank executives believe that within the next 3 years, there will a substantial effect of blockchain and cryptocurrencies on the banking and financing sector [56]. Another similar kind of survey reported that blockchain will be implemented in 15% of the banks present all over the world by the end of 2018 [57]. IBM reported that in the next 4 years, blockchain will be implemented commercially in 66% of the global banks [58]. Blockchain-enabled smart contract applications can easily be extended in building a P2P or crowdfunding insurance model. The new model is expected to focus on supply and demand matching and risk calculation aspects, where insurers will build platforms for potential customers to post their customized requirements for insurance plans. Insurers would apply their risk assessment techniques to perform necessary calculations. Once the calculations are finalized, insurers can place their premium estimations giving a chance for investors to subscribe to the plan.

■ **Medical and health care**
  In the health-care industry, blockchain can secure the valuable patient data. Sometimes, the health sector uses patient information for improving the intelligence of health-care systems without any prior permission from the patient. This privacy issue can be solved by a decentralized and secured blockchain technology [59]. Again, Deloitte has surveyed the health care opportunities in *Blockchain: Opportunities for Health Care* [60], which identified blockchain as a promising new distributed framework to amplify and support the integration of health care information. Blockchain-based systems have the potential to reduce costs of current intermediaries between doctors and patients. In the health–care industry, blockchain technology use cases can be quality medicine, patient care and outcomes research, and global standard health-care system. The application field can be clinical data sharing, public health data storage, research and clinical trials, administrative and financial health information, and doctor and food identification and prioritization. For example, wearables and IoT devices collect patient information, and blockchain can secure this by replacing individual cloud to the shared ledger. Another example can be when a patient with several health issues undergoes a severe operation, blockchain consensus technique can be applied among specialist doctors to finalize the medical decision.

■ **Energy and power grid**
  Blockchain decentralized and privacy-protected scope can authenticate and manage the billing process in power grid billing systems. James Basden

describes two use cases of blockchain that can be used in the future power grid sector: (i) Participants of a microgrid project living in a city can sell electricity produced by their solar panels to the neighbors. Information and transactions of this application can be maintained by blockchain technology where each house can be considered as a "node" or miner in reference to the blockchain. (2) Selling of unused power during the break time of a company to another company of the same grid [61]. Private companies are deploying fossil fuel-based electricity generation companies. They are supplying power to the national grid where governments are facing difficulties in dealing with environmental pollutions, stealing, and corruptions. A shared database in this sector can track the exact flaws. Even the payment, billing, and user identity validation take longer times for this centralized power grid system. Blockchain transparency, census, and reputation log can remove this extra time taken for validation.

■ **Vehicle and transport**
Business related to vehicle sharing and renting will be highly affected by blockchain technology. Nowadays, from bicycle to car are deploying as a shared business in every country. The decision, rating, and approval can be done by a shared database like the blockchain technology. Scania truck suspension, booking, and maintenance system discussed by Lindberg can be a good example for other companies of similar type [62]. Sensing and smart vehicle communication algorithm was discussed by Sean Rowan where the vehicle-to-vehicle communication security was ensured by a similar algorithm like the blockchain private–public key [63].

■ **Marketplace**
The blockchain trustless business communication policy will have a huge impact on online marketplaces of the fourth industrial revolution. Payment system, client-to-seller relation, product guarantee, and review after business all can be blockchain based with more security and reliability. Fraud buyers and sellers will be easy to detect if it is a public blockchain. Buyers and sellers will be able to connect themselves without any middlemen and the payment system will be more secure too. The smart contract with a built-in reputation system can open markets such as OpenBazzar [64]. In the real estate business, blockchain can help in tracking, verifying, and transferring document and property, which can be done with the smart contract of blockchain [65].

■ **Internet of Things**
If we consider the success of Airbnb and Uber for the shared economy, we can make an estimate of how the IoT can be occupied by the blockchain technology. On the one side, we can share our devices, vehicles, buildings, and even services by the means of embedded sensors and network connectivity, and on the other side, blockchain helps us to keep a record of all these in a safer way [66]. IBM has started to use its shared cloud for product tracing.

From root-level producers to consumers, every stakeholder is tracked by IBM when he/she delivers goods. IBM has identified three main effects that the IoT industry will have due to blockchain: (i) build trust between parties, (ii) remove cost by avoiding middleman, and (iii) reduce settlement time in real time. When IoT handles our personal things (information), the communication among things must be secured. Blockchain census and shared storage can do the approval in a secured way as was mentioned by Konstantinos Christidis [67]. I-Scoop surveyed in 2017 and reported that IoT data and shared ledger can automate sectors such as health, insurance, and trade [68].

■ **Governance**
Due to the current political unrest and transparency issues, several studies tried to represent a government and voting system based on blockchain technologies. Blockchain-based decentralized governance, state authority, citizenship, and democracy were analyzed by a study [69]. The reports suggested that governance can be decentralized as an autonomous organization. For maintaining all the sectors of a complete government, it required huge amounts of money and manpower, and still, corruption and manipulation have been occurring. Blockchain can present a governance system without any central authority or organization. Governing bodies and policy makers can use this for their internal procurement and planning. At present, a central authority handles the communication between relevant stakeholders within and between the agencies, between the government and third parties, and between the government and the citizenry. Recordkeeping, value transfer, and smart contracts provided broader cases for possible adoption of blockchain in this sector. Some use cases are identity management for the smart citizens, land registration, and voting. Reports suggested that blockchain will save $15–20 billion annually in the financial services of future industries by the year 2022 [70].

10.4.3 Adaptation Issues and Open Research Challenges

Since both blockchain and Industry 4.0 are in their infancy, there will be technical and social issues and challenges on their adaptation. Since blockchain will have a robust impact on the fourth industrial revolution, it is high time to standardize the architecture and policies for blockchain and Industry 4.0.

■ **Transaction time**
For building a consensus (approval for transaction), there is a requirement of 10–60 minutes or even longer to get the approval for a transaction. This kind of situation is not acceptable for business in the current blockchain, so it has to be changed in order to get the business attention to blockchain. Long finality time (a transaction finalized time) is a big issue in making this technology fit for the smart factories of the fourth industrial revolution [71].

After a user decides to do a particular transaction, getting approval from others and eliminating simultaneous block creation require extra time, which is a big issue in the current blockchain architecture. According to blockchain. info, the average confirmation time of a BTC transaction, during December 2017, was 13 minutes. The lowest value calculated during that time was 9 minutes, but it can take even 18 minutes [72] which is very alarming for real-life businesses.

■ **Modification and edition**

Once information is added to the block, it sticks and there is no way to alter this information. But in business and industry, at some point, modifications or editions can be needed. Blockchain cannot provide such flexibility to the fourth industrial revolution. Since there can be no modification, there is no way of correcting or reversing a transaction, which sometimes makes it unfit for future smart businesses. In June 2016, a bug was identified in a smart contract (Ethereum) called "The DAO," but due to the lack of modification opportunities, it cost around $250 million to remove the bug [73]. Since it is a shared decision-based system where the party involved in POW cannot be always trusted, it can cause errors, but there is no way to return from that immutable blockchain information.

■ **Timestamping Authority (TSA)**

In a business environment, it is common and important to specify as well as record the date and time of a transaction. An important issue of current blockchain architecture, which must be resolved to suit Industry 4.0, is the lack of obligation with TSA or Time Assessment Authority. An accurate storing of time is very crucial for any business, but blockchain lags behind in this case [43]. From successful product manufacturing to delivery, everything must be well tracked. In the current blockchain architecture, it takes 10–60 minutes for a particular transaction to be completed. For example, a node (company A) wants to transfer money to another node (company B) for making a business deal. Company A initiated the transaction at 10:00 p.m., but it takes 15 minutes to generate a census (approval from all other nodes), and then blockchain can store the transaction time as 10:15 p.m., not 10:00 p.m. The actual time when the new block is created gets stored in the current architecture, and not the time of initiation.

■ **Storage consumption**

Blockchain participation with smaller capacity will be in trouble since this is a shared database system. Every node has the same copy of information and this can increase the cost of storage for devices such as phones and computers. For big companies, storage management will not be a problem, but a company with smaller capital and infrastructure will surely face problems in adapting to this. In December 2017, each node (block) already had 160 GB or more data, which is very alarming for the future. According to blockchain. info, in the year 2017, each block size exceeded 1.05 MB (average). It was just

600 KB during the end of 2016 and increased rapidly to become 3.6 MB at the end of 2017 [72]. This trend can demotivate stakeholders while deploying blockchain technologies into a real business. An architectural change is a must to resolve this problem.

■ **Energy consumption**

Resources (machine power) use high-configuration computers for information processing and transactions. Electricity consumption and the maintenance cost of these computers are huge. People worldwide bring more energy-hungry computers to mine the digital currency. BTCs estimated that the annual electricity consumption is 34.34 TWh. Electricity consumed per transaction is 240 kWh, which raises the question that whether industries will invest this much electricity for communication, transaction, and security [73]. The answer is probably yes since atomic energy is producing enormous electricity that can fulfil the needs of blockchain technology. Reports also suggested that the entire BTC network now consumes more energy than some countries lsuch as Serbia, Denmark, and Belarus. Another issue pointed out by the report was carbon footprint, which is 117.63 kg of CO_2 per transaction. Blockchain architecture and principle must be evaluated again to fit into the fourth industrial revolution. The biggest problem with POW is energy wastage. BTC, in particular, is voracious in its appetite for energy. Multichainblog.com revealed the energy consumption data for the month of October–November, 2017 [73]. On November 17, 2017, energy consumption for BTC was 28.5 TWh. The dangerous fact is that it was just 22 TWh on October 20, 2017. This rapid growth in energy consumption can limit the use of blockchain.

■ **Security issues**

The blockchain is mainly a P2P network technology with a strong security shield. Still, technical issues are arising, such as 51% error, eclipse attack, race attack, finery attack, brute force attack, and block discarding [43,74,75]. A 51% attack is generated when fraudulent people consume more than 50% of POS. Eclipse attack happens when the network is cut off. When a person tries to spend two BTCs at the same time, it is called race attack. Private mining to generate blockchain fork produces brute force attack. Studies also mentioned about some social security issues such as bribery attack, wallet stealing, and fake delay creation. When BTC was started, miners were honest and worked without any influence, but since the market started going high (1 BTC=US$9,000) powerful stakeholders started finding an alternate way for corruption. In Industry 4.0, security threats will be seriously taken; therefore, blockchain must fulfil the security needs of the future industry [52]. Stakeholders are paying money to bring about corruption, delay specific consensus, steal keys, etc. In the real business system, the third party involved resolves the issues. Since there are no middlemen in this technology, correcting issues are also difficult. Too many hackers are also getting involved for making easy money. Gordian recently reported a money laundering case of $500,000 where the attacker bought a fake Picasso. Such intermediate-less transactions can influence the economies of poor and corrupted countries where money laundering, black money, drug dealing, kidnapping, etc. will be easier and untraceable [43,74].

■ **Social challenges**

Factory structures and abilities differ from country to country. The technical senses are not the same for employees across different organizations. Technically sound people are needed for adapting blockchain in Industry 4.0. Company policy and budget should also meet the requirements for blockchain technology. Blockchain stores all the transactions in the block and makes them accessible to everyone, so this opens up a privacy issue. All transaction record is open, which may discourage its use by people or companies that do not want their personal data to be used for mining. Organizations do not want to open their transaction records for business policies, which can be financially dangerous in the future. PwC [44] reported that "Lack of digital culture and training is the biggest challenge facing companies." They also identified the three vital characteristics: transparency, legitimacy, and effectiveness. From owner to customer, everyone must change technically and mentally to welcome blockchain.

10.4.4 Challenges Associated with Law, Policy, and Standardization

The applications followed by issues were mentioned for blockchain and fourth industrial revolution, but the most important thing needed for a successful future for blending these two technologies together is setting up a law and policy for both blockchain and fourth industrial revolution (Industry 4.0). Vendor-specific blockchain technologies are coming from research organizations, banks, and factories with independent policies and architectures. For successful inclusion in Industry 4.0, they must be synchronized and must follow a specific pattern for compatibility. Until now, both blockchain and Industry 4.0 are vendor and use case specific in isolated production systems. In order to make a successful Industry 4.0 with blockchain, current independent approaches must be replaced by open and standardized policies. Service-level agreements are needed for getting proper services from blockchain technology. If Industry 4.0 does not finalize its standardization, then technologies such as blockchain, IoT, big data, smart simulator, AR, and VR will grow independently. This will cause serious trouble in future intercompatibility. The requirements of blockchain need to be clarified for business deployment. Industry, academia, and the public sector will have to design and implement similar kinds of blockchain, and there should be standardized training facilities among blockchain users and engineers [43]. Standardization process has already been started by the international organizations where a two-way communication between users and standard developers is a must before developing the standards and regulations. In June 2016, a workshop was conducted by the World Wide Web Consortium (www.w3.org) to discuss web and blockchain technology [76]. A coordination between ISO TC 307, ITU-T, and SWIFT took place in 2017 to standardize blockchain protocol-related issues. Federal Reserve System is also taking initiatives to standardize their monetary transactions via blockchain technology [77]. Unstable market values of cryptocurrencies will create problems in real-life blockchain implementation in the industry. Currently, bank charges are fixed and currency rates are also predictable. On the other hand, in cryptocurrency, fees are hard to predict due to frequent changes in its value. Taxation procedures, profit-making, price estimation, and cost analysis will be much more complicated. Financial stability is very much needed; otherwise, stakeholders will move away from blockchain due to higher business risks. Prices for the same product can vary significantly from one day to the next, which is very unusual for any business. According to blockchain.info, at the end of 2016, transaction fees cost around 136 (BTC, which was raised to 784 BTC at the end of 2017. This dissimilarity happened due to uneven changes in its market value. The same website stated that the market value for 1 BTC was US$3,777 on December 17, 2016, which went up to US$19,500 on December 17, 2017, without any legit variable. It is predicted that popularity, energy and storage consumption, and the price of other cryptocurrencies are the main factors affecting BTC's value [72].

10.4.5 Recommendations for Adaptation

Although opportunities are there but for turning it into a revolution, the culture of blockchain technology should be present from the root to the top level. When the first Internet emerged, it faced the same struggle, but technically sound people motivated the stakeholders. Similarly, the stockholders should know now what blockchain can provide. The applicable field, security, and, confidentiality must be clear to the investors. There must be collaboration and consideration among companies during the primary phase of investment. Parties mentioned in Figure 10.12 must adapt themselves for introducing a blockchain-based fourth industrial revolution. A collaborative work is needed for adapting this blockchain technology to the fourth industrial revolution. Blockchain service developers, industry stakeholders, researchers, trainers, customers, and governments all have to play their part. To overcome key challenges and accelerate the fourth industrial revolution, business, blockchain technology developers, and government stakeholders need to take immediate actions. Technology providers such as software companies and research and development centers must provide adequate training and demonstrations to make their products popular and acceptable. On the other hand, investors and factory owners must understand the necessity of this new technology along with its pros and cons. Finally, policy makers should remove the burden from cryptocurrencies. They must apply strong regulations to control its price. Similarly,

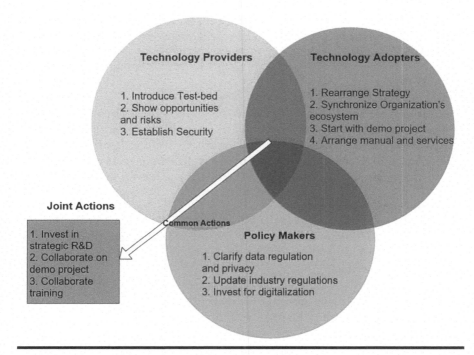

Figure 10.12   Recommendation to adapt blockchain.

from company level to country level, policy makers must synchronize the laws and regulations. They should also think elaborately about new technologies to cope with the current trends. The vital requirement for bringing about a successful fourth industrial revolution (Industry 4.0) is the cooperation among aforementioned parties (Figure 10.12). For example, if a bank wants to deploy a blockchain technology, there must be collaboration among the bank's customers, software developers, and other banks. If a fruitful cooperation takes places among them, only then bank owners can invest reliably.

10.5 Potential Use Case and Comparative Analysis

In the fourth industrial revolution, product is traceable from the raw material to the distribution stage. Point-to-point communication across different countries having different laws slows down the supply chain of every business. In May 2017, IBM and Maersk reported some cases in their survey. Maersk reported that for transferring one product from East Africa to Europe, they need to pass 30 organizations and 200 interactions, which makes their product delivery time longer [78]. Since companies such as DHL, FedEx, Maersk, and UPS need to deliver millions of products from region to region, they are also considering this blockchain technology as a possible solution. By involving the blockchain shared ledger system, they can trace and reduce the product supply time. Next we will discuss a digital product delivery system (DSC) as a blockchain use case.

10.5.1 Use Case: DSC

A similar use case was discussed by another survey done by the Japan Government [43]. In blockchain product delivery, every party involved in manufacture, retail, logistic department, human resource department, product marketing department, product delivery, and product consumption acts as a node. A shared database can track costing, quality, and feedback of a particular product which is essential for Industry 4.0.

- ■ **Information management**
  Blockchain can manage all the information related to the supply chain of an industry. Receipt, delivery report, identification numbers, and guarantee papers all can be protected by blockchain technology.
- ■ **Utilized function**
  Secured and shared data storage of blockchain technology has a lot to contribute in supply management. The three important blockchain functions used in supply chains [43] are "execution of applications using a dedicated script (smart contracts)," "ensuring traceability of data and enabling transparent transactions (shared ledger and consensus)," and "maintaining the ecosystem against any attacks by malicious users without a central authority (public and private key security)."
- ■ **Impact on industrial structure**
  Order placement for raw material, quotation supplying, delivery, checking, and payment methods are also traceable. If at any level of the chain, defective goods delivery reports are found against a particular supplier, then that information will be open and visible to all.
- ■ **Other possibilities**
  Retailers (downstream), wholesalers (middle stream), and manufacturers (upstream) communication procedure can be made independent by blockchain where everyone can contact each other. Here, the reputation or trust is not provided by a middleman and communication will happen from the root level to the top level if blockchain is used for supply chain management.

10.5.2 Comparative Analysis

Table 10.1 shows the comparative analysis of the effects that blockchain will have on the future industry.

- ■ **Industrial data management**
  Figure 10.13 shows a brief view of how current factories may change after the integration of blockchain in the fourth industrial revolution. Currently,

Table 10.1   Positive and Negative Effects of Blockchain on Future Industry

Positive Effects on Future Industry	Negative Effects on Future Industry
Information's availability and reliability will go up	Verification process time will be higher
Auditability, trust, and transparency will increase	Data storage will be limited or costly
Increasing confidence, decreasing fraudulence	Higher energy and power cost
Irrevocable transaction, increase accuracy of data	Cost for integrating blockchain in the factory will be higher
Paperless digital office	Worker may not be mentally ready
Industry will be able to do trustless exchange	Company's information technology sector needs to be redesigned
Company database will be consistent, timely, accurate, and easily accessible	Security thread can bring abrupt loss
Empowered workers with high morals	Immutability may create reputation-related problem
Interprocess integrity goes up	A powerful stakeholder can dominate start-ups in a negative way
Company-to-company transaction with less time	Workers may not be technically sound
No third-party or transaction cost	Lesser space for correction and modifications

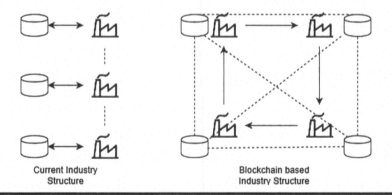

Current Industry Structure

Blockchain based Industry Structure

Figure 10.13   Current and future industry data access architecture.

each industry has its own database; therefore other companies can only have information that is supplied by that particular company. This creates data manipulation and system loss. Blockchain can replace a shared system where intercompany communication will be automatic. Industry 4.0 will certainly use this technique to make business interactions more transparent.

■ **Human resources and procurement management**

Potential contractors and partner identification and recruitment will be easier since both employer and employee can have a highly secured, distributed database. A company structure in recruitment can be changed as shown in Figure 10.14 where previous companies and academies can generate a reputation database and the next destination can be selected automatically from this data. Similarly, product and services can be ranked, which will generate more revenue for any reputed manufacturer in Industry 4.0 architecture.

■ **Trade and transaction management**

Middlemen from transactions will die out and industry's logistic and business architecture will be different. In current transactions (Figure 10.15), exporters and importers do business via banks. After blockchain-based shared storage provides direct transaction facilities, product development will be cost and time efficient.

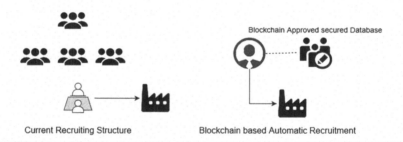

Figure 10.14 **Current and future industry recruitment architecture.**

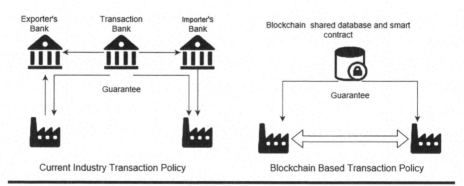

Figure 10.15 **Current and future industry transaction architecture.**

10.6 Conclusion

The blockchain is not a magic, but it is an innovative, general-purpose technology, offering a new way of value creation for almost all domains of industries. In this chapter, we have discussed the influence of blockchain and cryptocurrencies on Industry 4.0. First, we precisely mentioned the prerequisite of fourth industrial revolution, and consequently, we identified the key characteristics and components of blockchain technology that blends with the ongoing industrial revolution. While reporting the challenges and issues of blockchain technologies, we also mentioned that collaboration is a must among stakeholders for bringing about a solid blockchain standard. Finally, we have described the future scopes and applicable sectors for blockchain in the fourth industrial revolution. In summary, this chapter is a sole attempt toward highlighting the impact of blockchain on Industry 4.0. We believe that our discussion will help readers to easily understand the strategic, organizational, economic, informational, and technological aspects of blockchain and Industry 4.0.

References

1. Ganschar, O., Gerlach, S., Hämmerle, M., Krause, T., & Schlund, S. (2013). Produktionsarbeit der Zukunft-Industrie 4.0 [Production work of the future industry] (pp. 50–56). D. Spath (Ed.). FraunhoferVerlag, Stuttgart.
2. Kagermann, H., Lukas, W. D., & Wahlster, W. (2011). Industrie 4.0: Mitdem Internet der Dinge auf demWegzur 4. industriellen Revolution [Industry 4.0: With the Internet of Things on the way to the 4th industrial revolution]. *VDI nachrichten, 13*, 11.
3. The new High-Tech Strategy. (2014, December 03). Retrieved December 13, 2017, from www.hightech-strategie.de/de/The-new-High-Tech-Strategy-390.php.
4. Kagermann, H., Helbig, J., Hellinger, A., & Wahlster, W. (2013). Recommendations for implementing the strategic initiative INDUSTRIE 4.0: Securing the future of German manufacturing industry; final report of the Industrie 4.0 Working Group. Forschungsunion.
5. Bungart, S. (2014) Industrial Internet versus Industrie 4.0. Interview in: Produktion. Technik und Wirtschaftfür die deutsche Industrie. Retrieved from www.produktion.de/technik/automatisierung/industrial-internet-versusindustrie-4-0-338.html
6. Bauernhansl, T., Ten Hompel, M., & Vogel-Heuser, B. (Eds.). (2014). *Industrie 4.0 in Produktion, Automatisierung und Logistik: Anwendung, Technologien und Migration [Industry 4.0 in production, automation and logistics: application, technologies and migration]* (pp. 1–648). Springer Vieweg, Wiesbaden.
7. Dais, S. (2017). Industrie 4.0–Anstoß, vision, vorgehen. In B. Vogel-Heuser, T. Bauernhansl, and M. ten Hompel (Eds.), *Handbuch Industrie 4.0 Bd. 4* (pp. 261–277). Springer Vieweg, Berlin.
8. MacDougall, W. (2014). Industrie 4.0: Smart manufacturing for the future. Germany Trade & Invest.
9. C. Baur & D. W. (2015, June). Manufacturing's next act. Retrieved December 14, 2017, from www.mckinsey.com/business-functions/operations/our-insights/manufacturings-next-act
10. Davies, R. (2015). Industry 4.0.Digitalisation for productivity and growth. Briefing from EPRS. European Parliamentary Research Service.

11. L. G. (2015, May 18). What is industrie 4.0 and what should CIOs do about it? Retrieved December 14, 2017, from www.gartner.com/newsroom/id/3054921

12. Hofmann, E., & Rüsch, M. (2017). Industry 4.0 and the current status as well as future prospects on logistics. *Computers in Industry, 89*, 23–34.

13. Geissbauer, R., Vedso, J., & Schrauf, S. (2016). Industry 4.0: building the digital enterprise: 2016 global industry 4.0 survey. PwC, Munich.

14. Deloitte, A. G. (2015). Industry 4.0 challenges and solutions for the digital transformation and use of exponential technologies. *McKinsey Global Institute.*

15. Lee, J., Bagheri, B., & Kao, H. A. (2015). A cyber-physical systems architecture for industry 4.0-based manufacturing systems. *Manufacturing Letters, 3*, 18–23.

16. Gubbi, J., Buyya, R., Marusic, S., & Palaniswami, M. (2013). Internet of Things (IoT): A vision, architectural elements, and future directions. *Future Generation Computer Systems, 29*(7), 1645–1660.

17. Wollschlaeger, M., Sauter, T., & Jasperneite, J. (2017). The future of industrial communication: Automation networks in the era of the internet of things and industry 4.0. *IEEE Industrial Electronics Magazine, 11*(1), 17–27.

18. Hossain, M. S., & Muhammad, G. (2016). Cloud-assisted industrial Internet of Things (iiot)–enabled framework for health monitoring. Computer Networks, *101*, 192–202.

19. Energie, B. F. (2016, September 14). AutonomikfürIndustrie 4.0. Retrieved December 14, 2017, from www.bmwi.de/Redaktion/DE/Publikationen/Digitale-Welt/autonomik-fuer-industrie-4-0.html. Federal Ministry for Economic Affairs, Germany.

20. Wang, S., Wan, J., Li, D., & Zhang, C. (2016). Implementing smart factory of industrie 4.0: an outlook. *International Journal of Distributed Sensor Networks, 12*(1), 3159805.

21. Abramovici, M., Göbel, J. C., & Savarino, P. (2017). Reconfiguration of smart products during their use phase based on virtual product twins. *CIRP Annals-Manufacturing Technology.*

22. Lee, J., Kao, H. A., & Yang, S. (2014). Service innovation and smart analytics for industry 4.0 and big data environment. *Procedia Cirp, 16*, 3–8.

23. Pierdicca, R., Frontoni, E., Pollini, R., Trani, M., & Verdini, L. (2017) The use of augmented reality glasses for the application in industry 4.0. In L. De Paolis, P. Bourdot, and A. Mongelli (Eds.), *Augmented Reality, Virtual Reality, and Computer Graphics. AVR 2017. Lecture Notes in Computer Science,* Vol. 10324. Springer, Cham.

24. Rehnberg, M., & Ponte, S. (2017). From smiling to smirking? 3D printing, upgrading and the restructuring of global value chains. *Global Networks.*

25. Huber, A., & Weiss, A. (2017, March). Developing human-robot interaction for an industry 4.0 robot: How industry workers helped to improve remote-HRI to physical-HRI. In *Proceedings of the Companion of the 2017 ACM/IEEE International Conference on Human-Robot Interaction* (pp. 137–138). ACM, Vienna, Austria.

26. Nakamoto, S. (2008, October). Bitcoin: A peer-to-peer electronic cash system.

27. Hackett, R. (2016, May 23). Wait, what is blockchain? Retrieved December 15, 2017, from http://fortune.com/2016/05/23/blockchain-definition/

28. Kosba, A., Miller, A., Shi, E., Wen, Z., & Papamanthou, C. (2016, May). Hawk: The blockchain model of cryptography and privacy-preserving smart contracts. In *2016 IEEE Symposium on Security and Privacy (SP)* (pp. 839–858). IEEE, San Jose, CA.

29. Szabo, N. (1997). Formalizing and securing relationships on public networks. *First Monday, 2*(9).

30. Zheng, Z., Xie, S., Dai, H., Chen, X., & Wang, H. (2017, June). An overview of blockchain technology: Architecture, consensus, and future trends. In G. Karypis and J. Zhang (Eds.), *2017 IEEE International Congress on Big Data (BigData Congress)* (pp. 557–564). IEEE, Honolulu, HI.

31. Pilkington, M. (2015, September 18). Blockchain technology: Principles and applications In F. Xavier Olleros and M. Zhegu (Eds.), *Research Handbook on Digital Transformations.* Edward Elgar, 2016. Retrieved from SSRN, https://ssrn.com/abstract=2662660

32. Johnson, D., Menezes, A., & Vanstone, S. (2001). The elliptic curve digital signature algorithm (ECDSA). *International Journal of Information Security*, *1*(1), 36–63.

33. C. Miguel & L. Barbara. Practical byzantine fault tolerance. In *Proceedings of the Third Symposium on Operating Systems Design and Implementation*, Vol. 99, New Orleans, USA, 1999, pp. 173–186.

34. Kiayias, A., Russell, A., David, B., & Oliynykov, R. (2017, August). Ouroboros: A provably secure proof-of-stake blockchain protocol. In J. Katz and H. Shacham (Eds.), *Advances in Cryptology – CRYPTO 2017. CRYPTO 2017. Lecture Notes in Computer Science*, Vol. 10401. Springer, Cham.

35. Chen, S., Chen, C. Y. H., Härdle, W. K., Lee, T. M., & Ong, B. (2017). Econometric analysis of a cryptocurrency index for portfolio investment. In *Handbook of Blockchain, Digital Finance, and Inclusion* (Vol. 1, pp. 175–206). Academic Press, San Diego, CA.

36. D. Schwartz, N. Youngs, and A. Britto.(2014). "The Ripple protocol consensus algorithm", [PDF file] Ripple Labs Inc White Paper. Retrieved from https://ripple.com/files/ripple consensus whitepaper.pdf

37. Sporny, M. (2017, April). LD-DL'17 workshop keynote talk by many sporny: Building better blockchains via linked data. In *Proceedings of the 26th International Conference on World Wide Web Companion* (pp. 1429–1429). International World Wide Web Conferences Steering Committee.

38. O'Dwyer, K.J., Malone, D. (2014). Bitcoin mining and its energy footprint. ISSC 2014/CIICT 2014, imerick, June 26–27.

39. Vasin, P. (2015). Blackcoin's proof-of-stake protocol v2. 2014. Retrieved from http://blackcoin.co/blackcoin-pos-protocol-v2-whitepaper.pdf

40. Zamfir, V. (2015). Introducing Casper "the friendly ghost". Ethereum Blog. Retrieved from https://blog. ethereum.org/2015/08/01/introducing-casper-friendly-ghost

41. Vigna, P., & Casey, M. J. (2016). *The Age of Crypto Currency*. Picador St Martin's Press, New York. Retrieved from https://theageofcryptocurrency.com/

42. Kiviat, T. I. (2015). Beyond bitcoin: Issues in regulating blockchain tranactions. *Duke LJ*, *65*, 569.

43. The Results of a Survey on Blockchain Technologies and Related Services were compiled. (2016). Retrieved December 17, 2017, from www.meti.go.jp/english/press/2016/0531_01.html. Japan's Ministry of Economy, Trade and Industry (METI).

44. Geissbauer, D., & Vedso, J. (2016, April). Industry 4.0. Retrieved December 16, 2017, from www.pwc.com/gx/en/industries/industry-4.0.html

45. Challenges and solutions for the digital transformation and use of exponential | Deloitte Taiwan | Manufacturing. (2015, September 2). Retrieved December 16, 2017, from www2.deloitte.com/tw/en/pages/manufacturing/articles/industry4-0.html

46. Mattila, J., & Seppälä, T. (2016). Digital trust, platforms, and policy. *ETLA Brief No.*, *42*.

47. Mishra, D. P., Samantaray, S. R., & Joos, G. (2016). A combined wavelet and data-mining based intelligent protection scheme for microgrid. *IEEE Transactions on Smart Grid*, *7*(5), 2295–2304.

48. Azaria, A., Ekblaw, A., Vieira, T., & Lippman, A. (2016, August). Medrec: Using block-chain for medical data access and permission management. In *International Conference on Open and Big Data (OBD)* (pp. 25–30). IEEE, Vienna, Austria.
49. Peters, G. W., & Panayi, E. (2016). Understanding modern banking ledgers through block-chain technologies: Future of transaction processing and smart contracts on the internet of money. In P. Tasca, T. Aste, L. Pelizzon, and N. Perony (Eds.), *Banking Beyond Banks and Money. New Economic Windows*. Springer, Cham.
50. Korpela, K., Hallikas, J., and Dahlberg, T. 2017. Digital supply chain transformation toward Blockchain integration. In *50th Hawaii International Conference on System Sciences (HICSS 2017)*, Waikoloa, HI, pp. 4182–4191.
51. Boylan, D. (2017, August 17). Pentagon eyes bitcoin blockchain technology as cybersecurity shield. Retrieved December 16, 2017, from www.washingtontimes.com/news/2017/aug/17/pentagon-eyes-bitcoin-blockchain-technology-as-cyb/
52. Chhetri, S. R., Rashid, N., Faezi, S., & Faruque, M.A.A. (2017). Security trends and advances in manufacturing systems in the era of industry 4.0. IEEE/ACM ICCAD, pp. 1039–1046. doi:10.1109/ICCAD.2017.8203896.
53. Yakowicz, W. (2015, September 8). Companies Lose $400 Billion to Hackers Each Year. Retrieved December 16, 2017, from www.inc.com/will-yakowicz/cyberattacks-cost-companies-400-billion-each-year.html
54. Rutter, K., & Rutter, C. (2017, December 11). Kevin Rutter. Retrieved December 16, 2017, from www.r3.com/research/
55. Guo, Y., & Liang, C. (2016). Blockchain application and outlook in the banking industry. *Financial Innovation*, *2*(1), 24.
56. How blockchains could change the world. (2016, May 15). Retrieved December 16, 2017, from www.mckinsey.com/industries/high-tech/our-insights/how-blockchains-could-change-the-world
57. Blockchain Could Start Making Some Real Waves the Banking Industry Next Year. (2016, November 28). Retrieved December 16, 2017, from http://fortune.com/2016/09/28/blockchain-banks-2017/
58. Jia, C. & Feng, H. (2016) *Blockchain: From Digital Currencies to Credit Society [M]*. CITIC Publishing Group, Beijing, China.
59. Yue, X., Wang, H., Jin, D., Li, M., & Jiang, W. (2016). Healthcare data gateways: found healthcare intelligence on blockchain with novel privacy risk control. *Journal of Medical Systems*, *40*(10), 218.
60. Krawiec, R. J., Housman, D., White, M., Filipova, M., Quarre, F., Barr, D., ... Tsai, L. (2016, August). Blockchain: Opportunities for health care. *In Proc. NIST Workshop Blockchain Healthcare* (pp. 1–16).
61. Basden, J., & Cottrell, M. (2017). How utilities are using blockchain to modernize the grid. *Harvard Business Review*, Retrieved from https://hbr.org/2017/03/how-utilities-are-using-blockchain-to-modernize-the-grid
62. Lindberg, J. (2017). Blockchain technology in Scania Services: An investigative study of how blockchain technology can be utilized by Scania. Blockchain technology in Scania Services : An investigative study of how blockchain technology can be utilized by Scania (Dissertation). Retrieved from http://urn.kb.se/resolve?urn=urn:nbn:se:uu:diva-327959
63. Rowan, S., Clear, M., Gerla, M., Huggard, M., & Goldrick, C. M. (2017). Securing vehicle to vehicle communications using blockchain through visible light and acoustic side-channels. CoRR, abs/1704.02553.

64. Online Marketplace | Peer-to-Peer Ecommerce. (n.d.). Retrieved December 16, 2017, from www.openbazaar.org/
65. Blouin, M. R., & Serrano, R. (2001). A decentralized market with common values uncertainty: Non-steady states. *The Review of Economic Studies, 68*(2), 323–346.
66. Huckle, S., Bhattacharya, R., White, M., & Beloff, N. (2016). Internet of things, blockchain and shared economy applications. *Procedia Computer Science, 98*, 461–466.
67. Christidis, K., & Devetsikiotis, M. (2016). Blockchains and smart contracts for the internet of things. *IEEE Access, 4*, 2292–2303.
68. Bieler, D. (2017). Blockchain and the Internet of Things: the IoT blockchain picture. Retrieved December 16, 2017, from www.i-scoop.eu/blockchain-distributed-ledger-technology/blockchain-iot/
69. Atzori, M. (2015). Blockchain technology and decentralized governance: Is the state still necessary? Retrieved from http://dx.doi.org/10.2139/ssrn.2709713
70. White, M., Killmeyer, J., & Chew, B. (2017, September 11). Will blockchain transform the public sector? Retrieved December 17, 2017, from www2.deloitte.com/insights/us/en/industry/public-sector/understanding-basics-of-blockchain-in-government.html
71. Peters, G. W., & Panayi, E. (2016). Understanding modern banking ledgers through blockchain technologies: Future of transaction processing and smart contracts on the internet of money. In P. Tasca, T. Aste, L. Pelizzon, and N. Perony (Eds.), *Banking Beyond Banks and Money. New Economic Windows*. Springer, Cham.
72. Bitcoin Charts & Graphs—Blockchain. (2017, December 17). Retrieved December 17, 2017, from https://blockchain.info/charts
73. The Blockchain Immutability Myth. (2017, May 4). Retrieved December 17, 2017, from www.multichain.com/blog/2017/05/blockchain-immutability-myth/
74. Usborne, S. (2017, May 15). Digital gold: why hackers love Bitcoin. Retrieved December 17, 2017, from www.theguardian.com/technology/2017/may/15/digital-gold-why-hackers-love-bitcoin-ransomware
75. Conti, M., Lal, C., & Ruj, S. (2017). A survey on security and privacy issues of Bitcoin. *IEEE Communications Surveys & Tutorials*.
76. MIT Media Lab. (2016, June 30). Retrieved December 17, 2017, from www.w3.org/2016/04/blockchain-workshop/
77. Mills, D. C., Wang, K., Malone, B., Ravi, A., Marquardt, J. C., Badev, A. I., ... Ellithorpe, M. (2016). Distributed ledger technology in payments, clearing, and settlement.Finance and Economics Discussion Series 2016–095. Washington: Board of Governors of the Federal Reserve System. Retrieved from https://doi.org/10.17016/FEDS.2016.095
78. Four blockchain use cases transforming business. (2017, May 25). Retrieved December 17, 2017, from www.ibm.com/blogs/internet-of-things/iot-blockchain-use-cases/

Chapter 11

Dark Data for Analytics

Abid Hasan
Institute of Business Administration

Contents

11.1 Introduction

The whole world is now more linked and shared than ever before. As the Internet becomes even more indispensably attached to our everyday lives, we start to tread on the path that leads to a technology-driven future. We are also creating huge amounts of data in the process, both willingly and unwillingly. Humongous amounts of data are being generated that most of us are not even aware of because most of them are unstructured data hiding in plain sight. A company must increase productivity, decrease cost, be up to date with market opportunity, and influence potential customers to keep up with the evolving environment. All of these goals can be achieved if we can tap into the realm of dark data, i.e., unstructured, unused, and unexplored big data. Dark data analytics is still new and untapped. It is a unique opportunity to go beyond the traditional routine spreadsheet analytics. There are both risks and opportunities in dark data. Let us look at a simple but insightful example about how an employee of Target used its unstructured, unused, and unexplored customer data to gain a business advantage.

Target, a discount store retailer, found out about the pregnancy of a girl even before her father did only by analyzing the buying patterns of pregnant women [1]. Target assigns a unique ID number to its customers that is linked with their email IDs, names, and credit card numbers, and it remains in their database. When this event happened, competitions were fierce among the retail stores for acquiring pregnant customers so that they would purchase everything related to their babies in the future and persuade them to become loyal and long-lasting customers. So, the store that reached a pregnant woman before anyone else hit the jackpot and gained a profitable buyer. Target statistician, Andrew Pole, was given the responsibility to find a way so that they could reach out to pregnant women before any other store could. He was given the job of predicting customer pregnancy. So, he observed the buying behaviors among the ladies who signed up for their baby registries in the past. And surprisingly, there were significant differences between a regular and a pregnant woman's buying patterns. Crawling through the database, Pole identified about 25 products with differentiable characteristics. All of them were analyzed together by Pole. After that he was able to assign each shopper a "pregnancy prediction" value based on their buying pattern. Now, let us go back to the story where the girl was sent an email with coupons for baby products and her father got angry at Target for sending this email as his high-school-going daughter could not be pregnant. A few days later, Target called him to apologize, but instead of the Target authority, the father was apologizing as he did not know about his daughter's pregnancy beforehand. Now, this may seem interesting and very much profitable for Target, but this event also posed privacy questions. Should a retail store know about someone's pregnancy even before the family does? Many questions were raised which made them change their strategy to mix pregnancy-related advertising with day-to-day ads so that people did not feel that their privacy was being violated [1]. Even though this event raised controversy, we can see that the data was available all the time, but it was hidden, and all it needed was some attention.

Dark data offers the possibilities to shape the business in the future. From this example, it is clear that how much opportunity lies in the untapped world of dark data. But dark data analytics is not as easy as it sounds. There are different tools and techniques out there to derive value from dark data. Hadoop and DeepDive are noteworthy solutions to the problem of dark data. Corporate solutions are also provided by prominent companies to transform and extract value from dark data. Solutions also vary according to the source and type of data. Data is going to be the driving force in the near future and to be in the driving seat. We need to ensure that this huge amount of dark data is handled effectively and efficiently.

11.1.1 Chapter Roadmap

Rest of the chapter is organized as follows: Section 11.2 explains how data goes dark in the first place. Section 11.3 contains a discussion on risks that dark data possesses, followed by the various opportunities of dark data discussed in Section 11.4. Section 11.5 describes the tools and techniques for collecting and analyzing dark data and portrays ways of eliminating dark data. Section 11.6 discusses different dark data solutions provided by different companies. Section 11.7 deals with International Data Corporation's research on an organization's ability to derive value from dark data. Section 11.8 contains recommendations on managing dark data, and Section 11.9 concludes the chapter.

11.2 Origin of Dark Data

Dark data is also called big data that is sitting idle. Now, it can be really costly if companies miss out on this opportunity. Let us explore how dark data is created in the first place. Before dark data, there was big data. Dark data is technically unused and unexplored big data. Big data, in short, is the collection of a large volume of structured and unstructured data. Businesses are flooded with these types of data on a daily basis. How companies handle and use the data is much more important than the creation of big data itself. Big data can be analyzed to produce actionable insights that can lead to better business decisions and strategies.

Every minute, Google conducts 3.6 million searches, 100 million emails are sent by spammers, 527,000 photos are sent through Snapchat, 456,000 tweets are published, and 46,740 pictures are shared on Instagram [2]. This is just a fraction of what lies ahead of us in terms of big data creation. Every day 2.5 quintillion bytes of data are created. And 90% of all the data in the world was created in the past 2 years. Big data has different dimensions such as volume, velocity, variety, and veracity [3]. From the above examples, we can understand the huge volume of data that is created from different sources, varieties of data—like simple queries—that generate customer insights, and numerous photos and tweets that help create social insight. A huge amount of data created within a minute indicates the velocity, and

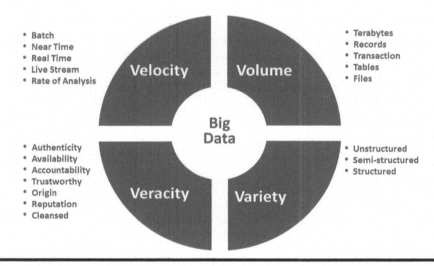

Figure 11.1 Four V's of big data. (Adapted from [4].)

lastly the spam emails that alert us not to trust every source indicate veracity or the accuracy of the source. Besides, these data can be irregular and inconsistent with seasonality. All of these make it really difficult to search, process, store, and analyze. Due to the lack of awareness, proper knowledge, accessibility measures, and extraction methods, big data turns into its evil twin, i.e., dark data (Figure 11.1).

Dark data includes emails, documents, presentation files, including both internal and external archived sensor data from Internet of Things (IoT), spreadsheets, backups of operation database, images, partial documents, audio files, CCTV surveillance footage of a superstore, geographic data, partial codes, zip files, log files, and everything that is unused, underutilized, neglected, or forgotten in the system. Networking devices generate a huge amount of information. If this huge amount of data is not analyzed, it will simply go dark. Due to our inability to handle data efficiently and inconsistency in the format of the data that analytics do not support, we cannot turn these into actionable information [5].

To some extent, data buried in the deep web can be considered as dark data, too. Deep web is not indexed by our typical search engines and includes data from academia, government agencies, legal documents, scientific studies, subscription only information, financial records, user communities, and many more. And dark web is something inside the deep web that is completely untraceable and hidden, and it cannot be accessed with the standard web browsers [6].

11.3 Risks of Dark Data

Dark data is produced, collected, and stored in a business, and it is never used again. In most of the cases, dark data remains dormant, but it is present, unknown, inactive, and unmanaged. The data remains dark when it is forgotten. Unmonitored and unsecured data always poses threat because there are different compliance reasons, and there is also the risk of sensitive information falling into the wrong hands. Hackers can easily hack into the system when the location and even the content is unknown to the authority, and it can be deadly in terms of reputation and business profits, and may result in complete shutdown. Dark data poses serious security risks in this ever-connected world where one can easily hack into a system and cause havoc. A company can be unaware of the existence of a data just to find out about it only after it is exposed to the public. How can one protect or hide something that they do not even know about? Also, when a company is asked to provide some data, it really hurts their reputation when they are unable to do that. Apart from the obvious risks of losing business opportunities derived from dark data, we also have to be aware of the other risks associated with it [7].

11.4 Dark Data Analytics: An Untapped Opportunity

Networking machines generate a huge amount of data from servers, firewalls, monitoring tools, and from other operations. We can keep the data from going dark by using it to analyze the security features of the network and also to monitor activity patterns so that network infrastructure is optimized [5].

We need to combine data along the value chain of the manufacturing process. Also, by combining analytics, we can create a "digital thread," which will be extended from customers to the suppliers [8]. Greater visibility along the value chain will help us analyze dark data that will lead to actionable insights. Data collected from machine logs or from equipment sensors, product telematics, and consumer data from clickstream can help the company forecast future supply needs and react fast to optimize the production process and delivery [8]. By using the dark data from different sensors and telematics, companies can separate production issues that remain hidden inside the manufacturing process. When the company sees and analyzes the total process with proper data collected from all parts of the value chain it will definitely increase productivity and profitability.

Customer interactivity data are really crucial, like when they contacted, which communication medium they used, duration of the interaction, whom they contacted, and anything related to customer-support. Rather than using this data when it is needed, one can adapt and integrate this information into the analytics workflow to predict when and how future customers are going to connect [5].

Now, if a company has a mainframe system and thinks that it is impossible to use the current analytics software to derive meaning from it, they are wrong. They can offload these system logs from their current system into Hadoop and pull out the "legacy" data from the dark [5].

While analyzing data we only think about textual ones. But in today's world, the amount of non-textual data is staggering. There are video, audio, photo, and even emojis that can tell a lot about social patterns. One can analyze the associated metadata, translate audio to text, use photo recognition, and categorize emojis into different intensities of feelings expressed to gain more insight and understand the content. Now, it requires a lot of effort than for the textual ones and may not be worth it in many cases, but it does not need to turn into dark data. At the very outset, we can filter out and sort the data from the most important to the least, which will definitely result in the most time-efficient outcome. And in a world of sharing nontextual information, which is only going to increase in the future, it is very unlikely that effort to mitigate dark data will go in vain. So better late than never; it is high time that we took nontextual data seriously and built a self-sustainable and long-lasting system around it [5].

11.4.1 Implication of Dark Data in the Health Sector

Prevention is always better than cure. With the help of credit card data, hospitals are now predicting sickness [9]. Carolinas HealthCare, a nonprofit hospital network in North and South Carolina, has been purchasing customer data from brokers. They are feeding all this information including their credit card information into algorithms to identify high-risk patients so that they can intervene even before someone is sick. Our health is determined by the food we eat and, in this case, the saying is put into practice. They are using a multivariable regression model to identify the sick people. They are the first of its kind who are using credit card data for taking health decisions. Now, there are obvious privacy issues where patients are not comfortable with hospitals having their personal information, so time will tell whether this practice becomes successful or the use of private information [10] is stopped.

Think about a situation where a doctor tells you to change a particular behavior or a medication so that your life expectancy may increase up to 6 years. In the United States, with the help of big data, it is possible to predict which patients are going to be readmitted into a hospital within 30 days of release. Remedial action is also predicted for individual patients. We are generating a huge amount of data with fitness trackers, calorie counters, and health-related applications. Data such as duration of our sleep, heart rate, walking distance, burnt calorie, and consumed calories is available. Retail stores have our consumption data and we have already seen how Target predicted pregnancy from buying habits. If the available dataset is more, it will lead to more accurate predictions and this will help us eliminate surprises and anticipate unexpected outbreaks and demands [11]. Now, there are ethical concerns where personal data may be sold by/to a recruiting agency or a bank and all of this might affect his/her chances of getting a job or even a mortgage. On the other hand, many are not bothered about it as this is, in the end, helping them to serve public health goals and may be useful for the greater good [12].

A huge amount of data is being produced by different devices and sensors that are used for health-related issues, but most of this data is still unused. With proper user permission, we can eliminate the legal issues and then develop a model that will predict future sickness. It can be done by monitoring people's consumption patterns and also by observing historical data on how a certain type of consumption leads to different outcomes. We can observe Mr A's health compared to Mr B's, based on their food habits over a year and deduce the reason for different or similar outcomes. Now, think about millions of user data accumulated in a single system and analyze it to find a relationship between food habits and health. We will be able to predict health issues successfully and help prevent diseases, instead of curing it after it has already happened.

Indiana University Health (IU Health) wants to personalize individual health care and improve overall health outcomes. To achieve this goal, they are exploring the world of unstructured and non-traditional data. The relationship between the hospital and patient has been based on individual visits and treatments. A holistic approach is missing in the current system. IU Health wants to build loyalty among patients and provide efficient but affordable health care solutions with the help of unexplored data. For that they need to have a 360° understanding about their patient. Both verbal and written free-form notes are given to patients by their consultants and all of that remains unmanaged. With the help of voice recognition, text analysis, and deep learning those unmanaged data can be utilized for the patient's betterment in the future. These historical medical records will enrich the file of a patient by adding relevant information. All of this will allow IU Health to develop an in-depth understanding about patient needs and formulate a model on how patients can use the health-care services more efficiently. They are also trying to find patterns of sickness, access to health care, and historical mapping of a local area's health outcomes. Cognitive computing and both external data and patient data can find out how socioeconomic factors may affect someone's relationship with health-care providers. In the end, they want to use this scattered and unused dark data and unveil its potential to improve individual health care as well as the overall health of the population [13].

11.4.2 Dark Data for Gaining Market Advantage

Information is really crucial for intelligent investment decisions. While some information is easily accessible, others are not. Due to its nature, dark data is mostly inaccessible to most of us, but to gain competitive advantage over others, we need to discover the hidden potential of dark data. Indus Valley Partners have arranged market-related data into different parts according to its visibility. When the data is well displayed, structured, is easily available, and can be analyzed, it is called light market data. To access gray data, we need to have contacts and means to access them. Now, dark data is not easily accessible and requires advanced tools and technologies. Sentiment analysis of social media, supply chain analysis, and satellite imaging can be sources for new insights. The challenge is to unveil dark data's potential before anyone else can in order to gain market advantage [14].

11.4.3 Dark Data for Social Media Insights

Dark data can help unravel trends in social media and find out the strengths and weaknesses of a particular brand among their target audiences. It can open new doors of opportunities to improve operations and optimize user experience. The challenge is to find out the symphony among the noise in social media and put it to use. Most of the social data are now unstructured, i.e., dark. But they are also organic in nature [15]. Social post sharing, online reviews, posting photos in a bar or restaurant, commenting or mentioning a friend, all of these are done naturally and that's why these are really important. After visiting a restaurant, purchasing a laptop or mobile, buying a car, receiving a service, and experiencing almost anything related to a brand, one may tweet with a hashtag or someone may give a post on Facebook, and others may share photos on Instagram. All of these represent perception about a brand—how people are accepting or rejecting them, criticizing or praising them, referring or forbidding someone to buy from them, and loving or hating them. This huge pool of unstructured data is the source of actual and honest social media insights that a brand can rely on. This dark data can help a brand to strengthen its online presence by working on its flaws.

It is also now possible with sentiment analysis to find out the words associated with a brand. If your brand is doing good and customers are satisfied, then it is most likely that your brand name will be associated with positive words. And, in case of bad reputations, the chances are high that negative words will be seen with your brand name. In simple words, with sentiment analysis, we can gain valuable insights from dark data about the sentiments of the masses toward any particular brand or, in general, about any keywords, like which words are coming up with the keywords "customer service." Now, the answer can be either positive or negative customer service, and we can also find out if any brand name is associated with it. This can help a company to identify its problems and rectify them so that in the future there will be more positive sentiments and reviews among the users, thus leading to increased revenues [15].

11.4.4 Retailers Providing Personalization with the Help of Dark Data

You will be surprised to know that for every dollar that is spent in an offline store, $0.56 of it is influenced by digital media [16]. So, it is really important to deliver expected digital experiences that a customer wants. The available dark data from customers' digital lives can provide retailers with valuable insights that can help develop merchandising, product promotion, and development, and can enhance user experiences tailored for individual people. Stitch Fix is making use of all the data available with permission from the user to analyze their sense of style and then sending them clothes matched to their styles on a regular basis. They analyze user's Pinterest board, social media sites, and all the digital footprint, and scan images to understand their sense of style. They begin the process with a detailed questionnaire about their choice and preference in clothing. Sixty data scientists work together to analyze all of it and produce a detailed understanding about their customers. Kroger Co., a grocery supermarket chain, is using its customer's purchasing history to give on-time suggestions about purchasing a product on a 4-inch display mounted in the aisles [13].

Have you wondered how ads are shown on Facebook related to a product, right after you have searched it on Google? How are they even doing that? No wonder that your particular interest is channeled through the mediums and is used in marketing different products. You are visiting a website and a few minutes later their ad is shown on Facebook. They are exploiting every possible source of customer information to get to potential buyers. They are not giving any chance for the creation of dark data, so others also should not sit idle and watch valuable data turn into dark data. Data is now the competitive currency in today's digital transformation [6]. Consumer behavior has changed dramatically over the years. Digital marketing has taken over traditional marketing and every bit of customer information is now critical for company success.

11.5 Different Ways to Eliminate Dark Data

11.5.1 Tools and Technique for Collecting and Analyzing Dark Data

One of the main reasons why organizations fail to tackle dark data is the lack of resources. Tools and techniques for analyzing audio and video, computer vision, pattern recognition, and machine learning are not always available to them. Luckily, some common tools can be used to analyze dark data, which include Apache Hadoop, SAP HANA 2, IBM Watson, and Cognitive Services by Microsoft in Azure. DeepDive, an open-source solution, created by Stanford University can extract value from dark data and can be integrated with other databases with the help of SQL tables. Stanford University also created Hidden Web Exposer, a prototype engine, for scraping the deep web for information. Deep Web Technologies (AGT) and BrightPlanet offer tools to harvest data from the deep web [6].

According to IDC, by 2020, one billion terabytes of data will be generated. And, it is coming from various resources, for example, 4–5 TB of data is generated every day by the New York Stock Exchange, and 240 billion photos are hosted by Facebook, which is growing per month at 7 PB. There is a lot out there, but we are struggling to collect, store, and analyze it all. Our storage capacity has increased over the years, but the speed at which we access or read the data from the drives has not been increased that much. In the 1990s, a typical drive storage was around 1,370 MB and its transfer speed was 4.4 MB/second. So, data could be read in 5 minutes approximately. In 2015, storage increased to 1 TB and its transfer speed became 100 MB/second. Now, it takes 2.5 hours to read all of it and this is really a long time. We can read data simultaneously from multiple sources to reduce the time when drives work in parallel and provide shared access to each other. But there are two problems when we connect multiple disks: One is the high chance of hardware failure and another is to combine data from different disks during the analysis. And, this is where Hadoop steps in [17]. One of the main reasons behind the popularity of Hadoop is that Google, Facebook, Amazon, and Yahoo use it on the largest sets of data in the world. Hadoop also addresses the two main problems stated above with its two main components. Hadoop Distributed File System helps to manage data by splitting and putting it on different nodes, then replicating and managing it. Map Reduce processes and calculates the data on each node [18].

We need to have a way to transform data into different forms according to the needs of different analytics platforms. Syncsort's Big Data solutions suite enables one to access data, to translate, and integrate it with the help of DMX-h to move it easily into Hadoop. It allows integration with traditionally dark environments such as mainframes [5].

Hadoop clusters and NoSQL databases have the ability to process this huge amount of data, which makes it possible to integrate dark data into the application and unlock business value. A Hadoop-based data warehouse in Edmunds.com Inc. has speeded up the old time-consuming process that made the data invalid by the time it was analyzed. It has opened up new dimensions of data and helped in reducing the operating cost. People who work with keyword acquisition for paid searches and online presence can now probe real-time data to analyze the change in buying patterns, which will eventually affect the marketing tactics. And, according to the blog post of Philip Potloff, chief information officer at Edmunds, the newly established system saved more than $1.7 million between February and mid-June. Merv Adrian, a Gartner analyst, said that increasing number of companies are going to audit archives of data to point out the dark ones and streamline them to possible business requirements. We know that the transactions are occurring, but we do not know what is happening around them and that is something we need to figure out so that we can turn the dark data into a potential business gold mine [19].

11.5.2 A Brief Introduction to DeepDive

We can extract value from turning unstructured dark data into structured data by using the DeepDive system. This system takes in dark data and makes it usable for standard data management tools such as OLAP, Tableau, R, or Excel [20]. This is the result of the DeepDive project at Stanford University, led by Christopher Ré [21]. We have access to huge amounts of scientific data, but it is not possible for us to read everything and extract insights from all of that. It is required to read pages after pages to get a single answer and then read again for another question. Now, to go through all the resources and make a structure out of it, we need machines that can process it like humans. In DARPA's MEMEX, law enforcement agencies use

DeepDive to fight human trafficking. The assumption was that trafficked individuals offer sexual services at a lower cost than others. Ads are given online in plain sight in different websites. In this case, DeepDive is used for searching all over the Internet for low-cost sexual services that is related to trafficking. All of this resulted in the real perpetrators getting arrested [22]. While training data is used by most of the machine learning techniques, DeepDive learns from distant supervision that is less costly than the traditional method [23]. DeepDive uses machine learning techniques, but it is different from traditional systems in many ways. DeepDive asks users for features rather than algorithms and can extract data from millions of sources. It allows developers to write simple rules and adapt by learning from the user feedbacks. It can achieve higher quality than humans. PaleoDeepDive has achieved a winning performance in extracting complex knowledge by assembling synthetic paleontological databases in entity relation extraction competitions [21]. Let us see how DeepDive functions following the four steps: The first step is data processing that includes adding raw input data, giving the raw data a structure, and then feature representation. The second step is distant supervision of the dataset to enable machine learning. It is also known as data programming for extracting features, training classifiers, and predicting relations. After that, the third step is to specify the model on which DeepDive will perform learning and inferencing. We need to specify the connections and features of the variables that the system will predict for us and DeepDive will perform statistical inference over the model. Lastly, it will determine the probability of each variable being true. In the last step, we will have to measure its accuracy, i.e., accuracy of the model—estimating the precision with Mindtagger, browsing the data with Mindbender, and monitoring the statistics with dashboard and calibration plots [24].

11.5.3 Six Steps to Identify and Manage Dark Data

According to ARMA International President, Fred A. Pulzello, we can follow these six steps to manage dark data [25].

1. We have to identify the source of the data and define it. System-generated data is more likely to be helpful compared to employee-generated data. We need to collect in a conducive form that is analyzable. But there is always a chance that these efforts may go in vain.
2. The next step is doing a cost–benefit analysis to understand the usefulness of the data in hand. The data should serve a definite purpose, and we should avoid the temptation to preserve the data after the purpose is met.
3. Now, we have to select what data we will keep and what we will delete. We have to find out which ones are useful and can be useful in the future, and, on the other hand, we have to delete data with no apparent value. It is wise to think that some of it might come in handy in the future, but storing it may create chaos and confusion when it gets mixed up with important data.

4. We also have to justify why we deleted some data by mapping it to the retention and disposition schedule. The data that is not yet addressed is addressed by creating new categories on the retention schedule. This is important because some policy may or may not address issues that may arise.
5. We have to execute our defensible disposition plan and make sure it is actually done. But it is important to keep the documents, mentioning the "why" and the "when" of deletion.
6. Every year, we need to look back and calculate whether the repurposed data is adding any value to the organization or not. It not, then there is no reason to use it again and it should be buried in a proper, defensible manner.

Dark data may seem like a buzzword, but it is going to be a part of every organization in recent future as the volume of electronically stored information is only going to increase. The best way to respond to that problem is to implement an information governance program. It will properly and efficiently manage all of the organization's data produced throughout its life cycle. It will also recognize the possibility of any dark data occurrence and implement measures to make it usable or to properly delete it [25].

We can also get the value out of dark data in three steps. We have to find, review, and determine the value. Now, the first step is the hardest one. Different costs such as architectural cost are associated with it, and there are legal issues; this three-step data analysis process needs to be done by disrupting the ongoing workflow of an organization. All of this makes the executives reluctant in finding dark data. Now, to do all this with minimum disruption, we need to search across every file and folder, then categorize it attribute wise, provide administrative access through all the storage platforms, and lastly report according to the usage and purpose so that the value can be determined. One of the most important things is to ensure smooth integration of data from all over the platform. Dark data have unfulfilled value that can provide actionable insights which can lead to profits [7].

The four key steps in information governance are identifying the sources of data, analyzing key categories and issues, managing accordingly—like deleting unnecessary data, analyzing data with potential value, and securing sensitive data—and lastly monitoring the whole process with relevant metrices and evaluating the whole process. After completing these four steps, we have to utilize the feedback to improve and evolve [26].

11.6 Dark Data Solution Provided by Companies

11.6.1 AI Foundry's Agile Solutions for Transformation of Dark Data

AI Foundry is a Kodak Alaris business unit. By integrating information, people, and processes they transform enterprise operations for increased insight and improved decision-making. Dark data leads to chaos. It also results in bad customer service, loss of productivity, and the risk of confidential or personal information leak. Now we need to transform this dark data into operational data. The first step is to separate the outdated, redundant, and trivial data. Every organization have data scattered throughout the system, maybe in Google Drive, Dropbox, SharePoint, or a content management system. AI Foundry's enterprise crawler looks carefully through the data stores and identifies the redundant files, duplicate files, personally identifiable contents, and extraneous log or temp files. They believe that removing this junk can clean 30% or more of the redundant data that is mixed up and hidden within the important organizational data. The second step is to group documents into different categories that have similarities between them just like the library shelves. The third step is to add metadata and indexes or, in other words, data about the data that includes retention periods, security issues, and indexes. Step fourth step is to search intelligently with keywords, phrases, or categories as they are already indexed and have metadata. The last and fifth step is to use it for business, i.e., work smartly with the organized and searchable system [27].

11.6.2 Dark Data Fracking by Datumize

The mission of Datumize is to become the number one company in the world in terms of enlightening dark data. For that, recently, they have developed data fracking. The overall process is simple: capture, process, and integrate. Dark data can be of two types: temporary data and closed proprietary data. Data that contains value about activity within a short time period and is generated in ERP, CRM, or B2B is generally temporary data. This data will be lost if not captured immediately and they are extracted with the help of network sniffing techniques. On the other hand, closed proprietary data locked inside machines are extracted via specific protocol-level methods. These protocol-level methods are developed for dark data formation. After capturing both types of dark data, they are ready to be processed. This may include cleaning unnecessary data, aggregating to reduce data volume and increase semantic usefulness, or transforming to a format. After processing, it will look like a standard information, i.e., a refined product which is ready to be used. Now, this usable data is going to be used in a wide range of applications and in several departments in an organization through different technologies. It can be integrated with other applications to create new analytical products. All of this will increase efficiency and give better and faster decision-making [28].

11.6.3 Nuix Information Governance Solution

Nuix is a software company based in Australia, providing information governance solution. According to Nuix white paper on information governance, there are mainly four steps to derive the business value from dark data [29].

1. First, we need to shed light on the dark data by understanding its nature and prioritizing it. How much do we have, in which formats, where is it, how old it is, and what does it contain? We need technological tools to index and normalize it. After that, with automated tools and targeted searches, we have to classify everything into three categories: redundant data, risky data, and data with business value. By keeping an inventory, it will be easy to prioritize and set objectives for the next phase. It is not possible to address all the pain points at once. First, we need to address projects with higher returns on investment and then process the rest.

2. The first phase will allow the organization to make informed decisions. We need to analyze and review different data sources that warrant deeper inspection with powerful searching and advanced analytical tools. After that, they can generate a list of targeted sources to act on.

3. After the first two steps, we should know what to do with different sources of dark data. This is where analysis is turned into actions. Risky and sensitive data must be reviewed by HR, legal, risk, or compliance departments, alerting respective personnel. Organizations should dispose or delete all the redundant, obsolete, or trivial data with no legal or business value. All other data should contain some sort of business value that can be used by connecting it through an enterprise search tool, moving or copying it to modern archive, quarantining some with a suitable security profile, or by migrating it into a management software based on the requirement. In simple words, this step is all about channeling the data smoothly throughout the organization according to the specific business needs of a particular department.

4. Next, we need to implement sustainable policies after the generation of a complete index of unstructured data throughout the previous stages. With regular updates and iterations of its proven processes, an organization can be "evergreen" and can maintain a "living index" of real-time user-generated communications. It will be able to search instantly for eDiscovery and investigations.

All of this will allow an organization to reduce data volume, which will decrease the time and cost of initiatives such as audits, eDiscovery, or investigations even by 50%. It will also minimize the risk from dark data and maintain compliance and allow us to adhere to policies. Lastly, but most importantly, it will help us to extract the values from dark, unstructured data that can bring unimaginable benefits to an organization. The overall aim of information governance is to take control over all the data that goes around in an organization and develop a self-sustaining process for the future to reduce the amount of dark data as much as possible because volume of data is only going to increase exponentially in the coming days [29].

11.6.4 Deloitte: Insight's Way to Start Extracting Value from Dark Data

Very soon most of the companies will be overwhelmed with the amount of data generated by IoT devices. The chances are high that it will be mostly unstructured.

Now, it is not possible to overhaul the whole system and be data driven overnight, rather it is a continuous process. Small steps toward the big goal can lead to data-driven insights for now and game changing opportunities for the future. The first step is to ask the appropriate questions rather than rummaging through everything that one has in his/her disposal. Now, we need to identify the potential sources of dark data that can answer the questions, for example, if a marketing team wants to increase sales in a certain region, then its analytics team can look for relevant data on that target region only. The data can include video footage of customer traffic or product placement pictures. Next, we need to look outside for available demographic or local data outside the organization. For example, a doctor can give advice to his/her asthma patients by reviewing the weather data and assist the patient through a flare-up during the pollen season. Employers can find out the relationship between commute time to workplace and job satisfaction by using geospatial tools, employee turnover, and traffic patterns. A company also needs to have expert data scientists in the team to handle all these steps for turning dark data into operational data. But the insights generated by the data scientist as a printout of advanced Bayesian statistics will not be comprehendible by most of the business heads, so we need to represent these results in an easier form. Most people inside an organization need to understand the complex insights before they can turn insight into action, and visualization tools can help in this aspect in the form of an infographic or a dashboard. After developing new strategies, it is wise to extend it throughout the value chain, from suppliers to customers, for holistic upgradation [13].

11.7 International Data Corporation's Research on Organization's Ability to Derive Value from Dark Data

A research done by International Data Corporation (IDC) shows that 90% of all digital information is unstructured. It is hidden in different formats and in different places. But if used properly they can boost sales, reduce costs, and connect with customers more efficiently. IDC wanted to identify organizations that could derive more value from this untapped information than any other organization. Their survey was done across six countries and included 2,155 organizations. They also did 11 in-depth interviews with organizations in United States and Europe. They coined the term knowledge quotient (KQ). KQ is a score to identify an organization's ability to derive value from information. KQ is composed of four different components: process, technology, socialization, and culture. Process refers to the ability to access, analyze, and share pertinent information. Information can be initiated both inside and outside the organization. Technology is the availability, satisfaction, and quality of unstructured information software that is used in accessing, sharing, and

Figure 11.2   The KQ. (Adapted from [30].)

analyzing in the processing part. Socialization is the organization's ability to share and reuse the information. Culture is how management is recognizing information as a key organization asset and also supporting and funding likewise. Important lessons are learned from this research on how one can unlock the hidden value and also increase its KQ. Connecting both structured and unstructured data sources by creating information access and analysis strategy, we can implement the search strategy that will cover all our sources. We also need to make an organization culture so that the information is embraced, used, shared, and disseminated as a key asset. Text analytics along with auto categorization, tagging, and taxonomy generation should be used to extract additional value from the unstructured information to establish a connection with the structured data repositories. Lastly, key performance indicators are also important to determine success. Definite measurements and methodologies can help in this aspect [30] (Figure 11.2).

11.8 Recommendations on Managing Dark Data

Dark data is only going to increase across all the organizations if proper steps are not taken. It can be redundant at times, it can contain private and sensitive information, and most importantly it can possess immense opportunity for an organization. We have already discussed how important value dark data holds in today's business environment, if properly handled. From the understanding of the relevant literature, some things are really important while working with dark data. We need to find the source from where data is going dark. And, it will be best if we can channel data to the respective systems at the point of production. As for example, weather updates, log files, sensor data, website traffic, customer queries, prescriptions, blood reports, video footage, shared images, or audio files can either serve a definite purpose or bear no value. So, we need to put a filter right when it is being produced so that it isn't overlooked or forgotten later. All the data will pass through a system and then will be divided according to needs and deleted after a particular time period when it no longer has any potential. Sometimes, we do not know whether we will need some information or not. In that case, it is wise to ask the right questions and understand the nature and value of the data. If not done properly, we can need up wasting time on useless information. So, asking the right question by identifying business needs is really important. After that, categorizing the data according to its purpose is crucial. There are technologies that can turn unstructured data into analyzable data, and after that, the existing big data tools can do the rest. But before that, we have to feed the system the right data and ask the right questions to make brilliant use of it. We will get rid of dark data from our organization only when we build a self-sustainable system to stop data from going dark in the first place. Then it will only be big data, not dark data.

11.9 Conclusion

In this chapter, we discussed how dark data has become a pressing issue due to its sheer volume and nature. Whether they are aware of it or not, every organization has a huge amount of unused, unexplored, and unstructured information at its disposal. Proper knowledge about one's business and about how to use this data in improving business is really necessary. Ignorance can be costly in this case, in terms of both risks and returns. Opportunity in data analytics is endless, and there are also different ways and systems to manage dark data. Hadoop and DeepDive are the potential solutions to this dark data problem. Information governance also warns us about managing the total information chain properly to ensure that data does not go dark and is not left unchecked. Dark data analytics is still an untapped opportunity for us, but if we can manage all our data sources properly, then we can mitigate the risks and use this wonderful opportunity.

References

1. K. Hill. How Target Figured Out a Teen Girl Was Pregnant Before Her Father Did. 16 February 2012. Available: www.forbes.com/sites/kashmirhill/2012/02/16/how-target-figured-out-a-teen-girl-was-pregnant-before-her-father-did/#20d6cae36668. [Accessed 16 December 2017].
2. J. Koetsier. Data Deluge: What People Do on the Internet, Every Minute of Every Day. 25 July 2017. Available: www.inc.com/john-koetsier/every-minute-on-the-internet-2017-new-numbers-to-b.html. [Accessed 13 December 2017].
3. R. Jacobson. 2.5 Quintillion Bytes of Data Created Every Day. How Does CPG & Retail Manage It?—IBM Consumer Products Industry Blog. 24 April 2013. Available: www.ibm.com/blogs/insights-on-business/consumer-products/2-5-quintillion-bytes-of-data-created-every-day-how-does-cpg-retail-manage-it/. [Accessed 13 December 2017].

4. Ennovision. Ennovision.co.uk. 20 May 2017. Available: http://ennovision.co.uk/big-data-and-analytics/. [Accessed 10 January 2018].

5. C. Tozzi. Dark Data Use Cases: Examples of Putting Dark Data to Use. 17 May 2017. Available: http://blog.syncsort.com/2017/05/big-data/4-dark-data-examples-use-cases/. [Accessed 15 December 2017].

6. K. McNulty. Expanding the Definition of Dark Data and Mining It with Dark Analytics. 30 June 2017. Available: www.prowesscorp.com/expanding-the-definition-of-dark-data-and-mining-it-with-dark-analytics/. [Accessed 18 December 2017].

7. S. Mackey. The Rise of Dark Data and How It Can Be Harnessed. 1 March 2017. Available: www.kdnuggets.com/2016/03/rise-dark-data-how-harnessed.html. [Accessed 16 December 2017].

8. P. Dennies. TeradataVoice: Factories Of The Future: The Value Of Dark Data. 19 February 2015. Available: www.forbes.com/sites/teradata/2015/02/19/factories-of-the-future-the-value-of-dark-data/#d2cb76f555a3. [Accessed 13 December 2017].

9. S. Pettypiece and J. Robertson. Hospitals Are Mining Patients' Credit Card Data to Predict Who Will Get Sick. 3 July 2014. Available: www.bloomberg.com/news/articles/2014-07-03/hospitals-are-mining-patients-credit-card-data-to-predict-who-will-get-sick. [Accessed 16 December 2017].

10. D. O. Credit Card Purchasing Data Helps Hospitals Predict Your Health. 22 November 2015. Available: https://digit.hbs.org/submission/credit-card-purchasing-data-helps-hospitals-predict-your-health/. [Accessed 16 December 2017].

11. W. Parslow. How Big Data Could Be Used to Predict a Patient's Future. 17 January 2014. Available: www.theguardian.com/healthcare-network/2014/jan/17/big-data-nhs-predict-illness. [Accessed 17 December 2017].

12. J. Sarasohn-Kahn. Here's Looking at You: How Personal Health Information is Being Tracked and Used. July 2014. Available: www.chcf.org/publications/2014/07/heres-looking-personal-health-info/. [Accessed 17 December 2017].

13. T. Kambies, P. Roma, N. Mittal and S. K. Sharma. Dark Analytics: Illuminating Opportunities Hidden within Unstructured Data. 7 February 2017. Available: www2.deloitte.com/insights/us/en/focus/tech-trends/2017/dark-data-analyzing-unstructured-data.html.

14. T. Coughlin. Analysis of Dark Data Provides Market Advantages. 24 July 2017. Available: www.forbes.com/sites/tomcoughlin/2017/07/24/analysis-of-dark-data-provides-market-advantages/#7fb43222872b. [Accessed 17 December 2017].

15. M. Lange. Dark Data on Social Media: Insights That Shed Light on Your Business. 6 October 2017. Available: www.marketingprofs.com/articles/2017/32911/dark-data-on-social-media-insights-that-shed-light-on-your-business. [Accessed 17 December 2017].

16. J. Stevens. Internet Stats & Facts for 2017. 17 August 2017. Available: https://hostingfacts.com/internet-facts-stats-2016/. [Accessed 17 December 2017].

17. A. Shah. Hadoop Explained Simply!—Edvancer Eduventures. 15 February 2016. Available: www.edvancer.in/what-is-hadoop/. [Accessed 15 December 2017].

18. A. Bloom. Demystifying Apache Hadoop in 5 Pictures. 1 July 2013. Available: https://content.pivotal.io/blog/demystifying-apache-hadoop-in-5-pictures. [Accessed 15 December 2017].

19. J. Vaughan. Big Data Systems Shine Light on Neglected 'Dark Data'. 20 August 2013. Available: http://searchdatamanagement.techtarget.com/feature/Big-data-systems-shine-light-on-neglected-dark-data. [Accessed 15 December 2017].

20. C. Zhang, J. Shin, C. Ré, M. Cafarella and F. Niu. Extracting Databases from Dark Data with DeepDive. In *Proceedings of the 2016 International Conference on Management of Data—SIGMOD'16,* pp. 847–859, 2016.
21. DeepDive. DeepDive. 2017. Available: http://deepdive.stanford.edu/. [Accessed 19 December 2017].
22. C. Ré. DeepDive: A Dark Data-System. 28 Decemebr 2016. Available: www.youtube.com/watch?v=NjdT34L0-uU. [Accessed 19 December 2017].
23. DeepDive. Distant Supervision. 2017. Available: http://deepdive.stanford.edu/distant_supervision. [Accessed 19 December 2017].
24. DeepDive. DeepDive. 2017. Available: http://deepdive.stanford.edu/example-spouse. [Accessed 19 December 2017].
25. F. A. Pulzello. Six Steps to 'Dark Data' Information Governance. September 2014. Available: http://searchcompliance.techtarget.com/tip/Six-steps-to-dark-data-information-governance. [Accessed 19 December 2017].
26. S. Ryan. Illuminating Dark Data. 2013. Available: https://conferences.heanet.ie/2013/files/65/Lightning%20Talk%20-%20Shane%20Ryan%20-%20Illuminating%20Dark%20Data.pdf. [Accessed 20 December 2017].
27. Aifoundry. Dark Data Transformation—AI Foundry. 1 April 2014. Available: http://aifoundry.com/agile-solutions/dark-data-transformation/. [Accessed 16 December 2017].
28. Datumize. Data Fracking. Improve your Access to Dark Data. 2017. Available: https://datumize.com/wp-content/uploads/2017/08/Datumize-DataFracking.pdf. [Accessed 19 December 2017].
29. NUIX. INFORMATION GOVERNANCE: Building Business Value from Dark Data. 2015. Available: www.techworld.com.au/whitepaper/372690/information-governance-building-business-value-from-dark-data/?type=other&arg=0&location=featured_list. [Accessed 19 December 2017].
30. D. Schubmehl. Unlocking the Hidden Value of Information—IDC Community. 15 July 2014. Available: https://idc-community.com/groups/it_agenda/bigdataanalytics/unlocking_the_hidden_value_of_information [Accessed 06 August 2018].
31. T. Srivastava. What is Hadoop? | Big Data Hadoop Technology. 21 May 2014. Available: www.analyticsvidhya.com/blog/2014/05/hadoop-simplified/. [Accessed 15 December 2017].

DATA ANALYTICS APPLICATIONS

Chapter 12

Big Data: Prospects and Applications in the Technical and Vocational Education and Training Sector

Mutwalibi Nambobi and Md. Shahadat Hossain Khan
Islamic University of Technology

Adam A. Alli
Islamic University in Uganda

Contents

12.1 Introduction

Many big data algorithms, applications, and techniques constitute the buzzword "big data," which find its way beyond computer science into the essential tools for business, government, and very recently in education. The word big data was coined in 2001 by researchers to describe voluminous and complex datasets that cannot be processed by traditional means. Since then, organizations and, later on, academic institutions have created avenues to build tools that assist in defining (i) goals around their big data, (ii) milestones in the maturity and use of big data applications, (iii) capacity of use, and (iv) areas that require the use of big data. Given that big data analytics is growing rapidly, we are not at liberty to understand what big data is all about and whether it is useful, but the main concern is to understand how we can yield its use in different areas of society that prove to be useful in the development of society. Considering this developmental issue, the Technical Vocational Education and Training (TVET) sectors are very much interested in big data applications to get benefits from it.

TVET, which is gaining acceptance in many countries as a part of tertiary education, is dedicated to converting skilled manpower for the economic development of any country. The TVET sector constantly needs to be evaluated and transformed so that it can follow the fast pace of changing trends in different sectors of the market, which in turn can create a variety of demands in the workplace [1,2]. A recent survey shows that 80% of the data created in the world is unstructured and this assertion does not isolate TVET institutions. One challenge associated with this massive generated data is how to structure them and make use of them as an asset in boosting educational process in the TVET industry. The second challenge is how we can store it. Though a number of technologies have been developed to support the analytics and storage function of big data, which include but not limited to Apache Hadoop, Map Reduce, Pig, Hive, HBase, Sqoop, Spark, Oozie, etc., they are still expensive for small institutions, more specifically in the TVET institutions.

12.1.1 What Is Big Data?

Big data is one of the major trends that have radically altered the way education will be conducted in future. The concept of big data has been widely accepted as an important and inexorable technology to facilitate change, and therefore, it is no longer processing the province of computer science niche alone. Big data technologies enable easy storage of information and accumulation of data repositories with time. When this information is of varying sizes, very extensive, and of highly complex magnitude, it becomes big data [3,4]. According to Michalik et al. [5], big data is defined by its size; it comprises a large, complex, and independent collection of datasets, each with the potential to interact. In addition, an important aspect of big data is the fact that it cannot be handled with standard data management techniques due to inconsistency and unpredictability of the possible combinations.

In other words, big data can be defined as data that is growing too large and fast, different, complex, important, and valuable for providing interesting insights and patterns. Big data characteristics are summarized as volume (size), variety (sources, formats, and types), and velocity (speed and frequency), and add complexity to the data, which is, in fact, another attribute in concern [6]. Big data is context-specific having different data formats, such as structured, semistructured, and unstructured data that ranges from sector to sector. The common challenge is that all these sectors must be able to make use of the data by processing and enabling data-driven improvements through high-level big data analytics [7,8].

In order to improve the current practices, TVET institutions will increasingly need to capture and analyze data from diverse sources so as to respond to diverse data flows, such as data coming from learning management systems (LMSs), smart devices (phones, wearable devices etc.), call center voice and access point messages, image and video feeds picked up from online classes, emails, transaction data and social networks, and other learning platforms/sources where students and teachers are continually interacting and engaging in learning and teaching activities [9]. Besides, from a technical point of view, the key challenge in the education industry is to adapt and learn from big data. In this case, two things need to be considered: *data coming from different sources and vendors* and the *current platforms* that were not designed for this data. From a practical point of view, staff and institutions need to learn the new data management and analysis tools and new skills that are required to visualize and analyze data from the analytics platforms.

With a number of big data technologies becoming available for institutions, TVET sectors can now leverage data to (i) understand how long it took for a student to access content after starting the course, (ii) visualize the time of day they interacted with the data or with each other, (iii) find out how long they spent looking at specific content, (iv) seek whether they collaborated with each other or logged on to the same forums, (v) find out whether they asked questions and what type of questions were asked, and (vi) understand which format did they engage in during their course. Using the information obtained from big data platforms, users (teachers and administrators) can process data quickly and establish insights into the interesting patterns about their students. These sorts of pattern interactions produce huge data that have significance in improving the quality of technical education. As more data gets analyzed, the decision makers in TVET sectors particularly need to find out ways to interpret the data in a meaningful way so that they can predict the future direction in a learner's learning behavior.

Graduates from TVET institutions are deployed straight in the field of work. These graduates are a source of data for TVET institutions about how and what should be included in the curriculum to match the current market demands. Using big data analytics, it is easy to collect data from the market and other TVET institutions, and thereafter analyze them in a meaningful way that has a direct impact on the future labor market prediction and market demands.

In many cases, the TVET curriculum of developing countries follows teacher-centered teaching and uses a conventional teaching method, i.e., the same teaching content, the same teaching methods, and the same time for delivery are used [10]. Therefore, it places less emphasis on students' understanding of taught subjects. Previous literature reports that such curriculum often leaves gaps in the development of a learner. Using big data analytics on how students interact during learning can change the way learning and development is achieved by students and this process can predict the course of action between teachers and students. This, in turn, insinuates in finding ways to provide tailored instructions to individual students who have difficulties in learning. In the past, many students have failed to reach anywhere near their potential because of the inability to correctly find the deficiencies in learning potential. Big data presents tools necessary for teachers and students to better understand each other in the learning environment, which in turn gives students better opportunities for success in learning.

In brief, many technologies are making way in our society, among them Internet of Things (IoT), social media, virtual reality, and 3D printing, which will be useful to TVET sectors. These technologies will use and create avenues to produce a myriad of data that contain huge information, attributes, and features that can be used in TVET sectors when proper analytics and strategy are applied.

12.1.2 Chapter Roadmap

In this chapter, we present the prospects and applications of big data in the TVET sector. Big data technologies present a myriad of opportunities and practices in teaching, learning, and administration of TVET institutions. Using big data in management and teaching in the TVET sector does not only provide the ability to make informed decisions but also enable the prediction of learners' behavior, thus leading to customized learning among others. The rest of the chapter has been organized as follows: Section 12.1 provides an overview of big data. Section 12.2 presents big data technologies that are commonly available in the industry to activate big data functionalities such as data input, cleaning, performing analytics through modeling, the framework, the learning cycle, possibilities, and benefits of big data technologies in TVET. Section 12.3 presents tools and analytical platforms for educational purposes. Section 12.4 provides recommendation and conclusion.

12.2 Big Data Technologies

Big data technology consists of technologies such as Hadoop, Map Reduce, Pig, Hive, HBase, Sqoop, Spark, and Oozie (see Table 12.1) that provide organizations with big data tools to extract, prepare, visualize, and perform analytics that will change the way TVET institutions will perform their business in the future. Like other educational technologies such as instructional technology, behavioral technology, and instructional design technology [11], big data is visualized to have a significant impact on TVET sectors in particular and other educational sectors in general. Impact of big data on TVET sectors includes but not limited to self-assessment of students, gathering information about the students' progress, evaluation and monitoring, etc. Naturally, big data and other educational technologies provide a platform upon which learning can be achieved by understanding and measuring the progress of learners in learning and of the instructors in teaching, except for big data technologies where value is added through analytics. With analytics, it is possible for TVET students to set realistic goals in learning based on their previous interactions via LMS, to improve their educational performances,

Table 12.1   Learning Theories for TVET Sectors

	Learning Theory	*Description*
1.	Behaviorism	Based on this theory, learners provide response to external stimulus, and therefore, learning occurs through repetition and reinforcement. The main purpose of this theory is to change apprentices' skills (behavior). Therefore, when designing a teaching and learning experience, this theory concentrates on shaping the student behavior. Collecting and analyzing (huge) data from LMS will forecast learners' changing behaviors and will measure learners' changed behaviors.
2.	Cognitivism	This theory links with the mental process of the learner. When designing big data algorithms, emphasis should be laid on how information is received, organized, stored, and retrieved by the brain when designing prediction and recommendations systems. According to Piaget's instruction, the teaching and learning environment should be organized, sequenced, and presented in a manner so that students understand the process. The accumulated huge data from the TVET sectors is therefore analyzed to find out learners' ability to grasp knowledge in a particular TVET context.

(Continued)

Table 12.1 (*Continued*)   Learning Theories for TVET Sectors

	Learning Theory	Description
3.	Constructivism	Learning is more meaningful when apprentices are able to interact with a problem or a concept. This theory assumes that a learner has prior knowledge, and thereafter, students discover things on their own (self-directed) by using the prior knowledge. This theory focuses on creating new knowledge and ideas in TVET sectors, which come into practice when learners' engagement, motivation, and interactions could be ensured. Self-directed active learning is ensured via myriad technology supported tools in TVET sectors. These sorts of learning experiences provide huge data that need big data and learning analytic in TVET sectors.
4.	Deconstructionism	According to the theory of deconstructionism, one may discover meaning from a reading text. This concept could be used in big data applications in TVET sectors. "Big data offer a way for teachers to understand students' learning characteristics, in order to determine the comparative efficacy of different types of learning opportunities and offer support to the undesirable leaners" [15].

and to track their progress. There are many other benefits that may not reflect in this section. Therefore, Section 12.2.1 provides literature that enables the reader to understand and measure the value that is added to TVET by big data technology.

12.2.1 Big Data Architecture Framework

Big Data Architecture Framework comprises components that address the big data ecosystem in TVET. Big data aspects that are considered in this framework are orthogonal and complementary. The following architecture captures the flow of big data implementation in real time. It has the following five main stages (Figure 12.1):

- Input data
- Big data management
- Big data analytics and tools
- Big data infrastructure (BDI)
- Big data security and privacy

The first stage describes the input data that is going to be processed on the big data platform. Different forms of data are inserted at this stage. It can be structured

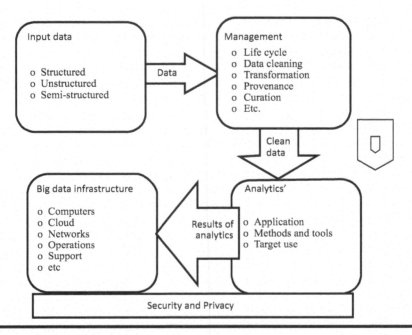

Figure 12.1   Big data architecture framework.

or unstructured with varying data formats like text, audio, video, etc. In the second stage, the focus goes on managing the raw data that is processed in the first stage. It utilizes the big data life cycle management system to process the data in the flow. The third stage contains big data tools and configurations needed to process the large datasets into useful information. Some tools are commonly accessible, such as Hortonworks (https://hortonworks.com) or Cloudera (www.cloudera.com), to run the analytics algorithms on the large input files. The fourth stage performs multiple tasks, for instance, BDI contains different forms of storing devices, infrastructure, services delivery, and operational support for the processed data. The fifth stage is responsible for the security and privacy of results of the analytics process. It is necessary to secure the results analyzed by the BDI. So, security mechanisms such as Kerberos security or other encryptions and crypto-algorithms are used to secure big data systems.

Technology is moving at a fast pace creating a big gap or a big disruption. Technical education also faces the same challenge in training technicians using these technologies at places of work. This gap creates a constant change in the way TVET is delivered. The main goal of TVET is to prepare the skilled manpower for the future world of work. The current and future work force would face a number of dynamics that make TVET institutions fail in finding out what exact skills are required by its graduates in the future for a particular profession. Especially, TVET stakeholders of many developing countries may not provide straight answers to questions such as: *What future skills will be required in a particular discipline? What will be the*

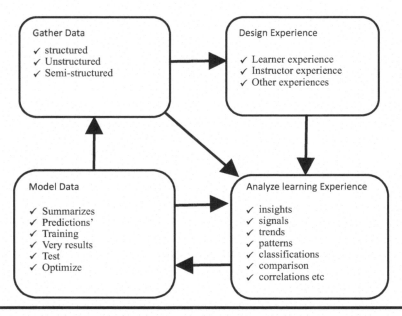

Figure 12.2 Big data learning experience cycle.

demography of workers? What industry or industrial capabilities will be needed? What human intellectual developments TVET should be focused on? In order to address these issues, TVET education should be connected with recent trends. Special focus therefore should be given on understanding the art of teaching, classroom management, and learners' requirements in teaching TVET, to bridge the gap between TVET institutions and industrial practices. It further links TVET practices to existing theories, teaching design, learning experience, data collection, analysis of the learners' data, model development, and redesigning the learning experiences. All the stated activities and possibilities are somehow connected to big data analytics. These practices could be shown in Figure 12.2, which is updated from the studies of [12,13].

12.2.2 Big Data Learning Experience Cycle

Teaching and learning has shifted from a teacher-centered to a student-centered model very rapidly within the last decade [14]. The way TVET students used to learn before is not the way students are learning or perceiving learning in the present time. The main reason for this shift is due to having diverse possibilities through technology in education and very recently in technical education. The new and innovative technology supported tools have been greatly modernized and they keep changing rapidly; therefore, it requires improvements and upgrades. The Figure 12.2 shows that learning is based on continual improvement, which is linked with the use of diverse modes of technology. For these reasons, students' learning styles and preferences in TVET sectors are changing, and therefore, students' learning experiences are connected with diverse learning theories that were not seen before. The main learning theories are briefly described in Table 12.2 to link them with the learning experience of the existing students.

These theories provide a systematic process and applications of big data technologies to facilitate the acquisition of skills and knowledge in various learning environments in the TVET sectors.

Table 12.2   Tools for Big Data in TVET

	Tools	Application in TVET
1.	No Database SQL (Oracle)	Oracle NoSQL Database gives a superior ability to model a variety of problems, it provides an excellent platform to perform learning analytics in TVET, given that it is scalable and designed to provide high reliability. Besides being integrated with a wide range of Oracle products, NoSQL fits well with the open source application. This simplifies development and deployment of multiple solutions developed from multiple platforms. It retrieves the data that is modeled by means other than the tabular relations. This tool is used in TVET to perform learning analytics on students and instructors' data as they continue to engage in learning as well as other related datasets. Web: www.oracle.com/technetwork/database/database-technologies/nosqldb/overview/index.html
2.	Storm	Storm is a multidimensional tool whose application includes real-time analytics, machine learning, extract load and transform, and remote procedure call, among many other big data tools. Given that it is open source, scalable, fault tolerant, and available for use free of cost, storm is favorable for use by TVET institutions that cannot afford expensive tools for analytics. Storm is very good in processing real-time data. It has attracted many use cases of storm including data monetization, real-time customer management, cybersecurity analytics, operational dashboards, and threat detection. For the above reason, it can give an attractive tool to use cases that involve learning analytics in TVET sector. Web: http://storm.apache.org

(Continued)

Table 12.2 (*Continued*)   Tools for Big Data in TVET

	Tools	Application in TVET
3.	Hadoop	Apache Hadoop is an open source software platform that can be directly used in TVET sectors. For personal and career development, TVET educators and apprentices may use this platform. It is a framework that allows for the distributed processing of large datasets across clusters of computers using simple programming models. It is designed to scale up from single servers to thousands of machines, each offering local computation and storage. Web: http://hadoop.apache.org
4.	SenseiDB	Sensei is a distributed data system that is built to support many social sites' data. SenseiDB can be used to build TVET applications that include hands-on experiments on distributed systems. Such applications will help students and teachers in many contexts. Among the context is the ability of students to link theory to practice and the time students take to conceptualize a learning item and/or the students' preferences. Web: http://senseidb.github.io/sensei/overview.html
5.	Voldemort	Voldemort contains ACID (atomicity, consistency, isolation, and durability) properties. These four properties can be implemented on TVET application to deal with transaction databases. Web: www.project-voldemort.com/25oldemort/
6.	Cassandra	Cassandra is a scalability tool that provides high availability without compromising on performance. It is durable, scalable, decentralized, and performant. These powerful features of Cassandra make it reliable for big data applications in the TVET sector. This tool is widely used to manage large amounts of data. Therefore, when plans for processing large data in TVET are required, Cassandra gives the best alternative. Web: http://cassandra.apache.org
7.	S3	Amazon Simple Storage Service (Amazon S3) is used to store and retrieve any amount of data at any time from anywhere on the web. In situations where institutions do not have sufficient infrastructures for big data analytics, AWS S3 gives an alternative option at affordable cost.

(Continued)

Table 12.2 (*Continued*)   Tools for Big Data in TVET

	Tools	Application in TVET
		Since considerable TVET institutions are located in countries whose BDI is still wanting, the use of S3 provides space for storage, database, analytics, machine learning, and other services. Web: https://aws.amazon.com/s3/
8.	MongoDB	MongoDB works on the concepts of collection and documentation. It gives a platform with expressive query language that has strong consistency, scalability, and flexibility. This makes MangoDB suitable for use in TVET sectors for any purpose in document analysis and other advanced analytics. Web: www.mongodb.com/
9.	MapReduce	MapReduce is a programming model to process huge data on the Hadoop platform. We can implement this technology in TVET by providing the knowledge on Hadoop cluster and its programming language. Web: www.ibm.com/analytics/hadoop/mapreduce
10.	Cloudera	Cloudera is an open-source Hadoop distribution. It provides Hadoop services in one system. This tool is useful in TVET to give sessions on all Hadoop services such as HDFS, MapReduce, Oozie, and Spark. Web: www.cloudera.com
11.	Hortonworks	The Hortonworks is used for big data analysis in the ultimate cost-effective and open-source architecture for all types of data. This tool also provides Hadoop services such as HDFS, Ambari Cluster, MapReduce, Oozie, and Spark. Web: https://hortonworks.com
12.	FlockDB	It is used for graph databases. This tool is useful for graphical data designing and processing in TVET sectors. Web: https://github.com/twitter-archive/flockdb

The steps (Figure 12.2) involved in designing learning experiences are described as follows:

i. **Continuous improvement:** Teaching and learning is changing at a very fast pace. The ways the students used to learn before cannot follow the same path today. The technology-enhanced teaching and learning greatly influence the process of teaching and learning. Therefore, improvements and upgrades are required not only in learning but also in educational management and collaboration [16]. A key challenge that teachers face is adapting their teaching techniques to the needs of different students, each of whom learns differently and at his/her own pace. Big data tools can be used for adaptive learning, i.e., it can be used for helping teachers adjust their pace of instructions to an individual student's interests, abilities, and prior knowledge.

ii. **Relating experiences to learning theories:** Teaching in face-to-face, blended, and online modes should be designed on the basis of learning theories for meaningful outcomes. The above stated theories (Table 12.1) have to be linked with both teaching and learning processes while considering big data applications. Therefore, a systematic process and the application of big data technologies facilitate the acquisition of skills and knowledge in various learning environments using different teaching and learning techniques and experiences.

iii. **Design teaching and learning experience:** Different nations have different learning styles, curriculums, and qualification framework. When designing online learning management systems to facilitate international learning, we have to consider or put in mind that different people interact differently on the system user interface [17–19]. In this case, big data developers have to customize data extraction and algorithms in relation to the environment and learners' interaction experiences.

iv. **Data collection:** Data collection is the systematic approach to gathering and measuring information from a variety of sources to achieve accurate results. Data collection enables an individual or an organization to answer relevant questions, evaluate outcomes, and make predictions about future probabilities and trends in TVET sectors. Data currently exist in different forms, both structured and unstructured. In fact, data is increasingly available to the extent that it no longer has to be collected, rather it just has to be connected using the available attributes, data behavior, and outcomes [20]. For example, to measure students' motivation toward a technical subject, individual student's attitudes (attribute) will be required. The researchers and educators need to connect it with the behavior and thereafter generate the outcomes.

Note: Data collected for any one at any point in time will limit the analysis that can be made. Data collected over time in which trends can be identified will enhance the abilities of instructors, administrators, and curriculum planners to make the right decision for strengthening current educational programs [21].

v. **Analysis of the data:** In the establishment of big data analytics, it is important to keep in mind that analyzing TVET data tends to be sophisticated and requires the establishment of standards [21]. TVET is associated with industrial tool engagement skills (hands-on) and theoretical knowledge. It is worth mentioning that different techniques are involved in analyzing data, such as predictive analysis, network analysis, and association and cluster analysis, which can be utilized in finding educational questions, decision-making, forecasting, and improving teaching practices [22].

vi. **Model development:** The data modeling is composed of the following main aspects:
   a. Conceptual modeling: get involved in the sector
   b. Logical modeling: define attribute
   c. Information modeling: identify the attribute required to describe a thing or entity
   d. Physical modeling: combine and flatten the data
   e. Deployment modeling

   The structural institutional data can be known, such as core business concepts (I know where my business comes from, both theoretically and practically), relationship (can be many to many), institutional drivers (agents), and attribute (student ID, demography), and the like. On the other hand, semistructured or unstructured data means some attributes are unknown. Therefore, there is need to take the known key and separate it with the context that describes it. This is observed in the ensemble data modeling [23,24]. In this case, if the attribute is important to someone, then he/she keeps it. Developers during designing models use different methods, like try and error (trying many possibilities or variables available using linear and non-linear relationships). This is done through model transformation and generalization. For example, different models will work on different clusters of students such as urban technical students and village technical students. They both have different user interactivities and accessibilities in this case.

vii. **Redesigning the learning experiences:** In this phase, big data technologists have to validate the model, assess the model, and find the relationship [25,26]. For example, this is done by collecting research data such as students' attitudes and survey data and then correlating it with models of students' behaviors to learn the dominant characters of students that can predict their behavior. When redesigning the learning experience, we have to consider the sequence available, the association rules, and causal data to achieve the desired learning outcomes.

12.2.3 Benefits of Big Data

12.2.3.1 Enabling Personalized Learning

Studies like those of Skinner and Plato have documented about the necessity of personalized learning [27], i.e., learning which is controlled by an individual learner. Currently, the adaptive and personalized learning processes for students include: personalized e-learning, intelligent tutoring systems, adaptive courses, historical performance and demographics data integrated with external data captured from the social network, and the behavioral studies. The above can be analyzed to show interesting aspects of the individual learning process [28]. Grubisic [29] found over 5,500 pieces of literature that are related to these sorts of adaptive and personalized learning processes, which are computer software generated. The main goal of the education software available in adaptive and personalized learning processes is to accomplish adaptability. Most technical schools in developed nations apply some form of this in reading classes or standardized testing to place students in the appropriate reading or remedial reading classes as needed. These processes are used to identify the specific needs or support services so that students in technical education have a better chance at graduating and retaining knowledge. Personalized learning also helps facilitators to know which students need teachers' assistance the most. In many cases, students do not willingly talk about their difficulties or are not responsive in class. TVET institutions will able to turn this potential for early intervention through personalized learning experiences [28]. The importance of personalized learning is further emphasized on:

> It cannot deny that personalized learning is setting the trend for future development of education. Big data in education makes the process of learning become possible to meet every student's need through a personalized recommendation system which could recommend adapted learning resources and proper path, as well as give academic advice [15].

12.2.3.2 Proper Decision-Making

At the moment, big data and data-driven decisions in TVET are primarily used in developed nations for predictive modeling, identification of the optimal patterns of learning, tracking individual information, and research [30]. Earlier, decision makers and educators were trying to assess teaching and learning by answering questions like the following:

i. Where are the students?
ii. What are the students doing?
iii. What do they know?
iv. How are they thinking?

These questions were very useful but not sufficient. In the TVET sector, we also have to ask the following:

i. Where is the student going?
ii. Is he/she going to pass or fail the technical course?
iii. Is he/she ready for the next course?
iv. What are the motivational factors in relation to teaching and learning?
v. Are the TVET graduates ready for their careers?
vi. Are the TVET graduates competent for the world of work?

All the above aspects lead toward the success of any course in TVET. Big data in the TVET sector shows potential in providing learning support and facilitates learning across learning management systems. When trying to assess the success of any course, it is important to look at learners' misconceptions and the goals of learning. Decision makers intervene to help learning take place. Intervention from teachers, researchers, parents, and counselors provides feedback about: *Which students finish their classes? And who learns?* This provides improvements to the TVET curriculum. Literature shows that different individuals learn in different ways. Let us consider three different learning styles as an example. Auditory learners are more likely to learn effectively by hearing, e.g., reading loudly to enhance recitation; visual learners learn best by seeing, e.g., watching graphics and demonstrations, and reading; and kinesthetic learners obtain knowledge best through "hands-on" experiences, e.g., attending activities and writing notes.

It has been presented that students' collaborative work on the same assignment that follows different interaction patterns affects the performance and assessment of the group work in collaborative learning. Continuous focus, self-reflection, live collaboration, and fairly even distribution of workload are naturally more likely to lead to more refined and coherent assignments and, consequently, lead to better learning outcomes. But again there are some regulations that are widely accepted in improving learning effectiveness, e.g., regular reviewing, more practice, and active collaboration and discussion, and so forth. In relation to TVET apprentices, learning behavior, knowledge composition, and knowledge acquisition are different from case to case. It is thus vital to identify the optimal learning patterns for individual students or groups to maximize learning performance and to identify key impact factors that would allow the generalization and formulation of the best practice guidelines in this space [17].

12.2.3.3 Measure Return on Investment

Upon application of big data methods, a large amount of student related information become instantly available to institutions via LMS. Allowing LMS to gain from focused analytics, assists these institutions in decision-making. Daniel [31] reports that investment in big data yields surprising returns through examining the contributions of big data and analytics on a micro, meso, and macro levels. Now data is available, and in many cases, it is real time across all sectors including the TVET sector, that is to say, data can be available as public data (government), institutional data (vocational schools and colleges), business data (industries), and social data (Facebook, Twitter, LinkedIn, etc.).

On the micro level, these analytics are useful in improving the condition of teaching and learning as well as in comprehending the student learning activities. Researchers and educators can track the data that students have left behind through their social connections, library searches, test scores, LMS, and the like over certain periods of time. Analysis of this data shows or predicts future patterns of learning and teaching and related problems. On the meso level, performances can be measured by collecting data about the improvement in graduate rates. Another example would be the measurement of students' overall performances in specific teachers' classes over a period of time.

Additionally, since large institutions should prepare reports for investors and stakeholders of TVET, it is required to focus on a broad macro view of institutional performance. Therefore, TVET institutions need to address key areas such as teaching and learning that have to be reported to the stakeholders. Benefit is seen in the development of models that can assess an institution's current state of performance while providing accurate predictions for future performance outcomes.

In relation to the existing model, descriptive models enable TVET facilitators to detect student trends in admission, rate of improvement, and graduation rates. A predictive model, the second type, is that whose purpose is to discover previously undetected relationships in data and to predict future outcomes. For example, schools might be able to ascertain at-risk students during their academic programs at primary and secondary levels. These prescriptive models provide the foundation for action plans constructed upon knowledge acquired from both types of models; thereby, allowing institutions to accurately appraise their current situations and make data-driven choices about other possibilities. All this facilitates a great return on investment in TVET sectors when properly utilized.

12.2.3.4 Performance Prediction

We predict the future in order to improve the present context, otherwise why should we predict in the first place? Performance prediction can be done by sending reports to TVET facilitators/tutors or parents and by gaining an actual picture of class engagement and motivation in the teaching and learning situation. This also provides information about answering questions such as: (i) *How are the students prepared for future learning?* (ii) *Which student will succeed now or later as the class continues?* These types of information could be achieved through assessment of topics, knowing which students ask for help often in the LMS, and which ways and how frequently each student gets involved in learning via LMS.

Synthesizing and applying knowledge to solve unseen problems enhance the quality of student learning. Literature shows that TVET sectors are mostly less preferred [8]. By using big data in an appropriate way, TVET institutions can improve student performance. For instance, it controls directly and indirectly the dropout rates and therefore increases the graduation rates. These could be possible by establishing student relationships within the TVET learning environment and ensuring interactions with peers and instructors via LMS. This will further provide a way of gathering information about the performance of particular populations within the student groups. In brief, identifying learners' performance in a particular domain of TVET sector will assist the overall improvement of this domain [5].

12.2.3.5 Determination of Student Behavior

Student behavior, as suggested by BF Skinner, Thorndike, and Pavlov, can be distinguished by following certain fundamental principles and guidelines. They are as follows:

1. Reinforcement of learning.
2. Improve and control undesirable behavior following principles of classical or operand conditioning and laws of learning.
3. Eliminate all incorrect responses and fix only the right responses.

Student behavior is shaped through the feedback on learners' performance such as complaints, approval, encouragement, and engagement [30]. It is important that TVET administrators, when handling attitude and career preparation, ask the following questions: (i) *What attitude possesses great social outcomes?* (ii) *What student behavior generates a positive or negative outcome?* (iii) *What do we need to know for learning?* Use of big data in this sector helps educational administrators and facilitators to find out answers to the stated questions.

Figure 12.3 is a block diagram that presents the combination of authentic student observations and their interactions. Analyzing through big data tools and algorithms will predict a pattern for student behavior. This symbolic strategy also helps educators to distinguish disengaged students, struggling students, disrupting students, and fluctuating material. In LMS, it was reported earlier that different countries tend to use different fashions and user interfaces. Designing the right model to trace the interaction of the students will help you know which students are off-task and also their connected posing time. Such interfaces will directly assist students and further provide information to the educators. Knowing what

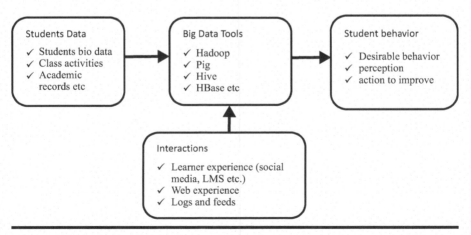

Figure 12.3   Determining student behavior.

particular students are doing provides an informal cheat code to the educators (administrators) such as the following: (i) *What do students find interesting on the Internet?* (ii) *What games do they like playing?* (iii) *What do they watch and what social network do they associate with in the teaching and learning contexts?*

These sorts of acts and information assist the facilitators to know more about the level of student behavior and their level of performance, hence providing a platform where the student feels recognized and wanted.

12.3 Tools, Algorithms, and Analytic Platforms for Educational Purposes

At present, there are many big data tools available in the market. These tools claim to provide cost efficiency, time management, and analysis of data to find out interesting patterns. This is also termed as open analytics. Technology has provided the ability to collect data either directly from students or from observations or choices made by students and to analyze this information so that educators can give individual attention to each learner [32]. Table 12.2 provides the names of possible tools connected with big data in TVET sectors.

12.4 Recommendation and Conclusion

Data is growing exponentially, and therefore, the amount of data stored during the past 2 years is more than that done in any other time of history. With this pace, at one point storage will be exhausted. To handle this huge volume of data, a distributed file system will be suitable. Educational authorities, particularly in TVET sectors, are scared about the governance issues connected to big data technologies, for instance, lack of competency level in handling the use of analytics and their interactions, lack of skills and awareness of teachers, difficultly in synchronizing the TVET systems to the growing pace of data, etc.

In a nutshell, data is not only getting big, but it also presents itself in different complex structures: (i) structured data (organized in data forms and data schemas that are fixed like data found in relational databases), (ii) semistructured data (partially organized, lack of the formal structure of data modeling such as JSON files and XML), and (iii) unstructured data (unorganized and unknown schema, and multimedia files such as videos, photos, and sensor data). Subjecting this big data to computations becomes a bottleneck (storage capacity vs disk transfer performance) [31].

In this chapter, therefore, we have documented prospects, tools, and applications of big data in the TVET sector. It is noted that application of learning analytics in the TVET sector brings many advantages to learners, instructors, and administrators which include but not limited to personalized learning, providing insights into the learners' behavior, and consequently providing directions for the instructors to tailor the way they teach. Considering learning analytics in TVET sector will enable the administrators to visualize the actual pattern of TVET graduates, and eventually be able to properly document future success factors of TVET. Lastly, we provide useful information for readers, educators, curriculum developers, policy makers, and other TVET stakeholders on implementing big data technologies to ensure the quality TVET education.

Besides, big data technology facilitates the creation of new knowledge and enhancement of competences in TVET sectors.

References

1. E. Clift, V. Liptak, and D. Rosen. Educational ideas and the future of higher education: The quest for a new business model. In *Von der Kutsche zur Cloud–globale Bildung sucht neue Wege*, edited by Manfred Schönebeck and Ada Pellert. Springer, Wiesbaden, Germany, 2016, pp. 7–37.
2. D. E. C. B. Ms.Deepa. A. Big data analytics for accreditation in the higher education sector. *International Journal of Computer Science and Information Technologies(IJCSIT)*, vol. 8, pp. 357–360, 2017.
3. D. C. Gibson and D. Ifenthaler. Preparing the next generation of education researchers for big data in higher education. In *Big Data and Learning Analytics in Higher Education*, edited by Ben Kei Daniel. Springer, Switzerland, 2017, pp. 29–42.
4. L. M.-s. Ni, J. Xiao, and H. Tan. The golden age for popularizing big data "平民化"——大数据技术发展的新目标. *Science China Information Sciences*, vol. 59, p. 108101, 2016.
5. P. Michalik, J. Stofa, and I. Zolotova. Concept definition for Big Data architecture in the education system. In *2014 IEEE 12th International Symposium on Applied Machine Intelligence and Informatics (SAMI)*, 2014, pp. 331–334.
6. R. Kitchin and G. McArdle. What makes big data, big data? Exploring the ontological characteristics of 26 datasets. *Big Data & Society*, vol. 3, p. 2053951716631130, 2016.
7. Y. Wang, L. Kung, W. Y. C. Wang, and C. G. Cegielski. An integrated big data analytics-enabled transformation model: Application to health care. *Information & Management*, vol. 55, pp. 64–79, 2018.
8. M. Nambobi. *Big Data: Information is the new Oil mine in Africa*. 2017. Available: https://nambobi.com/big_data.
9. G. Bello-Orgaz, J. J. Jung, and D. Camacho. Social big data: Recent achievements and new challenges. *Information Fusion*, vol. 28, pp. 45–59, 2016.
10. A. Alli and M. Nambobi. *Adopting ICT and Green Skills in Teaching and Learning: BTVET in Uganda*. CreateSpace Independent Publishing Platform, North Charleston, SC, 2017.
11. S. Mangal. Essentials of Educational Technology. PHI Learning Pvt. Ltd., New Delhi, 2009.
12. Y. Song. The research on individual adaptive English studying of network education platform based big data technology. In 2015 *14th International Symposium on Distributed Computing and Applications for Business Engineering and Science (DCABES)*, 2015, pp. 260–263.
13. W. Vollenbroek, K. Jagersberg, S. Vries, and E. Constantinides. Learning Education: An 'Educational Big Data'approach for monitoring, steering and assessment of the process of continuous improvement of education. 2014.

14. M. S. H. Khan and L. Markauskaite. Approaches to ICT-enhanced teaching in technical and vocational education: a phenomenographic perspective. *Higher Education*, vol. 73, pp. 691–707, 2017.
15. X. Yu and S. Wu. Typical applications of big data in education. In 2015 *International Conference of Educational Innovation through Technology (EITT)*, 2015, pp. 103–106.
16. N. J. Michuda. Mining big data to create a tool for empirical observation of continuous safety improvement in a construction company-A progressive case study in the lean environment. 2016.
17. S. Allais. The implementation and impact of national qualifications frameworks: Report of a study in 16 countries. ILO, Geneva, Switzerland, 2010.
18. C. Portugal. Design, user-experience and teaching-learning. In International Conference of Design, User Experience, and Usability, 2014, pp. 230–241.
19. K. Fisher and C. Newton. Transforming the twenty-first-century campus to enhance the net-generation student learning experience: using evidence-based design to determine what works and why in virtual/physical teaching spaces. *Higher Education Research & Development*, vol. 33, pp. 903–920, 2014.
20. C. Cecchinel, M. Jimenez, S. Mosser, and M. Riveill. An architecture to support the collection of big data in the internet of things. In 2014 *IEEE World Congress on Services (SERVICES)*, 2014, pp. 442–449.
21. C. R. Finch and J. R. Crunkilton. *Curriculum Development in Vocational and Technical Education. Planning, Content, and Implementation*. ERIC, Washington, DC, 1999.
22. X. Li, X. Zhang, W. Fu, and X. Liu. E-Learning with visual analytics. In 2015 *IEEE Conference on e-Learning, e-Management and e-Services (IC3e)*, 2015, pp. 125–130.
23. B. Gupta, M. Goul, and B. Dinter. Business intelligence and big data in higher education: Status of a multi-year model curriculum development effort for business school undergraduates, MS graduates, and MBAs. *CAIS*, vol. 36, p. 23, 2015.
24. H. Hultgren. *Modeling the Agile Data Warehouse with Data Vault*. New Hamilton, Brighton, UK, 2012.
25. M. J. Koehler and P. Mishra. Teachers learning technology by design. *Journal of Computing in Teacher Education*, vol. 21, pp. 94–102, 2005.
26. P.-W. On and R. McKethan. Redesigning the course in an online delivery based on students' perception of online learning experiences. In *Society for Information Technology & Teacher Education International Conference*, 2008, pp. 609–611.
27. M. A. McEachern. The utopias of Plato, Skinner, And Perkins Gilman: A comparative analysis in theory and art. Doctoral Dissertation, Faculty of Education, University Of Lethbridge, Lethbridge, Canada, 1997.
28. L. Cen, D. Ruta, and J. Ng. Big education: Opportunities for big data analytics. In *2015 IEEE International Conference on Digital Signal Processing (DSP)*, 2015, pp. 502–506.
29. A. Grubisic. Adaptive courseware: A literature review. *Journal of Universal Computer Science*, vol. 21, no. 9, pp. 1168–1209, 2013.
30. X. Huang, W. Ge, and Y. Liu. Design and implementation of E-training decision-making system. In *2015 International Conference of Educational Innovation through Technology (EITT)*, 2015, pp. 24–28.
31. B. Daniel. Big data and analytics in higher education: Opportunities and challenges. *British Journal of Educational Technology*, vol. 46, pp. 904–920, 2015.
32. M. Grush. (2014, September 1). Big data: An evolution in higher education's technology landscape. *Strategic Directions*.

Chapter 13

Sports Analytics: Visualizing Basketball Records in Graphical Form

Muye Jiang
University of Ottawa

Gerry Chan and Robert Biddle
Carleton University

Contents

13.1 Introduction

Statistics has long been an inherent component in professional sports. Sports visualization is growing, yet most games tend to leave the statistics in numerical format and use very few in-game visual representations. Basketball is a game that still leaves the statistics in numerical and text format. An enormous amount of data is generated in one basketball game. Live basketball play-by-play records in the National Basketball Association (NBA), for example (Figure 13.1), are organized in a tabular format listing events that occur during a game [1]. To search for a particular event, a user must scroll up and down a long list of records and calculate the amount of time at 12-min intervals per quarter. This makes it very difficult for users such as coaches, players, audiences, sports reporters, and analysts to search for particular events. We believe that live basketball records could be represented in a better format.

To our knowledge, no designer has attempted to redesign the format for showing live basketball records. There is one visualization for showing the performance of basketball players for an entire season [2] (Figure 13.2) and one design scheme for showing three different game levels (season, game, and session) [3], as well as some research regarding the potential applications of information visualization for representing sports statistics [4,5], but no designer has yet focused on a design for

TEAM A (6-1)		TEAM B (6-2)
	START OF 1ST **QUARTER**	
	(12:00) JUMP BALL PLAYER VS PLAYER (PLAYER GAINS POSSESSION)	
Player Violation: Kicked Ball (Player)	11:49	
	11:32	Player 3pt Shot: Missed
Player 3pt Shot: Missed	11:10	
	11:08	Player Jump Shot: Missed
Player Rebound (Off: 0 Def: 1)	10:59	
Player Layup Shot: Missed Block: Player (1BLK)	10:55	
	10:50	Player Rebound (Off:0 Def:1)
	10:43 [TEAM A 2-0]	**Player Layup Short: Made (2 PTS)**
Player 3pt Shot: Missed	10:29	

Figure 13.1   NBA play-by-play basketball records [1].

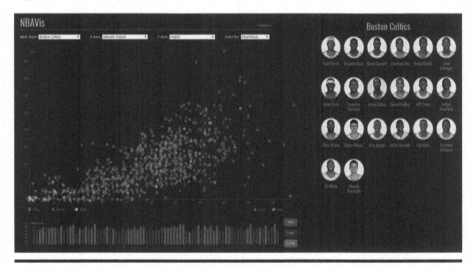

Figure 13.2   Visualization for performance of basketball players for an entire season [2].

visualizing team performance during a specific game. We propose a new format for representing in-game basketball records: a graphical chart, which we called *BasketBallVis* (Figure 13.3), is composed of three primary components: (1) a line chart, (2) track lines, and (3) dynamic elements. We believe that our new design approach is of value to users for supporting rapid detection of events and score advantage during and after a game because no scrolling or mental computation is needed here. To test the value of our new design approach, we conducted a user study to evaluate the efficiency and effectiveness for supporting visual search and

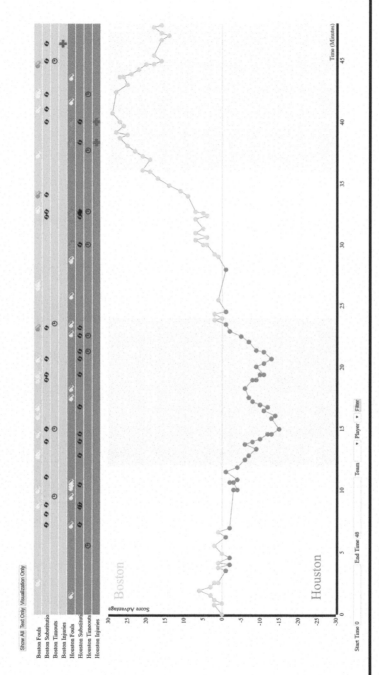

Figure 13.3 Graphical chart for visualizing basketball records of a specific game designed and used for testing, which we named "BasketBallVis."

query. Our results show that the graph we designed and tested is clear, usable, and visually appealing. We found evidence that it is both easier and faster to find critical information about the game using the graph as opposed to the traditional text chart. We have empirical evidence to support the assertion that the graph yields better user experience than a traditional text chart, particularly for experts than for novices. This graph displays basketball records clearly, and during a game, users will likely find it quick and useful for finding information they wish to know.

The main goal of this project was to design a visualization that will better aid visual search and query and test its effectiveness. Due to the large amount of scrolling and computation[1] required for the use of a text chart, it was hypothesized that the new graph chart (Figure 13.3) will be more usable than a conventional text chart (Figure 13.1) in many ways. For example, no scrolling is required while using the graph chart and, thus, users will be able to detect an event almost instantaneously. Also, no computation of time is required because a continuous track line is conveniently located at the top of the graph chart. In addition, to no need for scrolling and computation, visualization elements such as colors, symbols, patterns, and hover queries have been applied to the graph to aid visual search and query.

13.1.1 Chapter Roadmap

The subsequent sections of this chapter are organized as follows: Section 13.2 provides the background information about basketball and related literature. Section 13.3 outlines the design approach along with the design principles, technology, and user tasks. Section 13.4 provides details regarding the user study, while Section 13.5 explains the method that was employed for comparing a traditional text chart vs. graph. Section 13.6 presents a report of the results of the study, and Section 13.7 offers interpretation of the results, limitations, and suggestions for future research.

13.2 Background and Related Work

For most sports with complex rules such as basketball, baseball, ice hockey, and so on, one game generates a large amount of data. These data are usually stored in a text or numerical format. Saving records in text or numerical format takes less storage space compared to saving images and videos, but this makes tasks such as analyzing and utilizing data extremely time-consuming for users. When it comes to making decisions during a live basketball game, time is a critical factor because most users need to respond very quickly. For example, coaches need to generate attack or defense strategies according to a current game status in a short amount of time—usually less than 1 min. The domain of information visualization—"the use of computer-supported, interactive, visual representations of abstract data to amplify cognition" [6]—offers good solutions to save time and help users see trends in the data because the use of good visualization principles, such as colors and hover queries, could increase visual salience and support rapid search and query [7].

We focused our sports data visualization research on basketball games because basketball has a fixed game time for each quarter and its scores changes dramatically, usually three or four times each minute, all the time. These basketball characteristics make it a perfect choice for visualizing game data. However, very little research has explored the area of sports using data visualization, and topics of these research projects focus on other specific games, such as baseball [8]. In contrast, game data visualization is very popular in Esports [9]. High-level professionalized Esports, such as Starcraft II [10] (Figure 13.4) or Dota 2 [11] (Figure 13.5), are also popular in game data visualization and are very detailed and well rounded. The visualization (Figure 13.3) introduced in this chapter was inspired by one of these professionalized Esports called League of Legends [12] (Figure 13.6).

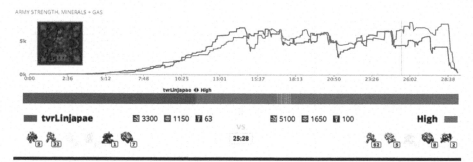

Figure 13.4   Starcraft II [10]—Real-time strategy game performance visualization [13].

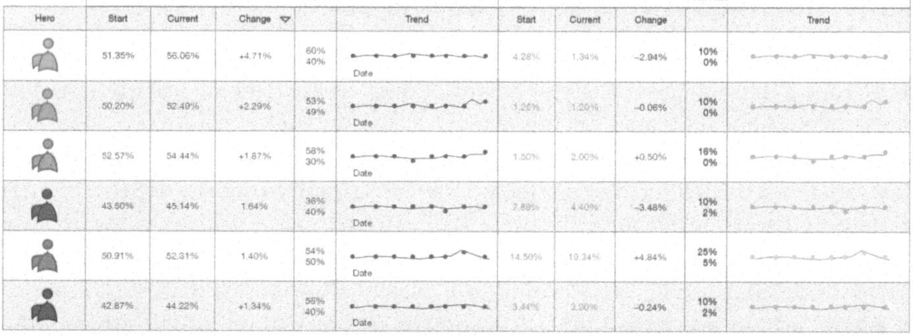

Figure 13.5   Dota 2 [11]—Trends organized by week [14].

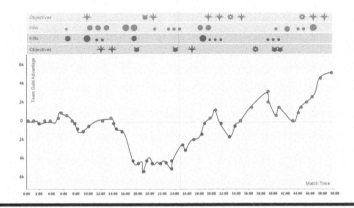

Figure 13.6   Team gold advantage visualization in League of Legends [12] match history record.

Figure 13.6 is a screenshot of League of Legends [12] game data visualization showing records of match history. It contains two main parts: (1) a track line and (2) a graph. The first part is the red and blue track lines located at the top of the whole visualization. The track line is used for recording important events that happened at different times for the red team and blue team. The second part is the line chart which is used for recording the team gold advantage that serves as a reference for the game's current status because the leading team always has the team gold advantage. We believe that data generated during a live basketball game share many similar characteristics with the data generated in League of Legends [12].

A standard NBA basketball game has four quarters and each quarter lasts for 12 min. There are two teams on the basketball court. Each team consists of five on-court players and several substitution players. Like most other ball games, a basketball game has only one ball, and the two teams will try their best to gain control of the ball and shoot the ball into their opponent's basket in order to gain scores. The team with higher scores will have a score advantage and the team that has the score advantage at the end of the fourth quarter wins. A basketball game usually contains many important events, which occur at different times of the game, such as fouls, substitutions, and timeouts. These events change the trend of the game.

In general, there are four types of basketball game data users. The first type of users are coaches. Coaches need the game's data to evaluate the game's current status and to make attack or defense strategies. The game's data also contain some vital information such as specific player performance, number of fouls, and the amount of stamina left. Coaches will use this information to plan substitutions and improve their strategies. The second type of users are players. Unlike coaches, players usually focus their attention on more simple game data, like the number of fouls they have and their matchup player's performance. The third type of users are basketball analysts and reporters. They need the game data to explain to the audiences what is happening on the basketball court. Sometimes, they will use the teams' or players' previous game data and compare it to the current game data to predict the final result of the current game and evaluate players' performance. The last type of user is audiences. They simply focus on the performance of their favorite team(s) or player(s) because they experience enjoyment when their favorite team wins or if their favorite player scores a lot of points.

Little research has explored the merits of using visualizations for representing sport statistics. Legg et al. [15] designed an algorithm for the layout of metaphoric glyphs at different spatial scales called "MatchPad" and examined its effectiveness for supporting rapid information seeking in a Rugby context. The researchers found that MatchPad was useful for coaches and analysts in making important match decisions in a short time period and was successful at helping examine events in detail while maintaining a clear overview of the game situation. They concluded that glyph-based visualization offers an efficient and effective way for conveying large amounts of event records. In a different study, Dietrich et al. [8] developed a new visual analytics tool called "Baseball4D" for analyzing, visualizing, and tracking the performance of baseball players. Although the design was not empirically tested, the authors believe that their design is valuable for teams and coaches to study gameplay and player performance. Losada et al. [16] created an interactive visual prototype called "BKViz" for analyzing basketball games which focuses on the processing and presentation of play-by-play data. To validate the tool, the researchers consulted with experts and received much positive feedback with respect to the usefulness of their design, such as the capability of comparing game situations where multiple players are or are not on the court together, filtering of events to reveal when various plays occur, and linking of multiple interactive visualizations to show the potential of predicting a variety of conclusions. Although informative, there are a lot of basketball performance visualizations, but they are all created after the games rather than during the games (live).

13.3 Design Details

For basketball game data visualization, it should complete two major missions. The first mission is converting the text format data into unified data structure and the second mission is using the data structure to create charts and graphs. We separated our program into two parts according to the two missions.

13.3.1 Converting Text Format Data

Text format basketball game data recorded what happened at a specific time. Figure 13.7 [1] is an example of text format data. And, we called the data stored in one row in Figure 13.3 as an "event." Although there are many kinds of events, such

TEAM A			TEAM B
	START OF 1ST QUARTER		
	(12:00) JUMP BALL PLAYER VS PLAYER (PLAYER GAINS POSSESSION)		
Player Jump Shot: Made (2PTS)	11:15 [TEAM A 2-0]		
	11:08 [TEAM A 2-2]	Player Driving Layup Shot: Made (2PTS)	
Player Floating Jump shot: Made (2PTS)	10:50 [TEAM A 4-2]		
	10:28	Player Foul: shooting (1PF) (2FTA) (B Forte)	
Player Free Throw 1 of 2 (1PTS)	10:28 [TEAM A 5-2]		
Player 3pt Shot: Made (5PTS) Assist: Player (1 AST)	10:06 [TEAM A 8-2]		

Figure 13.7   **The event surrounded by a yellow box shows the time that an event occurred at 1:10 (each quarter for lasts 12 min and 1:10 = 12:00–10:50), the type of event is "scoring," and the team that created this event is Boston Celtics. The event also contains some detailed information, such as the name of the player and the player's scoring method [1].**

as scoring and substitutions, these events share some common characteristics. We designed our data structure according to these common characteristics. Dictionary structures were used to store events' information. This dictionary structure contains four keys: the first key is "time" that represents the moment when this event happened; the second key is "team" that represents the team or the team's player that generated this event; the third key is "type" that represents what this event is, such as "timeout" and "injury"; and the last key is "detail" which is a sub-dictionary, and its keys are based on this event's "type"—for an "injury" event, its keys are "injured player's name" and "type of injury."

13.3.2 Drawing Charts and Graphs

The visualizations used to create BasketBallVis (Figure 13.3) are a combination of (1) a line chart, (2) track lines, and (3) dynamic elements.

13.3.2.1 Line Chart

The most important component of our visualization is the line chart. Time appears on the x-axis because the two basketball teams (home and guest) that are playing this game use the same timescale, and overtimes are rare in basketball games. The most interesting feature of this chart lies on the y-axis. Usually, chart designers will plot each team's current scores on the y-axis. But, each team's scores mean very little to all the users (players, coaches, analysts, reporters, and audiences); instead, the score difference between the two teams (or we can also call it score advantage) is the critical information that users need. As a result, we decided to show score advantage on

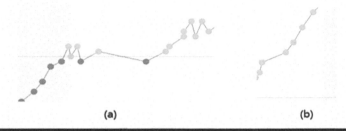

(a)   (b)

Figure 13.8   Pre-attentive features applied to the design of BasketBallVis. (a) The blue circles represent the home team has the score advantage, while the green circles represent the visiting team has the score advantage. (b) Green circles that are farther from the horizon (pink line) means that the visiting team has a larger score advantage at that time.

the *y*-axis, and the points above the *x*-axis represent that the guest team has the score advantage, whereas the point below the *x*-axis represents that the home team has score advantage. To make the points in the line graph more meaningful, we added more features to these points to contain more information. Since players and coaches need quick and accurate access to this information, we selected two pre-attentive features suggested by Ware [7] (Figure 13.8). The first feature is color to show which team has score advantage (Figure 13.8a). The second feature is distance to the horizon to show how large the score advantage is (Figure 13.8b).

Like the points, the score line is also a major part of a line chart, and we utilized the line's orientation to represent the game's tendency. If the line is getting closer to the top of the chart during a specific period, it means the guest team is gaining an upper hand during this period (Figure 13.3: from time 30:00 to time 48:00). Otherwise, it means the home team is gaining an upper hand (Figure 13.3: from time 10:00 to time 20:00). In addition to color and size, we also found a way to utilize the chart's background. Each basketball game consists of four quarters, and each quarter is exactly 12 minutes long. Thus, different background colors were used to represent each quarter. Low-saturated light colors were used here because this could make crucial small subsets, such as points, and the line more visible and distinct from the background [7].

13.3.2.2 Track Lines

Track lines are used here to record the critical events of each team. There are four kinds of critical events: injuries, substitutions, fouls, and timeouts. Although visual appeal is not important for players and coaches, it is so for the audiences. A well-designed symbol set can be appealing (meets audience' requirements) and readily found [7] (meets players' and coaches' requirements); thus, symbols were integrated into the graph (Figure 13.9a). According to Ware [7], symbols should be distinct

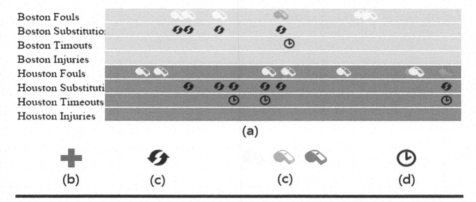

Figure 13.9 (a) The four blue track lines to events belonging to the Boston team and the four green track lines to events belonging to the Houston team. (b) A red cross is commonly associated with first-aid and medical services, so it was used to denote player injury. (c) Two rotating arrows forming a circle is usually a symbol for swapping and recycling. We used it to represent players' substitutions. (d) Basketball referees will blow a whistle when players commit an offense or a foul, so we used whistles to represent players' fouls. The colors of the whistles represent the number of fouls the players have at that time. (e) A clock is used for showing time and we used it to represent timeout.

from the background and other symbols. Four symbols were created for denoting each critical event by following this principle (Figure 13.9b–e).

13.3.2.3 Dynamic Elements

The events mentioned before usually contain more detailed information than the event's type and the time when the event happened. But displaying all these detailed information at the same time would make our graph too complex and unfocused. Thus, we chose to introduce interactions and dynamics into our graph. Since coaches and players need to access information fast, "Hover Queries" [7], which supports one of the quickest epistemic actions [17] in our graph, was applied. When a user places the mouse cursor over a symbol on the track line or over a point on the line graph, a pop-up message appears to reveal player and score information (Figure 13.10a and b).

13.3.3 Technologies

Our program is based on HTML, CSS, and JavaScript programming language that are the core technologies for web development. Recall that our program consists of two parts. For the first part, since the text game data provided by the NBA's official

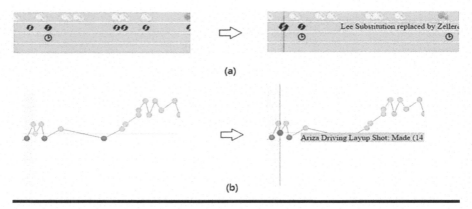

Figure 13.10 **(a) This small window contains more information regarding a particular substitution event. "Lee" and "Zeller" are the two players' names. (b) This small window contains more information about a scoring event. "Ariza" is the player's name and "Driving Layup shot" is the scoring method.**

website [1] utilizes a unified format, we used JavaScript language's original string methods to convert the data into our designed structure. For the second part, we used SVG (Scalable Vector Graphics) to draw our visualization because SVG specification is an open standard developed by W3C (World Wide Web Consortium) and it has many good characteristics. For example, SVG is based on vector images and is very flexible. The visualization's dynamic parts were implemented by the D3.js JavaScript library [18]. D3's core idea is based on data-driven documents [18] so it is convenient to manipulate the document's elements. For some of our program's functions, such as filtering a specific player's game record on the visualization, we filtered the game's data, and D3 helped us remove the unbound game record (other players' record) from the visualization.

13.3.4 System Usage

The visualization is for supporting visual search and query during a live basketball game. There are two kinds of usage for the visualization. The first kind of usage is general usage that is designed for all kinds of users. The second usage is specific usage that is designed for specific kinds of users.

13.3.4.1 General Usage

General usage is focused on the score advantage. When users want to know the score advantage at a specific time, they will start with the x-axis (time-axis). Users will find the specific location on the x-axis first and use it as a reference to find the closest scoring event circle in the line chart. Then, users will try to identify the circle's color and the distance between the circles with respect to the horizon.

Finally, users will get the result which team has the advantage by the color and the result is how much the score advantage is by the distance.

13.3.4.2 Specific Usage

Players, since they usually focus on their own performance, will use the visualization's filtering function to filter the events which are related to them. They can also know the number of fouls they have accumulated by looking at the color of the whistles located on the foul's track line.

Coaches will use the slope of the line charts to evaluate his decisions and strategies. For example, if the coaches called a player substitution at 5 minutes of the game, he should look at the line's slope during the 5 and 10 minutes of the game. If the slope is inclined toward his team direction, this means the substitution is a good decision. On the other hand, if the slope is inclined toward the opposite team's direction, this means the substitution is a bad decision. Aside from the evaluation usage, the visualization can also help the coaches make decisions. For example, if he finds his most valuable player's record contains an orange or red whistle at the first or second quarter of the game, he should call a substitution to prevent the most valuable player from getting six fouls and get fouled out too early in the game.

Basketball analysts and reporters can compare the shape of the current game's line charts of the two teams with the shape of the previous game's line charts to predict which team will win the current game. Furthermore, they can also use the line chart's slope to explain which team is having the current advantage.

13.4 User Study

The dependent variables of this study are search efficiency, clarity, usability, and visual appeal, while the independent variables are two types of charts: text and graph. The research question of this study is: Can basketball records and events be better represented using a graph and symbols rather than text format? Following are six hypotheses:

H1: It will be easier to search for information on a graph than on a text chart.
H2: It will be easier to identify information on a graph than on a text chart.
H3: It will take less time to find information on a graph than on a text chart.
H4: A graph will be more usable than a text chart.
H5: A graph will be more visually appealing than a text chart.
H6: A graph will yield better user experience than a text chart.

13.4.1 Design and Participants

A 2 (chart type: text vs. graph) by 2 (user type: novice[2] vs. expert[3]) within participant, counter-balanced design was used. University students were recruited via convenience and opportunistic sampling. Posters were posted around the university campus and email notices were sent to colleagues in our class asking for their participation. Twelve participants (ten males, two females; six experts, six novices) ranging in age from 23 to 29 years old ($M = 25.08$ years, $SD = 2.07$ years) volunteered to participate in the study. Six user representatives in each user category were sufficient for the purposes of this evaluation because of eventual data saturation [19]. All participants were graduate students studying in the fields of engineering, psychology, and computer science.

13.4.2 Measures

A combination of subjective and objective measures was gathered for analysis. Subjective measures included search efficiency, clarity, usability, learnability, and visual appeal. These were integrated into two post-record questionnaires: one for evaluation of the conventional text chart (Figure 13.1) and the other for evaluation of the new graph (Figure 13.3). The post-record questionnaire also included one question that evaluated overall experience and one final question to provide suggestions for improving the chart. Time was recorded as an objective measure of search efficiency.

13.4.2.1 Search Efficiency and Clarity

Five custom items (Table 13.1) using a 5-point Likert scale (1 = strongly disagree to 5 = strongly agree) were developed to evaluate the ease of visual search and the clarity of information. As an objective measure, the length of time it took to find an event and report the team that is taking the lead was recorded for each chart. More time it takes to find an event and report the team that is taking the lead on a chart indicates poor search efficiency, whereas less time it takes to search and report information indicates good search efficiency.

Table 13.1   Post-Record Questionnaire Statements That Evaluated Ease of Search and Clarity

Measures	Questionnaire Statements
Search	It was hard to find the information I was looking for.
Clarity	It was easy to identify the trend of the game.
	The chart was hard to understand.
	I could tell right away when team A had the largest score advantage.
	It was unclear which team was taking the lead at a specific time (e.g., 20 minutes).

13.4.2.2 Usability and Learnability

The System Usability Scale (SUS) [20] is a ten-item scale measuring the level of usability (e.g., *I thought the chart was easy to use*) and learnability (e.g., *I think I would need the support of a technical person to be able to use this chart*) of a system ($r = 0.99$ and 0.78, respectively). It consists of five positively worded items and five negatively worded items. Participants were asked to indicate their responses on a 5-point Likert scale with responses ranging from 1 = strongly disagree to 5 = strongly disagree. As suggested by Lewis and Sauro [21], item 8 was changed from "cumbersome" to "awkward," and the word "system" was replaced with the word "chart" to better fit the nature of the study.

13.4.2.3 Visual Appeal

Lindgaard et al. [22] developed a 9-point scale (1 = very unappealing to 9 = very appealing) for measuring characteristics (e.g., *interesting—boring; good design—bad design*) of visual appeal, ($R^2 = 0.94$, $p < 0.001$). These characteristics were integrated as statements (e.g., *the chart was interesting*) into the post-record questionnaires consisting of three positively worded items and two negatively worded items. To maintain consistency with other statements in the questionnaire, participants were asked to indicate their responses on a 5-point Likert scale with responses ranging from 1 = strongly disagree to 5 = strongly agree.

13.4.2.4 User Experience and Improvement

The last section of the post-record questionnaire consisted of two questions: (1) a closed-ended question that assessed the overall experience of the chart using a 10-point Likert scale, 1 = bad to 10 = good, and (2) an open-ended question asking participants to provide feedback for improving the chart.

13.4.3 Materials and Apparatus

Charts were displayed using a web browser (Google Chrome) on a 15-inch, 1920 × 1080 pixels notebook computer running Windows 10. A different notebook computer that displayed a built-in stopwatch in a web browser (Google Chrome) was used to record time. A mouse with a scroll wheel was connected to the computer for better interaction. Participants completed paper questionnaires and a time record sheet was used to organize time data.

13.4.4 Procedures

Ethical approval for the current research was obtained from the university's Research Ethics Committee. The experiment was approximately 30 minutes long and was divided into two parts: an exploration session followed by an experimental session. In a closed laboratory setting, six participants explored and evaluated the graph chart followed by the text chart, while this order was reversed for the reminder of participants. For participants who were unfamiliar with basketball, the experimenter briefly explained the mechanics of the game and the scoring system. After initializing the informed consent, participants scrolled through and explored a chart for about 1 minute. Next, participants were asked and timed on a series of eight questions relating to the chart they explored and completed a post-record questionnaire. The same procedure was repeated with a different chart type. Finally, participants completed a demographics questionnaire, were debriefed, and thanked for their participation.

13.5 Results

Data were analyzed using IBM SPSS Version 22.0 and figures were generated using Microsoft Excel 2010. Prior to analysis, data were screened for missing values, outliers, and out of range values. Subjective results (Table 13.2) were drawn from the analysis of the post-record questionnaires, whereas objective results were obtained from the analysis of time. Nonparametric tests were selected to perform the analysis because the use of an ordinal scale in the post-record questionnaires and the shape of the distributions were skewed. A p-value threshold of 0.05 was set for all statistical tests[4].

13.5.1 Search and Clarity

To decide which chart type (text or graph) was easier to find information with respect to the user type (expert or novice), a Friedman test was conducted on each of the statements in the post-record questionnaire that evaluated search efficiency and clarity. Results (Table 13.3) showed no significant differences for search, but it showed significant differences for the two statements that evaluated clarity.

Next, post hoc analyses were conducted using a Wilcoxon's signed-rank test to further examine where the differences lay. The statement, "It was easy to identify the trend of the game," showed marginally significant results (Figure 13.11) for both experts ($Z = -1.84, p = 0.07$) and novices ($Z = -1.83, p = 0.07$). The statement, "I could tell right away when team A had the largest score advantage", showed marginally significant results (Figure 13.12) for experts ($Z = -1.83, p = 0.07$) and significant results for novices ($Z = -2.12, p = 0.03$). Both of these results suggest that the graph is clearer than the text chart.

Time was used as an objective measure of search efficiency. To compare which chart type (graph or text), was easier to perform visual search with respect to the user type(expert or novice), two separate Wilcoxon's signed-rank tests were conducted on time. Statistically significant results (Figure 13.13) shown for both

Table 13.2 Descriptive Statistics for Level of Agreement on a 5-Point Likert Scale (1 = Strongly Disagree to 5 = Strongly Agree) with Respect to Post-Record Survey Statements

	Total Sample Size (N = 12)	Descriptive Statistics				
Measure	Post-Game Survey Statements	Mean	SD	Median	Skewness	Kurtosis
Search	It was hard to find the information I was looking for.	1.83	1.19	1.00	0.96	2.21
Clarity	The chart was hard to understand.	2.00	1.13	2.00	0.76	2.13
	It was easy to identify the trend of the game.	4.50	0.52	4.50	0.00	0.92
	I could tell right away when team A had the largest score advantage.	4.67	0.65	5.00	−1.61	4.15
	It was unclear which team was taking the lead at a specific time (e.g., 20 minutes).	2.75	2.01	1.50	0.27	1.04

Note: Descriptive statistics for graphical chart for novice and experts.

Table 13.3 Mean Rank Results of a Freidman Test for Chart Type with Respect to User Type on Level of Agreement on a 5-point Likert Scale (1 = Strongly Disagree to 5 = Strongly Agree) in the Post-Record Survey

Measure	Post-Record Survey Statements	Text		Graph		χ^2	p
		Expert	Novice	Expert	Novice		
Search	It was hard to find the information I was looking for.	2.33	3.42	1.75	2.50	5.94	0.11
Clarity	The chart was hard to understand.	2.24	3.25	1.83	2.50	4.21	0.24
	It was easy to identify the trend of the game.	2.00	1.67	3.67	2.67	9.00	0.03*
	I could tell right away when team A had the largest score advantage.	2.25	1.25	3.42	3.08	12.89	0.01**
	It was unclear which team was taking the lead at a specific time (e.g., 20 minutes).	2.25	2.92	2.50	2.33	1.08	0.79

*$p < 0.05$; **$p < 0.01$.

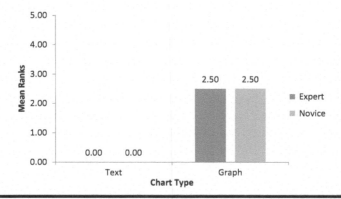

Figure 13.11   Mean rank results of a Wilcoxon's signed-rank test for the statement: "It was easy to identify the trend of the game."

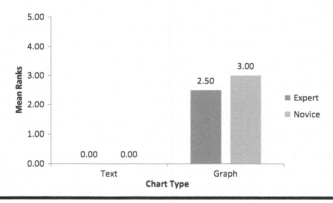

Figure 13.12   Mean rank results of a Wilcoxon's signed-rank test for the statement: "I could tell right away that team A had the largest score advantage."

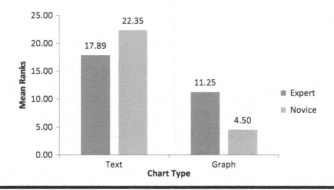

Figure 13.13   Mean rank results of a Wilcoxon's signed-rank test for search efficiency. Lower mean rank scores indicate less search time.

experts ($Z = -4.71$, $p = 0.00$) and novices ($Z = -5.53$, $p = 0.00$) suggest that the graph is more efficient for performing visual search than the text chart.

13.5.2 Usability and Learnability

First, an overall SUS score was computed by subtracting all the negatively worded items from 5 and all the positively worded items from 1, followed by multiplying the sum of item score contributions by 2.5.[5] To compare which chart type was more usable with respect to the user type, two separate Wilcoxon's signed-rank tests were conducted on the overall SUS score. Marginally significant results (Figure 13.14) shown for both experts ($Z = -1.78$, $p = 0.08$) and novices ($Z = -1.75$, $p = 0.08$) suggest that the graph is slightly more usable compared to the text chart.

13.5.3 Visual Appeal

Before conducting the analyses, the scores were averaged for the positively worded items, where higher scores on the measure corresponded to higher levels of visual appeal. Since the original 9-point scale was replaced with a 5-point scale, a reliability analysis was conducted to test the internal consistency of the data. A Cronbach's alpha of 0.895 indicates high internal consistency. To compare which chart type (text or graph) was more visually appealing with respect to the user type (expert or novice), two separate Wilcoxon's signed-rank tests were conducted on an averaged visual appeal score. Marginally significant results (Figure 13.15) shown for both experts ($Z = -1.89$, $p = 0.06$) and novices ($Z = -1.84$, $p = 0.07$) suggest that the graph chart is more visually appealing than the text chart.

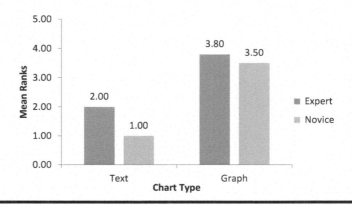

Figure 13.14 Mean rank results of a Wilcoxon's signed-rank test for level of usability and learnability.

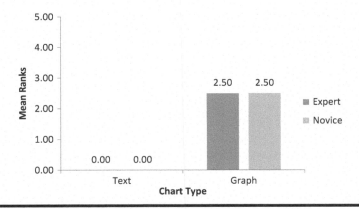

Figure 13.15 Mean rank results of a Wilcoxon's signed-rank test for visual appeal.

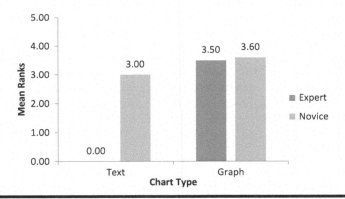

Figure 13.16 Mean rank results of a Wilcoxon's signed-rank test for overall experience.

13.5.4 Overall Experience

To compare which chart type (graph or text) elicited better overall experience with respect to the user type (expert or novice), two separate Wilcoxon's signed-rank tests were conducted on the question: "On a scale of 1 (bad) to 10 (good), please rate your overall experience with this chart" in the post-record questionnaire. Statistically significant results (Figure 13.16) shown for experts ($Z = -2.23$, $p = 0.03$) suggest that the graph yields better experience compared to the text chart, and nonsignificant results shown for novices ($Z = -1.59$, $p = 0.11$) suggest that both the graph and the text chart yield the same experience.

13.5.5 Subjective Report

Results in this section are comments that were gathered from the open-ended question in the post-record questionnaire. They are all related to improving the graph. One participant noted that additional information about the game, such as steal, block, and missed shot, is needed. Another participant recommended that the colors on the graph should match the official colors of the team. Furthermore, several participants reported a slight confusion with the score advantage due to the negative signs below the midline on the y-axis. Participants also suggested adding more interactive elements on the graph, such as providing a link to a video clip of an event or providing a legend for indicating the meaning of colored whistles.

13.6 Discussion

The purpose of this study was to explore the possibility of representing live basketball records in graphical format. A graphical representation was designed leveraging a variety of visualization principles, such as colors, patterns, symbols, and hover queries [7]. The design was tested against a traditional text chart on measures of clarity, search efficiency, usability, visual appeal, and user experience with respect to two user types—experts and novices. Because of the application of good design principles for supporting visual search and query, it was hypothesized that the graph would be more efficient, usable, visually appealing, and yield better user experience than the text chart. In general, results showed that the graph was rated better than the text chart on all measures. Recall the six hypotheses of this study that are as follows:

H1: It will be easier to search for information on the graph than on a text chart.
H2: It will be easier to identify information on a graph than on a text chart.
H3: It will take less time to find information on a graph than on a text chart.
H4: A graph will be more usable than a text chart.
H5: A graph will be more visually appealing than a text chart.
H6: A graph will yield better user experience than a text chart.

The finding that participants rated their ability to detect information such as the trend of the game and score advantage to be faster while using the graph than a text chart supports H1, H2, and H3. Additionally, the finding that irrespective of the user type, expert or novice, it took less time to search and report details on the graph than on the text chart also supports H1, H2, and H3. These findings suggest that the graph is more efficient for supporting visual search and query than a traditional text chart. Likewise, H4 and H5 were supported in that both experts and novices rated the graph to be more usable and visually appealing compared to the text chart. Finally, H6 was partially supported in that findings differed depending on user type. Experts rated their overall experience with the graph to be better than with the text chart, whereas novices rated their overall experience of both chart types to be about the same.

The findings of this study have implications for information visualization and design. One major finding was that the graph was more efficient for performing visual search and queries than a traditional text chart. This suggests that the graph was well designed. Good use of visualization principles (colors, symbols, patterns, and hover queries) enabled participants to easily find what they were asked to search for. Thus, the traditional text chart could potentially be replaced by a graph. Basketball is a quick-paced game and coaches need to make important decisions within a limited timeframe. Making injudicious decisions could result in lost of a game. A more usable, search efficient, visually appealing, and clearer way of displaying records, could reduce the chances of making unwise decisions and could increase the chances of winning a game. With respect to the finding that novices did not have a preference for graph or text chart with respect to overall experience, it is likely that novices have never been exposed to or used a graph or text for looking up basketball records, and, thus, chart type did not make a difference. Perhaps there needs to be some understating and enthusiasm for the game before one can appreciate the merits of the graph.

From a human–computer interaction perspective, the results of this study provide some interesting insights for designers and users. The main goal of interaction design is to help users quickly become experts by making the user-interface as easy to use as possible. Although marginally significant, the graph was rated more usable than the text chart. Particularly for experts, the graph elicited better use experience than the text chart. It is possible that until now no designer has attempted a way to improve the display of live basketball records. Results of this study provide statistical evidence that users can quickly become familiar with this new graph and, possibly, use it more effectively than a traditional text chart. As for the subjective reports, although most comments were associated with minor aesthetic issues, recall that one novice participant suggested adding more interactive elements on the graph, such as providing a link to a video clip of an event. This finding is interesting because simply by looking at and interacting with basketball records evoked an interest in the game. From a design perspective, the interactive elements in the graph could have encouraged further exploration.

13.6.1 *Limitations and Future Work*

One of the main limitations of this study is with respect to participant characteristics: all participants were graduate students, the relatively small sample size, and the comparison of only two user types: experts and novices. Players, coaches, sports analysts, and reporters play an important role in basketball, particularly coaches because they must assess the game situations and make critical decisions in a short amount of time and, thus, the results of this study may not generalize to other user types. A future study could aim to recruit more participants and other user types. Another limitation is that the experiment was conducted in a closed laboratory setting and, thus, results may not be valid in the field. To increase the ecological validity, a future study could examine the usefulness of the graph during a live basketball game. One more limitation of this study is the reliance on subjective measures with the exception of time as an indication of search efficiency. To further test the efficiency and effectiveness of the graph for supporting visual search and query, additional objective measures such as the level of accuracy or the number of errors made during search could be gathered. Moreover, time was recorded rather loosely: the experimenter simply asked the question, and when a response was heard, a timestamp was recorded. Recording time this way allows for much variability with respect to individual differences. A more precise method for recording time could be managed by a computer. For example, present each question on a full screen and provide a "start" button to allow the user initiate time. Once the user has an answer, provide a "stop" button to end time.

More generally, the graph can be adapted for other sports and application areas. Baseball, for example, is another sport that generates a great deal of data during a single game and, perhaps, the same graph designed in this research project could be modified to show live baseball records. As for other application contexts, recall that the graph was inspired by a graphical visualization from a multiplayer online game: League of Legends [12]. What was learned in this research could in turn inform the design of video or online game visualizations, such as the progress and performance of teams and players.

13.7 Conclusions

We sought to improve the format of how live basketball records are represented. After comparing both the conventional text chart and a newly designed graph, we found that a graph is clearer, more usable, and visually appealing than a conventional text chart. Not only does a graph better represent live records, but it also invites interaction and further exploration. Due to the limited amount of research in the area of sports visualizations, we would like to encourage other designers and researchers to explore other possibilities of showing sports statistics using different visualization methods in other sports contexts. In closing, this is a preliminary attempt at improving the format of live basketball records and it provided some new insights into the advantages of using visual methods for showing in-game sports statistics, as well as the application of information visualization principles for designing graphical charts.

Acknowledgments

We thank all the participants who kindly volunteered to participate in this research.

Declaration of Conflicting Interests

The authors declared no potential conflicts of interests with respect to the authorship and/or publication in this chapter.

Funding

The authors received no financial support for the research and/or authorship of this chapter.

Notes

1 Time begins at 12 minutes—countdown from 12:00 to 00:00 per quarter (4 quarters in total, total time = 48 minutes). To know when an event occurs, a user must add and subtract time. For example, to determine which team has the largest score advantage at 30 minutes into the game, a user must add 12 + 12 + 12 to reach the third quarter and subtract 6 from 36.
2 Novice = with very limited to no knowledge of basketball.
3 Expert = basketball amateurs; play and watch basketball frequently and uses text chart while watching NBA game.
4 $^{*}p < 0.05$; $^{**}p < 0.01$
5 Example formula in Microsoft Excel spreadsheet: $((((J5)-1)+(5-(K5))+((L5)-1)+(5-(M5))+((N5)-1)+(5-(O5))+((P5)-1)+(5-(Q5))+((R5)-1)+(5-(S5)))*2.5$

References

1. "NBA Media Ventures, LCC." Retrieved from www.nba.com/games/20151023/MEMORL/gameinfo.html?ls=iref:nba:scoreboard#nbaGIPlay.
2. F. Li. "NBAVis."
3. W. Chen et al. "GameFlow: Narrative Visualization of NBA Basketball Games." *IEEE Trans. Multimed.*, vol. 18, no. 11, pp. 2247–2256, 2016.
4. A. Cox and J. Stasko. "SportVis : Discovering Meaning in Sports Statistics through Information Visualization." *Hum. Factors,* pp. 10–11, 2006.
5. R. Therón and L. Casares. "Visual Analysis of Time-motion in Basketball Games." *Lect. Notes Comput. Sci. (including Subser. Lect. Notes Artif. Intell. Lect. Notes Bioinformatics)*, vol. 6133 LNCS, pp. 196–207, 2010.
6. K. Card, D. Mackinley, and B. Shneiderman. "Readings in Information Visualization: Using Vision to Think." p. 716, January 1999.
7. C. Ware. *Information Visualisation: Perception for Design*. 2012.
8. C. Dietrich, D. Koop, H. T. Vo, and C. T. Silva. "Baseball4D: A Tool for Baseball Game Reconstruction & Visualization." In 2014 *IEEE Conf. Vis. Anal. Sci. Technol. VAST* 2014- *Proc.*, pp. 23–32, 2015.

9. V. R. M. Feitosa, J. G. R. Maia, L. O. Moreira, and G. A. M. Gomes. "GameVis: Game Data Visualization for the Web." In Brazilian Symp. Games Digit. Entertain. SBGAMES, pp. 70–79, 2016.

10. "StarCraft II Guide." Control, 2011. Available: https://starcraft2.com/en-gb/.

11. "Valve- Dota 2." www.valvesoftware.com/games/dota2.html.

12. G. Guide. "League of Legends." *Riot Games*, 2014. Available: www.gamesinformations. com/wp-content/uploads/2016/09/LeagueofLegendsGuide-2.pdf.

13. "GGTracker." Available: http://ggtracker.com/landing_tour.

14. "Heros Trends." Available: www.dotabuff.com/heroes/trends.

15. P. A. Legg et al. "MatchPad: Interactive Glyph-Based Visualization for Real-Time Sports Performance Analysis." *Comput. Graph. Forum*, vol. 31, no. 3pt4, pp. 1255–1264, 2012.

16. A. G. Losada, R. Theron, and A. Benito. "BKViz: A Basketball Visual Analysis Tool." *IEEE Comput. Graph. Appl.*, vol. 36, no. 6, pp. 58–68, 2016.

17. D. Kirsh and P. Maglio. "On Distinguishing Epistemic from Pragmatic Action." *Cogn. Sci.*, vol. 18, no. 4, pp. 513–549, 1994.

18. M. Bostock, V. Ogievetsky, and J. Heer. "D3 Data-driven Documents." *IEEE Trans. Vis. Comput. Graph.*, vol. 17, no. 12, pp. 2301–2309, 2011.

19. J. Nielsen and T. K. Landauer. "A Mathematical Model of the Finding of Usability Problems." In *Proc. SIGCHI Conf. Hum. Factors Comput. Syst.—CHI'93*, pp. 206–213, 1993.

20. J. Brooke. "SUS: A "Quick and Dirty" Usability Scale." In *Usability Evaluation in Industry*, Jordan, P. W., Thomas, B., Weerdmeester, B. A., and McClelland (Eds.), pp. 189–194. Taylor & Francis, London, UK, 1996.

21. J. R. Lewis and J. Sauro. "The Factor Structure of the System Usability Scale." *Lect. Notes Comput. Sci. (including Subser. Lect. Notes Artif. Intell. Lect. Notes Bioinformatics)*, vol. 5619 LNCS, pp. 94–103, 2009.

22. G. Lindgaard, G. Fernandes, C. Dudek, and J. Browñ. "Attention Web Designers: You Have 50 Milliseconds to Make a Good First Impression!" *Behav. Inf. Technol.*, vol. 25, no. 2, pp. 115–126, 2006.

Chapter 14

Analysis of Traffic Offenses in Transportation: Application of Big Data Analysis

Charitha Subhashi Jayasekara, Malka N. Halgamuge, Asma Noor, and Ather Saeed

Charles Sturt University

Contents

14.1 Introduction

Due to the rapid advancement in technology, the amount of data and the speed of data collection are swiftly increasing. Especially in the traffic and transportation field, multiple techniques are used to collect data on a daily basis. For instance, surveillance cameras are operating 24 hours and speed cameras are recording vehicle speeding offenses. Furthermore, offense details and traffic violations can be automatically recorded or logged manually by the police. Therefore, at the end of each day, extremely large datasets known as big data are created in different formats with structured, semistructured, and unstructured data. However, with the use of different data analysis techniques, this data can be analyzed to identify patterns and trends. Also, this analysis is useful to draw attention to any anomaly that can be noticed in the dataset. The biggest benefit is that processing a large collection of data provides better accurate results, delivering more precise outcomes when appropriately analyzed. Those identifications are helpful for various purposes such as preventing future issues, making predictions, understanding needs, improving safety, and making laws.

With the purpose of improving the road safety, this chapter has used descriptive statistical analysis methods and regression modeling to analyze a dataset of traffic offenses. According to statistics from 2007 to 2016 announced by the Victorian Police, Australia [1], the number of impounds is increasing with each calendar year. The data shows an increase of 62.4% in vehicle impounds during this period, with incidences more than doubling over a 10-year period. Moreover, the Australian Bureau of Statistics reports [2] that the number of vehicles in Australia has grown by 2.1% from 2015 to 2016 with 18.4 million registered motor vehicles in Australia as of January 31, 2016. Consequently, the growing number of vehicles is a reminder that the specialists need to pay more attention to road accidents and traffic violations. At the same time, law enforcement authorities are encouraged to come up with more viable and efficient traffic laws that provide better infrastructure facilities to minimize the accidents. When there is better infrastructure, the authorities can make better and more reasonable decisions that could prevent future traffic offenses. Therefore, there is a strong necessity to conduct research in the field of traffic offenses to increase preventative measures.

Previous studies in this field have focused on driver behaviors, pedestrians, driver attitudes, and road safety technologies, but overall there needs to be more attention as this is quite an under-researched area. Most of the researches [3–6] in this area provide a deeper understanding of areas such as each individual's behavior, current technologies related to traffic, and individual offense types. However, despite the significance of this work, there is a lack of research interest in seasonal traffic violations. The psychological state, moods, and emotions of a person can be different during different seasons [7,8]; thus, this needs to be taken into consideration when an offense occurs. For instance, the mood of a person on a Friday night can be different from a Monday morning, and this aspect needs more research attention in order to reduce road danger depending on the time of year it occurs. Therefore, the current analysis has been conducted to analyze how traffic offenses differ during different times and days in a month. In addition, the top 15 violations were analyzed separately to help understand what type of offenses happened the most during peak time periods as it will be helpful in further optimizing danger reduction.

In order to find out whether there is a relationship between the offenses and the time of occurrence, the study started with the null hypothesis, which suggested that there was no relationship between the two variables. Computing technology and the data mining algorithm of regression modeling were then used to determine the acceptance or rejection of the null hypothesis. This technique has been used by many researchers for predictive modeling [9–11] as it helps to identify the increase or decrease in a certain group of data group by creating a regression equation. The selected attributes were categorical and well suited for regression modeling to identify patterns of data distribution in the dataset. The regression equations showed whether and how the number of traffic offenses changed during the given time period proving that the null hypothesis could be rejected by using the equation, as it was possible to calculate the approximate number of offenses on a given time.

Furthermore, the dataset used for the study included various types of traffic offenses that occurred on a particular date and at a particular time. After preprocessing, there were approximately 300 types of offenses and out of them, the majority occurred due to 15 types. Therefore, these 15 types were the focus of this analysis.

The study can be useful for many studies related to traffic control and road safety. Particularly, the results of this study will be useful for the traffic authorities when creating transport strategies to minimize road hazards, and it can also be used for further analytical studies related to traffic offenses.

14.1.1 Chapter Roadmap

The chapter is organized as follows: **Section 14.1** introduces the aim of this chapter. It shows the importance of big data analysis and how it can be used in the traffic and road safety area to get improved decision-making. **Section 14.2** explains the material and methods used. Once the data was collected it was necessary to understand the data types, which methods were most appropriate, and how the expected outcomes could be generated. Furthermore, the software tools that were used are described. **Section 14.3** includes the statistical tests and results. It shows the regression models created and the generated expressions. **Section 14.4** is the discussion section that explains the trends found and decisions made using the results. **Section 14.5** is the conclusion that provides final thoughts on this chapter. It briefly summarizes the rest of the chapter and also explains how the tests can be improved in the future.

14.2 Material and Methods

Data for this research was obtained through openly licensed public datasets from the Australian government website: data.gov.au. The dataset acquired from this site consisted of 574,166 instances of traffic reparations in Australia. Each instance had 27 attributes and the data was collected from July 1, 2015, to June 30, 2016 (Figure 14.1).

14.2.1 Data Inclusion Criteria

The attributes used for analysis are described in Table 14.1. Other attributes such as penalty written on notice, corporate fee amount, and expiation offense code were not incorporated into the data as they were not related to the focus of the study. Furthermore after preprocessing, 521,811 of the offenses were deemed suitable for use in analysis.

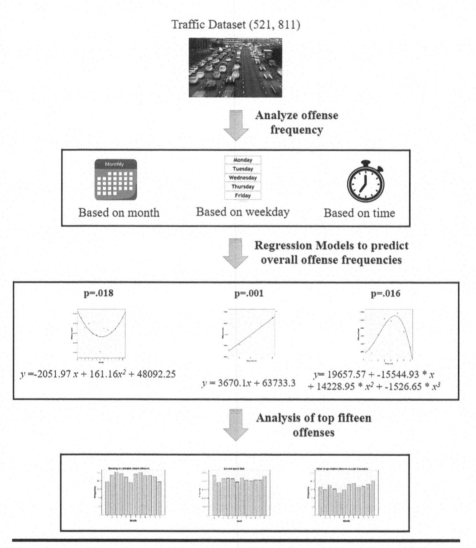

Figure 14.1 Analysis of 521,811 traffic offense data to understand seasonal offenses using regression models.

14.2.2 Data Preprocessing

The raw data was preprocessed before being used for the data analysis. Since there are 916 types of traffic offenses they were categorized depending on the type of offenses into 301 groups. Table 14.2 shows some of the offenses added under the "Exceed speed limit" category.

Table 14.1 Selected Attributes for the Analysis

Attribute	Data Type	Description
Offense type	Categorical (nominal)	Type of offense as recorded by the police, e.g., exceed speed limit, alcohol-related offenses
Year of occurrence	Categorical (ordinal)	Year the offense occurred e.g., 2015, 2016
Month of occurrence	Categorical (Ordinal)	Month the offense occurred e.g., January, February,...
Weekday of occurrence	Categorical (ordinal)	Day the offense occurred e.g., Monday, Tuesday,...
Time of occurrence	Categorical (interval)	Time the offense occurred. Time has been rounded to the nearest 30 minutes. e.g., 0000, 0030,...

Table 14.2 A Sample Portion of Offense Categories

Category	Offense Description
Exceed speed limit	Exceed signed speed by 1–9 kmph
Exceed speed limit	Exceed signed speed by 10–19 kmph
Exceed speed limit	Exceed signed speed by 20–29 kmph
Exceed speed limit	Exceed signed speed by 30–44 kmph
Exceed speed limit	Exceed speed by 45 kmph or more
Alcohol-related offenses	Blood alcohol concentration: 0.08–0.149
Alcohol-related offenses	Blood alcohol concentration: above 0.15
Alcohol-related offenses	Probationary driver exceeding 0.00 blood alcohol concentration
Alcohol-related offenses	Possess liquor in public place contrary to prohibition
...	...

14.2.3 Data Analysis

The main aim of this analysis was to understand the seasonal traffic violation patterns that explain the relationship between the offenses and the time of occurrence. Additionally, the analysis also aimed to measure the frequency of offenses that occurred during different times of the year.

The IBM SPSS (version 23) software was chosen for the data analysis since it has a number of features for statistical analysis, including predictive modeling suitable for big data analytics.

There are several data analyzing methods and it is important to select the correct method depending on the dataset and expected outcome. Considering the dataset used in this chapter, all the data used was categorical and the counts of observations were of different categories. Therefore, regression analysis was selected as the data analysis method. The two major types of regression analysis used in this analysis will be discussed next.

14.2.3.1 Linear Regression

Linear regression can be used to determine the relationship between one dependent variable (denoted by y) and one or more independent variables (denoted by x). Its formula generates a straight line. In this research, it was used to show the relationship between weekdays and offense frequency on each weekday. As an example, $y = mx + b$ represents a linear regression model.

14.2.3.2 Nonlinear (Polynomial) Regression

Nonlinear regression is used to represent a relationship between one dependent variable (denoted by y) and one or more independent polynomial variables (denoted by x) such as squared or cubed (x^2 or x^3) and coefficients. This creates a quadratic or cubic curve. In this research, it was used to show the relationships between months and offense frequency for each month and time periods and its offense frequency. As an example, $y = bx + cx^2 + a$ represents a nonlinear regression model.

14.2.4 Data Analysis Algorithms

The data classification was done according to the frequency types, and then the types were calculated. After that, the frequencies were sorted according to the date and time of occurrence before creating regression models.

Furthermore, three algorithms were used to carry out the analysis. At the end of each algorithm, three different regression equations were created.

Algorithm 1 shows how the regression model was generated to analyze the monthly offense frequency.

Algorithm 1: Offenses against Month of Occurrence

```
int [] offense frequency » Offense frequencies of each month
int [] month » Numeric values of months (from 1 to 12)

get a dataset of offenses within a year
```

```
generate regression model

int y » Offense count
int b » Regression slope
int c » Regression slope
int x » Month
int a » Regression intercept

determine values for b, c, and a using regression model
generate regression equation using the determined values of
b, c, and a
compute y for given x using the generated regression
equation
print y
```

Algorithm 2 shows how the regression model was generated to analyze the weekly offense frequency.

Algorithm 2: Offenses against Weekday of Occurrence

```
int [] offense frequency » Offense frequencies of each day
of the week
int [] month » Numeric values of days of the week (from 1 to 5)

get a dataset of offenses within a year
generate regression model

int y » Offense count
int b » Regression slope
int x » Day of the week
int a » Regression intercept

determine values for b and a using regression model
generate regression equation using the determined values of
b and a
compute y for given x using the generated regression
equation
print y
```

Algorithm 3 shows how the regression model was generated to analyze the offense frequency during different time slots.

Algorithm 3: Offenses against Time Slot of Occurrence

```
int [] offense frequency » Offense frequencies of each time
slot
```

```
int [] month » Numeric values of a time slot (from 1 to 8)

get a dataset of offenses within a year
generate regression model

int y » Offense count
int b » Regression slope
int c » Regression slope
int d » Regression slope
int x » Timeslot
int a » Regression intercept

determine values for b, c, d, and a using regression model
generate regression equation using the determined values of
b, c, d, and a
compute y for given x using the generated regression equation
print y
```

14.2.5 Statistical Analysis

The hypothesis test is important when selecting a dataset and the test was done for this analysis using the SPSS tool. For the current research, the selected null hypothesis (H_0) and the alternative hypothesis (H_1) were:

H_0: There are no differences among the months/ day of week/ time and offense
   frequency
H_1: There is a difference between the months/ day of week/ time and offense
   frequency

Table 14.3 shows the p-values of each group used to generate results. All the p-values are less than 0.05. Therefore, the null hypothesis can be rejected.

14.3 Results

The analysis of the frequency of traffic offenses and the time periods in which they occurred was the main focus of the study. A descriptive statistical analysis was used to measure the frequencies and regression models created to analyze the data.

Table 14.3   *p*-Values among Groups Used for the Test

Type	P-Value of Offense Frequency
Month	0.018
Day of week	0.001
Time	0.016

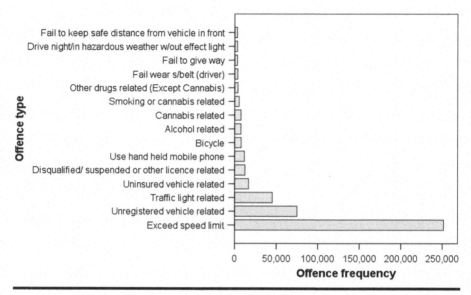

Figure 14.2   First 15 traffic offenses with the highest frequencies of occurrence.

14.3.1 Top 15 Traffic Offenses

Although there were 301 categories of offenses, approximately 88% of them belonged to 15 types of offenses. Therefore, an analysis was performed on the top 15 types as shown in Figure 14.2.

According to the results, drivers who exceeded the speed limit showed the highest number of offenses with 251,529 cases. Therefore, 48.2% of the cases from the total offense count belonged to speeding.

Moreover, the analysis also showed that there were offenses that could have been prevented earlier as they did not relate to the moment it occurred. For example, failing to wear a seatbelt or driving an unregistered vehicle could prevent the accident earlier, although exceeding the speed limit or traffic light violation can happen suddenly while driving. Therefore, further analysis was carried out to identify the direct time of the offenses.

14.3.2 Directly Time-Related Offenses

The time at which the offense occurred was taken into consideration when categorizing the data with offenses identified as either "directly time dependent" or "not directly time dependent." For example, unregistered and uninsured vehicles offenses could have been prevented earlier so they are "not directly time dependent," while vehicles passing through a red traffic light are "directly time dependent." Table 14.4 shows the list of offenses categorized according to the time dependency.

Table 14.4 Time Dependency of the First 15 Offense Counts

Time Dependency	Offense Type	Number of Offenses
Directly time dependent	Exceed speed limit	251,529
	Traffic light-related offenses	45,213
	Use of handheld mobile phone	11,810
	Bicycle offenses	7,796
	Fail to give way offenses	3,307
	Drive at night/in hazardous weather w/out effective light	3,268
	Fail to keep safe distance from vehicle in front	3,102
	Alcohol-related offenses	7,647
	Cannabis-related offenses	7,615
	Smoking- or cannabis-related offenses	5,362
	Other drug-related offenses (except cannabis)	3,981
	Fail to wear s/belt (driver)	3,742
		354,372
Not directly time dependent	Unregistered vehicle-related offenses	75,150
	Uninsured vehicle-related offenses	16,789
	Disqualified/suspended or other license-related offenses	12,470
		104,409

According to Figure 14.3, 77% of offenses were directly related to the time at which they occurred. This gives a strong indication that time is an important factor to be considered when discussing traffic offenses.

14.3.3 Offenses against Year of Occurrence

The number of offenses that occurred during the period 2015–2016 is illustrated in Figure 14.4, and it is noticeable that there was no significant difference with only a 0.96% decrease in the number of offenses in 2016.

Figure 14.3 **Percentages of time dependency of offenses.**

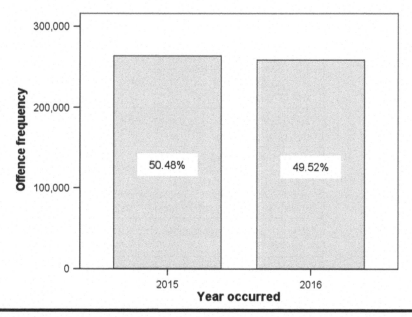

Figure 14.4 **Traffic offense frequency against year of occurrence.**

14.3.4 *Offenses against Month of Occurrence*

14.3.4.1 *Regression Model*

The total number of offenses during each month was analyzed as shown in Figure 14.5.

A regression analysis was carried out to determine the change in the number of offenses in each month. The analysis created a nonlinear quadratic curve as illustrated in Figure 14.6.

Table 14.5 shows the model summary and parameter estimates.

According to the results, the R-squared value was 0.591 and it was approximately a 60% fit model. Furthermore, the p-value was 0.018.

The regression model obtained was $y = ax + bx^2 + c$, where y is the offense count, b and c are regression slopes, x is the month, and a is the regression intercept. Therefore, in order to determine the number of offenses per day during each month, the equation $y = -2051.97 x + 161.16x^2 + 48092.25$ can be used.

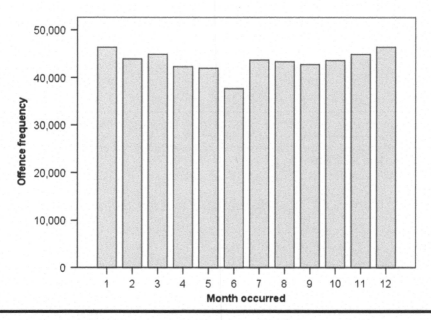

Figure 14.5 **Traffic offense frequency against month of occurrence.**

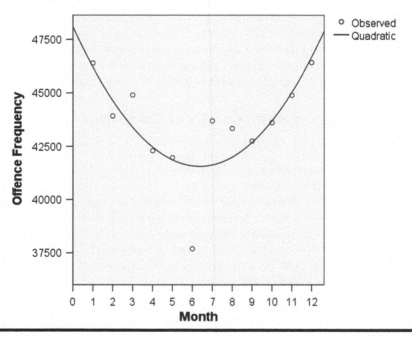

Figure 14.6 **Regression model for monthly offense frequency.**

Table 14.5 Monthly Offense Frequency Regression Model Summary and Parameter Estimates

Equation	Model Summary					Parameter Estimates		
	R Square	F	df1	df2	Sig.	a	b	c
Quadratic	0.591	6.500	2	9	0.018	−2051.974	161.166	48,092.250

Note: The dependent variable is monthly offense frequency, and the independent variable is month.

14.3.4.2 Top 15 Traffic Offense Frequencies against Month

The top 15 traffic offense counts were analyzed against each month as shown in Figure 14.7. It gave a clear view of how each offense varied over time.

14.3.4.3 Obtained Results

This study found that there was a significant difference in offense frequencies in different months of the year. However, June shows the least number of offenses, while January and December show the highest. Therefore, from the beginning of the year, the number of violations decreases, and it increases when the year ends. The difference between the highest and the lowest number of offenses was around 8,000.

Considering the top 15 traffic offenses, offenses such as alcohol- and bicycle-related offenses showed the lowest number of occurrences during the middle of the year, whereas offenses such as failing to keep a distance from the vehicle in front and driving without effective lights were higher in the same period.

14.3.5 Offenses against Weekday of Occurrence

14.3.5.1 Regression Model

Offenses were also analyzed on each day of the week. Figure 14.8 shows the offense frequency of each day of the week.

Using weekdays and the number of offenses, a regression analysis was done to analyze the increase in detail. It creates a linear model as shown in Figure 14.9.

Table 14.6 shows the summary and parameter estimation of the model.

The R-value of the model was 0.992, and it was very close to 1. Therefore, there is a strong connection between the number of offenses and the day of a week making it a better fit to the created model.

The regression model obtained was $y = bx + a$, where y is the offense count, b is the regression slope, x is the day of week, and a is the regression intercept. Therefore, to predict the number of offenses in a day during weekdays, the equation $y = 3670.1x + 63733.3$ can be used.

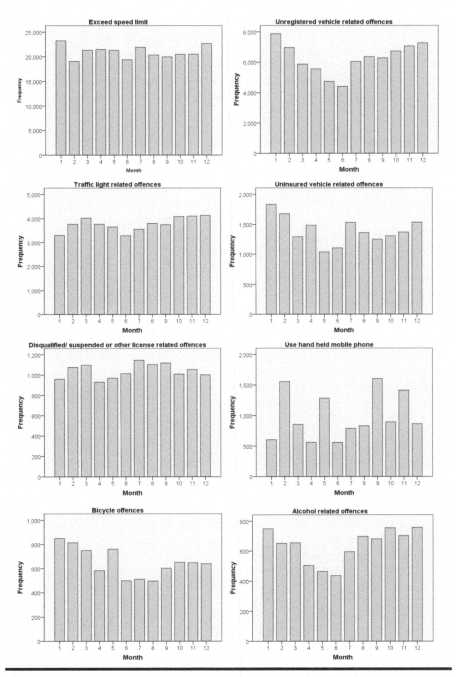

Figure 14.7   Monthly frequencies of top 15 traffic offenses.

(Continued)

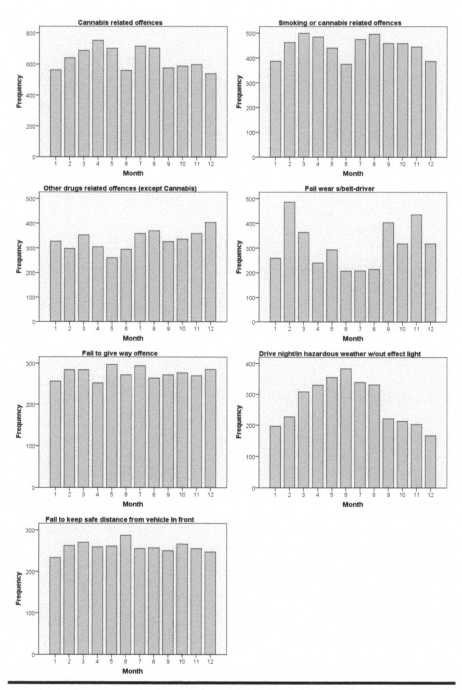

Figure 14.7 (CONTINUED) Monthly frequencies of top 15 traffic offenses.

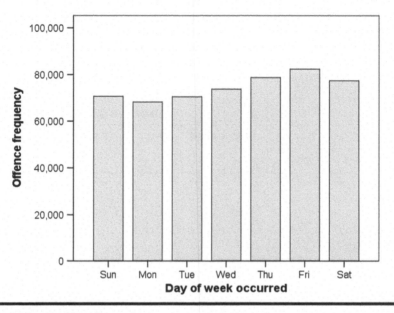

Figure 14.8 Traffic offense frequency against day of occurrence.

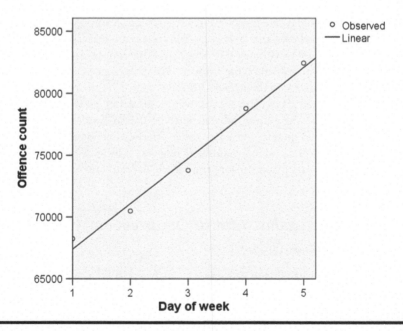

Figure 14.9 Regression model for daily offense frequency.

Table 14.6 Daily Offense Frequency Regression Model Summary and Parameter Estimates

	Unstandardized Coefficients			Model Summary			
	Coefficient Value	Std. Error	Sig.	R	R Square	Adjusted R Square	Std. Error of the Estimate
a	63733.3	904.588	0.000	0.992	0.984	0.978	862.49
b	3670.1	272.743	0.001				

14.3.5.2 Top 15 Traffic Offense Frequency against the Day of the Week

Figure 14.10 shows the frequency of each traffic offense according to the day of the week. It clearly illustrates the variation in the number of occurrences over a week. In the graphs, 1–7 represent the days starting from Sunday to Saturday.

14.3.5.3 Obtained Results

Thursday and Friday showed the highest number of incidences, whereas Monday was the lowest, although there is no significant fluctuation among the 7-day counts. However, the graph shows that there is a very clear increase in the number of offenses during the week (Monday to Friday). In other words, each day number of offenses increases by almost the same amount. The difference between the Monday and Friday counts was approximately 15,000.

However, all seven days of the week were considered to analyze the top 15 offenses. According to the graphs, offenses such as alcohol- and drug-related violations are higher on weekends, but most other offenses do not show a significant increase. Also, offenses involving handheld devices, failing to wear the seatbelt, and failing to keep a safe distance from the vehicle in front are outstandingly lower during weekends.

14.3.6 Offenses against Time of Occurrence

14.3.6.1 Regression Model

The frequency of offenses during the day was analyzed in Figure 14.11.

However, in order to improve the analysis, the 48 time records (00:00, 00:30, 01:00, 01:30,…) were grouped into eight time slots as presented in Table 14.7.

Figure 14.12 clearly shows the variation in offense frequencies during each time slot.

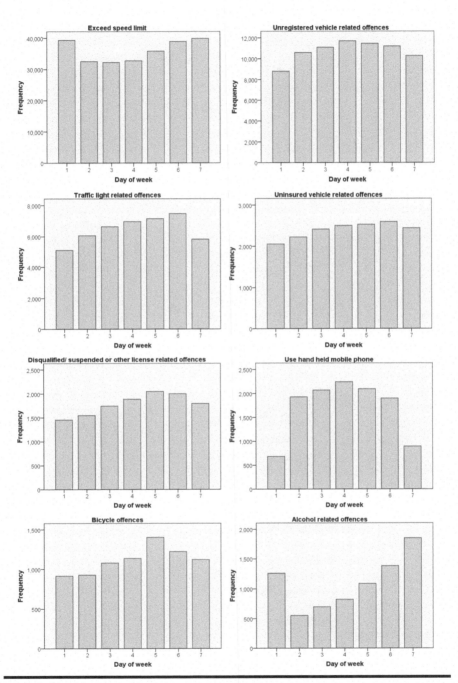

Figure 14.10 Daily frequencies of top 15 traffic offenses.

(*Continued*)

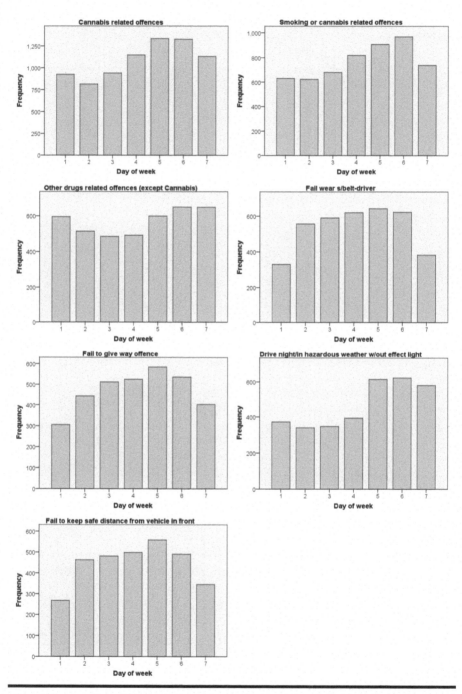

Figure 14.10 (CONTINUED) Daily frequencies of top 15 traffic offenses.

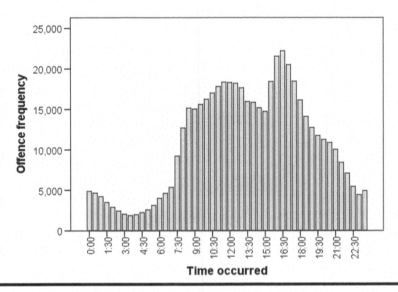

Figure 14.11   Traffic offense frequency against time of occurrence.

Table 14.7   Grouped Time Slots

Grouped Time Slot Number	Time period
1	0:00–3.00
2	3:30–6:00
3	6:30–9:00
4	9:30–12:00
5	12:30–15:00
6	15:30–18:00
7	18:30–21:00
8	21:30–23:30

For further analysis, a cubic graph was created through a regression curve estimation as illustrated in Figure 14.13 to understand the variation better.

Table 14.8 shows the summary and parameter estimates.

The R-squared value is 0.905, which indicated that there was a strong connection between the time slots and the number of expiations in each time slot. Furthermore, the p-value of 0.016 showed that the relationship was significant. Using the resulted parameter, the regression equation shown below was created.

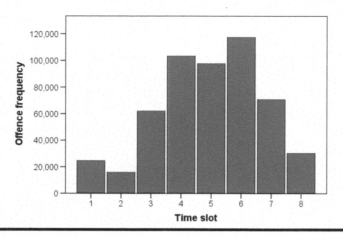

Figure 14.12 Traffic offense frequency against time slot of occurrence.

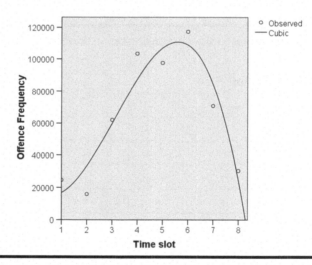

Figure 14.13 Regression model for timely offense frequency.

Table 14.8 Timely Offense Frequency Regression Model Summary and Parameter Estimates

	Model Summary					Parameter Estimates			
Equation	R Square	F	df1	df2	Sig.	a	B	c	d
Cubic	.905	12.702	3	4	.016	19,657.57	−15,544.93	14,228.95	−1,526.65

Note: The dependent variable is timely offense frequency, and the independent variable is timeslot.

The obtained regression model is $y = a + bx + cx^2 + dx^3$, where y is the offense count; b, c, and d are regression slopes; x is the time slot; and a is the regression intercept. Therefore, in order to predict the number of offenses in a particular time period, the equation $y = 19657.57 + -15544.93x + 14228.95x^2 + -1526.65x^3$ can be used.

14.3.6.2 Top 15 Traffic Offense Frequency against Time Period

Figure 14.14 shows the hourly frequencies of the top 15 traffic offenses. The graphs illustrate the disparity of offense frequencies among different time slots within a day. Each time period is grouped as outlined in Table 14.7.

14.3.6.3 Obtained Results

Compared to month and day of the week, time shows a highly significant fluctuation. The number of offenses increases slowly from the morning, peaking at 17:00, then dropping suddenly by midnight. That is, according to Figure 14.12, the number of offenses is highest from 15:30 to 18:00 and lowest between 03:30 and 06:00.

Although most of the offenses occurred during the daytime, bicycle-, alcohol-, drug-, and smoking-related traffic violations are outstandingly higher during midnight. Furthermore, the number of offenses of failing to wear a seatbelt, give way offenses, and failing to keep a safe distance from the vehicle in front shows fluctuations during the night time. To find the time periods of each offense, a cross-tabulation was used as shown in Table 14.9.

Table 14.9 shows the maximum number of offenses by type that occurred on Thursdays and Fridays. Offenses such as traffic light- and speeding-related incidences that occur due to carelessness and impatience are highest from 15:30 to 18.00, whereas alcohol- and drug-related offenses show a variance. Therefore, in a separate graph, alcohol- and drug-related offenses during each time slot are presented in Figure 14.15.

According to Figure 14.15, alcohol-related offenses are higher in the evening up until midnight, whereas smoking- and drug-related offenses begin to rise from noon.

14.3.7 Summary of the Proposed Regression Models

Summary of the three regression models (proposed) generated to predict the frequency of traffic offenses is represented in Table 14.10.

14.4 Discussion

The aim of this research was to identify the frequency of offenses during different seasons of the year. This will help to identify possible reasons for the variation in

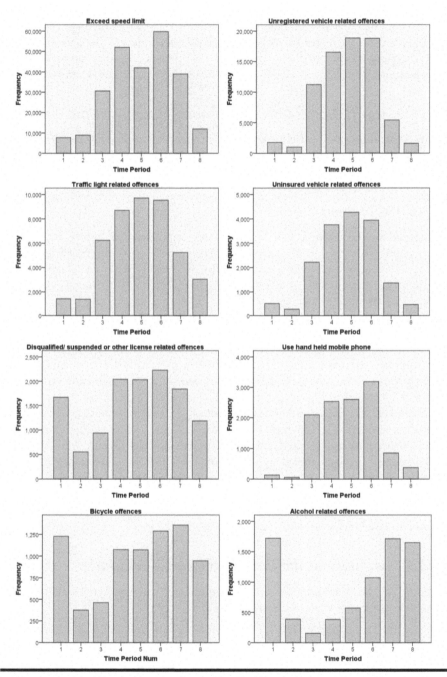

Figure 14.14 Hourly frequencies of top 15 traffic offenses.

(Continued)

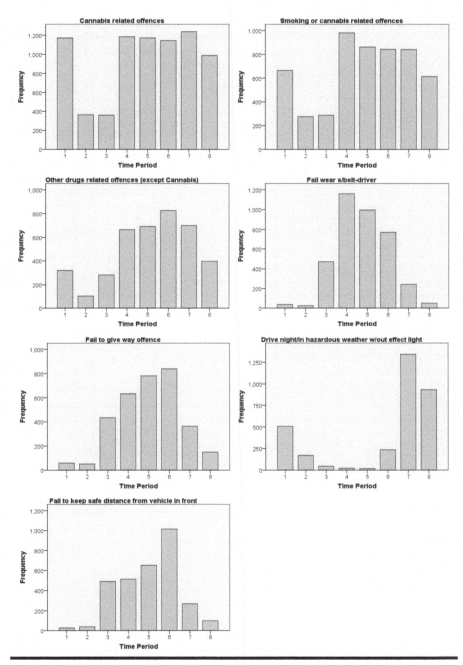

Figure 14.14 (CONTINUED) Hourly frequencies of top 15 traffic offenses.

Table 14.9 Mostly Occurred Time Periods of Offenses

Offense Type	Month	Day of the Week	Time Slot
[a]Bicycle offenses	January	Thursday	18:30–21:00
[a]Exceed speed limit	January	Saturday	15:30–18:00
[a]Fail wear s/belt-driver	February	Thursday	9:30–12:00
[a]Smoking- or cannabis-related offenses	March	Friday	9:30–12:00
[a]Cannabis-related offenses	April	Thursday	18:30–21:00
[a]Fail to give way offense	May	Thursday	15:30–18:00
[a]Drive at night/in hazardous weather w/out effective light	June	Friday	18:30–21:00
[a]Fail to keep safe distance from vehicle in front	June	Thursday	15:30–18:00
[a]Use of handheld mobile phone	September	Wednesday	15:30–18:00
[a]Alcohol-related offenses	December	Saturday	0:00–3.30
[a]Other drug-related offenses (except cannabis)	December	Friday	15:30–18:00
[a]Traffic light-related offenses	December	Friday	12:30–15:00
Uninsured vehicle-related offenses	January	Friday	12:30–15:00
Unregistered vehicle-related offenses	January	Wednesday	12:30–15:00
Disqualified/suspended or other license-related offenses	July	Thursday	15:30–18:00

[a] Directly time-related offenses.

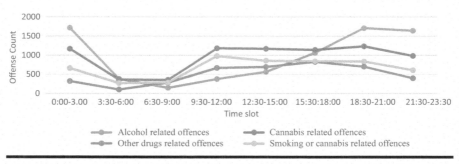

Figure 14.15 Alcohol-, smoking-, and drug-related offenses against time slot.

Table 14.10 Summary of the Proposed Regression Models

Item	Figure No.	Best-Fit Model	Coefficient (a)	Coefficient (b)	Coefficient (c)	Coefficient (d)	R^2 Value
Offenses against month of occurrence	6	Polynomial $F(x) = bx + cx^2 + a$	48,092.25	–2,051.97	161.16	–	0.591
Offenses against weekday of occurrence	9	Polynomial $F(x) = bx + a$	63,733.3	3670.1	–	–	0.984
Offenses against time of occurrence	13	Polynomial $F(x) = a + bx + cx^2 + dx^3$	19,657.57	–15,544.93	14,228.95	–1,526.65	0.905

offenses and to attain a better understanding of seasonal patterns of traffic violations so that research can help reduce road danger.

The major finding determined from the results was that the offense frequencies are approximately similar in both 2015 and 2016, but the offense frequency during different times of the year varies.

In terms of the month when offenses occurred, the holiday season of December and January had the highest overall offense rates. The amount of alcohol consumption can be taken as one of the reasons for the increased offenses during this time [12,13] as the alcohol-related offenses are dramatically higher in these periods. Furthermore, several studies [14–16] have shown that driving under the influence of alcohol is one of the major reasons for traffic accidents and alcohol can result in other offenses, such as exceeding the speed limit. A Norwegian study [17] showed that alcohol-related accidents are more dangerous than drug-related offenses, such as taking a medicinal drug, cannabis, amphetamine, or methamphetamine. However, cannabis-related offenses are higher in April compared to other months. In the cannabis culture, the "weed day" or "420 days" falls on April every year to protest for the legalization of marijuana and people use more Marijuana during this period [18]. This can lead to more cannabis-related offenses during this period of the year. In addition, during summer people tend to go outdoors and enjoy the hedonistic existence of festivals [13], thus exposing themselves to more traffic offenses, unlike in winter when people are usually home. Compared to June, the months of December and January have approximately 10,000 more recorded offenses proving that more offenses happen during the summer season. Also, the use of handheld mobile phones distracts drivers, thus causing traffic offenses [15], and the frequency fluctuates throughout the year; unlike other offenses, it is dramatically low during the December and January periods. Also, the number of offenses caused by driving at night in hazardous weather without effective lights is higher during May to August, which is the winter season that is darker than the other months of the year. Next, narrowing down from months to weeks, the discussion focuses on how the offense count varies during each day of a week.

The analysis of offenses during weekdays shows an overall traffic violation rise from Monday to Friday, whereas the frequencies stay the same over the weekend. From the start to the end of the week, the offenses increase by 5.4%. People are more reinvigorated and ready to start the week on Monday, but by Friday weekend parties and alcohol consumption increase resulting in a rise in traffic violations. A study done with a group of Chinese workers showed that daily work stress is strongly related to the use of alcohol [19]. In other words, after working through the week, stress drives them to consume alcohol. Furthermore, among students, Thursday is known as "Thirsty Thursday" [20] as it is the time to party and drink alcohol. At the same time, there is also an increase in alcohol-, cannabis-, smoking-, and other drug-related offenses, starting from Thursdays that last up to Sundays. Furthermore, alcohol and drug consumption lead to speeding offenses that occur more frequently during the same days of the week. In addition, both pedestrians and drivers are exposed to road dangers due to irresponsible alcohol intake, especially during the festive season. The use of handheld mobile phone offenses dramatically drops by approximately 70% on the weekends compared to weekdays. This is because during the business hours and in the busy weekdays people use their mobile phones more even while driving. This distraction can cause drivers to violate traffic light laws, exceed speed limits, fail to keep a safe distance from the vehicle in front, and not wear a seatbelt. Moreover, driving at night in hazardous weather without effective lights is highest from Thursday to Saturday. This could be caused by people tending to stay longer at parties during this period rather than the other days and it leads them to drive at night, which could make the drivers sleepy and lead to traffic accidents [21]. Next, an analysis of the time periods in which traffic violations occur will be discussed.

Considering the overall frequencies, the time from 09:30 to 18:00 showed the highest number of traffic violations. There was an 83% increase from the period of 03:30 to 06:00, with the highest number of recorded offenses occurring between 1530 and 1800. Exceeding the speed limit, traffic light-related offenses, the use of handheld devices, failure to give way, and failure to keep a safe distance from the vehicle in front are also higher from 15:30 to 18:00. This is the peak traffic time when people return home from work violating more laws and increasing road danger. For instance, getting stuck in a long queue of vehicles at a traffic signal gives drivers an urge to pass the lights as soon as possible, which can result in traffic-related offenses, such as exceeding speed limits and failing to give way. The alcohol-related offenses are highest between 18:30 and 03:00 as people consume alcohol after regular business hours and this explains the reason for most of these offenses. However, the number of smoking-, cannabis-, and other drug-related offenses were highest most of the time, except during 03:30 to 09:00. Unlike alcohol, cannabis and certain drugs stay in the body for a longer period. Therefore, officers can detect the drugs even when they were taken hours ago. For instance, on an average, cannabinoid level is detectable for up to 9.8 days [22] in the body of a frequent cannabis user. Furthermore, failure to wear a seat belt is highest from 09:30 to 12:00; as the regular offices start around 9:00, the drivers might forget to wear seat belts in their hurry to reach office on time.

With the discussion of traffic offenses during different time periods of a year it is proved that application of big data analysis is important and can be used to obtain thoughtful and reasonable decisions. Data science is a broad subject starting from a simple descriptive analysis to deep learning neural networks. Depending on the factors such as data types, necessary results, and available infrastructures, different techniques and methods can be used for the analysis [23–27].

This research will help scholars understand the correlation between times and incidences that lead to time specific traffic violations so that further actions can be taken by creating feasible policies to reduce them.

14.5 Conclusion

This study showed that there was a significant fluctuation in the number of traffic offenses depending on the time and day of occurrence. Using 521,811 traffic offense data instances, this study clearly illustrated that the traffic offense count increases during festival times, weekends, and during the evening. Moreover, further analysis shows variations in the different types of violations. For instance, it distinctly showed that speeding offenses are higher during the evenings and drugs-related traffic offenses are higher from noon to midnight. The analysis will be helpful for police officers, traffic authorities, psychologists, and other researchers interested in traffic-related offenses since it intends to deliver improved solutions to reduce road danger and enhance road safety. Also, sustainable transport policies can be created with active transport strategies to optimize danger reduction. However, based on this study, further research can be carried out to find out the psychological aspects that lead to offenses during different times.

In addition to the insights on traffic violations, this research also proved that big data analysis is very useful for making important decisions. Unlike assumptions, analyzing real data is helpful in coming to more practical conclusions and in predicting future trends. Therefore, the theories that were applied to traffic and transportation in this chapter can be similarly used to a vast range of domains to scrutinize real-world problems in detail.

References

1. Corporate Statistics, Victoria Police. (2017). *Vehicle Impoundment Statistics 2007–2016.*
2. Australian Bureau of Statistics. (2016). *9309.0- Motor Vehicle Census, Australia.*
3. Bucchi, A., Sangiorgi, C., & Vignali, V. (2012). Traffic psychology and driver behavior. *Procedia—Social and Behavioral Sciences, 53*, 972–979. http://dx.doi.org/10.1016/j.sbspro.2012.09.946.
4. Precht, L., Keinath, A., & Krems, J. (2017). Effects of driving anger on driver behavior: Results from naturalistic driving data. *Transportation Research Part F: Traffic Psychology and Behaviour, 45*, 75–92. http://dx.doi.org/10.1016/j.trf.2016.10.019.
5. Papadimitriou, E., Yannis, G., & Golias, J. (2009). A critical assessment of pedestrian behaviour models. *Transportation Research Part F: Traffic Psychology and Behaviour, 12*(3), 242–255. http://dx.doi.org/10.1016/j.trf.2008.12.004.
6. Hu, T., Xie, X., & Li, J. (2013). Negative or positive? The effect of emotion and mood on risky driving. *Transportation Research Part F: Traffic Psychology and Behaviour, 16*, 29–40. http://dx.doi.org/10.1016/j.trf.2012.08.009.
7. Babson, K., & Feldner, M. (2015). *Sleep and Affect* (1st ed.).
8. Hammar, L. M., Emami, A., Engström, G., & Götell, E. (2010). Reactions of persons with dementia to caregivers singing in morning care situations. *The Open Nursing Journal, 4*, 35.
9. Li, X., Er, M., Lim, B., Zhou, J., Gan, O., & Rutkowski, L. (2010). Fuzzy regression modeling for tool performance prediction and degradation detection. *International Journal of Neural Systems, 20*(05), 405–419. http://dx.doi.org/10.1142/s0129065710002498.

10. Ahmadi, H., Pham, N., Ganti, R., Abdelzaher, T., Nath, S., & Han, J. (2010). Privacy-aware regression modeling of participatory sensing data. *Proceedings of the 8th ACM Conference on Embedded Networked Sensor Systems—Sensys '10.* http://dx.doi.org/10.1145/1869983.1869994.

11. Duwe, G., & Freske, P. (2012). Using logistic regression modeling to predict sexual recidivism. *Sexual Abuse: A Journal of Research and Treatment, 24*(4), 350–377. http://dx.doi.org/10.1177/1079063211429470.

12. Wellings, K., Macdowall, W., Catchpole, M., & Goodrich, J. (1999). Seasonal variations in sexual activity and their implications for sexual health promotion. *Journal of the Royal Society of Medicine, 92*(2), 60–64. http://dx.doi.org/10.1177/014107689909200204.

13. Stamps, D., & Carr, M. (2012). Holiday season for a healthy heart. *Critical Care Nursing Clinics of North America,* 24(4), 519–525. http://dx.doi.org/10.1016/j.ccell.2012.07.007.

14. Dai, J., Teng, J., Bai, X., Shen, Z., & Xuan, D. (2010). Mobile phone based drunk driving detection. *Proceedings of the 4th International ICST Conference on Pervasive Computing Technologies for Healthcare.* http://dx.doi.org/10.4108/icst.pervasivehealth2010.8901.

15. Pöysti, L., Rajalin, S., & Summala, H. (2005). Factors influencing the use of cellular (mobile) phone during driving and hazards while using it. *Accident Analysis & Prevention, 37*(1), 47–51. http://dx.doi.org/10.1016/j.aap.2004.06.003.

16. Wellings, K., Macdowall, W., Catchpole, M., & Goodrich, J. (1999). Seasonal variations in sexual activity and their implications for sexual health promotion. *Journal of the Royal Society of Medicine, 92*(2), 60–64. http://dx.doi.org/10.1177/014107689909200204.

17. Gjerde, H., Normann, P., Christophersen, A., Samuelsen, S., & Mørland, J. (2011). Alcohol, psychoactive drugs and fatal road traffic accidents in Norway: A case–control study. *Accident Analysis & Prevention, 43*(3), 1197–1203. http://dx.doi.org/10.1016/j.aap.2010.12.034.

18. Doherty, E., & Haddou, J. (2016). Green light for dope-smoking picnics. *Heraldsun.com.au.* Retrieved August 6, 2017, from www.heraldsun.com.au/news/law-order/police-allow-dopesmoking-melbourne-picnics-dubbing-them-freedom-of-expression/news-story/787528d80a7e92926cdf467c12eadaa5.

19. Liu, S., Wang, M., Zhan, Y., & Shi, J. (2009). Daily work stress and alcohol use: Testing the cross-level moderation effects of neuroticism and job involvement. *Personnel Psychology, 62*(3), 575–597. http://dx.doi.org/10.1111/j.1744-6570.2009.01149.x.

20. Henderson, A. (2010). Push to reinstate "Thirsty thursday" grog ban. *ABC News.* Retrieved August 6, 2017, from www.abc.net.au/news/2010-10-22/push-to-reinstate-thirsty-thursday-grog-ban/2308276.

21. Åkerstedt, T., Hallvig, D., Anund, A., Fors, C., Schwarz, J., & Kecklund, G. (2013). Having to stop driving at night because of dangerous sleepiness—awareness, physiology and behaviour. Journal of Sleep Research, 22(4), 380–388. http://dx.doi.org/10.1111/jsr.12042.

22. Johansson, E., & Halldin, M. (1989). Urinary excretion half-life of 1-Tetrahydrocannabinol-7-oic acid in heavy marijuana users after smoking. *Journal of Analytical Toxicology,* 13(4), 218–223. http://dx.doi.org/10.1093/jat/13.4.218.

23. Singh, A., Halgamuge, M. N., & Lakshmiganthan, R. (December 2017). Impact of different data types on classifier performance of random forest, Naïve Bayes, and k-nearest neighbors algorithms. *International Journal of Advanced Computer Science and Applications (IJACSA),* 8(12), 1–10.

24. Halgamuge, M. N. (November 2017). Machine learning for bioelectromagnetics: Prediction model for weak radiofrequency radiation effect from mobile phone on plants. *International Journal of Advanced Computer Science and Applications (IJACSA),* 8(11), 223–235.

25. Wanigasooriya, C., Halgamuge, M. N., & Mohamad, A. (September 2017). The analyzes of anticancer drug sensitivity of lung cancer cell lines by using machine learning clustering techniques. *International Journal of Advanced Computer Science and Applications (IJACSA)*, 8(9).
26. Gupta, A., Mohammad, A., Syed, A., & Halgamuge, M. N. (August 2016). A comparative study of classification algorithms using data mining: Crime and accidents in denver city the USA. *International Journal of Advanced Computer Science and Applications (IJACSA)*, 7(7), 374–381.
27. Bashyal, C., Halgamuge, M. N., & Mohammad, A. (January 2018). Review on Analysis of the Application Areas and Algorithms used in Data Wrangling in Big Data. Lecture Notes on Data Engineering and Communications Technologies Cognitive Computing for Big Data Systems Over IoT, Frameworks, Tools and Applications, Springer, 14, Chapter 14, ISBN: 978-3-319–70687-0.

Chapter 15

Intrusion Detection for Big Data

Biozid Bostami
Islamic University of Technology
Mohiuddin Ahmed
Canberra Institute of Technology

Contents

Big data, a technology which stores the data in distributed cloud infrastructures, is changing the business logic and application models. The valuable information that big data contains is driving the decisions businesses are making toward data-driven processes. However, when it comes to security, it is the concern of the owners and users. Security and privacy can be increased by securing the computing environment. In network security scheme, intrusion detection systems (IDSs) play a vital role. This chapter explores the collaborative intrusion detection systems that enhance the security of the big data and also handle the cloud vulnerabilities. Cyberattack sources are heterogeneous. Correlating cyberattack incidents generated from different sources and time can provide a concrete view and an increased awareness about the vulnerabilities of cyberattacks. Conventional intrusion detection systems are not suitable for distributed environments and they cannot detect cooperative attacks. For defending against the correlated attacks collaborative intrusion systems are introduced that analyze the suspicious behaviors collected from other IDSs to increase the efficiency of intrusion detection.

Coordinated attacks are also a common scenario in big data. Such attacks like large-scale stealthy scans, worm outbreaks, and distributed denial-of-service (DDoS) attacks occur simultaneously over multiple networks and this makes it nearly impossible for a standalone intrusion detection system (IDS) to detect such attacks as it can only monitor certain portions of the network. In this chapter, we have presented a brief summary of the research done on coordinated attacks with collaborative intrusion detection systems (CIDSs).

Finally, this chapter will be helpful for both the security and data analytics professionals, academics, and graduate level students.

15.1 Big Data and Intrusion Detection System

We live in an era where every aspect of our life is influenced by data. From streaming music to analysis of health problem diagnosis, everything is dependent on data. With the emergence of big data, it is now possible to analyze data and give a quick response. With big data scalability, availability is no longer a problem. There are three Vs that define big data: velocity, volume, and variety. Volume represents the amount of data. Data processing speed represents the volume of big data. Variety in big data is represented by the complexity raised by the heterogeneous sources of data. Big data has opened up new doors for inventions and future products. But the flip side of the coin is that big data is also the prime target of data security issues for criminal activities and malware. Intrusion detection is one of the main cybersecurity issues in the field of big data. In order to protect the data from different types of cyberattacks, organizations implement intrusion detection systems. The system that detects different kinds of intrusions and protects systems from different attacks acts as the second line of defense. An IDS monitors a host or a network and analyzes it for signs of intrusions that are manifested by malicious behavior or security policy violations. Thus, its goal is the detection of any attempt to compromise confidentiality, integrity, availability, or simply to bypass the security mechanisms of a computer or network [3]. But traditional intrusion detection systems are not suitable for the distributed architecture of big data. That is why collaborative intrusion detection systems are proposed. Collaborative intrusion detection systems monitor from different endpoints of the network and takes decision collectively, which is much more secure than traditional intrusion detection approaches. In this chapter, we will explore state-of-the-art methods and techniques in network intrusion detection and the advances and challenges of big data analytics in intrusion detection to explore new techniques that aid in intrusion detection analysis.

15.1.1 Chapter Roadmap

In this chapter, we give an overview of the intrusion detection systems for the big data architecture. In this chapter, the key aspects of big data analytics are presented in detail. Section 15.2 starts with the definition of big data. Section 15.3 reflects the challenges associated with big data. Section 15.4 provides introduction to intrusion detection systems. Section 15.5 discusses about the classification of intrusion systems. In Section 15.6, we introduce collaborative intrusion systems for big data. Section 15.7 focuses on the architecture of the collaborative intrusion systems. Section 15.8 presents the building blocks, Section 15.9 describes different types of attacks of CIDS, and Section 15.10 gives a brief idea about the importance of CIDS in a cloud environment. In Section 15.11, we discuss about some of the well-known coordinated attacks and in Section 15.12, we present the research done by different researchers and explore their limitations and strong points. Finally, in Section 15.13, we conclude the chapter by discussing about the opportunities.

15.2 What is Big Data?

The concept of big data has been around for years [1]. It is used by different communities like technological enterprises, scientific organizations, research scholars, data analysts, and technical practitioners, etc. They all have different definitions of big data. Big data can be defined as a collection of large datasets that cannot be processed using traditional computing technologies, such as tools/software [2]. It is highly connected with the system configuration, i.e., RAM and HDD capacity [4]. NIST [6] defines big data as following: "Big data means the data of which the data volume, acquisition speed, or data representation limits the capacity of using traditional relational methods to conduct effective analysis or the data which may be effectively processed with important horizontal zoom technologies, which focuses on the technological aspect of Big data." IBM and Microsoft [5,7] also define big data in terms of the three Vs model: "In the 3V model, Volume means, with the generation and collection of masses of data, data scale becomes increasingly Big; Velocity means the timeliness of Big data; Variety indicates the various types of data, which include semi-structured and unstructured data such as audio, video, web page, and text, as well as traditional structured data." In many literature, big data is described in terms of Vs as volume, variety, variability, velocity, and veracity [9]. Volume represents the amount and dimensionality of the data. The diverse sources of data are the main attractions for companies in the fields of health care, social networking, finance, or genetics. Variety refers to the heterogeneity and mixing of data. In big data analysis, the data do not follow any ordered form. These data can be highly structured, semi-structured, or unstructured like video, audio, or images [10]. Velocity involves the streaming of big data from sources for analysis and decision-making. Veracity is related to the certainty, precision, approximation, ambiguities, and latency. Due to veracity, results derived from big data cannot be proven, but they can be assigned a probability [9]. Variability is more related to the variety in terms of semantics and communication protocol [10]. In a summarized way we can define big data as datasets that could not be captured, managed, and processed by general computers within an acceptable scope [10]. In the next section, we will be focusing on the security issues of big data.

15.3 Security Issues with Big Data

The big data era brings a set of challenges in data acquisition, storage, management, analysis, privacy, security, and so on. We will be focusing on the security and data privacy section. Cybersecurity is critical as computerized systems are evolving into a distributed nature. One of the most significant concerns in cybersecurity is intrusion detection. In order to prevent attacks, awareness of an attack is essential to be able to defend against attackers. Cyber defense can be improved by introducing intrusion detection systems that monitor the network and detect abnormality and suspicious activities and also take appropriate actions against them. Intrusion detection can be helpful in providing early warnings and in minimizing damage. In the next section, we will focus on the overview of intrusion detection systems.

15.4 Intrusion Detection System

The first layer of defense for data security consists of authentication, firewall, cryptography, authorization, etc., whereas the intrusion detection system is considered as the second line of defense [2]. To protect vital information, organizations implement intrusion detection and prevention systems (IDPS) [12]. An intrusion prevention system acts like an intrusion detection system with additional features for preventing repetitions of malicious events. By turning off the prevention feature, an intrusion prevention system can act as an intrusion detection system. An IDS can monitor different types of protocols. An IDS that monitors protocols like hypertext transfer protocol (HTTP) is known as protocol-based intrusion detection system (PIDS). Some IDSs are designed to monitor application-specific protocols, for example, database structured query language (SQL) protocol also known as application protocol-based intrusion detection system (APIDS). IDSs can be configured so that their behavior and output are altered according to the network host types and event sources [49].

Four types of data, which are honeypot data, http packet, DNS reply, and IP flow record, are used for correlation and monitoring. Flow record can provide information for botnet communications. Core router, NetFlow, provides all the communication over the Internet and enterprise networks and vice versa. HTTP packets contain uniform resource identifiers along with the payloads embedded in them, which can be studied to detect and prevent malicious communication over the network. DNS replies are monitored to detect and prevent malicious attacks at particular domains. A honeypot that emulates services and fake production data can be used to find out the attacker's target, IPaddress, network protocol, and scanning methods from the logging files [13].

In the following section, we will be describing the classification of intrusion detection systems.

15.5 Classification of Intrusion Detection Systems

Based on the location point and anomaly detection techniques intrusion detection systems can be classified into different types. We will be describing them in the following section.

15.5.1 Location-Based Classification

Depending on the location of deployment in a network, IDSs can be classified into two categories. They are host-based intrusion detection system and network-based intrusion detection system [14].

Host-based intrusion detection system is responsible for monitoring individual devices or hosts. It monitors all the incoming and outgoing traffic to Internet and vice versa of the attached host as well as monitors the internal system calls. But it is not aware of the overall network situation. That is the limitation of host-based intrusion detection systems.

Network-based IDSs (NIDS) situated at the edge points of the network are responsible for monitoring the traffic at those points. NIDs use the packet sniffers and analyze the data to correlate the intrusion. Whenever suspicious packet or traffic is detected the alarm is triggered. But, NIDs are unaware of the internal network activities.

15.5.2 Evaluation Criteria-Based Classification

Depending on the evaluation methods of intrusion detection, the intrusion detection system can be classified into three major types: signature-based intrusion detection, anomaly-based detection, and hybrid intrusion detection system.

Signature-based intrusion is also known as misuse detection. It considers the behavior as a mode and matches whether the behavior of the subject conforms to a mode. The modes are also known as signature features. That's why it is called signature-based intrusion detection. The network specialist can design newer modes based on the attack signature or the behavior, if any unknown attack is found and studied. This type of intrusion detection is very good at detecting the attacks with known signatures and it creates less number of false positive alerts. But if the attack signature is altered then it cannot detect the attacks as efficiently.

Anomaly detection analyzes the historical data over a period of time and builds up the pattern to detect abnormal behavior over the network. The main drawback of this system is in designing and training of the algorithm. The anomaly detection algorithm can use the unsupervised learning approach that does not need the labelled pattern but creates high false alarms [16]. Anomaly-based detection is limited to the network layer only; it cannot detect the attack if the payload is involved, for example, an attack on Microsoft IIS induces the users to download a malicious script file. Since there are no invalid packet header fields involved, header-based techniques will not trigger any alarm. Malicious payload, remote-to-local (R2L), and user-to-root (U2R) belong to application level attacks; if the payload is ignored in anomaly-based detection, poor performance in detecting payload associated attacks is obvious [17].

The hybrid-based detection approach is a combination of both anomaly-based detection and signature-based detection to improve the performance of the detection and prevention systems [18] (Tables 15.1 and 15.2).

Table 15.1 Overview of the Signature-Based Method and the Anomaly-Based Method for Intrusion Detection [18]

Methodology	Description	Limitation
Signature-Based Detection	Takes decisions based on known attacking pattern or signatures.	• Need to update to identify the new attacks. • False negative rate is high.
Anomaly-Based Detection	Learns from known activity and alerts when significant deviation is noticed.	• Designing the algorithm is costly. • False positive rate is high.

In the following section, we will be focusing on the intrusion detection systems designed for distributed architecture like big data, which is known as the collaborative intrusion detection system, and on its necessity.

15.6 Collaborative Intrusion Detection and Big Data

A collaborative intrusion detection network (CIDN) is a network of connected intrusion detection systems (IDSs). It allows the exchange of intrusion alerts, suspicious files, blacklists, and detection rules among the IDSs. CIDS acts like a dynamic distributed system where the participating IDSs form new organizational structures like teams and play different roles to accomplish a common goal which is not achievable through single participation. Enterprise networks like big data and cloud computing environments is built upon the distributed nature with multiple entry points. This widely adopted topology ensures and enhances the accessibility and availability of the network. But this topology possesses security vulnerabilities that are exploited by the attackers with advanced attack schemes, like cooperative intrusions. Unlike traditional attack schemes, cooperative intrusions are directed by the botnets and attacks are launched simultaneously by the slaved machines. Attack instances are organized by the attacker at all the entry points of the enterprise network to penetrate the system. Since the attack traffic is evenly distributed these cooperative intrusions can evade detection by the traditional standalone IDSs. This is because the standalone IDSs do not raise an alarm if the traffic at every entry point does not deviate from normal behavior. After exploring all the ports of the network, the cooperative attack targets the vulnerable services within the network. Even an attacker can initiate attacks on all the vulnerable services simultaneously over the network. To match these types of attacks, intrusion detection needs to improve.

Table 15.2 Performance Evaluation of Three Detection Methods [19]

Detection Techniques	Alarm Rate	Speed	Resource Consumption	Flexibility	Scalability	Robustness
Anomaly	High	Low	High	High	High	High
Signature	Low	High	Low	Low	Low	Low
Hybrid	Moderate	Moderate	High	High	High	High

15.6.1 Why Is It Necessary?

Traditional standalone IDSs are likely to be invaded by the cooperative attacks, so their performance is poor in the distributed environment cloud computing or big data. By correlating suspicious evidence between different IDSs, collaborative intrusion detection systems (CIDSs) improve the efficiency of intrusion detection. Unlike conventional standalone IDSs, IDSs located at a local network's entry points share the information among themselves. In practice, the IDS is organized within the CIDS over a large network following a decentralized or hierarchical pattern. Communication takes place between each IDS directly or via a central coordinator through the applied mode. By aggregating the network information received from other IDSs in the CIDS, a complete attack diagram of the network is generated. The central coordinator, which analyzes the aggregated information, generates a complete attack diagram of the network. Collaborative intrusion and malware detection offers an anonymous communication scheme. Participating IDSs can share information with the interested partners based on the intrusion ontology. CIDS also provides a decentralized group formation algorithm and a robust collaborative model.

In the following section, we will be describing the architecture of collaborative intrusion detection systems and their classification.

15.7 Architecture of CIDS

Early IDSs were designed to monitor a single host or port over a network by carrying out local analysis. There was no scope for communication. Clearly, those design approaches are not suitable for distributed networks. They were not designed to establish connection between events occurring in different places simultaneously. Thus, collaborative IDS (CIDS) was proposed for the protection of large networks and large IT ecosystems. CIDS is a collection of several monitors acting as sensors and collecting data. They usually contain several analysis units that are responsible for intrusion detection from the collected data coming from sensors. Complex task done by the network administrator is significantly reduced by the CIDS because it provides high accuracy in intrusion detection [8]. Based on the specification, monitoring and the analysis unit can be co-located. In this chapter, we will assume that a monitor is built with both the monitoring unit and the analysis unit. By ensuring cooperation between the monitors, CIDS becomes more scalable than traditional IDS. Following their communication architecture, CIDS can be classified into three different categories: centralized, decentralized, and distributed CIDS.

15.7.1 Centralized Architecture

In this architecture, several IDSs are attached to their respective hosts for monitoring the traffic and behavior (as shown in Figure 15.1). Monitored data is then shared with

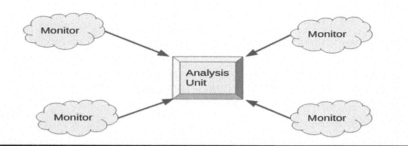

Figure 15.1   Centralized architecture.

the central unit for analysis. The data sent to the central monitor can be either local traffic or they can be alerts produced by intrusion detection. Hence, alert correlation algorithm is applied on the alerts sent by other monitors or the detection algorithm is applied by the central unit.

But this architecture has some limitations. As a standalone IDS, with the increasing size of the system, centralized CIDS cannot be scaled easily. This architecture works for small-scale enterprise networks. It has two major drawbacks. If the central unit fails then complete alert correlation will fail as well since it is dependent on the central unit. It is commonly known as the single point of failure (SPoF). The second drawback is that all the edge monitors send the monitored data to the central unit. If the data flow exceeds the capacity of the central unit then some data might get loss and the performance might decrease.

15.7.2 Hierarchical Architecture

For overcoming the drawbacks of a centralized design, the hierarchical architecture was proposed. In this architectural design, the CIDSs are placed in a hierarchical model that is based on multiple small communication groups. This group formation is done by some of these features: (1) administrative controlling, (2) geographical position, (3) similarity of the platform, and (4) intrusion type. Every communication group acts as a subset of the overall hierarchy. Every group has a parent analysis node that is responsible for correlating all the alerts and traffic data belonging to the respective group. After data from edge node is collected by the parent node of a group then it forwards the processed data to the higher order node in the hierarchy for analysis. Usually, IDS situated at the base level of the hierarchy acts as the detecting unit. IDSs situated at the higher levels act as detection units as well as correlation units. Higher-level nodes do all the analysis on the data sent by the lower level nodes. After correlation and analysis of the alerts and the traffic data, the result is sent to the higher level and this continues until it reaches the maximum level from where the decision is distributed to the lower levels.

The hierarchical architecture (as in Figure 15.2) works better than the centralized design, but it still has some drawbacks. The whole system can be hampered

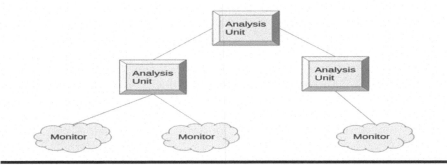

Figure 15.2   Hierarchical architecture.

if the higher-level nodes stop their functionality. In that case, the whole hierarchy will fail. Moreover, at the top level, it is difficult to scale, keeping pace with the increased network. Again, due to input data abstraction at the top-level nodes, there is limited detection coverage.

15.7.3 *Distributed Architecture*

In the distributed architecture, the task of analysis is distributed among all the monitors in the network, making sure that each monitor has its own analysis unit and is not directly dependent on other nodes for analysis. The distributed architecture is similar to the peer-to-peer (P2P) architecture in which the data correlation, data aggregation, and data analysis are done in a distributed manner with the participation of all the monitors.

The fully distributed architecture focuses on the scalability property of CIDS. But there are still many challenges and open issues related to accuracy of detection, scale, and load balance.

- **Accuracy:** Depending on the information dissemination, some attack information does not get access to the place where the decision is made for a particular attack. That is why to get the same accuracy rate as compared to the centralized approach, we need to take into account the trade-offs between false alarm and rate of detection. The common goal of intrusion detection research is to achieve maximum accuracy and minimum false alarm proportion. But most of the distributed approach focus on the architectural design rather than on detection accuracy.
- **Scale of Alert Correlation:** One of the key features of intrusion detection is alert correlation. The fully distributed approaches usually use the source IP address for representing the alert information. This is known as the single dimension feature where a single attribute is used for correlation. However, it cannot provide information for large-scale attacks. So, scaling of alert correlation is still an open issue.

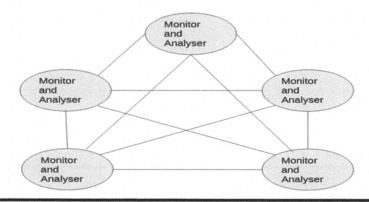

Figure 15.3 Distributed architecture.

- **Load Balance:** Another open issue in the distributed architecture is to balance load across all the IDSs so that no single IDS is overloaded by the traffic (Figure 15.3).

In the following section, we will be focusing on the building blocks of collaborative intrusion detection systems.

15.8 Building Blocks of CIDS

Designing a CIDS is a challenging task. These challenges minimize the data exchange rate; maximizing the detection rate; taking decision on communication scheme for data sharing; distribution of alert information; aggregation of the data, etc. Based on the challenges, the structure of CIDS is separated into five building blocks: (1) local monitoring, (2) membership, (3) data dissemination, (4) data aggregation and correlation, and (5) global monitoring.

15.8.1 Local Monitoring

Local monitoring can be of two types: host level monitoring and network level monitoring. In case of host level monitoring, only the associated hosts behaviors are considered. On the other hand, network level monitoring aims to cover the whole network from attacks by deploying CIDS at selected points on the edge that are closer to the ingress or egress routers of the network. A combination of both host level and network level deploy can further increase the detection accuracy.

Monitoring can be divided into active monitoring and passive monitoring. Passive monitoring comprises host level monitoring or networking level monitoring. Honeypots are used for passive monitoring for detecting the presence of promising attack targets. Although honeypot's false positive is zero, the false negative rate is quite high.

In local monitoring, the analysis unit uses a detection mechanism from the data collected by the sensors. The detection mechanism can be signature based or can be anomaly based. Even combination is also possible, which was proposed as Bro IDS [48].

Local monitoring act as a vital part in designing an optimal CIDS because the data collected by the local monitors is utilized by the other blocks.

15.8.2 Membership Management

The task of membership management unit is to establish overall connectivity between all the neighboring monitors. Membership management can be of static type or it can be dynamic by nature. In its static nature, whenever a new component is added the network administrator needs to alter the overlay of the network. Connections are predetermined in static membership. On the other hand, in dynamic membership component a new component is added with the help of a central server that provides a global view or follows the membership protocol. This protocol is run locally at each CIDS. Since the membership controls the connectivity among the neighboring CIDSs the architecture of the network is also dependent on this unit. Based on the connectivity, the network architecture can be centralized, hierarchical, or completely distributed as described in the previous section.

15.8.3 Correlation and Aggregation

When the local monitors collect the data, it has to be analyzed for correlating the alerts, and the aggregated alert data information is needed to be sent to other monitors for further analysis.

Correlation can be of two types: (1) single monitor correlation and (2) monitor-to-monitor correlation. In case of single monitoring mechanism, the alert data information is not shared with the neighboring CIDSs. The local alert information is either sent to the administration interface or is redirected to the central units for further analysis. Alternatively, alert data information is shared with the neighboring CIDSs for correlating the information with their local data. In this, detailed information is shared among the monitors and not only among the list of IP addresses. One of the major challenges is correlating the multidimensional alert patterns [32]. Different examples can be given where the single dimensional attributes are not enough, e.g., when multiple nodes are attacked simultaneously or when a part of the system is attacked or sacrificed information from the victimized unit is not very helpful. That is why combination of different attributes are needed, like source and destination IPs, payload, port numbers, etc.

There are four different approaches for alert data correlation. Here we will give a brief description of them.

- **Similarity-based correlation:** In this approach, the alert data is compared between different sets for scoring the similarity. The more the score, the more correlated the alerts are. The similarity is usually checked with known alert information.
- **Attack scenario-based correlation:** The attack scenario-based approach can detect attacks at multiple levels. This approach maintains a dataset of known attacks. Such approaches can be found in the works of Dain and Cunningham [39], Garcia et al. [40], and Eckmann et al. [41]. These algorithms are trained under the dataset and that is why it shows high accuracy in detecting known attacks, whereas unknown attacks cannot be detected by this mechanism.
- **Multistage alert correlation:** Multistage alert correlation aims to detect unknown attacks based on the presumption that attacks are correlated, i.e., one attack is the first stage of preparation for another attack to follow. Multistage approach creates a library of attack steps that is used to correlate attack scenarios. The multistage approach is based on the correlation of attacks, i.e., it cannot detect attacks that do not have a correlation with one another. The accuracy of correlation is affected by the IDS false alerts. Moreover, creating the library can be sometimes costly.
- **Filter-based correlation:** To remove the overhead of costly and library dependent attack correlation approaches, a filter-based approach was proposed [46]. In this approach, the attacks are prioritized based on the impact using some filtering algorithms. To reduce the false positive rate, filters are used to filter out the irrelevant information [47]. In order to protect the system, detailed information about the respective systems must be known for the correlation, but sometimes it is not possible to provide such information. The information about the system measures the rate of accuracy.

15.8.4 Data Dissemination

CIDSs that focus on correlating alerts and aggregating information need to be efficiently distributed. Data dissemination is highly dependent upon the architectural design of the membership unit. In centralized design, the data flow is always the same. There the alert information always flows to the central analysis unit. On the other hand, the decentralized design monitors and maintains a hierarchy between them and sends the alert information in a bottom-up fashion. Distributed design provides high level of freedom for data sharing on a flat overlay. In a distributed approach, information can be shared in both directions for monitors having interest in similar information. The information among the groups can be shared via gossiping approach [44] or by flooding selectively/partially using random walks [45] or by flooding the total CIDS network. Some distributed approaches use distributed hash table to maintain the information flow.

15.8.5 Global Monitoring

The capabilities of a particular CIDS are based on global monitoring. Global monitoring aims to detect the distributed attacks. Based on the detection scope, global monitoring can be of two types: (1) generic type and (2) specific type. The generic type aims to detect multiple types of attacks. Specific types are used for specialized attacks. In a nutshell, global monitoring aims to detect malicious behavior over the CIDSs that are connected with each other representing the collaborative detection abilities.

15.9 Attacks on Collaborative Intrusion System

Even though collaborative intrusion detection systems are used to protect systems from cyberattacks, these systems can also be the target of cyberattacks. That is why one must be aware of the weaknesses and vulnerabilities of these systems. Based on the scope of the attackers, there can be two types of attacks on CIDS: (1) external attack and (2) internal attack.

15.9.1 External Attacks

The origin of the external attack is outside the network that is being monitored by the CIDSs. The external attacks aim to explore the presence of the CIDS monitoring points to plan future attacks to bypass the CIDS or to exploit the vulnerable services of CIDS to degrade the quality of service. External attacks can be classified into two types: (1) disclosure attack and (2) evasion attack.

15.9.1.1 Disclosure Attack

The disclosure attack aims at gathering the location information of the CIDSs in the target network. A disclosure attacker expects a feedback from the CIDS. These feedbacks can be of different types like the attack results publicly available in some website over the Internet. Yoichi et al. [50] in their work proposed a passive approach that takes the feedback from public websites. In their work, they gain information about the CIDS location as well as other information by analyzing the feedback graph that is updated periodically. An active approach was proposed by Shmatikov et al. where disclosure attack gathers information from public sites by the method named probe-response attacks [51]. In disclosure attacks, the attacker uses a known attack signature to identify the attack feedbacks. Evasion attacks are followed by the disclosure attacks. We will be discussing the evasion attacks in the next section.

15.9.2 Evasion Attack

The evasion attack aims to avoid the IDS so that no alert is initiated. There are many methods to achieve this goal. From the point of intrusion detection techniques, the evasion attack is divided into two types: (1) signature-based evasion and (2) anomaly-based evasion.

- **Signature-based evasion:** Signature-based evasion aims to bypass the IDS in which the detection mechanism is depending on a known signature. In order to bypass such IDSs, the attacker changes the signature of the attack slightly so that it no longer triggers the IDS alert for now it does not belong to the known attack set of the particular IDS. Some of the methods are described below.
  - **Attack Obfuscation:** In this method, the attack signature code is transferred to a equivalent code that is not known to the detection unit [43]. There are many tools available for testing obfuscation, for example, the metasploit framework.
  - **Packet Splitting:** In this method, the segmented IP packets are used because they cannot be assembled by the operating system properly and IDS cannot raise any alert [43].
  - **Overlapping Packet:** In this method, packets from known and safe data sources are overlapped by the attacking packets. Since operating systems can distinguish between the overlapping packets that is why no alert is generated.
  - **False Positive Flooding:** In this approach, IDS is attacked by a large number of parallel attacks having known signatures, which hide the actual attacks so that the IDS overlooks the actual attacks. There are many tools available and it requires a large number of known false positives.
- **Anomaly-based evasion:** Anomaly-based detection is capable of detecting unknown attacks based on historical data. Any deviation from the normal behavior triggers the alert in anomaly-based detection. In order to evade the anomaly-based detection, the attacker must train the attack data is such a way so that the attack does not deviate from the normal data [38]. There are several ways to carry out anomaly-based attacks: (1) injecting training data, (2) mimicry attacks, and (3) polymorphic blending attack.
  - **Injecting training data attack:** Injecting training data attack introduces the attack signature in the training phase of the algorithm. So when the actual attack occurs in the future the IDS considers is as a normal behavior.
  - **Mimicry attack:** Mimicry attack aims to evade the IDS by making the attack act as a normal request so that the IDS doesnot trigger any alert information [38,42].
  - **Polymorphic blending attacks:** It is similar to the mimicry attack, but it aims to exploit the fact that due to complexity the anomaly-based

algorithm only analyzes a particular area of the traffic. So, the attacker first creates a normal traffic profile and then blends the attack with it. Fogla et al. [37] in his work showed methods using PAYL, a byte frequency-based anomaly IDS, as a case study and demonstrates that polymorphic blending attacks are indeed feasible.

15.9.2.1 Internal Attack

The origin of the internal attack is located inside the monitored network by an insider. An insider can belong to a compromised CIDS monitoring unit or it can be a compromised host in the network. A compromised host within the protected network sets up a secret channel with an attacker outside the network. All the traffic between the compromised host and the attacker is hidden from the monitors [53,54]. The channel used by the compromised host is not usually used for communication, for example, unutilized bits of the packet header or the timing information. Internal attacks can become more harmful if a component of the CIDS is compromised. A compromised/malicious CIDS monitor can expose the location of other monitoring agents and it can compromise other monitoring agents by taking advantage of the vulnerability of the CIDS protocol. It can lead to a total takeover of the whole system at worst.

A generic countermeasure against malicious insiders in the distributed systems is the adoption of reputation systems [55,56], such as EigenTrust [57]. In this case, each of the monitors creates a level of trust depending on detection behavior or other defined properties. If the trust level goes below a certain threshold, the monitor is considered less trustworthy and preventive steps can be taken, for example, blacklisting of the malicious monitor. Several proposals have been given for trust management to avoid internal attacks [58–61]. Another problem with the reputation system occurs when the highly trusted monitors are compromised, which is known as the betrayal attack [58]. In another attack known as the sleeper attack, the compromised CIDS acts very gently until they gain a certain level of trust and then the target attack is carried out [62]. Internal attacks are even more harmful when combined with external attacks. Figure 15.4 summarizes the scenario.

In the following section, we will focus on the contribution of CIDS in the cloud infrastructure followed by a short introduction of the cloud.

15.10 Cloud Framework and Collaborative Intrusion Detection System

Cloud framework is a multi-tenant infrastructure which is shared by several users. As defined by NIST, "Cloud Computing is a model for enabling ubiquitous, convenient, on-demand network access to a shared pool of configurable computing

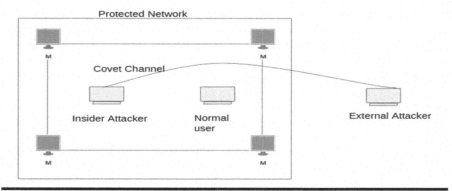

Figure 15.4 **Different attacks and attackers' location in secure networks.**

resources (e.g., networks, servers, storage, applications, and services) that can be rapidly provisioned and released with minimal management effort or service provider interaction." Cloud computing servers are basically operating systems (OS) where the users are clustered into separate groups by using virtual machines. Since the virtual machines reside in an operating system that is why threats of VM-to-VM attacks increases. With the presence of a collaborative cloud computing model, a large amount of data transfer occurs either between the local VMs or between the different clouds. These are highly attracted to the attacker and are primary targets of MITM or probing attacks. This information leakage can be followed by attacks like DDoS, worm spread, etc. which can affect not only the compromised clouds but also the connected cloud regions. Even the attacker can take advantage of other services of cloud computing to attack their victims. A collaborative intrusion detection system takes into consideration the suspicious activities and attack signatures from multiple sources of IDS to protect the cloud systems. The CIDS provides:

- Improvements in the security of the large-scale distributed environment.
- CIDS has less computational cost because they share information.
- The amount of false alarm gets reduced over the network.
- It can protect other cloud regions by sharing lists of malicious VMs over the network.

In the following section, we will be looking into the coordinated attacks. We will only present a short introduction to them.

15.11 Coordinated Attacks

Coordinated attacks are carried out by the attacker with the aim of monetary gain [36]. Some of the known coordinated attacks are large-scale stealthy scans, worms, and DDoS attacks. With the help of automation, it is easy to exploit different vulnerable services simultaneously [52]. The highly distributed nature makes these attacks more difficult to detect. In the following section, we review three main coordinated attack methods by exploring their topology, purpose, target services, etc.

15.11.1 Large-Scale Stealthy Scans

The large scale stealthy scans aim to gaining information about the target network. It gains information about ports and IP addresses that are to be exploited by the attacker [35]. To avoid the detection algorithm, the attacker randomized the scanning order or lowered the scan frequency over the targeted network. There are two types of stealthy scans: (1) block scan and (2) horizontal scan. Horizontal scan explores the targeted ports for vulnerability over the range of hosts. For example, TCP port 139 scans explore the NetBIOS vulnerability. Block scan targets a set of services for exploring the vulnerability. These attacks occur in a randomized order over the network and the attack topology is one to many. The randomizing scan helps them to avoid detection algorithms.

15.11.2 Worm Outbreaks

A worm is a special type of program that has the ability to replicate itself and without any user interaction it can send copies to other computers over the network. The worm outbreaks aim to gain two main goals: (1) degrading the system performance of the targeted network and (2) creating compromised hosts for launching future attacks. There are many known worms and some new worms are being created. It is difficult to detect the worms because the newer worms may have completely unknown structures. However, these worms attack in two phases: in the first phase the worm infects the target and during second phase it propagate to new hosts by self- replicating. Some common worms are: SQL-Slammer, Code Red 2, W32/Sasser, etc.

15.11.3 Distributed Denial-of-Service Attacks

Distributed denial-of-service (DDoS) attacks are well-known and powerful coordinated attacks that can disrupt the services of the victimized hosts. The attacker's primary target for launching DDoS attacks is to gain financial benefits, which may be claimed from the victims or from the opponents of the victims. A DDoS attack has two stages. The first stage, which is known as the recruiting stage, is where the attacker searches for the vulnerability of the targeted hosts to compromise them and installs attacking tools on the victim machine. In the second stage, which is the attacking stage, the attacker sends commands to attack the third-party service which is the main target of the attack and the service gets disrupted. The attacking topology is one to many. Distributed SYN floods and distributed reflector attacks are the common attacking methods of DDoS.

Distributed SYN attack targets the TCP in a three-way handshake. In this approach, the attacker introduces SYN packets from invalid sources into the target host in order to open many half-open connections until the target memory stack is so full that no new request can be accepted even from a valid source. These invalid requests are sent to the target source within a very short time frame and from several compromised machines.

The distributed reflector attack uses the web servers and router to attack the target host but hides the main source of the attack and also increases the attack traffic [34]. The attacker sends spoofed packets from the compromised host to the reflectors and these reflectors initiate the real attack by sending back the SYN-ACK packet. If no reply is found then the reflector sends multiple retransmitted packets which actually increases the attack traffic.

In the following section, we will discuss several studies that have been done on the intrusion detection systems by different researchers.

15.12 State-of-the-Art Existing Literatures

Much research has been carried out, of of which some focused on the architecture of CIDS while others proposed different algorithms of intrusion detection. We will be focusing a few of them here.

Among the early proposals for CIDS was the distributed intrusion detection system (DIDS) by Snapp et al. [33], which follows a centralized architectural design. DIDS makes use of a mechanism of distributed monitoring and the analysis is done according to the centralized system. DIDS has three components: central unit, network monitoring unit, and host monitoring unit. The main unit of this system is the central unit that uses detection mechanism on the data coming from other units. The accuracy is comparatively poorer and suffer from SoPF. Also, here the scaling is costly.

SURFcert IDS is also a centralized CIDS, which uses the honeypots to produce minimum false positives [31]. This system creates private virtual networks with the central analysis unit and the monitoring units. The virtual links are monitored by one or many honeypots and that is why the false positive rate is close to zero. However, not all the attacks are detected by this system. Moreover, there is no alert correlation method and honeypots are not scalable. Since the detection is done locally, SURFcert does not perform well in global detections.

Another CIDS was proposed that is known as the distributed intrusion detection system using mobile agents (DIDMA) [30]. It uses the mobile agents for aggregation and correlation methods and the static agents as monitoring units. Static agents monitor the network and whenever any alert is generated the central unit creates a mobile agent that updates the global list containing the node address that suffers from similar attacks. DIDMA uses the signature-based detection which is why it can detect unknown attacks efficiently. Moreover, creation of mobile agent can become costly if multiple nodes are attacked simultaneously and it may create communication disruption. Again, the central unit is a SPoF. Again, if any host is compromised then the mobile agents will become affected too.

The graph-based intrusion detection system (GrIDS) proposed a tree-like infrastructure where networks are clustered into many zones called departments [21]. GrIDSs maintain a hierarchical model. Each department detects and analyzes the intrusion. Each department has a parent node associated with it. Locally detected attacks are sent to the parent nodes for future analysis. GrIDS uses policy rules to detect alerts. That is why it may not detect attacks of unknown policies. Moreover, the system performance can degrade for insider attacks as well as for the DDoS attacks. However, GrIDS has a privacy protection mechanism that restricts access to the departments, and also the system is very scalable.

Another hierarchical CIDS that can be used as a framework for different attack detection engines is known as the autonomous agents for intrusion detection (AAFID), it was proposed in Refs. [28,29]. The system has several transceivers and monitors. The lower-level monitors monitor the network and send the feedback to the transceivers for alert aggregation and correlation. The transceivers control the local monitors as well as configure them. After aggregation, the report is sent to the higher-level monitors. The higher level monitor is responsible for auditing transceivers. The higher-level monitors can suffer from a single point of failure. Again, the authors did not give any details about the aggregation, correlation, and dissemination methods in their prototype.

Hierarchical intrusion detection (HIDE) was proposed in Ref. [27], which is based on anomaly-based detection. The detection uses the statical preprocessing and neural network classification. The monitors use the statistical approach to detect the alert with reference to the model provided and after that the neural network is used to determine whether an attack is normal or not. Lastly, final reports are generated and provided to the user via the user interface. HIDE generates high level of false positives. Moreover, the accuracy of the system depends on the design of the algorithm. Zheng Zhang et al. [27] also points out that system cannot detect the low volume attack traffic efficiently, which is a vital limitation.

Janakiraman et al. proposed a distributed collaborative intrusion detection system, named intrusion detection and rapid action (INDRA) [25]. It follows the peer-to-peer overlay and can detect generic attacks. INDRA uses the public-subscriber method to exchange data between the monitors. The monitors in INDRA have monitoring units to detect attacks and analysis unit, which generate alerts and take action against the attacks. It disseminates the alert information with the help of scribe [23]. Scribe creates a separate node for each class of attack and the monitors subscribe to those nodes. INDRA has a feature for adding plugins for new classes of attacks, but these need a manual approach of administration. Moreover, compromised monitors can degrade the accuracy of the system. The authors suggested that keeping a blacklist consisting of suspicious peers can maintain the overall system performance.

Zhou et al. introduced the large-scale intrusion detection (LarSID) in his work [22,26]. It is a peer-to-peer-based CIDS and it uses the publish-subscribe method on top of the distributed hash table. The local monitors monitor the network and maintain a list of malicious IP addresses. The local list is shared if a certain number of malicious IP addresses is added to the list. All the monitors communicate over SSL. Moreover, they introduce the public key infrastructure (PKI) for authentication. Even it can be scaled according to network size. The main drawback is that it has no global monitoring ability, it can only detect attacks with common sources.

A hybrid architectural-based CIDS named distributed overlay for monitoring Internet outbreaks (DOMINO) was proposed in Ref. [24]. It consists of three components: (1) axis overlay, (2) satellite communities, and (3) terrestrial contributors. Axis overlay is considered as the central component and it consists of trusted peers, which only use PKI authentication for communication. These monitors can do the analysis of the traffic. These nodes introduce threshold filtering to deal with the insider attacks. Satellite communities are localized versions of DOMINO protocols. These are dependent on the axis nodes. Terrestrial contributors include all the nodes, even their non-trusty peers. DOMINO uses signature-based detection and also uses honeypots. The alert data information is shared in XML format periodically. There may arise a communication overhead if the interval between the broadcasting is too short. Again, the system has no policies for insider attacks.

Locasto et al. proposed a peer-to-peer-based intrusion system named worminator [15,20]. In worminator, each peer has a monitoring unit and every host is a network-based IDS. Distributed correlation scheduling algorithm selects peers for information sharing and information sharing is done by the bloom filter. Bloom filters are used to exchange compressed alert data and to ensure security. However, the scheduling algorithm was not given in detail by the authors.

CIDS for detecting distributed attack patterns, which is known as quicksand, was introduced in Ref. [11]. It uses a hybrid approach for attack detection at the global level, but at the local level each IDS is signature-based or anomaly-based. The system has a central unit for attack signature storage and update. Authors proposed the attack specification language (ASL) for describing the attack signatures of the distributed attacks. With the help of ASL, the relationship between the attack and the host is transformed into an acyclic graph. The central unit then disseminates the pattern graphs to the monitors. The local monitors detect the attacks based on the updated pattern. The accuracy of the system depends on the graphs patterns, so false positives might degrade the level of accuracy.

In the following section, we present the summary for different collaborative intrusion detection systems in Table 15.3.

Table 15.3 CIDS

Name	Local Monitoring	Membership Management	Aggregation and Correlation	Data Dissemination	Global Monitoring
DIDS	Host specific	Central	Unique Peer Monitoring	Central Unit Dependent	General Detection
SURFcert	Honeypot	Central	Not Specified	Central Unit Dependent	General Detection
DIDMA	Signature Specific	Central	Peer-to-Peer Monitoring	Selective Broadcast	General Detection
GrIDS	Both Host and Network Specific	Hierarchy-Based	Peer-to-Peer Monitoring	Broadcasting	Malware Specific
AAFID	Host specific	Hierarchy-Based	Peer-to-Peer Monitoring	Unknown	General Detection
HIDE	Anomaly Dependent	Hierarchy-Based	Unique Peer Monitoring	Broadcasting	General Detection
INDRA	Signature Specific	Structured Distribution	Not Specified	Publisher-Subscriber-Based	General Detection
LarSID	Unknown	Structured Distribution	Peer-to-Peer Monitoring	Publisher-Subscriber-Based	Service-Based Detection

(Continued)

Table 15.3 (*Continued*)   CIDS

Name	Local Monitoring	Membership Management	Aggregation and Correlation	Data Dissemination	Global Monitoring
DOMINO	Honeypot	Unstructured Distribution	Not Specified	Selective Broadcast	General Detection
Worminator	Hybrid	Unstructured Distribution	Unique Peer Monitoring	Selective Broadcast	Malware Specific
Quicksand	Hybrid	Unstructured Distribution	Peer-to-Peer Monitoring	Selective Broadcast	General Detection

15.13 Future Direction and Conclusion

In the end, we can conclude by saying that there is no suitable approach for protecting large networks from collaborative attacks. Centralized CIDS approach is suitable for small to medium size networks as they can be deployed in different networks. However, they suffer from a single point of failure (SPoF) and they are hard to scale when the monitor number increases. Decentralized and distributed approach is promising for large networks, but they are limited to specific attacks. More research is required to improve data correlation and also to improve detection accuracy. The challenge is that intrusion detection attempts to find anomalies in data without knowing exactly what these anomalies look like. Hence, data correlation techniques are required that do not presume knowledge about the attributes on which the correlation is performed. An additional challenge is the expense of deploying CIDS. So, with further research we could face these sophisticated attacks.

References

1. Xiufeng Liu, Nadeem Iftikhar, and Xike Xie. 2014. Survey of real-time processing systems for Big data. In *Proceedings of the 18th International Database Engineering & Applications Symposium (IDEAS'14)*, Ana Maria Almeida, Jorge Bernardino, and Elsa Ferreira Gomes (Eds.). ACM, New York, pp. 356–361.
2. Mustafa Amir Faisal, Zeyar Aung, John R. Williams, and Abel Sanchez. 2012. Securing advanced metering infrastructure using intrusion detection system with data stream mining. In *Intelligence and Security Informatics. PAISI 2012. Lecture Notes in Computer Science*, Vol. 7299, Michael Chau, G. Alan Wang, Wei Thoo Yue, Hsinchun Chen (Eds.). Springer, Berlin.
3. Bazara I. A. Barry and H. Anthony Chan. 2010. Intrusion detection systems. In *Handbook of Information and Communication Security*. Springer, Berlin, pp. 193–205.
4. Daniel A. Reed and Jack Dongarra. 2015. Exascale computing and big data. *Communications of ACM* 58(7), 56–68
5. Big Data Information. www.nist.gov/el/cyberphysical-systems/Big-data-pwg
6. What is Big Data. www.ibm.com/Big-data/us/en/
7. Understanding Microsoft Big data solutions. https://msdn.microsoft.com/en-us/library/dn749804.aspx
8. John R. Goodall, Wayne G. Lutters, and Anita Komlodi. 2004. I know my network: collaboration and expertise in intrusion detection. In *Proceedings of the 2004 ACM Conference on Computer Supported Cooperative Work (CSCW '04)*. ACM, New York, NY, pp. 342–345.
9. Mohiuddin Ahmed, Adnan Anwar, Abdun Mahmood, Zubair Shah, Michael J. Maher. 2015. An investigation of performance analysis of anomaly detection techniques for big data in scada systems. *EAI Endorsed Transactions on Industrial Networks and Intelligent Systems* 15(3), 1–16.
10. Subramanian Neelakantan and Shrisha Rao. 2008. A threat-aware signature based intrusion-detection approach for obtaining network-specific useful alarms. In 2008 the Third International Conference on Internet Monitoring and Protection. Bucharest, pp. 80–85.

11. Christopher Krügel, Thomas Toth, and Clemens Kerer. 2002. Decentralized event correlation for intrusion detection. In *Information Security and Cryptology (ICISC)*. Springer, Berlin and Heidelberg, vol. 2288, pp. 114–131.

12. R. Zuech, T.M. Khoshgoftaar, R. Wald. 2015. Intrusion detection and big heterogeneous data: A survey. *Journal of Big Data* 2(1), 3.

13. Samuel Marchal, Xiuyan Jiang, Radu State, Thomas Engel. 2014. A big data architecture for large scale security monitoring. In *2014 IEEE International Congress on Big data (BigData Congress)*. IEEE, pp. 56–63.

14. Varun Chandola, Arindam Banerjee, and Vipin Kumar. 2009. Anomaly detection: A survey. *ACM Computing Surveys* 41(3), 1–58.

15. Michael E. Locasto, Janak J. Parekh, Angelos D. Keromytis, and Salvatore J. Stolfo. 2005. Towards collaborative security and P2P intrusion detection. In *IEEE Workshop on Information Assurance and Security*. IEEE, pp. 333–339.

16. J.F. Nieves and Y.C. Jia. 2009. Data clustering for anomaly detection in network intrusion detection. *Research Alliance in Math and Science*, 1–12.

17. Like Zhang and Gregory B. White. 2007. An approach to detect executable content for anomaly based network intrusion detection. In *Parallel and Distributed Processing Symposium, 2007. IPDPS 2007*. IEEE International, pp. 1–8.

18. Ahmed Youssef and Ahmed Emam (2011). Network intrusion detection using data mining and network behaviour analysis. *International Journal of Computer Science & Information Technology* 3(6), 87–98.

19. Ahmed Patel, Mona Taghavi, Kaveh Bakhtiyari, Joaquim Celestino Júnior. (2013). An intrusion detection and prevention system in cloud computing: A systematic review. *Journal of Network and Computer Applications* 36(1), 25–41.

20. Michael E. Locasto, Janak J. Parekh, Salvatore Stolfo, and Vishal Misra. 2004. Collaborative distributed intrusion detection. Technical report, Columbia University.

21. Steven Cheung, Rick Crawford, Mark Dilger, Jeremy Frank, Jim Hoagland, Karl Levitt, Jeff Rowe, Stuart Staniford-Chen, Raymond Yip, and Dan Zerkle. 1999. The design of GrIDS: A graph based intrusion detection system. Technical report, Department of Computer Science, University of California at Davis.

22. Chenfeng Vincent Zhou, Shanika Karunasekera, and Christopher Leckie. 2005. A peer-to-peer collaborative intrusion detection system. In *International Conference on Networks*. IEEE.

23. I.T. Antony, Miguel Castro, Peter Druschel, A.-M. Kermarrec, A.I.T. Rowstron. 2002. Scribe: A large-scale and decentralized application level multicast infrastructure. IEEE *Journal on Selected Areas in Communications* 20(8):1489–1499.

24. Vinod Yegneswaran, Paul Barford, and Somesh Jha. 2004. Global intrusion detection in the DOMINO overlay system. In *Proceedings of the Network and Distributed System Security Symposium, NDSS 2004*.

25. Ramaprabhu Janakiraman, Marcel Waldvogel, and Qi Zhang. 2003. Indra: A peer-to-peer approach to network intrusion detection and prevention. In *WETICE'03: Proceedings of the Twelfth International Workshop on Enabling Technologies*. IEEE Computer Society.

26. Chenfeng Vincent Zhou, Shanika Karunasekera, and Christopher Leckie. 2007. Evaluation of a decentralized architecture for large scale collaborative intrusion detection. In *The Tenth IFIP/ IEEE International Symposium on Integrated Network Management (IM 2007)*, pp. 80–89.

27. Zheng Zhang, Jun Li, C.N. Manikopoulos, Jay Jorgenson, and Jose Ucles. 2001. HIDE: A hierarchical network intrusion detection system using statistical preprocessing and neural network classification. In *IEEE Workshop on Information Assurance and Security*. IEEE, pp. 85–90. ISBN 0780398149.

28. Eugene H. Spafford and Diego Zamboni. 2000. Intrusion detection using autonomous agents. *Computer Networks* 34(4), 547–570
29. Jai Sundar Balasubramaniyan, Jose Omar Garcia-fernandez, David Isacoff, Eugene Spafford, and Diego Zamboni Ý. 1998. An architecture for intrusion detection using autonomous agents. In *IEEE Computer Security Applications Conference*, pp. 13–24.
30. Pradeep Kannadiga and Mohammad Zulkernine. 2005. DIDMA: A distributed intrusion detection system using mobile agents. In *International Conference on Software Engineering, Artificial Intelligence, Networking and Parallel/Distributed Computing*. IEEE, pp. 238–245.
31. http://ids.surfnet.nl
32. Chenfeng Vincent Zhou, Shanika Karunasekera, and Christopher Leckie. 2007. Evaluation of a decentralized architecture for large scale collaborative intrusion detection. In *The Tenth IFIP/IEEE International Symposium on Integrated Network Management (IM 2007)*, pp. 80–89.
33. Steven Snapp, James Brentano, Gihan Dias, Terrance Goan, Todd Heberlein, Che-Lin Ho, Karl Levitt, Biswanath Mukherjee, Stephen Smaha, Tim Grance, Daniel Teal, and Doug Mansur. 1991. DIDS (Distributed intrusion detection system)—Motivation, architecture, and an early prototype. In *Fourteenth National Computer Security Conference*, pp. 167–176.
34. Vern Paxson. 2001. An analysis of using reflectors for distributed denial-ofservice attacks. *ACM SIGCOMM Computer Communication Review* 31(3), 38–47.
35. Stuart Staniford, James A. Hoagland, and Joseph M. McAlerney. 2002. Practical automated detection of stealthy portscans. *Journal of Computer Security* 10(1–2), 105–136.
36. CERT Coordination center (CERT/CC). 2003. Module 4-types of intruder attacks.
37. Prahlad Fogla, Monirul I. Sharif, Roberto Perdisci, Oleg M. Kolesnikov, and Wenke Lee. 2006. Polymorphic blending attacks. In *USENIX Security Symposium*, pp. 241–256.
38. Kymie M.C. Tan, Kevin S. Killourhy, and Roy A. Maxion. 2002. Undermining an anomaly-based intrusion detection system using common exploits. In *Recent Advances in Intrusion Detection*. Springer, Berlin and Heidelberg, vol. 2516, pp. 54–73.
39. Oliver Dain and Robert K. Cunningham. 2001. Fusing a heterogeneous alert stream into scenarios. In *Proceedings of the 2001 ACM Workshop on Data Mining for Security Applications*, pp. 1–13.
40. Joaquin Garcia, Fabien Autrel, Joan Borrell, Sergio Castillo, Frederic Cuppens, and Guillermo Navarro. 2004. Decentralized publish-subscribe system to prevent coordinated attacks via alert correlation. In *Sixth International Conference on Information and Communications Security*, pp. 223–35.
41. Steven T. Eckmann. 2002. Statl: An attack language for state-based intrusion detection. *Journal of Computer Security* 10(1), 71–103.
42. David Wagner and Paolo Soto. 2002. Mimicry attacks on host-based intrusion detection systems. In *ACM Conference on Computer and Communications Security—CCS'02*. ACM Press, New York, pp. 255–264.
43. Tsung-Huan Cheng, Ying-Dar Lin, Yuan-Cheng Lai, and Po-Ching Lin. 2012. Evasion techniques: Sneaking through your intrusion detection/prevention systems. *IEEE Communications Surveys & Tutorials* 14(4), 1011–1020.
44. Ayalvadi J. Ganesh, A.-M. Kermarrec, and Laurent Massoulié. 2003. Peer-to-peer membership management for gossip-based protocols. *IEEE Transactions on Computers* 52(2), 139–149.
45. Vivek Vishnumurthy and Paul Francis. 2006. On heterogeneous overlay construction and random node selection in unstructured P2P networks. In *Proceedings IEEE INFOCOM 2006. 25TH IEEE International Conference on Computer Communications*. Barcelona, pp. 1–12.

46. Phillip A. Porras, Martin W. Fong, and Alfonso Valdes. 2002. A mission-impact-based approach to INFOSEC alarm correlation. In *Recent Advances in Intrusion Detection. RAID 2002. Lecture Notes in Computer Science,* Vol. 2516, Andreas Wespi, Giovanni Vigna, and Luca Deri (Eds.). Springer, Berlin.
47. Zhi-Hua Zhou. 2011. When semi-supervised learning meets ensemble learning. *Frontiers of Electrical and Electronic Engineering in China* 6(1), 6–16.
48. Vern Paxson. 1999. Bro: A system for detecting network intruders in real-time. *Computer Networks* 31(23–24), 2435–2463.
49. Richard Zuech, Taghi M. Khoshgoftaar and Randall Wald. 2015. Intrusion detection and big heterogeneous data: A survey. *Journal of Big Data* 2(1), 3.
50. Yoichi Shinoda, Ko Ikai, and Motomu Itoh. 2005. Vulnerabilities of passive internet threat monitors. In *Proceedings of the 14th USENIX Security Symposium*, pp. 209–224.
51. Vitaly Shmatikov and Ming-Hsiu Wang. 2007. Security against probe-response attacks in collaborative intrusion detection. In *Proceedings of the Workshop on Large Scale Attack Defense (LSAD'07)*. ACM, New York, pp. 129–136.
52. Stefan Savage, Geoff Voelker, Michael Vrable, and Nick Weaver. 2005. Internet Outbreaks: Epidemiology and Defenses.
53. Butler W. Lampson. 1973. A note on the confinement problem. *Communications of the ACM* 16(10), 613–615.
54. Sebastian Zander, Grenville J. Armitage, and Philip Branch. 2007. A survey of covert channels and counter-measures in computer network protocols. *IEEE Communications Surveys 9*, 44–57.
56. Claudiu Duma, Martin Karresand, Nahid Shahmehri, and Germano Caronni. 2006. A trust-aware, P2P-based overlay for intrusion detection. In *Proceedings of the International Conference on Database and Expert Systems Applications (DEXA'06)*. IEEE, pp. 692–697.
57. Sepandar D. Kamvar, Mario T. Schlosser, and Hector Garcia-Molina. 2003. The eigen-trust algorithm for reputation management in P2P networks. In *Proceedings of the 12th International Conference on World Wide Web (WWW'03)*, p. 640.
58. Carol Fung, Olga Baysal, Jie Zhang, Issam Aib, and Raouf Boutaba. 2008. Trust management for host-based collaborative intrusion detection. *Managing Large-Scale Service Deployment* 5273(2008), 109–122.
59. Claudiu Duma, Martin Karresand, Nahid Shahmehri, and Germano Caronni. 2006. A trust-aware, P2P-based overlay for intrusion detection. In *Proceedings of the International Conference on Database and Expert Systems Applications (DEXA'06)*. IEEE, pp. 692–697.
60. Poly Sen, Nabendu Chaki, and Rituparna Chaki. 2008. HIDS: Honesty-rate based collaborative intrusion detection system for mobile ad-hoc networks. In *Proceedings of the 7th Computer Information Systems and Industrial Management Applications*. IEEE, pp 121–126.
61. Michael Brinkmeier, Mathias Fischer, Sascha Grau, and Guenter Schaefer. 2009. Towards the design of unexploitable construction mechanisms for multiple-tree based P2P streaming systems. In *Kommunikation in Verteilten Systemen (KiVS)*. Springer, Berlin, pp. 193–204.
62. Manuel Gil Pérez, Félix Gómez Mármol, Gregorio Martínez Pérez, and Antonio F. Skarmeta Gómez. 2013. RepCIDN: A reputation-based collaborative intrusion detection network to lessen the impact of malicious alarms. *Journal of Network and Systems Management* 21(1), 128–167.

Chapter 16

Health Care Security Analytics

Mohiuddin Ahmed and
Abu Saleh Shah Mohammad Barkat Ullah
Canberra Institute of Technology

Contents

16.1 Introduction

The health care sector is now embracing a plethora of newer technologies and, eventually, producing a huge amount of data. Managing these data for effective health care systems is a challenge [1]. Health care data analytics is a multidisciplinary field where scientific investigation is carried out to study social factors, financing systems, health technologies, and personal behaviors. The objective of health care analytics is to make health care effective, affordable, safe, accessible, and patient-oriented [2,3]. The motivation behind the health care analytics is to benefit both the patients and the health care providers. Health care brings together experts from a wide range of disciplines such as medicine, social science, statistics, engineering, policy, governance, etc. However, one of the challenges faced by health care sector is in detecting and identifying cyberattacks and reducing cyber incidents [4]. Due to the emerging malicious Internet users, i.e., cyber criminals, health care is being affected. Some of the alarming cyber incidents are listed below:

- In 2015, cyber criminals took control of the personal information for 80 million patients and stole tens of millions of records [4].
- According to 2017 Verizon Data Breach report [4], ransomware was ranked 22 for being the most common type of malware in 2014. However, in 2017, it became fifth.
- Using phishing techniques, hackers compromised nearly 90,000 patients' personal information at the University of Washington in 2013 [4].
- A new type of hijacking in health care is known as the medical device hijack (called MEDJACK) [4]. A recent victim of MEDJACK is UCLA Health, where personal data of 4.5 million patients were exposed.

Consequently, in the era of IoT, health care technology is changing in major ways that creates more space for the cyber criminals to evade. It is estimated that the number of health care IoT devices will increase from 95 million in 2015 to 646 million in 2020, which is almost 7-times in 5 years. Therefore, these devices will lead to more accessible data or, in other words, to "big data." It is important in the health care sector that the big data gets utilized properly to predict epidemics, cure diseases, and avoid preventable diseases [2,3].

The aforementioned facts about IoT and big data emphasize the development of robust cybersecurity strategies than ever before, especially for health care, as the impact is most adverse when the data and devices are controlled by cyber criminals [7–14]. To the best of our knowledge, this chapter is the first of its kind that covers cybersecurity in the health care domain extensively. Although there are a few reports published by different organizations, such as Verizon, KPMG, Symantec, etc., these reports [5] are not comprehensive enough to become helpful for the research community.

16.1.1 Chapter Roadmap

The rest of the chapter is organized as follows. Section 15.2 covers the digitalization of health care, i.e., industry 4.0. Section 15.3 discusses the cyberattacks in the health care sector. Section 15.4 contains the ways hackers get access to a hospital network, followed by counter measures in Section 15.5. Section 15.6 concludes the chapter.

16.2 Health Care in the Era of Industry 4.0

Due to the advancement of information technology across a wide range of application domains, we are observing significant changes in health care as well. Many other examples can be found in a recent report by Deloitte [5]. Nowadays, it is a common trend to adopt e-health care systems that intersect cyber-physical systems and industry 4.0 design principles [6]. In other words, we can think of health 4.0. Health 4.0 encompasses human beings and virtual components such as algorithms, databases, biosensors, etc. In addition to health 4.0, in the health care industry, blockchain can secure valuable patient data. Sometimes, the health sector uses patient information for improving the intelligence of health care systems without any prior permission from patients. This privacy issue can be controlled by a decentralized and secured blockchain technology. Again, Deloitte has surveyed health care opportunities in *"Blockchain: Opportunities for Health Care"* [5], which identified blockchain as an effective framework to support the integration of health care information. Blockchain-based systems have the potential to reduce costs of current intermediaries between doctors and patients. In the health industry, blockchain technology use cases can be quality medicine, patient care and outcomes research (PCOR), and global standard health care system. The application fields can be clinical data sharing, public health data storage, research and clinical trials, administrative and financial health information, and doctor and food identification and prioritization. For example, wearables and IoT devices are collecting patient information; blockchain can secure that by replacing individual cloud to the shared ledger. Another example can be, when a patient with several health issues undergoes a severe operation blockchain consensus technique can be applied among specialist doctors to finalize the medical decisions.

In this scenario, hackers are far more interested as the incorporation of industry 4.0 opens a lot of opportunities for them [7–14]. Financial gain by hacking health care systems is far more than any other systems as the information is sensitive and the compromised organization can do nothing but comply with the demands of the hackers. A cyberattack on a medical device can lead to misguided analysis and wrong treatment of the patients. An attack on the cyber-physical systems of a health care facility may jeopardize regular operations and affect critical utilities such as electricity, water, heating, air conditioning, etc. Both medical devices and cyber-physical systems faced a number of cyberattacks recently, and even after the adoption of newer defense strategies, these attacks have not stopped.

16.3 Taxonomy of Cyberattacks in The Health Care Domain

Cyberattacks in the health care domain can be classified into three groups in general. The first type of attack is on medical devices where the devices connected to the hospital network are compromised by cyber criminals who then exploits the victims. The second type of attack is on cyber-physical systems, e.g., the smart infrastructure of the health care facility. The third type of attack is alarming and it's called insider threat. The hospital employees are sometimes found exploiting their access to the network and other devices, which leads to severe damages by the cyber criminals [1]. Figure 16.1 below depicts the simple taxonomy of attacks in health care. In the next subsections, we briefly discuss the three major types of cyberattacks.

16.3.1 Attacks on Medical Devices

Due to the advancement in information technology, the health care sector embraced a lot of smart medical devices [15]. However, the hackers also found a new target, i.e., the medical devices. The cyberattacks on medical devices are also known

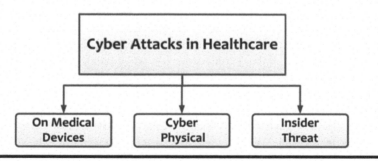

Figure 16.1   Taxonomy of cyberattacks in health care.

as MEDJACK [4] Launching a cyberattack on medical devices can be compared with exploiting the equipment in an industry setup. However, the consequences are more severe in terms of health care devices. Next, we briefly discuss some of the major attack types on medical devices.

16.3.1.1 Magnetic Resonance Imaging (MRI)

According to Ayala et al. [1], when a cyber criminal tampers with the MRI controls, a patient or hospital employee can be injured via the MRI machine. An MRI device has the option to displace implanted devices, heat devices through radio frequency, or obscure the intended imaging [16]. Therefore, all passive implants are treated with specific information before their use within the magnetic resonance environment. In a nutshell, a compromised MRI machine can lead to ill-physical consequences and financial penalties for the health care facility.

16.3.1.2 Robotic Surgical Machine

Robots are widely used in a variety of application domains; therefore, health care is also enjoying the benefits of robots to operate complex tasks [17]. For example, a robotic surgeon can conduct surgical procedures such as cardiology, rectal surgery, gynecology, neurosurgery, vascular and transplant surgery, etc. Now, the cyber criminals target the computing device that controls the robot and video feeds used during the operation. If the devices are compromised by the hackers, then the repercussion is extremely dangerous and hackers might ask for a high amount of ransom here in this instance.

16.3.1.3 Active Patient Monitoring Devices

Patient monitoring devices are popular nowadays due to the remote monitoring facility provided to the physicians. These devices are used to execute a number of health care tasks, such as identification of arrhythmias, diabetes, etc. However, the hackers did not ignore these devices at all. If an attacker can take control of a device that receives and/or displays crucial information, then it is possible to use the device with malicious intent to endanger some patients' life.

16.3.2 Cyber-Physical Attacks

Apart from the medical devices, the hackers are also interested in compromising the cyber-physical devices. For example, the hospital building can be targeted [18]. There has been a lot of research on cyber-physical systems. However, in the scope of health care facilities, there is no significant research. These attacks have the potential to do significant physical damage to hospital equipment and to create a constraint for regular patient treatments.

16.3.2.1 Attacks on Building Controls System

In a health care facility, building controls system (BCS) is responsible for monitoring and operating equipment, such as air conditioning, carbon dioxide, noise levels, etc. [18]. It is imperative to maintain a comfortable and safe environment for the patients and simultaneously consider energy efficiency for the hospitals. In this scenario, if the control of such sensitive systems goes into the hands of a hacker it will jeopardize the regular operations of hospitals and will lead to ill-treatment of the patients admitted in the hospital or wrong analysis by the physicians. The hacker may shut down the elevators, water supply, close the air vents, turn up the heat, and many other unimaginable acts. The situation may get worse in case any emergency operation is hampered due to these acts.

16.3.3 Insider Threat

Insider threats are emerging types of attacks as it has been found in the last few years that the legitimate users of the health care facilities are being exploited by the cyber criminals. Therefore, these insiders have the credibility to cause physical damages to medical equipment and hospital facilities [19]. Insider threats to critical infrastructure are more serious than outsider threats because an outside attacker is less likely to know the hospital network vulnerabilities and weaknesses than an insider would. Health care personnel with complete access to the hospital network can easily perform reconnaissance on the network to identify vulnerabilities and may inform the hackers. In summary, an insider attack is a malicious attack on a network or computer system by a person with authorized system access. There is an increasing number of incidents due to these types of attacks. However, the current strategies are not enough to identify and detect these attacks.

16.4 Hacker's Entry

In this section, we cover two important aspects by which the hacker gains information to access the health care network. Figure 16.2 displays a simple taxonomy and major ways to collect critical information about the network and to access the network.

16.4.1 Reconnaissance

Network reconnaissance is an effective way to test potential vulnerabilities in a computer network [20–23]. Although it is a legitimate activity for the network operator who is seeking to protect it, the hackers take advantage of it. The hackers are interested to know more about the health care networks before launching the attacks to devise strategies to bypass the protective shields. Next, we briefly discuss

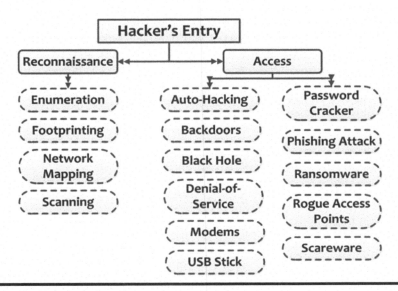

Figure 16.2 Hacker's entry.

some popular techniques used for reconnaissance purpose and about how hackers get to know more about the health care network.

16.4.1.1 Footprinting

One of the easiest ways to gather information about any network is to just use "who is" [20]. Using "who is" it is possible to know about the organization's employee directory that is the source of information for hackers to conduct social engineering. Also, other important information obtained may include knowledge about the Internet technologies being used, the operating system and hardware being used, IP addresses, e-mail addresses and phone numbers, and policies and procedures. The main objective of footprinting is to learn as much as you can about a system, its remote access capabilities, ports, services, and the security arrangements for the organization.

16.4.1.2 Network Mapping

There is an open source utility for network discovery and security auditing, called Nmap (Network Mapper) [21]. Apart from systems and network administrators, cyber criminals also find it useful for:

- Network inventory
- Management of service upgrade schedules
- Monitoring host or service

This tool provides a number of functions for probing computer networks, host discovery, service and operating system detection. The Nmap users are continuing to develop and refine the tool. According to [21], Nmap is designed to rapidly scan large networks. However, it also works well with single hosts. Nmap can be used in almost every operating system and their binary packages are available for Linux, Windows, and Mac OS X. Besides the command line-based Nmap, it also includes the following:

- **Zenmap**: Advanced GUI.
- **Ncat**: Tool for data transfer, redirection, and debugging.
- **Ndiff**: Utility for comparing scan results.
- **Nping**: Tool for packet generation and response analysis.

16.4.1.3 Scanning

Port scanning is a popular technique to extract critical information, such as what are the open ports and services available on a network host [22]. The security auditors also use this technique to audit computers for vulnerabilities; however, it is also used by hackers to target victims. For reconnaissance purpose, port scanning is used to send requests to connect to the targeted computers and to track the open ports or which respond to the request. Based on the port scanning information, hackers know where to attack, especially the denial of service attack can be launched very easily. Cyber criminals utilize port scanning since it is one of the easiest ways to discover services on the target that they want to break into. Due to the lack of security countermeasures in hospital networks, it is one of the most convenient ways for people with malicious intents to launch cyberattacks in the health care networks.

16.4.2 Hacker's Access Hospital Network

In this section, we discuss some of the major ways in which the hackers can access the hospital network. There are a number of ways by which a hacker gains access to an active medical device or the network. For example, a successful spear phishing campaign would let the hackers know about the network administrator, technicians, and a lot of other information that is supposed to be private and secure.

16.4.2.1 Phishing Attack

Phishing is a method to trick the victims. For example, the hackers send legitimate-looking emails in an attempt to gather classified information from the victims. Usually, the messages are framed in such a way that it seems to come from well-known addresses. Websites that are frequently spoofed by phishers include popular websites [24]. The ignorant employees of a health care facility will be easily compromised by these types of attacks. For example, spear phishing targets certain hospital personnel and lures them to open emails that appear to come from a colleague. When such emails are opened and some links are clicked, and the hospital computers are compromised [24].

16.4.2.2 Ransomware

Ransomware is considered as extortion in cyber space; it is also known as crypto viral extortion that restricts access to the infected computer system and it gives the hackers power to demand a ransom. These types of attacks are extremely dangerous as it may so happen that the affected computer can be a server holding patient files, which are being used as active monitoring devices. The hackers use malware to infect the computers [25]. They demand a ransom of $17,000 to restore their operation. After investigation it is found that an employee opened an infected email or downloaded the malware from a pop-up ad, which facilitated the virus to be planted in the network. Currently, there are two different types of ransomware. The first is through a program named Locky. Locky exploits spam email campaigns where an email is sent across the system that contains infected MS Word documents. Once the victim opens the document, macros will install on the host computer and begin infecting the network. The second ransomware is via the Samas program, which attacks web servers directly.

16.4.2.3 USB Stick

USB sticks are considered as gateways to plant malwares in any computing environment. Cyber criminals often try to hand the infected USB sticks to hospital employees via social engineering. Once the employee uses the USB stick in any of the hospital's networked computer, the malware is planted and then they can gain as much information as they want via remote access. Infecting the USB sticks with virus is another way of affecting the networked computers and getting access to them. Consequently, the cyber criminals can identify the active medical devices. Then, they are able to execute a wide range of malicious attacks, such as shutting down the active medical devices or threatening to cause serious damage to the devices unless a ransom is paid [26].

16.4.2.4 Password Cracker

A common approach to access any network is to crack the passwords of different access points [27]. Cyber criminals use two major types of methods to guess passwords: (i) brute-force and (ii) dictionary searches. Brute force is a widely used approach by hackers to try different combinations until the right password is found. In dictionary search, the hacker looks at each word in the dictionary for the correct password. Password dictionaries contain a wide range of subjects, such as policy, politics, games, movies, music, etc. There are other methods also, such as salting, rainbow tables, and guessing, which are effective in cracking the passwords for any system. In a health care network, the employees often use naive passwords that are easy to crack due to the ignorance about the emerging attacks and social engineering.

16.4.2.5 Black Hole Attack

When a router is compromised, the packets which are supposed to be relayed are dropped instead. These attacks are called packet drop or black hole attack as the legitimate traffic is lost. We can think of it as a type of denial of service attack since the users are deprived of the expected information. These attacks can have serious consequences. For example, while a physician is waiting for medical history or health records, the lost packets will cause a delay in providing medical advices. Moreover, in lossy networks, it is a common phenomenon to have packet drops; therefore, it is difficult to detect the black hole attacks. Being able to distinguish these attacks from normal packet drops is the main challenge and, in the research community, there is ongoing research to devise an effective technique to detect such attacks [28].

16.4.2.6 Rogue Access Points

One of the overlooked devices in any networked environment is an access point [29]. Organizations are more focused on the Internet-based components; however, if a cyber criminal installs a device to connect to the network, the repercussions are equally dangerous. The health care facilities usually have a hardwired and wireless network. Among the numerous devices, access points are easy targets for a hacker to replicate and install to get access to the network. These access points are called rogue access points, which open the door for the hackers to compromise the network remotely. The credibility of the rogue access points were overlooked in the past; however, it is high time to devise strategies to detect such vulnerabilities.

16.5 Countermeasures

Countermeasures for health care cybersecurity is not much different from that for any other domain. However, as reiterated time and again throughout the chapter, the consequences of cyberattack are far more dangerous as it involves human lives. There have been many studies and research for securing health care facilities from cyber criminals; however, there is always room for improvement. We can think of the countermeasures in two categories: detection and prevention.

Detection of cyberattacks in health care has recently got attention and newer attacks are emerging, such as false data injection attacks. A recent research showcased the impact of false data injection attacks in health care [4]. In terms of detection of cyberattacks, there are numerous tools and techniques in the literature [7–14]; however, the challenge is to devise strategies to detect the zero-day attacks. A few notable tools are listed below that are embraced by security analysts and researchers across the globe:

- **Wireshark**: A very handy network traffic analyzer tool [30].
- **Snort**: A popular network intrusion detection system [31].
- **Bro**: An open source Linux-based monitoring system [32].
- **OSSEC**: Another open source network traffic analysis tool that has released a stable version recently [33].
- **Antivirus**: There are plenty of antivirus software; however, we are yet to see any custom-tailored one for health care network or medical devices [34,35].

The list is not comprehensive; however, it is a good starting point for the practitioners. Now, when we delve into "prevention", we need to be aware of the proverb that "prevention is better than cure." There are many IPS (intrusion prevention systems) that are capable of detecting and preventing the system. Apart from the regular systems which are available, it is also notable that there are hardly any specific IPS for health care networks. Based on the discussion above, it is clear that there is a lack of IDS and IPS designed for health care systems.

Apart from the specific IDS and IPS, it is also important to establish a strong security culture among the people working in the health care sector. As a part of the security countermeasures, it is imperative to educate and train everyone involved in the health care sector. It is often said that the most vulnerable point of any networked/digital system is its users. The researchers who worked with the psychology of information technology users have repeatedly showcased that the attitude of the users is one of the main reasons for cyber incidents. Since the mass user cannot predict the repercussions of cyber incidents, it is a challenge to raise the awareness. Following steps can be executed to enhance security:

- Frequent training and education on cybersecurity.
- Accountability for information security must be one of the core values of the organization.
- The appropriate usage of mobile devices. Due to the Internet of Things, the hacker can compromise a mobile device that may be connected to many other medical devices. Therefore, the consequences are unimaginable.
- Maintaining proper and updated computer management. All the devices connected to the health care network must be regularly updated and scanned using antivirus.
- Role-based access to sensitive information. For example, one physician should not have access to the health records of patients who are not assigned

to him/her. If the hacker can compromise the physician's account, it is possible that, all the sensitive information will be in the hand of criminals.
■ Last but not the least, it should be a regular practice to be prepared for the zero-day attacks and contingency plans. For example, what happens if there are ransomware attacks, false data injection attacks, cyber-physical attacks, etc.

16.6 Conclusions

Since cybersecurity is an important application domain of data analytics, in this chapter, we have summarized our investigation on health care. The chapter showcased the current status of cyber incidents in the health care sector, followed by state-of-the-art health care systems. The taxonomy of attacks in the health care sector provides a better understanding for the health care professionals. The discussion on how hackers gain access to the hospital networks also provides meaningful insights for the readers. To detect and identify the customized cyberattacks in the health care sector, a discussion on countermeasures has been included that will help the researchers in this area to devise newer strategies and robust intrusion detection systems.

References

1. L. Ayala. *Cybersecurity for Hospitals and Healthcare Facilities: A Guide to Detection and Prevention*. Berkely, CA: Apress, 2016.
2. J. Archenaa and E. M. Anita. "A survey of big data analytics in healthcare and government." *Procedia Computer Science*, vol. 50, pp. 408–413, 2015. big Data, Cloud and Computing Challenges.
3. S. M. R. Islam, D. Kwak, M. H. Kabir, M. Hossain, and K. S. Kwak. "The internet of things for health care: A comprehensive survey." *IEEE Access*, vol. 3, pp. 678–708, 2015.
4. M. Ahmed and A.S.S.M. Barkat Ullah. "False data injection attacks in healthcare." In *15th Australasian Data Mining Conference*, AusDM, 2017.
5. Connected Health. Available at www2.deloitte.com/content/dam/Deloitte/uk/Documents/life-sciences-health-care/deloitte-uk-connected-health.pdf, accessed: February 10, 2018.
6. A. Hari and T. V. Lakshman. "The internet blockchain: A distributed, tamper-resistant transaction framework for the internet." In *Proceedings of the 15th ACM Workshop on Hot Topics in Networks, ser. HotNets'16*. New York: ACM, 2016, pp. 204–210.
7. M. Ahmed. "Thwarting dos attacks: A framework for detection based on collective anomalies and clustering." *Computer*, vol. 50, no. 9, pp. 76–82, 2017.
8. M. Ahmed. "Collective anomaly detection techniques for network traffic analysis." Annals of Data Science, January 2018.
9. M. Ahmed, A. Mahmood, and J. Hu. "A survey of network anomaly detection techniques." *Journal of Network and Computer Applications*, vol. 60, pp. 19–31, 2015.
10. M. Ahmed and A. Mahmood. "Network traffic analysis based on collective anomaly detection." In *9th IEEE International Conference on Industrial Electronics and Applications*. IEEE, 2014, pp. 1141–1146.

11. M. Ahmed and A. Mahmood. "Network traffic pattern analysis using improved information theoretic co-clustering based collective anomaly detection." In *International Conference on Security and Privacy in Communication Networks*. Springer International Publishing, 2015, vol. 153, pp. 204–219.

12. M. Ahmed, A. Anwar, A. N. Mahmood, Z. Shah, and M. J. Maher. "An investigation of performance analysis of anomaly detection techniques for big data in scada systems." *EAI Endorsed Transactions on Industrial Networks and Intelligent Systems*, vol. 15, no. 3, pp. 1–16, May 2015.

13. M. Ahmed, A. N. Mahmood, and J. Hu. "Chapter 1: Outlier detection." In *The State of the Art in Intrusion Prevention and Detection*. New York: CRC Press, January 2014, pp. 3–21.

14. M. Ahmed, A. N. Mahmood, and M. R. Islam. "A survey of anomaly detection techniques in financial domain." *Future Generation Computer Systems*, vol. 55, pp. 278–288, 2016.

15. A. Ray and R. Cleaveland. "An analysis method for medical device security." In *Proceedings of the 2014 Symposium and Bootcamp on the Science of Security, ser. HotSoS '14*. New York: ACM, 2014, pp. 16:1–16:2.

16. J. Siegmund, C. K¨astner, S. Apel, C. Parnin, A. Bethmann, T. Leich, G. Saake, and A. Brechmann. "Understanding understanding source code with functional magnetic resonance imaging." In *Proceedings of the 36th International Conference on Software Engineering, ser. ICSE 2014*. New York: ACM, 2014, pp. 378–389.

17. T. Zhou, J. S. Cha, G. T. Gonzalez, J. P. Wachs, C. Sundaram, and D. Yu. "Joint surgeon attributes estimation in robot-assisted surgery." In *Companion of the 2018 ACM/IEEE International Conference on Human-Robot Interaction, ser. HRI '18*. New York: ACM, 2018, pp. 285–286.

18. S. Wendzel, T. Rist, E. Andr´e, and M. Masoodian. "A secure interoperable architecture for building-automation applications." In *Proceedings of the 4th International Symposium on Applied Sciences in Biomedical and Communication Technologies, ser. ISABEL '11*. New York: ACM, 2011, pp. 8:1–8:5.

19. M. D. Carroll. "Information security: Examining and managing the insider threat." In *Proceedings of the 3rd Annual Conference on Information Security Curriculum Development, ser. InfoSecCD '06*. New York: ACM, 2006, pp. 156–158.

20. A. Sridharan and T. Ye. "Tracking port scanners on the ip backbone." In *Proceedings of the 2007 Workshop on Large Scale Attack Defense, ser. LSAD '07*. New York: ACM, 2007, pp. 137–144.

21. K. Rankin. "Hack and/: Dynamic config files with nmap." *Linux J.*, vol. 2010, no. 194, June 2010.

22. J. Ye and L. Akoglu. "Discovering opinion spammer groups by network footprints." In *Proceedings of the 2015 ACM on Conference on Online Social Networks, ser. COSN'15*. New York: ACM, 2015, pp. 97–97.

23. S. Standard, R. Greenlaw, A. Phillips, D. Stahl, and J. Schultz. "Network reconnaissance, attack, and defense laboratories for an introductory cyber-security course." *ACM Inroads*, vol. 4, no. 3, pp. 52–64, September 2013.

24. Q. Cui, G.-V. Jourdan, G. V. Bochmann, R. Couturier, and I.-V. Onut. "Tracking phishing attacks over time." In *Proceedings of the 26th International Conference on World Wide Web, ser. WWW '17*. Republic and Canton of Geneva, Switzerland: International World Wide Web Conferences Steering Committee, 2017, pp. 667–676.

25. Y. L. Dion, A. A. Joshua, and S. N. Brohi. "Negation of ransomware via gamification and enforcement of standards." In *Proceedings of the 2017 International Conference on Computer Science and Artificial Intelligence, ser. CSAI 2017*. New York: ACM, 2017, pp. 203–208.

26. D. J. Tian, A. Bates, and K. Butler. "Defending against malicious usb firmware with goodusb." In *Proceedings of the 31st Annual Computer Security Applications Conference, ser. ACSAC 2015*. New York: ACM, 2015, pp. 261–270.
27. J. Blocki, M. Blum, and A. Datta. "Gotcha password hackers!" *In Proceedings of the 2013 ACM Workshop on Artificial Intelligence and Security, ser. AISec '13*. New York: ACM, 2013, pp. 25–34.
28. M. Shobana, R. Saranyadevi, and S. Karthik. "Geographic routing used in manet for black hole detection." *In Proceedings of the Second International Conference on Computational Science, Engineering and Information Technology, ser. CCSEIT '12*. New York: ACM, 2012, pp. 201–204.
29. G. XIE, T. He, and G. Zhang. "Rogue access point detection using segmental tcp jitter." In *Proceedings of the 17th International Conference on World Wide Web, ser. WWW '08*. New York: ACM, 2008, pp. 1249–1250.
30. V. Y. Hnatyshin and A. F. Lobo. "Undergraduate data communications and networking projects using opnet and wireshark software." In *Proceedings of the 39th SIGCSE Technical Symposium on Computer Science Education, ser. SIGCSE '08*. New York: ACM, 2008, pp. 241–245.
31. L. L. Reynolds, Jr, R. W. Tibbs, and E. J. Derrick. "A gui for intrusion detection and related experiences." In *Proceedings of the 43rd Annual Southeast Regional Conference - Volume 2, ser. ACM-SE 43*. New York: ACM, 2005, pp. 191–192.
32. R. Udd, M. Asplund, S. Nadjm-Tehrani, M. Kazemtabrizi, and M. Ekstedt. "Exploiting bro for intrusion detection in a scada system." In *Proceedings of the 2Nd ACM International Workshop on Cyber-Physical System Security, ser. CPSS '16*. New York: ACM, 2016, pp. 44–51.
33. A. Hay, D. Cid, and R. Bray. OSSEC Host-Based Intrusion Detection Guide. Rockland, MA: Syngress Publishing, 2008.
34. P. Szor. The Art of Computer Virus Research and Defense. New York: Addison-Wesley Professional, 2005.
35. G. Post and A. Kagan. "The use and effectiveness of anti-virus software." *Computers & Security*, vol. 17, no. 7, pp. 589–599, 1998.

Index